STUDIES IN CHRISTIAN HISTORY AND THOUGHT

Ecumenical and Eclectic

The Unity of the Church in the Contemporary World

Essays in Honour of Alan P. F. Sell

STUDIES IN CHRISTIAN HISTORY AND THOUGHT

A complete listing of all titles in this series
will be found at the close of this book.

Alan P.F. Sell

STUDIES IN CHRISTIAN HISTORY AND THOUGHT

Ecumenical and Eclectic

The Unity of the Church in the Contemporary World

Essays in Honour of Alan P. F. Sell

Edited by Anna M. Robbins

Copyright © Anna M. Robbins and the contributors 2007

First published 2007 by Paternoster

Paternoster is an imprint of Authentic Media
9 Holden Avenue, Bletchley, Milton Keynes, MK1 1QR, UK
and
PO Box 1047, Waynesboro, GA 30830–2047, USA

13 12 11 10 09 08 07 7 6 5 4 3 2 1

The right of Anna M. Robbins to be identified as the Editor of this Work
has been asserted by her in accordance with the Copyright, Designs
and Patents Act 1988.

All rights reserved. No part of this publication may be reproduced, stored in a retrieval system, or transmitted, in any form or by any means, electronic, mechanical, photocopying, recording or otherwise, without the prior permission of the publisher or a license permitting restricted copying. In the UK such licenses are issued by the Copyright Licensing Agency, 90 Tottenham Court Road, London W1P 9HE.

British Library Cataloguing in Publication Data
A catalogue record for this book is available from the British Library

ISBN 978-1-84227-432-3

Typeset by Anna M. Robbins
Printed and bound in Great Britain
by Nottingham Alpha Graphics

STUDIES IN CHRISTIAN HISTORY AND THOUGHT

Series Preface

This series complements the specialist series of *Studies in Evangelical History and Thought* and *Studies in Baptist History and Thought* for which Paternoster is becoming increasingly well known by offering works that cover the wider field of Christian history and thought. It encompasses accounts of Christian witness at various periods, studies of individual Christians and movements, and works which concern the relations of church and society through history, and the history of Christian thought.

The series includes monographs, revised dissertations and theses, and collections of papers by individuals and groups. As well as 'free standing' volumes, works on particular running themes are being commissioned; authors will be engaged for these from around the world and from a variety of Christian traditions.

A high academic standard combined with lively writing will commend the volumes in this series both to scholars and to a wider readership.

Series Editors

Alan P.F. Sell, Visiting Professor at Acadia University Divinity College, Nova Scotia, Canada

David Bebbington, Professor of History, University of Stirling, Stirling, Scotland, UK

Clyde Binfield, Professor Associate in History, University of Sheffield, UK

Gerald Bray, Anglican Professor of Divinity, Beeson Divinity School, Samford University, Birmingham, Alabama, USA

Grayson Carter, Associate Professor of Church History, Fuller Theological Seminary SW, Phoenix, Arizona, USA

Contents

Preface	xi
List of Contributors	xiii
Introduction	1

Ecumenical and Eclectic: Roots

Chapter 1
Reformed Foundations for the Unity of the Church in the Contemporary World · 7
Donald K. McKim

Chapter 2
The Sources and Significance of Richard Price's Distinction between Abstract Virtue and Practical Virtue · 25
D. O. Thomas

Chapter 3
'Fear where no fear is': Some Reflections on Heterodox Notions of Christian Unity · 43
Martin Fitzpatrick

Chapter 4
The Power of Christian Unity · 63
Andrew D. MacRae

Ecumenical and Eclectic: Reflections

Chapter 5
'A tradition handed on by preaching': The Allure of Broad Sermons – William Page Roberts of Vere Street · 85
Clyde Binfield

Chapter 6
The Theological Legacy of Lesslie Newbigin   129
David R. Peel

Chapter 7
Olive Wyon: Prayer, Vocation and Ecumenism   149
David Cornick

Chapter 8
C.H. Dodd and W.D. Davies: Two Welsh Congregationalists on the Nature of the Church   159
John Tudno Williams

Chapter 9
Jesus Before Parents: Finding the Right Priority When Seeking Unity in the Family   173
Peter Balla

Chapter 10
Weber, Troeltsch, and the Maintenance of Hegemony in the Marketplace of German Religion: A Preliminary Analysis   189
Irving Hexham

Ecumenical and Eclectic: Resonances

Chapter 11
Two Decades of Ecumenism in Europe: A Promising Past with an Uncertain Future   205
Keith Clements

Chapter 12
The Challenge of the Culture of Dialogue   221
Alan Falconer

Chapter 13
New Perspectives in the Lutheran-Reformed Dialogue   233
Botond Gaál

Chapter 14
Universalism or Tribalism? Christian Social Ethics in an Era of Globalisation 247
Anna M. Robbins

Chapter 15
A Case for the Cross? Passionate Apologetics 269
Gabriel Fackre

Bibliography of Alan P. F. Sell 283

Person Index 311

Subject Index 313

Preface

The initial impression I had of Alan Sell was that he was a scholar who knew more about most things historical, theological and philosophical than anyone I'd previously encountered. More than ten years on, having gained a doctorate under his supervision, and with the privilege of calling him a mentor and friend, that initial impression not only sticks, it has been proved and reinforced.

As one who is committed to Christ and to his church, Sell has projected an influence that is not only academically and ecclesiologically pervasive; it is also sometimes intensely personal. This was proved to me as I made contact with many of his acquaintances from around the world in an effort to put this festschrift together. It was a delight to be in touch with so many who deeply value his work and person, and who were in all contacts a delight in themselves. If a man is to be judged at all by the company he keeps, then the pleasant and encouraging contact I have had with his peers, friends and fans testifies to the positive qualities that characterise Sell's personality. He is known to be graciously pastoral while demonstrating integrity, sharp-witted humour, and intellectual rigour. There was universal agreement amongst his peers that he should be honoured for his significant contribution, and there was great eagerness amongst those contacted to be involved in the project.

This book has come to fruition only through the encouragement of the authors who have participated, and I thank them for promptness, expertise, and excellent scholarship. I am grateful too for their personal encouragement, and patience in the face of inevitable delays. I am thankful to my former students, Ms. Clare Woodhead who assisted in formatting the articles for publication, and Ms. Fiona Roques for administrative and indexing help which relieved a great deal of pressure, and to my colleague Dr. Conrad Gempf for casting his careful editorial eye over the proofs. Thanks goes also to Mr. Jeremy Mudditt, Rev. Dr. Anthony R. Cross and Dr. Robin Parry at Paternoster for their affirmation that the project was worthwhile, and assistance in seeing it to completion. Dr. Karen Sell was burdened with keeping the secret for a few days, and I thank her not only for her encouragement and discretion, but also for putting me in touch with a couple of important contacts. My greatest thanks in connection with this book must go to the one whom it seeks to honour. His influence has filtered not only into my theology, but the very direction of my vocation. With profound gratitude, and on behalf of the authors, I respectfully offer him these essays, and pray that he will be blessed by them.

Anna M. Robbins
London School of Theology

List of Contributors

Peter Balla, Chair of New Testament Studies, Károli Gáspár Reformed University, Budapest

Clyde Binfield, Professor Emeritus in History, University of Sheffield

David Cornick, General Secretary of the United Reformed Church

Keith Clements, General Secretary of the Conference of European Churches

Gabriel Fackre, Abbott Professor of Theology Emeritus at Andover Newton Theological School

Alan Falconer, Minister of St. Machar's Cathedral, Aberdeen, formerly Director of Faith and Order with the World Council of Churches

Martin Fitzpatrick, formerly Senior Lecturer and Senior Research Fellow, Department of History and Welsh History, University of Wales, Aberystwyth

Botond Gaál, Professor of Christian Dogmatics and Christian Theology, University of Debrecen

Irving Hexham, Professor of Religious Studies at the University of Calgary

Andrew MacRae, Director of the Doctor of Ministry Programme, and formerly Principal of Acadia Divinity College, Acadia University

Donald McKim, Academic and Reference Editor at Westminster John Knox Press

David Peel, Development Strategy Officer for the United Reformed Church, formerly Principal of Northern College, Manchester

Anna Robbins, Lecturer in Theology and Contemporary Culture at the London School of Theology

D. O. Thomas, retired as Reader in Philosophy from the University of Wales, Aberystwyth. He passed away in 2005.

John Tudno Williams, Honorary Fellow in Biblical Studies, Department of Theology and Religious Studies, University of Wales, Lampeter

Introduction

The unity of the church in the contemporary world is a matter of pronounced importance. As philosophies and practices fragment at local levels, the church continues to work out what it means to be unified on a globally and locally. Of course, the unity of the church is a crucial biblical theme with implications for how we live as Christians today. Much has been written around this topic from the perspectives of 'old ecumenism' and of 'post denominationalism'. It is an issue that has motivated much of the work of Alan Sell, as he has explored its dimensions through theology, philosophy, and history, particularly through the history of dissent. Throughout his work, he has sought to expose unsatisfactory divisions amongst the people of Christ, to pose necessary challenges to those who hold sectarian attitudes, and offer constructive proposals for ongoing dialogue and other expressions of unity. Indeed, he has not only offered scholarly analyses of many relevant issues, he has also been an active participant in ecumenical dialogue globally. He has done all of this while maintaining the parameters of a theology of integrity in his work, not simply skimming over difficult questions that might prevent an easy agreement between those with divergent church loyalties. Instead, he has held together the gift of unity, as given by Christ through his Spirit to the church, with its demand that it be worked out in practice, even in the face of differences.

It is for that reason that the title of the present work is particularly appropriate. *Ecumenical and Eclectic* describes not only the essays of a diverse group of scholars who are happy to be called friends of Alan Sell, but it describes the body of his own work, and the style of his own theology. As the bibliography at the end of this book and the biographical notes in the preface attest, his interests and abilities as a scholar are as wide-ranging as he is prolific.

Alan Sell is a scholar of international repute, with an impressively long list of published books, articles, reviews and letters to his name, as the bibliography at the end of this volume attests. An entry for him in the *Dictionary of 20th Century British Philosophers* not only bears witness to his significance as a scholar, but elucidates some of the highlights of his varied contribution.[1] He was ordained to the Christian ministry in 1959 and held two pastorates, after his training at Northern Theological College, Manchester where he was awarded BA, BD and MA degrees. While pastoring, he continued his research on the interface of philosophy and religion, earning a PhD in 1967 from the University of Nottingham. He held a lecturing post at the West Midlands College of Higher Education before being appointed Theological Secretary of the World Alliance of Reformed Churches in 1983. He later occupied academic chairs at the University of Calgary and the University of Wales in Aberystwyth. He has not only lectured around the world, but received honourary doctorates from institutions in Hungary, Romania, the US and Canada. He was also awarded the prestigious Doctor of Divinity degree from the University of Manchester, and Doctor of Letters from Nottingham University, by submission and examination of his published scholarly works. He has been sought out by church leaders in need of his gifts in facilitating and clarifying ecumenical dialogue of many kinds, and his contribution to ecumenism is well known.

And so it is appropriate that Alan Sell be honoured with this volume of essays that seeks to make its own contribution to the discussion around the unity of the church in a way that reflects his broad interests, and also raises issues of continuing relevance for the church as we seek to come to terms with our existence as dissenters or otherwise in a post-Christian society.

The essays are organised under three themes. First, 'Ecumenical & Eclectic: Roots' opens with an essay by Donald McKim, who considers some of the Reformed foundations to be considered for the unity of the church today. In particular he focuses on some aspects of Calvin's thought, and draws out their implications for the contemporary situation. This article is followed by an examination of the nature of the distinction between abstract virtue and practical virtue as laid out by Richard Price. The relevance of this essay to unity is significant, as the distinction Price made between the two allowed him to maintain an attitude of dissent whilst acknowledging God's authority. This was the last work written by D.O. Thomas before his death in Aberystwyth, from where he had retired as Reader of Philosophy at the University some years before. It is with a deep sense of appreciation for his life of careful scholarship that this particular essay is included.

Subsequently, Martin Fitzpatrick offers some philosophical reflections on unity and dissent, focusing particularly on the thought of the unitarian Joseph Priestley, and the eighteenth-century Rational Dissenters. Fitzpatrick demonstrates how an attitude of dissent can contribute to the unity of the church, whilst acknowledging the limits of a unity based on a universal reason applied to doctrinal differences, particularly when the politics of the power of establishment are involved. Moreover he indicates through his study that there

---

[1] See Anna Robbins, "Alan P. F. Sell" *Dictionary of 20th Century Philosophers* (London: Thoemmes Press, 2005).

Introduction 3

is much we can learn from those with whose doctrine we may well disagree. Andrew MacRae then rounds out this section, as he offers a theological exposition on the power of Christian unity, considering its biblical foundations, ecumenical developments, and various recent manifestations, including some contemporary evangelical and Pentecostal movements. Despite their varied emphases, MacRae suggests that there is room for many types of ecumenical movements, all of which may contribute to the unity of the church, without being intrinsically divisive.

The next section of the book is entitled 'Ecumenical and Eclectic: Reflections', and includes a variety of essays representing historical, biblical, and sociological analysis. Clyde Binfield kicks off in Chapter 5 with a stimulating historical study examining the sermons of William Page Roberts at Vere Street, London. With an eye to the dynamics of the vibrant social and religious scene of late-Victorian London, Binfield demonstrates how change develops within a framework of continuity in the church. As such, it is able to bind the members of the church together, even as they experience significant transformation within and without the body of Christ. Next, there are two essays exploring the contributions of individuals who made an impact on the development of ecumenism in several ways. First, David Peel explores the legacy of Lesslie Newbigin, through an examination of his theology, and then David Cornick considers some of the ecumenical reflections of Olive Wyon. John Tudno Williams turns our attention to two Welsh New Testament scholars, C.H. Dodd and W.D. Davies, as he considers their thinking on the nature and unity of the church. Peter Balla follows on with the New Testament theme as he considers whether the authority of parents or Christ should have priority, and what the implications might be for unity in the family. This section is then completed with an essay by Irving Hexham, who explores the work of Weber and Troeltsch with respect to the development of the terminology of 'sect' and 'cult'. He suggests that such language is sectarian, and ideologically-loaded, and is therefore unhelpful to sociologists and theologians alike, who should seek to employ less value-loaded language in their work. This suggestion has implications for the ways in which Christians often find it easy to dismiss those whose doctrinal perspective differs from their own through the use of prejudicial language.

The third and final section of the book emerges as 'Ecumenical and Eclectic: Resonances'. This section seeks to look more concretely to the future, both in terms of the future of ecumenism, and the practices of the church. Keith Clements begins with an assessment of the current state of ecumenism in Europe, and highlighting the uncertainty of its future. In particular, he makes suggestions about the use and understanding of dialogue as a practice and expression of unity. Alan Falconer picks up this theme and explores some aspects of ecumenical dialogue, highlighting some types and the current crisis. Part of the response, he suggests, goes beyond churches merely talking to one another, to the necessity of fostering an overall culture of dialogue if ecumenism is to have a future at all. Botond Gaal then explores some of the particular features of the Lutheran-Reformed dialogue in Hungary, demonstrating the difficulty of opening up specific, closed doctrines for discussion in practice.

From an ethical perspective, Anna Robbins highlights the contemporary tension between a tendency towards pluralism and fragmentation, in the face of globalising forces. She suggests that a fragmented community is ill-equipped to address issues of global importance, but argues that the church is uniquely poised to serve as a network that empowers ethical engagement in an era of globalisation. Finally, in a creative exposition, Gabriel Fackre takes his cue from Alan Sell's apologetic method and seeks to apply it to the use of film in apologetics today. In the midst of the discussion, he highlights some key aspects of church unity, namely, how we think of Jesus Christ and how we seek to communicate Christ in the world today. It is perhaps in the proclamation of the gospel that the unity of the church in the contemporary world finds its most pertinent expression, and its greatest challenge.

These essays testify to the diversity of the church, and its thinkers. And yet they demonstrate how that diversity, when brought together in unity, is able to challenge, enrich, and develop the thought and action of the church for its worship of God and mission to the world. They show us how much we can learn from those who have gone before, as well as challenge us to embrace change in the practice of the enduring traditions of the church. They provide an impetus to continue to work out in practice what must be more than an intellectual assent to the high priestly prayer of Christ. Regardless of the intellectual and social context in which we find ourselves, the obligation of Christians to continually pursue and express the unity of the church is a commitment without compromise. Perhaps in its very nature, the task of expressing the unity of the church that is given in Christ, is to be thought of not only as ecumenical, but also thoroughly eclectic.

Ecumenical and Eclectic: Roots

CHAPTER 1

Reformed Foundations for the Unity of the Church in the Contemporary World

Donald K. McKim

It is a deep pleasure to contribute to this volume in honour of Alan Sell, one of my dear friends. There is no one I respect more as a theologian and whose work I appreciate more as a Reformed theologian. Alan's support and care through the years have been significant blessings for me. And I thank him.

The theme of this volume is 'The Unity of the Church in the Contemporary World.' It is a most appropriate theme in reflecting a major dimension of Alan Sell's work and ministry through the years. It is also a theme of particular interest and significance to the Reformed theological tradition, to which Alan Sell has contributed much. This well-chosen volume title is a theme on which much has been written. It is also one on which much more needs to be written—today and tomorrow.

My purpose here is to explore some 'Reformed foundations' for the affirmation that there is an essential unity to the Christian church. The focus will be on the thought of Calvin. A wider perspective could have been included. But Calvin's thought, which has been so constitutive for the Reformed tradition, serves as ground for the ecclesiology of later Reformed thinkers, including their thought on the unity of the church. This is a theme that has been central since Christianity's early creeds, and expressed in the clause from the Nicene Creed: I believe in the 'one, holy, catholic, and apostolic' church.

The value of looking to the foundations of this ecclesiological affirmation is that we become aware of the theological bases on which the range of expressions of ecclesiology we find in the contemporary world are built. The varieties of 'church experience' we encounter today with multitudes of denominations, sects, and 'fellowships' can make the 'diversity' of the church appear much more prominent than the 'unity' of the church. Since the unity of the church is a fundamental expression of Christian faith, it is helpful to look beyond the 'phenomena' of the contemporary world to the theological realities that undergird even expressions of diversity.

This is so particularly in the Reformed tradition. Here ecclesiology is a key theological focus and here, historically, 'diversity' has also been a hallmark. This 'diversity' has taken the shape of denominational splits and their residual effects. Reformed Christians in their churches have often found theological reasons to establish new ecclesiastical bodies. The best light that can be cast on these actions is to say that these are people who take theology seriously. But in the wider circle of Reformed ecclesiology where the unity of the whole church of Christ and all its members is a vital, central concern, the schisms and church splits are reminders of the sinfulness of (even!) Christians and the need to repent when the body of Christ is ruptured. The temptation to sectarianism is ever-present. The results of schism within the body of Christ continue to have effects, long after initial actions are taken. These splits are never 'cost-free.' In another context, Rowan Williams, Archbishop of Canterbury, reminded the worldwide Anglican communion: 'To put it as bluntly as I can, there are no clean breaks in the Body of Christ.'[1]

The basics of the 'unity of the church', as articulated by Calvin for the early Reformed Christians, provide orientation points for our assessments of the contemporary world and the Christian church, including Reformed churches. These Reformed foundations help us recognize the theological realities on which our understandings of ecclesiology are built. They call us back to the basics so we are better equipped to move forward in the future—towards the unity that God gives in Christ, and that towards which all history moves.

The Ecumenical Vision

In one sense, this study of Calvin's thought is an extended commentary on an important passage by Alan Sell in the chapter on 'The Ecumenical Vision' in his *A Reformed, Evangelical, Catholic Theology: The Contribution of the World Alliance of Reformed Churches, 1875-1982*. Sell wrote

> Recognizing that unity in Christ is God's gift and not a human achievement, Reformed ecumenists concur with all who believe that the goal is the *manifestation* of this God-given unity so that the world may believe. The church is called to be a sign in the world of that ultimate reconciliation of all things to God. Accordingly, the Reformed today typically maintain that the catholicity of the church entails its visible unity, which does not mean uniformity of expression, liturgy, and practice. On the contrary, it is recognized that differences of individual temperament and of cultural heritage are themselves gifts of God to be accepted gladly. But it is keenly felt that the proclamation of God's reconciliation by a manifestly unreconciled church is inherently incongruous and detrimental to mission. The goal, therefore, is the mutual recognition of ministries and memberships and, above all, the removal of those barriers dividing Christians at

---

[1] See 'Speech in Debate on the Windsor Report', Thursday 17 February 2005 at http://www.archbishopofcanterbury.org/sermons_speeches/050217.htm.

the Lord's table when certain doctrines of the ministry and of the sacraments cut across commonly held beliefs concerning the Trinity, the person and work of Christ, the work of the Holy Spirit, and the nature of the church as the people of God.[2]

Four elements are key here: 1) The church as a sign of God-given unity; 2) Recognition of varied cultural expressions in churches; 3) Mutual recognition of ministries and church memberships; 4) Removal of barriers in the Lord's Supper. As we will see, these elements emerge out of a thoroughly-grounded Reformed ecclesiology that owes its impetus to the contributions of Calvin and his own concerns and actions.

Sell's trenchant comments set the stage for the chapter in which he mines the writings of the World Alliance and its leadership through the years to sketch the ecumenical vision that has oriented Reformed churches in the contemporary world.

Calvin's Contributions

Calvin wrote much about the church and the contours of his thought are well-known. It is through 'faith in the gospel that Christ becomes ours and we are made partakers of the salvation and eternal blessedness brought by him,' Calvin explains.[3] Since we are ignorant and slothful people (and Calvin also adds that there is a 'fickleness' to our disposition), God has provided aids to help us in our weakness. These aids are found in the context of the church where the 'treasure' of the gospel is deposited (*Inst.* 4.1.1). Preaching and the sacraments are found in the church as God's divine accommodation to human weakness and as ways for us to draw near to God.[4] The church is where God draws people into the divine 'bosom' to nourish and help the people of God through ministry and also to guide them by 'motherly care until they are mature and at last reach the goal of faith.' Then Calvin famously adds: 'for those to whom he is Father the church may also be Mother' (*Inst.* 4.1.1).

Those who are drawn into the church are part of the church by 'God's secret election and his inner call' (*Inst.* 4.1.2). We must 'leave to God alone the knowledge of his church, whose foundation is his secret election.' This doctrine of election could be conceived as singular and insular, except that Calvin goes on to say that 'it is not sufficient, indeed, for us to comprehend in mind and

---

[2] *A Reformed, Evangelical, Catholic Theology: The Contribution of the World Alliance of Reformed Churches, 1875-1982* (Grand Rapids: Eerdmans, 1991), pp. 112-13.
[3] John Calvin, *Institutes of the Christian Religion*, ed. John T. McNeill, trans. Ford Lewis Battles, Library of Christian Classics 4.1.1 (Philadelphia: Westminster Press, 1960). All further references to the *Institutes* in the text are from this edition.
[4] On 'accommodation' in Calvin see Jack B. Rogers and Donald K. McKim, *The Authority and Interpretation of the Bible: An Historical Approach* (San Francisco: Harper & Row, 1979), pp. 98-100.

thought the multitude of the elect, unless we consider the unity of the church as that into which we are convinced we have been truly engrafted (Lat. *insitos*).' We recognize that the gift of faith, by which Christ becomes ours, and which is an outward expression of our election, does not 'single us out' for salvation, so much as it draws us into the 'multitude of the elect' who are all bound together in the 'unity of the church' (Lat. *Ecclesiae unitatem*). This focuses election towards a corporate view—towards election's nature as being that which constitutes the church itself and towards the end of election which is to draw together a people of God. This constitutes the reality of the church in the present (in both its 'visible' and 'invisible' aspects), as well as providing the ultimate eschatological benefit. For 'no hope of future inheritance remains to us unless we have been united (Lat. *coadunati*) with all other members under Christ, our Head' (*Inst.* 4.1.2). Future salvation ('inheritance') rests on our being united with others—by faith—in Christ. This takes shape in and through the church which is the body into which all believers are united.

Thus the 'unity of the church' takes center stage for Calvin in defining the nature of the church as well as the texture of 'election' in Jesus Christ, which is the source of the church, and the reality of faith, which is the means by which election in Christ is effected and recognized. From these basics, complementary aspects of the nature of the church's unity emerge for Calvin.

The Unity of the Church is Christ and is from God

There is an essential unity to the church because the church is grounded in Jesus Christ. He is the church's unity because he is the foundation of the church. All this is from God.

It is possible for the church to be 'catholic' or 'universal,' said Calvin, 'because there could not be two or three churches unless Christ be torn asunder [cf. I Cor. 1:13]—which cannot happen!' (*Inst.* 4.1.2). There is a 'catholic' church because there is 'one' church, the church of Jesus Christ. For

> all the elect are so united in Christ [cf. Eph. 1:22-23] that as they are dependent on one Head, they also grow together into one body, being joined and knit together [cf. Eph. 4:16] as are the limbs of a body [Rom. 12:5; 1 Cor. 10:17; 12:12, 27]. The church's unity takes shape as its members ('the elect') are continually being drawn together and as they continually express their dependence on Christ, their head. The church itself is not only the 'body of Christ' (1 Cor. 12:12) but all its members are the 'limbs' of the body as they grow together and are 'being joined and knit together.' So the unity of the church is at once a 'given'—in Jesus Christ; and a 'process'—a continuing work of being joined and knit and growing together.[5]

---

[5] The Latin is: *Quin sic electi Dei omnes in Christo sunt connexi, ut quemadmodum ab uno capite pendent, ita in unum velut corpus coalescant, ea inter se compage*

In commenting on 1 Corinthians 3:11: 'For no one can lay any foundation other than the one that has been laid; that foundation is Jesus Christ,' Calvin emphasized the church's one foundation to be Jesus Christ when he wrote that 'the Church must quite definitely be founded on Christ alone.'[6] For 'Christ is the one and only foundation of the Church.' This is because 'He is the one and only source of salvation and eternal life, because in Him we know God the Father, because the foundation of all our blessings is in Him, then if He is not acknowledged as such, He immediately ceases to be the foundation' (Comm. 1 Cor. 3:11). It is on Christ and 'Him alone the unity of the Church depends' (Comm. Eph. 1:22). We should not 'seek unity elsewhere than in Christ' (Comm. Eph. 2:15). For 'it is He to whom alone believers should look and on whom alone the unity of the body depends' (Comm. Col. 1:18). Christ is 'the one and only bond of sacred unity' (Comm. Acts 28:25). Christ is this bond, primarily through his death by which 'He drew all things unto Himself; and we are gathered into Christ's fold daily by the Gospel' (Comm. John 11:51). The church's unity is Christ who is the head.

The Unity of the Church is a Unity of Faith

Calvin continued to argue in his *Institutes* that as believers are 'joined and knit together,' so 'they are made truly one since they live together in one faith, hope, and love, and in the same Spirit of God. For they have been called not only into the same inheritance of eternal life but also to participate in one God and Christ [Eph. 5:30]' (*Inst.* 4.1.2). As he put it in his 'Necessity of Reforming the Church': 'The principle from which Paul derives unity is, that there is "one Lord, one faith, one baptism, one God and Father of all" who hath called us into one hope, (see Eph. 4:4, 5.) Therefore, we are one body and one spirit, as is here enjoined, if we adhere to God only, i.e., be bound to each other by the tie of faith.'[7] For 'God invites all with His one voice, so that they may be united in the same agreement of faith, and study to help one another' (*Comm. Eph. 4:4*). Faith is the means by which the unity of the church, which is a unity with Christ, is made real. In commenting on Ephesians 4:5, Calvin said

> Whenever you read this word 'one' here, understand it as emphatic, as if he said 'Christ cannot be divided; faith cannot be rent; there are not various baptisms, but

---

cohaerentes qua eiusdem corporis membra (*Inst.*, 4.1.2). The strong *co*-language emphasizes this 'being together'.

[6] John Calvin, *The First Epistle of Paul to the Corinthians*, eds David W. Torrance and Thomas F. Torrance, trans. John W. Fraser (Calvin's New Testament Commentaries; Grand Rapids: Eerdmans, rpt 1980), 1 Cor. 3:11 (p. 74). Further references to Calvin's New Testament commentaries will be to this series with the commentary references cited in the text. References to Calvin's Old Testament commentaries will be to the Calvin Translation Society translation.

[7] 'The Necessity of Reforming the Church', *Calvin's Selected Works,* 1: 272.

one common to all; God cannot be divided into parts.' Therefore it behooves us to cultivate among ourselves a holy unity, composed of many bonds. Faith, and baptism, and God the Father, and Christ, ought to unite us, so that we coalesce, as it were, into one man [person]....The unity of the faith, which is here mentioned, depends on the one eternal truth of God, on which it is founded (*Comm. Eph. 4:5*).

It is in 'the Church of God, where unity of faith ought to prevail' (*Comm. Acts 19:23*). The church is the locus where all believers' unity with Christ is expressed. Individual Christians are to act as 'one of the flock' since the 'saints' (believers) are 'gathered into the society of Christ.' This is the 'communion of saints' (*Inst.* 4.1.3). This unity of faith is defined for Calvin not only in terms of what believers believe: 'the knowledge of the Son of God' (*Comm. Eph. 4:13*)[8] or 'the eternal truth of God'[9] but also in the ultimate unity of the elect in Christ (*Comm. Ps. 147:2*; cf. *Comm. Isa. 51:16*). It is the "Gospel, which ought to be the bond of unity" (*Comm. Acts 14:4*).[10]

Yet Calvin is realistic to know that the unity of faith, while a reality, is also something elusive, given human frailty

> But ought not the unity of the faith to reign among us from the very commencement? It does reign, I acknowledge, among the sons of God, but not so perfectly as to make them come together. Such is the weakness of our nature, that it is enough if every day brings some nearer to others, and all approach together to Christ. The expression 'coming together', denotes that closest union to which we still aspire, and which we never reach until this flesh, which is always involved in many remnants of ignorance and unbelief, shall have been laid aside (*Comm. Eph. 4:13*).

Thus Calvin realistically acknowledges that while the unity of faith, as an expression of the unity of the church is a reality, on the basis of Jesus Christ, 'unity of faith' does not have a full manifestation in the visible church as it exists today. There must always be a process of 'coming together' to display the union of believers with Christ, with each other, and of the church with Christ. 'Ignorance and unbelief' are the culprits that hinder believers from coming together with each other. Calvin indicates that the slow work of 'day by day' establishing a closeness between believers in the church, is the best that

---

[8] See also the Antitode to 'The Articles of the Theological Faculty of Paris' in *Calvin's Selected Works*, 1: 132. Calvin saw the prophet Isaiah as anticipating the coming together of Jews and Gentiles in a unity of faith: 'Isaiah foretells that the Church will be greatly extended, when the Gentiles shall be received and united to the Jews in the unity of faith' (*Comm. Isa. 49:6*).

[9] 'The Necessity of Reforming the Church', *Calvin's Selected Works*, 1: 259. Cf. *Comm. Col. 2:2*.

[10] Calvin faulted the Papists for grounding unity only in the church and not in the authority of Scripture, 'as if the unity of the Church were itself founded elsewhere than on belief in Scripture' (*Comm.* John 19:24).

can be done. This happens only as the church and believers are focused on Christ, for the knowledge of the Son of God is the expression of the unity of faith and it is to Christ 'alone faith ought to look, on Him depend, in Him to rest and terminate.' For 'let us remember,' said Calvin, 'that true faith is so contained in Christ, that it neither knows, nor desires to know, anything beyond Him' (*Comm. Eph. 4:13*).

The Unity of the Church Acknowledges Diversities

Unity of the church, despite ignorance and sloth, and also the church divided into many places are the realities that Calvin affirmed. For him

> the church universal is a multitude gathered from all nations; it is divided and dispersed in separate places, but agrees on the one truth of divine doctrine, and is bound by the bond of the same religion. Under it are thus included individual churches, disposed in towns and villages according to human need, so that each rightly has the name and authority of the church. Individual men who, by their profession of religion, are reckoned within such churches, even though they may actually be strangers to the church, still in a sense belong to it until they have been rejected by public judgment (*Inst.* 4.1.9).

The ties that bind the church join and knit its members together despite the multiplicity of local churches in different places throughout the earth. The scattering of the early disciples who proclaimed the Word wherever they went—and later established local churches was the genesis of churches in different places. Calvin saw this as an example of 'the incredible providence of God that the dispersion of believers led many into the unity of the faith' (*Comm. Acts 8:4*). The church 'universal' is the church because the church is essentially 'one,' united, as he said in 'divine doctrine' and in the bonds of the same religion.

The geographical varieties are one form of diversity, but differences in Christian ministries and practices are others. Diversity within unity is a basic perspective for Calvin. He acknowledges this in commenting on Paul's address of his epistle to 'the churches of Galatia' (Gal. 1:2). Calvin said that 'where there is a Church there is unity of faith' (*Comm. Gal. 1:2*). The multiplicity of church bodies and of ministerial practices is not a hindrance to making that basic confession. Calvin commented on the churches of Galatia that

> where they professed Christianity, worshipped one God, used the Sacraments and had some kind of ministry, there remained the marks of the Church (*Ecclesiae insignia*). We do not always find in Churches such purity as were to be desired. Even the purest have their blemishes; and some not only have a few spots here and there but are almost completely deformed. We must not be so put off by the teaching and living of any society that, if we are not satisfied with everything that goes on, we at once deny it to be a church. Paul here teaches us a charitableness

which is very far from that. Yet when we acknowledge as Churches of Christ any societies which are laden with faults, we must at the same time condemn what is wrong in them. For it is not as if the perfection of everything to be desired in a Church is present wherever there is some kind of a Church (*Comm. Gal. 1:2*).

Neither the 'imperfections' of local church bodies, even to the point of being 'almost completely deformed' nor dissatisfaction with the 'teaching and living of any society' were for Calvin (following Paul) to be grounds for denying the presence of a 'church.' While condemnation of faults is expected, it should not reach the point where imperfections cause one to say that a church does not exist in a location. And, for Calvin, 'where there is a Church there is unity of faith' (*Comm. Gal.1:2*).

Diversities are found among churches in different places as well as within local church congregations themselves. This too goes back to Paul and his images of the church as the body of Christ in which 'there are many members, yet one body' (1 Cor. 12:20). Calvin commented that

Paul drives this home so often because the heart of the whole matter lies in these words; viz. The unity of the body is of such a kind as can only be preserved by having a variety of members; and, on the other hand, while the members differ from each other in their functions and abilities, it is in such a way that they are nevertheless connected to each other in order to preserve the unity of the body (*Comm. 1 Cor. 12:20*).

In his commentaries on 1 Corinthians and Ephesians, Calvin used the analogy of tones in music to make this point. He wrote about the diversities of gifts that 'the harmony of the Church lies in the fact that it is, so to speak, a unity of many parts; in other words, when the different gifts are all directed to one and the same end, just as in music different parts are adjusted to each other and combined so well that they produce one harmonious piece.' This is possible since there is 'a unity in difference, because One Spirit is the source of all the gifts' (*Comm. 1 Cor. 12:4*). When there are different ministerial functions in the church, as Paul writes to the Ephesians (4:11), Calvin said that Paul 'returns to the dispensation of the graces he had mentioned and declares more fully what he had touched on briefly, that out of this variety arises unity in the Church, as various tones in music make a sweet melody' (*Comm. Eph. 4:11*). The differences of gifts and functions of ministries within individual congregations are a focused example of the larger diversities of gifts and functions of ministries within the church universal. Yet theologically, these diversities are no hindrances to affirming likewise the unity of faith which is the means by which the essential unity of the church is recognized. On this practical level, surely the recognition of the ministries and church membership of other Christians is a key and crucial first step toward a genuinely expressed unity in Christ. The 'diversities' of practices, even when we perceive other Christian communions to be 'laden with faults,' should be transcended in the name of a common unity, a communion in diversity.

The Unity of the Church is a Gift Given and a Gift Sought

Calvin's views on the unity of the church are another example of the way his theology as a whole acknowledges both the divine initiative and the human response. This impulse is found throughout a number of his theological formulations.[11] The unity of the church is a gift given by God in Jesus Christ—who is himself, as the head of the church, the one in whom unity is found; and at the same time, also a gift to be sought by Christians with each other in local churches and beyond.

As a gift, the church is founded on Christ alone said Calvin. The church is 'called "catholic," or "universal," because there could not be two or three churches unless Christ be torn asunder [1 Cor. 1:13]—which cannot happen' (*Inst.* 4.1.2). In the church, 'authority belongs to Christ alone, so that we may all be dependent on Him; that He alone may be called Lord and Master among us, so that the name of no other person may be set up in rivalry to His' (*Comm. 1 Cor. 1:12*). Since the divine gift is Christ who alone is Lord, the apostle Paul was right to condemn 'those who draw away followers after themselves, and so split the Church into sects' (*Comm. 1 Cor. 1:12* cf. *Comm. Acts 20:30*). 'In short,' said Calvin, 'the unity of the Church rests mainly on this one thing: that we all depend on Christ alone, and that men therefore take, and remain in, a lower place, so that nothing may detract from His position of pre-eminence' (*Comm. 1 Cor.* 1:12).

For Calvin, trying to break the unity of the church by dividing the body of Christ is such a grievous sin because it rejects the divine gift of the essential unity of the church by seeking to tear Christ apart. This is what heretics have done. By their actions, 'all ambitious, unruly, contentious people who are led astray by sinful passions and disturb the peace of the Church; in short anyone who by his shameless pride breaks the unity of the Church is called a heretic by Paul' (*Comm. Titus 3:10*). They create rival bodies for 'all heretics have destroyed the unity of the Church by their sects, and thus there have been as many secessions from Christ' (*Comm. 2 Thess.* 2:3; cf. *Comm. 1 John 2:18*). 'Sectarianism' is to be vigorously rejected![12] Those who trouble the church by seeking to break its unity in Christ—as was happening with the church in Galatia to which Paul wrote—will face divine displeasure and punishment, said Calvin, 'Let all who introduce causes of trouble into Churches, who break the unity of faith, who destroy harmony, listen to this, and if they have any right

---

[11] See Donald K. McKim, 'The "Heart" and "Center" of the Reformed Faith', *Reformed Review*, 51.3 (Spring, 1998), pp. 206-19.

[12] Calvin said that 'unquestionably nothing is more opposed to the law of God than sects; for in it alone is communicated the truth of God, which is the bond of unity' (*Comm. Phil. 3:5*).

feeling, let them tremble at this word. For God declares by the mouth of Paul that no authors of such scandals will escape unpunished' (*Comm. Gal. 5:10*). In scathing words, Calvin wrote that 'separation from the church is the denial of God and Christ. Hence, we must even more avoid so wicked a separation' (*Inst.* 4.1.10).[13]

Schism and sectarianism have consequences, both now and in the future.

Most clearly, Calvin commented on the gift of the unity of the church in Christ when he expounded the phrase, 'Has Christ been divided?' from 1 Corinthians 1:13. He wrote

> This intolerable evil followed from the divisions that existed among the Corinthians. For only Christ ought to rule in the Church. And since the purpose of the Gospel is that we might be reconciled to God through Him, it is necessary first of all, that we should all be bound together in Him. Only a very few of the Corinthians, wiser than the others, continued to acknowledge Christ as their Master. All of them however boasted that they were Christians. In that way Christ was being torn to pieces. For we ought to be one body, if we want to be kept together under Him, as under the Head. For if we are split into different bodies we also break away from Him. To glory in His name in the midst of disagreements and parties is to tear Him in pieces. That cannot in fact be done. For never will He Himself turn away from unity and harmony, because 'He cannot deny Himself' (II Tim. 2.13). Having placed this contradictory situation before them, Paul wishes to make the Corinthians understand that they are alienated from Christ, because of their divisions. For He reigns in our midst, only when he is the means of binding us together in an inviolable union (*Comm. 1 Cor. 1:13*).

These strong comments, in exposition of the 'real-life' situation of the Corinthian church to which Paul wrote, display Calvin's recognition of the divine gift of the church's unity in Christ, the evils of attempting to break this unity, and the exhortation to recognize this union and work toward reflecting unity of faith in Christ. 'We ought to be one body,' wrote Calvin; 'if we split into different bodies we also break away from Him;' Christ 'reigns in our midst, only when He is the means of binding us together in an inviolable union.' The 'purpose of the Gospel,' after all, 'is that we might be reconciled to God through Him.' This reconciliation demands 'that we should all be bound together in Him.'

One can scarcely think of stronger sentiments to express the unity of the church than expressed here: 'There is nothing more out of keeping for Christians than their being divided from each other. For the most important

---

[13] Calvin continued: 'For when with all our might we are attempting the overthrow of God's truth, we deserve to have him hurl the whole thunderbolt of his wrath to crush us. Nor can any more atrocious crime be conceived than for us by sacrilegious disloyalty to violate the marriage that the only-begotten son of God deigned to contract with us [Cf. Eph. 5:23-32]. Calvin believed that 'Satan constantly leaves no stone unturned in order to break up the unity of the Church' (*Comm. 1 Cor. 11:19*).

principle of our religion is this, that we be in concord among ourselves' (*Comm. 1 Cor. 1:10*). This is a 'holy unity' (*Comm. 1 Cor. 1:11*; cf. *Comm. Col. 2:2*) given by the Spirit of God (*Inst.* 4.1.2; cf. *Comm. Eph. 4:3, 6*). This unity is the only source of peace for the church. When he commented on Colossians 3:15, Calvin said

> The clause, *to which ye are called*, declares what sort of peace this is: the unity which Christ has consecrated among us under His own rule. For God has reconciled us to Himself in Christ, so that we may live in harmony. He adds, *in one body*; meaning by this, that we cannot be in accord with God except by being united among ourselves as members of one body (*Comm. Col. 3:15*).

Yet it is a responsibility of the church and its members to seek this unity as well. There is a duty to make this unity real, in tangible ways. While there is in the church 'one Lord, one faith, one baptism' (Eph. 4:5)—all gifts of God, as the word 'one' emphasizes, it also 'behooves us,' said Calvin, 'to cultivate among ourselves a holy unity, composed of many bonds. Faith, and baptism, and God the Father, and Christ, ought to unite us, so that we coalesce, as it were, into one man' (*Comm. Eph. 4:5*). Diversities abound; others work and minister in different ways. These should be recognized because we are all one in Christ Jesus. These are the basics to which adherence should bring the recognition of unity among Christians—a unity which (though 'given'), also ought vigorously to be sought.

This quest for expression of the unity of the church begins with baptism and continues through Christian life as one receives the Lord's Supper. Calvin commented on Paul's statement that 'in one Spirit we were all baptized into one body—Jews or Greeks, slaves or free—and we were all made to drink of one Spirit' (1 Cor. 12:13) by saying that 'Paul therefore teaches that as soon as believers are initiated by the baptism of Christ they are already filled with zeal for cultivating unity with each other; then afterwards, when they receive the Holy Supper, they are again led, step by step, to the same unity, because they are all being revived by the same drink at the same time' (*Comm. 1 Cor. 12:13*). This is the life of the Christian in the church—to be baptized into the body of Christ and to be nourished by the Lord's Supper as life in the church progresses.[14] All this is initiated and made possible by the Spirit of God. That same Spirit is the Spirit of unity which instills Christians in the church with a 'zeal for cultivating unity with each other.' This is the constant goal to which all Christians are called and which the church itself should embody.

Since the church is one in Christ, there is an 'indivisible connection which all members of Christ have with one another' (*Inst.* 4.2.6). The connection is the bond of love through the Holy Spirit. 'Without mutual love, the body

---

[14] Calvin said, 'By baptism we are initiated into faith in him; by partaking in the Lord's Supper we attest our unity in true doctrine and love' (*Inst.* 4.1.7).

cannot be healthy,' according to Calvin (*Comm. Eph. 4:16*; cf. *Comm. 1 Cor. 13:4*). When we are 'ingrafted into the body of Christ, we really are members one of another' (*Comm. 1 Cor. 12:27*). Thus, said Calvin, 'Let there be love for each other, sympathy (Gr. *Sympatheia*) with each other, and consideration for each other. Let it be the common good that influences us, so that we may not ruin the Church by spite, or jealousy, or pride, or any discord; but let every single person rather devote all his energy to its consecration' (*Comm. 1 Cor. 12:27*).[15] Being united with Christ, believers are united with one another. Calvin says that 'a unity of that kind is properly called a (Gr. *koinonia*) or communion.' This is 'a spiritual union between Christ and believers'—'not a mere human fellowship' (Lat. *non tantum de mutual inter hominess communicatione*). It is necessary for us 'to be incorporated, as it were, into Christ in order to be united to each other' (*Comm. 1 Cor. 10:16*).

It is this unity in Christ for which Christ himself prays. In his great 'high priestly prayer' in John 17, Jesus prays 'that they may be one, as we are one' (Jn. 17:21). Calvin says that Christ

> places the end of our happiness in unity, and justly. For the ruin of the human race is that, alienated from God, it is also broken and scattered in itself. Conversely, therefore, its restoration lies in its proper coalescence in one body (*in corpus unum rite coalescat*); as Paul sees in Eph. 4.2, 16 the perfection of the Church in believers being joined together in one Spirit, and says that apostles, prophets, evangelists and pastors are given to restore and build up the body of Christ until it arrives at the unity of faith. And therefore he exhorts believers to grow into Christ, who is the Head from whom the whole body, joined together and connected by every bond of supply according to the operation in the measure of every part, makes increase of it to edification. Wherefore, whenever Christ speaks of unity, let us remember how foul and horrible is the world's scattering apart from Him. Next let us learn that the beginning of a blessed life is when we are all governed and live by the one Spirit of Christ (*Comm. John 17:21*).

This unity of believers in the church in the unity of faith is a unity shared in the fellowship of the church.[16] It is a unity to be 'cultivated' (*Comm. Eph. 4:5*; cf. *Comm. 1 Cor. 10:17*) since we Christians 'all meet together to share that symbol of that sacred unity' (*Comm. 1 Cor. 10:17*). We should 'cherish, as much as we can, unity with the whole body' (*Comm. Acts 6:1*). 'Servants of Christ' should 'take positive action to foster unity' (*Comm. Acts 15:2*). When Christians examine themselves in preparation to receive the Lord's Supper,

---

[15] Earlier, Calvin had commented that Paul is 'calling the Corinthians back to unity, when he reminds them that they have all obtained whatever gifts they have, from the one source; but at the same time he shows that no-one has so much as to be self-sufficient, and not need the help of other people' (*Comm. 1 Cor. 12:11*).

[16] Calvin said: 'So powerful is participation in the church that it keeps us in the society of God' (*Inst.* 4.1.3).

Calvin says they must bring 'faith and repentance' to the table. The imperative to work for unity is emphasized when Calvin wrote that 'Under repentance I include love, for there is no doubt that the man, who has learnt to deny himself in order to devote himself to Christ and His service, will also give himself whole-heartedly to the promotion of the unity which Christ has commended to us' (*Comm. 1 Cor. 11:28*). The Lord's Supper, which dramatizes the reality of unity in Christ is also the occasion in which efforts for the unity of Christians in Christ is to be expressed—as a sign of a repentance which features love as a primary component.

Yet again, Calvin is realistic as well. He asked, 'Ought not the unity of the faith to reign among us from the very commencement?' He answered, 'It does reign, I acknowledge, among the sons of God, but not so perfectly as to make them come together' (*Comm. Eph. 4:13*). Calvin knew, empirically from his own experience, as well as from the New Testament letters he interpreted, the ways in which the unity of the church can be fractured, by 'heretics' as well as by others within the body of Christ itself. Yet, it is the church's duty to overcome the situations and go beyond the persons who would fracture the unity of the body of Christ and lead those in the church astray. Calvin charged that 'it is for us to work hard and strive in every way to bring if possible the whole world to agree in the unity of the faith' (*Comm. John 10:8*). Christians must work for the unity of the church. This is an obligation for Christians from the earliest times to the present, and into the future. In contemplating the 'final coming of Christ,' Calvin asks: 'For what is the purpose of the coming of Christ but to gather us all together in one from this dispersion in which we are now wandering? Therefore the nearer His coming is the more we must bend our efforts that the scattered may be brought together and united and that there may be one fold and one Shepherd (John 10.16)' (*Comm. Hebrews 10:25*).[17]

Thus, the unity of the church in Jesus Christ is a unity that is a gift given as well as a sacred responsibility which rests on all Christians in the church—to enact this unity, through love and the ministry of the church—and thus to witness to the reality given in Jesus Christ.[18]

Calvin's Concerns

From these perspectives in Calvin's biblical and theological works, we have further testimony to the importance the Genevan reformer placed on the unity

---

[17] Calvin indicated that 'we who are the sheep of Christ repose in a safe place when we hold the unity of faith' (*Comm. Col. 2:8*).

[18] The context in which the gift-given and the responsibility-taken are carried out is the 'visible church,' which is the 'mother' of believers and is comprised of those 'spread over the earth who profess to worship one God and Christ' (*Inst.* 4.1.7; cf. 4.1.4). The 'invisible church' 'includes not only the saints presently living on earth, but all the elect from the beginning of the world' (*Inst.* 4.1.7).

of the church when we recall his own interests and efforts toward trying to establish unity in the whole church of Jesus Christ as well as among the various 'churches" that were emerging in the spread of the Protestant Reformation.

Calvin's reply to Cardinal Sadoleto's letter to the church at Geneva rejected the Cardinal's view that the Protestant reform was forsaking the church and trying to divide it. Calvin prayed

> With whom the blame rests it is for thee, O Lord, to decide. Always, both by word and deed, have I protested how eager I was for unity. Mine, however, was a unity of the Church, which should begin with Thee and end in Thee. For as oft as thou didst recommend to us peace and concord, thou, at the same time, didst show that thou wert the only bond for preserving it.[19]

Calvin claimed that

> though denounced as a deserter of the Church, and threatened, I was in no respect deterred, or induced to proceed less firmly and boldly in opposing those who in the character of pastors, wasted thy Church with a more than impious tyranny. My conscience told me how strong the zeal was with which I burned for the unity of thy Church, provided thy truth were made the bond of concord. As the commotions which followed were not excited by me, so there is no ground for imputing them to me.[20]

He concluded his 'Reply' with the wish: 'The Lord grant, Sadolet, that you and all your party may at length perceive, that the only true bond of Ecclesiastical unity would exist if Christ the Lord, who hath reconciled us to God the Father, were to gather us out of our present dispersion into the fellowship of his body, that so, through his one Word and Spirit, we might join together with one heart and one soul.'[21]

Calvin's 'devotion to "the church," which is reiterated with the greatest frequency' is always, wrote John T. McNeill, 'a devotion to "the catholic church" or the church of God in all her parts. Unified in the headship of Christ, she is to be extended into and beneficially operative in the whole world.'[22]

Yet Calvin's own antipathy toward the Roman Catholic Church, regarding it as a church in error where the Gospel is obscured meant that his own efforts

---

[19] John Calvin and Jacopo Sadoleto, *A Reformation Debate*, ed. John C. Olin (Grand Rapids: Baker Book House, rpt, 1982), p. 85. Also in *Selected Works of John Calvin: Tracts and Letters*, eds Henry Beveridge and Jules Bonnet (7 vols; Grand Rapids, Michigan: Baker Book House, rpt, 1983), 1:121.
[20] Calvin, *A Reformation Debate*, p. 86; *Selected Works* 1:121-122.
[21] Calvin, *A Reformation Debate*, p. 94; *Selected Works* 1:129.
[22] John T. McNeill, *Unitive Protestantism: The Ecumenical Spirit and Its Persistent Expression* (Richmond, Virginia: John Knox Press, 1964), p. 71. McNeill cites Calvin's commentary on Isaiah 55:5: 'The restoration of the church may be regarded as the restoration of the whole world.'

towards church unity are 'primarily directed toward the consolidation of Protestantism.'[23] Calvin's sojourn in Strasbourg where he imbibed the thought of Bucer was surely a contributing influence in bringing church unity into the forefront of his thought.[24] Calvin turned out to be, as Lukas Vischer noted

> tireless in his efforts to resolve disputes in the Reformation churches. Wherever his help was requested, he saw it as his natural duty to offer his services, and he was certainly not afraid of being accused of interfering in matters that were none of his business. 'We do this in obedience to our conscience, as our duty in the service of the Word' [Letter from the Venerable Company of Pastors of Geneva to the Council of Neuchâtel, September 29, 1541]. In this spirit, in 1541, for example, he sent a delegation to Neuchâtel to calm the unrest that had broken out there. The disputes in the refugee congregation in Frankfurt were an object of his concern over many years. He wrote numerous letters trying to reach a settlement and, in 1556, he traveled to Frankfurt in person to put an end to the conflict still smouldering there.[25]

Famously, Calvin wrote to Archbishop Thomas Cranmer in England who was proposing a general synod for the closer union of Reformed churches that when 'the members of the Church being severed, the body lies bleeding.' So much did this concern Calvin, he said, that 'could I be of any service, I would not grudge to cross even ten seas, if need were, on account of it.'[26] As McNeill puts it, 'the idea of a catholic unity dominated the church theory of Calvin.'[27]

---

[23] McNeill, *Unitive Protestantism*, p. 180. Lukas Vischer notes that 'this was also the crux of the matter in the encounters with the Roman adversary. For him the only point of these was to bring God's Word to bear. In the early years of his activities Calvin accepted conversations in which the differences between the 'two fronts' were negotiated: in Frankfurt (1539), in Hagenau (1540), in Worms (1541) and—as a delegate of the city of Strasbourg—in Regensburg (1541). Even though he was under no illusions that an agreement could be reached—the impatience that can be detected in his letters is evidence enough—every opportunity had to be taken to work through the controversy about the truth.' See Lukas Vischer, 'Pia Conspiratio: Calvin's Legacy and the Divisions of the Reformed Churches Today', p. 4 of 25, http://www.warc.ch/dt/erl13/12.html. Cf. his 'The Reformation Heritage and the Ecumenical Movement' and 'The Reformed Church and Its Witness Today', at the same website.

[24] See McNeill, *Unitive Protestantism*, pp. 182-184. On Bucer, see Martin Greschat, *Martin Bucer: A Reformer and His Times*, trans. Stephen E. Buckwalter (Louisville: Westminster John Knox Press, 2004), ch. 5.

[25] Vischer, 'Pia Conspiratio', p. 5 of 25.

[26] Calvin, Letter 294 to Cranmer, April 1552 in *Selected Works*, 5: 355. Cf. McNeill, *Unitive Protestantism*, p. 247.

[27] McNeill, *Unitive Protestantism*, p. 217. McNeill cites other examples of Calvin's efforts toward unity.

The Unity of the Church in the Contemporary World

Much has changed since Calvin's day, both for the ecumenical church and for the Reformed family of churches. Ecumenical dialogues have occurred and Christians in Reformed churches have been participants.[28] Insofar as the Reformed have entered into these conversations to find areas of agreement between and among communions, they are following the impetus of Calvin who affirmed the reality of the unity of the church catholic as well as the need to work toward unity as a practical goal.

As we have seen, the main elements to which Alan Sell pointed in his statement on 'The Ecumenical Vision' are basically grounded in Calvin. They are still aims to which Christians in Reformed churches ought to aspire.

- Because the Reformed affirm a basic unity of the church catholic, we are to recognize that our churches should be a sign of God-given unity in Jesus Christ.
- We should recognize the varied cultural expressions that the Reformed faith—and Christianity generally—inevitably take and seek community in diversity
- We should give mutual recognition of ministries and church memberships, since we should receive the gift of unity in Christ but also work for it.
- We should remove barriers in the Lord's Supper since it is in the Supper that the unity of faith in Jesus Christ is clearly expressed.

Those who honour Calvin have not always honoured these trajectories; and as Vischer has noted, there is a need to go 'beyond Calvin' in Reformed ecclesiology.[29]

But the task that Alan Sell outlined is still before us and 'the ecumenical vision' for Reformed churches is still that which pulls us ahead to the future. We are 'Reformed' as we act 'ecumenically.' We live, in Christ, to give expression of, and work towards, the unity of the church. We never believe in the 'success' of our efforts; we can only trust in God, by faith. Calvin's comment on Isaiah 18:7 ought to give us hope and strength for the task

> At the present day the Church is not far from despair, being plundered, scattered, and every where crushed and trodden under foot. What must be done in straits so numerous and so distressing? We ought to lay hold of these promises, so as to

---

[28] See the chronicles in Sell, *A Reformed, Evangelical, Catholic Theology*.

[29] See Vischer, 'Pia Conspiratio', p. 16 of 25 who says, 'Does Calvin show us the way forward in every respect? Of course not. The churches shaped by his legacy live in a different world. Actual as Calvin remains in many respects, new perspectives have developed that inevitably lead beyond him. Indeed, in retrospect, it can be seen that there are actually limits to Calvin's understanding of the church which have unintentionally and unwittingly fostered the divisions of the Reformed churches.' He goes on to list six points to be considered.

believe that still God will preserve the Church. To whatever extent the body may be torn, shivered into fragments and scattered, still by his Spirit he will easily unite the members, and will never allow the remembering and the calling on his name to perish. Out of those fragments which are now broken and scattered, the Lord will unite and assemble the people (*Comm. Isaiah 18:7*).

Soli Deo Gloria!

CHAPTER 2

The Sources and Significance of Richard Price's Distinction between Abstract Virtue and Practical Virtue

D. O. Thomas

Abstract virtue is, most properly, a quality of the external action or event. It denotes what an action is, considered independently of the *sense* of the agent; or what, *in itself* and *absolutely*, it is right *such* an agent, in *such* circumstances, should do; and what, if he judged truly, he would judge he ought to do.

Practical virtue, on the contrary, has a necessary relation to, and dependence upon, the opinion of the agent concerning his actions. It signifies what he ought to do, *upon supposition* of his having such and such sentiments.[1]

During the period Alan P.F. Sell held the Chair of Christian Doctrine at the United Theological College at Aberystwyth, he founded, directed and sustained the Centre for the Study of British Christian Thought. In the period from the foundation of the Centre in 1993 until his retirement in 2001, the monthly seminars during the winter season were a great boon for those interested in theological and philosophical questions, especially as the Department of Philosophy and the Philosophy Society at the University of Wales at Aberystwyth had been closed. Sell was superbly equipped for this office, not only because of his wide-ranging experience in educational matters, his reputation as a scholar and his extensive contacts in the academic world which enabled him to attract leading experts in the field to his seminars, but also because of his gifts as a chairman which include a quiet authority, a sure touch in the conduct of business and a welcome sense of humour.

---

[1] Richard Price, *A Review of the Principal Questions in Morals*, ed. D.D. Raphael (Oxford: Oxford University Press, 1948, revised edition 1974), p. 177.

Sell is a prolific author, with an amazing output over a wide range of theological, historical and philosophical subjects. The fields in which he has conducted extensive research include the theology and moral philosophy of the seventeenth and eighteenth centuries. Of particular interest to him has been the emphasis placed among Dissenters on the role of private judgement and the scope of individual responsibility. In the following I wish to discuss a topic which, I believe, is relevant to Sell's own interests, namely, some of the sources and the significance of the distinction Price drew between abstract virtue and practical virtue.

For Price the distinction is important because he wanted to maintain that a person's conduct may be virtuous when he acts conscientiously even though his conscience may be misinformed. It is true that a person must always do his best to see that his judgements are well-informed, but provided he satisfies that criterion, his action does not have of necessity to be, as some have thought, the best or the most appropriate action. In *Ethical and Political Thinking*, E.F. Carritt suggested that Price was perhaps the first to notice the importance of the question whether our obligations, and consequently our duties depend (a) upon the actual situation (including our capacities for affecting it, and the consequences of what we may immediately bring about) or (b) upon our moral estimate of what the supposed situation demands.[2] In an article entitled 'The Virtue of the Act and the Virtue of the Agent,' A.N. Prior challenged Carritt's claim that Price was original in making this distinction, and pointed to several possible sources – among them Samuel Rutherford, Matthew Henry, Joseph Butler and John Balguy – that might have suggested the importance of the distinction to him and from whom he could have derived the material which he used in his discussion of the problem in the eighth chapter of *Review*. Prior also drew attention to Thomas Reid's discussion of the subject in *Essays on the Active Powers* and the treatment of a comparable distinction in Greek, Roman and medieval thinkers.[3] In what follows I shall suggest some further possible sources for Price's treatment of the relevant distinction, one expressly indicated by Price himself, and others whom he acknowledged as sources of inspiration, with the aim of demonstrating that far from being original, Price was drawing upon traditions in moral philosophy that were well established in the seventeenth and early eighteenth centuries.

One indication that Price was drawing on previous discussions lies in the

---

[2] E.F. Carritt, *Ethical and Political Thinking* (Oxford: Clarendon Press, 1947), p. 14. This work was first published in 1947; in the preface Carritt acknowledges his debt to Price, 'apart from the well known classics on the subject, I think I owe most to Richard Price's *A Review of the Principal Questions and Difficulties in Morals*.' Carritt used the title of the first edition; in the second and third Price dropped the phrase 'and difficulties'.

[3] A.N. Prior, 'The Virtue of the Act and the Virtue of the Agent', *Philosophy*, XXVI, No 97 (April 1951), pp. 121-30.

title of his book: *A Review of the Principal Questions and Difficulties in Morals.* This suggests, although it would be easy to make too much of it, that Price thought of himself as surveying the main topics in moral philosophy that engaged the attention of his contemporaries.[4] Perhaps a stronger indication is that Price uses several different terms, or pairs of terms, for his concepts. For abstract virtue – what in itself and absolutely it is right an agent should do, and what, if he judges truly, he would judge he ought to do – Price also uses the terms absolute virtue. In addition, he refers to it as 'mere theoretical virtue' and again, as 'what is objectively right'. For practical virtue – what an agent ought to do, upon the supposition of his having certain sentiments – Price also uses the term relative virtue, and, for good measure, he claims that the distinction he draws between abstract (absolute) virtue and practical (relative) virtue is 'not entirely different' from the distinction some have drawn between actions that are 'materially good' and those that are 'formally so'.[5] Had Price been original in making the distinction between abstract and practical virtue, it is unlikely that he would have used so many different terms; it is much more likely that he was drawing upon well established traditions and finding inspiration in considerations that had proved fruitful in earlier discussions.

One of the sources for these pairs of terms – a source not mentioned by Prior – is to be found in a correspondence between Mrs Catharine Cockburn[6] and Dr Thomas Sharp, then Archdeacon of Northumberland,[7] on questions concerning the foundation of morals. In a footnote in the second edition of *Review*,[8] strangely, neither in the first nor in the third edition, Price draws the attention of the reader to these letters. In them the reader would find 'a distinction much the same with' the distinction he was making between abstract virtue and practical virtue. This correspondence[9] began with a letter from Dr Sharp to Mrs Cockburn, dated 8 August 1743 and continued intermittently until some time after 2 October 1747, Dr Sharp's reply to Mrs Cockburn's letter of 2 October 1747 being undated. In these letters they engaged in an amicable discussion, the hub of which is this. Mrs Cockburn, an indefatigable apologist for Samuel Clarke, wished to defend the view that the sole foundation of virtue is the 'immutable and essential difference of things'. The Archdeacon, on the other hand, maintained

---

[4] There is evidence to suggest that the title of the work suffered a late change to 'Review' from 'Inquiry'. See D.O. Thomas, John Stephens and P.A.L. Jones, *A Bibliography of the Works of Richard Price* (Aldershot: Scolar Press 1993), p. 8.
[5] Price, *Review*, p. 184 and p. 177.
[6] Mrs Catharine Cockburn, née Trotter (1679?-1749).
[7] Dr Thomas Sharp (1693-1758), Archdeacon of Northumberland, father of Granville Sharp.
[8] Price, *Review*, 2nd edn (1769), 293n.
[9] *The works of Mrs Catharine Cockburn*, with an account of her life by Thomas Birch (2 vols; London: 1751). The correspondence with Dr Sharp was published in Vol II, pp. 353-460.

that the principal not the sole foundation of moral virtue are the essential differences of things and fitnesses resulting necessarily from them, but not considered as separable or possibly separable from the will of God. And that the principal, not the sole foundation of moral obligation is the will of God, but not considered as separate, or possibly separable from the eternal and immutable ratios of things. And that the only proper ultimate foundation of moral virtue, and moral obligation is God himself; the only true foundation both of wisdom and goodness, and every thing, that is, either perfect, true, or right in physics, metaphysics, or morals.[10]

In defence of the view that the sole foundation of virtue is the immutable and essential difference of things, and to counter the Archdeacon's suggestion that if this were the case, there would be no reason why freedom and reason my not equally well be regarded as the foundation of virtue, Mrs Cockburn distinguishes what is necessary to virtue from what is necessary to moral agency

> Reason and freewill, I acknowledge, Sir, to be absolutely necessary to moral agency: they are qualifications without which there could be no such thing as the practice of virtue, and may, if you please be called foundations of virtuous practice. But this is quite another idea than the general abstract nature of virtue, the foundations of which we are enquiring about; and to the constituting and production of virtue in this sense, I see not that anything can be necessary, or at all contribute, but the immutable relations and essential differences of things, from which virtue, considered in its abstract nature, directly and solely arises.[11]

Mrs Cockburn anticipated many of the points that Price makes in his discussion of abstract and practical virtue – that there is a sense in which the agent's duty can be determined independently of his beliefs as to what his duty is – the notion of abstract virtue – and that there is a sense in which the agent's duty can only be determined by reference to those beliefs – the notion of practical virtue. She also anticipated Price's principle of the convinced conscience, namely, that a person ought always to do what he believes to be his duty, and she also anticipated much of Price's discussion of those virtues that are subsidiary to conscientiousness, namely, the disposition to seek out the truth and to inform oneself as best one can about one's duties, and the disposition to cultivate the habits of mind and heart that help to keep one in the paths of virtue. But she does not make explicit what is brought out in Price's discussion, namely, that a person may be wholly virtuous in following his conscience even though it is erroneous. She insists that a person must follow his conscience even though it is mistaken, but she does not emphasize that he may be not only sinless in so doing but also morally good.

In developing what he conceived to be the different foundations of virtue, Dr

---

[10] Cockburn, *Works*, II, pp. 372-73.
[11] Cockburn, *Works*, II, p. 376.

Sharp used the scholastic classification of causes. The material cause is 'the nature, truth, and relation of things, with their consequent fitness of application'; the formal cause is 'right reason with liberty'. The importance of distinguishing between these two lies in the fact that

> the actions even of reasonable creatures, however consonant (of themselves) to the nature, truth, and relations of things, if done through necessity, through ignorance, or, in one word, without moral intention, cannot be accounted virtue. However, they may be said to come within the matter of it, yet they have not the form of virtue.[12]

The Archdeacon's insistence upon the complementarity of material and formal virtue, and his insistence that an action cannot be virtuous unless it is formally so, tend to suggest that the action cannot be virtuous unless it is also materially so. Whereas Price claimed that if a person does what he sincerely believes he ought to do, his action may be morally good even though he is mistaken as to what his abstract duty is, it is not clear what the Archdeacon thought about the merits of an erroneous conscience, and the lack of clarity remains in his acknowledgement of his debt to Etienne Chauvin, author of *Lexicon Rationale, Sive Thesaurus Philosophicus*.[13] According to the Archdeacon, Chauvin maintained that the material principle of virtue

> is the nature of things in so far as it is a rule of conformity or a subject of moral practice...The formal principle is right reason; for...when every thing is considered and treated, as right reason teaches it should be considered and treated, then virtue comes forth in its perfection.[14]

In commenting upon Chauvin's distinctions, the Archdeacon claims

> We have got them a twofold ground of virtue (in the abstract idea) to stand upon, viz. the reasons of things, or fitnesses arising from the mutual relations of things to each other; and reason of agents, or the faculty of discerning those fitnesses and reasons of things. But virtue or practical morality cannot properly be said to be founded in either of these solely and wholly, but must arise from the voluntary and actual exercise of the reason of the agent in the great law of morals, which is nature's institution.[15]

Here we can see that Price's treatment of practical virtue differs from the Archdeacon's in that the latter's, like Mrs Cockburn's, emphasizes that the formal principle is essential to virtue, without holding that it may in certain circumstances be sufficient to moral goodness. As far as I know, Price never

---

[12] Cockburn, *Works*, II, p. 394.
[13] Rotterdam, 1692.
[14] Cockburn, *Works*, II, pp. 394-95.
[15] Cockburn, *Works*, II, p. 398.

explained why he dropped the reference to the correspondence between Mrs Cockburn and Dr Sharp from the third edition of *Review*. It may have been because he came to realize that although they used the terms abstract virtue and practical virtue, the use they made of them was different from his; that whereas they used them to distinguish two complementary elements in virtuous practice, without suggesting or even allowing that an agent could be morally praiseworthy even though he was ignorant of his objective duty. Whereas they allowed that a man ought always to follow his conscience, many Anglican Divines were reluctant to allow that such action is always virtuous. As an example, we may consider the views of John Sharp, Archbishop of York,[16] who maintained, in his contribution to a work entitled *A Collection of Cases and other Discourses, lately written to recover Dissenters to the Communion of the Church of England*,[17] that whereas a man ought always to follow his conscience even though it was mistaken, such action could not always be considered virtuous

> We do not indeed say, that every one is a good man that acts according to his Judgment; or that he is to be commended for all actions that are done in Pursuance of his Persuasion; no, we measure *Virtue* and *Vice* by the Rule according to which a Man ought to act, as well as by the Man's Intention in acting.[18]

Archbishop Sharp thus holds that where conscience is mistaken, a person may find himself in the uncomfortable position of sinning if he acts contrary to his conscience, and sinning if he acts in accordance with it. But, according to Price, not all actions done from an erroneous conscience are culpable: mistakes are not sinful where an honest-minded person may be mistaken, where he does not have sufficient means of information or adequate opportunities for instruction, or where he has done all he can in trying to understand his duty. A person has obligations to discover what his duty is, and he is sinless if he takes all reasonable steps to inform his conscience. But if he fails in this respect his ignorance and negligence are culpable. In such cases if seems that Price can be interpreted as holding that it is the ignorance and negligence that are culpable not the action that proceeds from them.[19] Sharp argues the contrary: where ignorance and negligence are culpable the action that proceeds from them, even though the agent is conscientious, is also culpable.[20] Sharp also holds that an erroneous conscience does not absolve a man from the obligations and duties that he has under the law, and here we see the force of construing moral

---

[16] John Sharp (1645-1714), became Dean of Norwich in 1681, and Archbishop of York in 1691. He was Spiritual Advisor to Queen Anne.
[17] See John Sharp, *A Collection of Cases and other Discourses, lately written to recover Dissenters to the Communion of the Church of England*, 3rd edn, (3 vols; London: 1718).
[18] Sharp, *A Collection*, I, p. 400.
[19] D.O. Thomas, *The Honest Mind* (Oxford: Oxford University Press, 1977), p. 94.
[20] Sharp, *A Collection*, p. 406.

obligations in the light of the principles of positive law or jurisprudence. Sharp insists that the maxim '*Ignorantia legis non excusat*' applies to the moral law and failure to act in accordance with objective rectitude or failure to perform contracts incurs penalties.

Sharp's main purpose is to clarify the grounds upon which a Dissenter is justified in not conforming to the Church of England, and since schism is such a grievous sin, a Dissenter has to be very careful that he stands on good ground in refusing to conform. Sharp does, however, allow that we should be slow to condemn a man who has made every reasonable effort to enlighten his conscience. Of the man who has tried to inform his judgement as well as he can, he writes, 'Though the man cannot be excused of schism, yet I trust he shall not be charged before God with the Formal Guilt of Schism any farther than the Error that has led him into it was contracted by his own Fault.'[21]

The main differences between Sharp and Price are (a) that Price does not require that abstract virtue is essential to virtuous conduct, even though it is a duty that one should strive earnestly to find out what abstract virtue requires; (b) that where one acts in accordance with an erroneous conscience and is negligent in so doing, it is the negligence that is culpable and not the action that proceeds from it. Sharp is quite convinced that in these circumstances both the negligence and the action that proceeds from it are culpable; (c) whereas Sharp thinks that the rectitude of conformity to the Anglican Church is easily demonstrable – a contention made more plausible by the assimilation of moral obligation to positive obligation – Price, like many Dissenters, would strenuously deny that conformity could be shown to be morally obligatory.

I have noted earlier that Price uses the pair of terms absolute and relative as an alternative to abstract and practical. One possible source for these terms, and the use made of them, may have been the controversy that occurred between Matthew Tindal, author of *Christianity as old as the creation*, which was published in 1730, and defenders of the validity of the Christian revelation, notably John Conybeare, whose *A Defence of Revealed Religion* appeared in 1732, and John Balguy whose *A Second Letter to a Deist* appeared in 1731. Tindal attacked all revealed religions, including Christianity, on the grounds that they are superfluous since all religious and moral truth can be determined by the exercise of reason. Conybeare, who was later to succeed Butler as Bishop of Bristol, argued that although the fundamental principles of morality are known to all, no man can simply by the exercise of reason, determine the whole of a perfect rule of conduct. Since men are variously endowed, since the capacity for rational activity differs from person to person, and since opportunities for education are unequally distributed, the ability to determine a rule of conduct also varies. A revelation is needed to remedy these deficiencies. Tindal's position is made plausible, Conybeare argued, by confusions in the conception of a Religion of Nature. It can be interpreted as 'a perfect Collection

---

[21] Sharp, *A Collection,* p. 427.

of all those moral Doctrines, and Precepts, which have a real Foundation in the nature and Reason of things', but it can also be interpreted as 'such a Collection of Doctrines and Precepts as is discoverable by us in the Use of our natural Faculties.'[22] It is because he conflates both of these conceptions that Tindal writes as though there is a perfect rule of conduct evident to every human being. In the former sense of the religion of nature, it is true, is an absolutely perfect rule, but since in its entirety it is known only to God, and since 'obligation cannot reach further than a capacity of knowledge', it is not wholly available to humans as a rule of conduct. What forms or helps to form our practical rule of conduct is a religion of nature understood in the latter sense, namely, the doctrines and precepts that at any one time an individual can discover by the exercise of reason. But the religion of nature thus understood is imperfect and its deficiencies need to be remedied by consulting what God has revealed to us through the prophets and pre-eminently through the Gospel. Whereas the religion of nature in the former sense yields an absolutely perfect rule, in the latter sense it yields a rule that is 'perfect in its kind', or as Conybeare otherwise expressed it, a rule that is relatively perfect, that is, perfect in the circumstances in which a man finds himself and as adjusted to his capacity for apprehending moral truths

> Things which have no Excellency in themselves, and therefore are not excellent in an absolute sense may yet have a relative Excellency, and when considered in this view, may contribute to the Excellency of the Scheme, the Design of which is not only to teach us the best Precepts, but to accommodate them to the present condition of Man.[23]

Failure to follow the absolutely perfect rule, Conybeare maintained, is not blameworthy, for it is in relation to the relatively perfect rule that we are accountable. This does not, however, absolve us from the duty to do our utmost to find out what the perfect rule requires. 'To him [God] therefore are they accountable for their Conformity to those Rules only, which they did know, or might have known to be his Will.'[24]

In *A Second Letter to a Deist*, John Balguy presented what Conybeare distinguished as two senses of the religion of nature as a distinction between the Law of nature and the Light of nature. He accused Tindal of confusing the two much as Conybeare did

---

[22] John Conybeare (1692-1755) became Bishop of Bristol in 1750. See his *A Defence of Revealed Religion*, 2nd edn (London: 1732), pp. 13-16. His antagonist, Matthew Tindal (1657-1733), a lawyer, was elected a Fellow of All Souls, Oxford in 1679.
[23] Conybeare, *Defence*, p. 217.
[24] Conybeare, *Defence*, p. 17.

If by the *Light of Nature*, you mean the *Law of Nature*, considered objectively, and in itself; I not only allow its *Sufficiency*, but its full *Perfection*. That Law which results from the External Reasons and Relations of Things, must needs be a compleat Rule of Action for all *intelligent Creatures*, and I beg leave to add, even for the *Creator* himself.[25] Properly speaking, the *Light of Nature* signifies that Share, that Portion of Moral Truth, which Men are naturally capable of discovering. Though the Sun be always the same in itself, yet the Light of it is variously enjoyed by Mankind; according to the Difference of their Sight, or Situation. And thus it is with Truth; which Men profess in larger or less Degree, according to their abilities, opportunities, Application, Conduct. In both cases that only can be said to be any Man's Natural Light; which he enjoys, or is capable of enjoying, by the Use of his natural Faculties.[26]

The distinction between the law of nature and the light of nature allows Balguy to distinguish, as Conybeare did, that which is absolutely good from the relatively good, 'that which is absolutely good, in itself, may be relatively deficient. Regard must therefore be had to the Conditions, the Circumstances, and Capacity of the Agent.'[27] Balguy brought out very clearly that what is relatively good is related to the capacities of the individual. Although one has but an imperfect knowledge of the perfect rule of conduct, if he improves his knowledge as much as he can, and practices accordingly, he is sure to discharge his duty, for no-one can have a duty to do 'what is not in his power to know'. However ignorant and uneducated one may be, the light of nature discloses some moral truths to him, and provided that he extends his knowledge of these as far as he can, and provided that he acts in accordance with them, his conduct will be acceptable to God.

The most ignorant and uninstructed Heathen must have had some Ideas of Justice, Probity, Gratitude, Mercy and the like. And I grant you, Sir, that even this little *Light of Nature* was, in some Sense *sufficient* for him. If we suppose him to have improved it as far as he was able, and to have practised accordingly, he could not fail of being approved in the sight of God; But, in another sense, it was manifestly *insufficient*; I mean, for bringing Mankind to that *Standard of Duty* which belongs to their Nature, and that *State of Perfection*, whereof they are capable.[28]

If they act in accordance with the best knowledge available to them, Balguy maintained, they are acceptable to God. Acceptance, however, is one thing; Perfection is another.[29]

Balguy's distinction between that which is absolutely good and that which is

---

[25] John Balguy (1686-1748) became Vicar of Northallerton in 1729. See *A Collection of Tracts* (London: 1774), p. 282.
[26] Balguy, *A Collection of Tracts*, p. 284.
[27] Balguy, *A Collection of Tracts*, p. 322.
[28] Balguy, *A Collection of Tracts*, p. 291.
[29] Balguy, *A Collection of Tracts*, p. 307.

relatively good recalls the distinction that Robert Sanderson makes in *De Obligatione Conscientiae* between those things that bind absolutely, binding primarily and of themselves – and those things that bind 'secondarily, and by consequences, not absolutely but relatively, not by their own Power, but by Virtue of some Divine Precept or Institution.'[30] Sanderson puts this distinction to two different uses: first, to distinguish, in a hierarchy of obligations, those fundamental principles of the Divine Law that derive their authority directly from the will of God, from those that have authority only in so far as they can be derived from fundamental principles; these secondary obligations are determined by human legislators, or are created by contracts between individuals, or are required by the law of scandal, that is by the need to avoid offending our fellow-men. The second use to which Sanderson puts this distinction is to mark off the fundamental principles that should govern human conduct – the common notions – from particular judgements, the conclusions of practical syllogisms, concerning what action should be taken in a given context. Sanderson defines conscience as 'A Faculty or Habit of the Practical understanding by which the mind of man, by the use of reason and argument applies the light which it has to particular moral action.'[31] He follows in the long established tradition[32] of distinguishing Synderesis, which he defines as a habit of first principles about good and evil, from Syneidesis, which he defines as knowledge of a conclusion of a practical syllogism. Sanderson notes that conscience is used in three different senses: (a) for the apprehension of first principles; (b) for knowledge of a conclusion derived from first principles; and (c) for the whole process of arguing from first principles to particular conclusions. The proper use, according to Sanderson, is (b) syneidesis (conscientia).[33] It might be thought that since both synderesis and syneidesis are forms of knowledge, that people cannot err in making moral judgements, but that is not what Sanderson holds. Although the apprehension of first principles is immediate and certain,[34] the conclusion might be vitiated by the mis-application of a principle.[35] 'You ought to relieve the needs of poor women and "Here is a poor woman in need" will, if conjointly asserted, entail "You ought

---

[30] See Robert Sanderson, 'The Nature and Obligation of Conscience Explained', contained in the second volume of *A Preservative against Schism and Rebellion in the most trying Times* (3 vols; London: 1722), II, p. 265. Robert Sanderson (1587-1663) became Bishop of Lincoln c.1660.

[31] Sanderson, *Preservative*, II, p. 28.

[32] On the history of the concept of synderesis see Robert A. Greene, 'Synderesis, the Spark of Conscience, in the English Renaissance', *JHI* 52.2 (April-June, 1991), pp. 196-219; and idem, 'Whichcote, the Candle of the Lord, and Synderesis', *JHI* 52.2 (October-December, 1991), pp. 617-644.

[33] Sanderson, *Preservative*, II, pp. 24-25.

[34] See Timothy C. Potts, *Conscience in Medieval Philosophy* (Cambridge: Cambridge University Press, 1980), p. 64.

[35] Sanderson, *Preservative*, II, pp. 39, 45.

to relieve the needs of this woman". But the conclusion will be false if the minor premise is false – that the lady in question is not a poor woman.' Sanderson is quite clear that conscience can be mistaken, and he is also clear that a man must act in accordance with his conscience, even if it is mistaken.[36] But an action in accordance with conscience is not necessarily morally good, nor is the agent necessarily morally praiseworthy if he acts in accordance with his conscience, even if he does what he can to inform his conscience correctly. In *De Obligatione Conscientiae* he writes

> The conscience therefore, by a sort of allowable ignorance (tho' perhaps otherwise erroneous) even in the Judgment of God himself, may be said to act so far uprightly, as it conforms to the Light of the Mind, which is its next and immediate Rule. But there is more required to complete the Integrity of the Conscience, and make her absolutely perfect; she must likewise conform to her first and *Supreme Rule*.[37]

Sanderson holds that the goodness of the intention is not enough to make an action morally good. To be morally good further elements must be present

> Since…no Action can justly be said to be Morally Good, unless the Matter be lawful, the Intention right and the Circumstances proper, it is evident, that a Good Intention alone is insufficient, and consequently no Act can be done with a safe Conscience, whatsoever the Intention be, that is either unlawful in the object, or defective in the Circumstance.[38]

Sanderson cites the case of Uzzah, who when the ark was being taken unlawfully on a cart, stretched out his hand to save it from falling to the ground, and was immediately struck dead by God for his presumption. There is no doubt that Uzzah's intention was most sincere and pious, but that did not save him from God's wrath and destruction.[39] Accordingly, it is evil to deliberately breach any of the Ten Commandments, whatever good may be thought to result from doing so, or whatever harm might be thought to be avoided in doing so. God's rules are not to be broken, whatever the apparent cost of keeping them. It is for this reason that sincerely thinking that some action is one's duty is not a sufficient justification for acting on that belief.

Another possible source not only for Price's distinction between objective and subjective rectitude, but for a great deal of his teaching on the subject, is to be found in Henry Grove's *A System of Moral Philosophy* which was published

---

[36] Robert Sanderson, *Sermons* (London: 1681). See particularly, the fourth sermon *Ad Clerum*, preached on 22 August 1634, p. 72. 'An erroneous conscience bindeth thus far that a man cannot go against it and be guiltless.'

[37] Sanderson, *De Obligatione Conscientiae*, p. 210. The Latin text is given in Whewell's edition of *De Obligatione Conscientiae* (Cambridge: 1851), pp. 101-102.

[38] Sanderson, *Preservative*, II, p. 85.

[39] Sanderson, *Preservative*, II, p. 96. 2 Sam.7: 6-7.

posthumously in 1749 from the author's manuscript. Price's name is included in the list of subscribers to the publication of this work.[40] Although Price does not refer to Grove's work when he discusses subjective rectitude he does refer to him on three occasions in *Review*. The first refers to Grove's refutation of the view, maintained by the Stoics, that right action in the abstract or absolute senses admits of degrees of rectitude.[41] Secondly, Price refers to Grove's *Wisdom the First Spring of Action in the Deity* (1734) on the question as to what may be inferred about the intentions of the Deity from our experience of the course of events in this world.[42] The third reference is to the discussion in the latter work of the question whether the most beautifully constructed universe would have any value if there were no beings capable of enjoying and appreciating it.[43] I hope to show that there are several other similarities in Grove's and Price's treatment of the subject. In his ethical thinking Price felt the need, in common with many of the Real Whigs of his time, to escape from the assumption that authority is founded only in will, whether human or divine. In moral philosophy, obligation and duty are founded in reason and in the essential nature of things. But to preserve the theocentricity of his ethics Price postulated that the moral law was founded not in God's will but in His nature. In this he was anticipated by Grove who, as Sell has pointed out, maintained

> We are obliged to love God, not merely because he hath commanded us to love him, but because he hath made us capable of loving him, and both by his perfections and his benefits challenges our love. Did these not oblige us to love him as soon as we were in a condition to make any reflection on them, no subsequent command could oblige us to it.[44]

This is not to deny, however, that moral duties are contained within a structure of authority. Every man is bound to do what God wills, and obey His commandments. What Grove emphasizes is that obligation and duty are grounded in a moral law that binds the Divine will itself.[45] Grove's moral philosophy is highly individualist in the sense that he stresses that the agent is to follow his own judgement. 'Every man is to guide himself and his actions by the Law; and that not as the Law appears to others, but to himself; or, which, is

---

[40] I am indebted to Mr John Stephens for this reference.
[41] Price, *Review*, 208n.; Grove, *System*, I, p. 262.
[42] Price, *Review*, 240n.
[43] Price, *Review*, 250n.
[44] Henry Grove (1684-1738) became a tutor at Taunton Academy in 1706. See Grove's ordination sermon for Thomas Amory and William Cornish preached at Taunton on 7 October 1730, *Works* I (1747), pp. 470-471, cited by Alan P.F. Sell, 'Henry Grove: A Dissenter at the Parting of the Ways', *Enlightenment and Dissent*, 4 (1985), p. 60.
[45] See Grove, *System*, II, p. 12, 'I affirm the Will of God to be the Rule of Conscience and the only Rule. This sovereign and holy Will is, I say, a Rule obliging the Conscience, however discovered, whether by Reason or Revelation.'

the same, by the Judgment and Light of his own Conscience.'[46]

Unlike Bishop Butler, Grove did not hold that the conscience is infallible and completely trustworthy as a guide to action.[47] Accordingly, since moral judgement is fallible, and what the agent takes to be his duty may not be what it really is, we need to distinguish the notion of objective duty from the notion of practical duty, the latter being what an agent ought to do, his beliefs as to what he ought to do being what they are. For the former notion Grove also uses the terms intrinsic and absolute, and for the latter he also uses the term relative.[48] Although his conscience is fallible, the agent is bound to follow it whether it is mistaken or not. 'A man sins if he goes against his erroneous conscience.'[49] Faced with the challenge that a man is held to sin if he breaks God's law, and that he sins if he does not follow an erroneous conscience, Grove resolves the paradox by distinguishing a general rule from a particular one. God's laws are a series of particular rules, which in practice are subordinate to the general rule that one must follow his own judgement of what it is that God requires of him.[50] If, on the other hand he follows his conscience, and if he does what he can to find out what his objective duties are, even though he is mistaken, he is not in danger of sinning and his conduct will be acceptable to God. 'The fundamental duty of all morality [is] a sincere endeavour to know and, as far known, to perform all the duties we stand obliged to.'[51]

Grove repeatedly insisted that fulfilling this 'fundamental duty' is not simply a matter of doing what the agent happens to believe is right at the moment of action. It is also essential that the agent applies the tests of reason to his beliefs, and in doing so cleanses the mind of irrational prejudices and those predispositions that are favoured by the pursuit of self-interest. It is also essential that the agent is candid, and this entails doing what he can to see that his judgement is well informed – he should be diligent in the 'search for truth'.[52] Grove follows in the jurisprudential tradition of holding that invincible ignorance excuses, but he is careful to point out that ignorance is only regarded as involuntary if the agent has made as much effort to inform himself of the truth as can be reasonably expected of him

> By an invincible ignorance is not meant an ignorance absolutely invincible but morally speaking; and such is the ignorance of the man, who makes use of all the

---

[46] Grove, *System*, II, p. 15.
[47] See Joseph Butler, *Works*, ed. Samuel Halifax (2 vols; Oxford: 1849), II, pp. 31-43; Thomas, *Bibliography*, pp. 87-88.
[48] Grove, *System*, II, p. 42 for absolute and relative.
[49] Grove, *System*, II, p. 32.
[50] Grove, *System*, II, p. 32.
[51] Grove, *System*, I, p. 30.
[52] Grove, *System*, II, p.27.

pains, and care, and caution, to inform himself of the truth, that can be expected from one as desirous of it.[53]

Grove makes it clear that the reason why blameworthiness attaches to failure to do one's practical or relative duty, and not to failure to do one's objective duty, is that it is only one's practical duty that is available as an action in accordance with conscience. One cannot be legitimately expected to do as one's duty what is not known as one's duty: One cannot do more than inquire impartially, and then honestly act according to the best judgment we can make of things, after having inquired into them; all beyond this is impossible, and therefore no part of our duty.[54] Grove follows Grotius, as Price was also to do, in holding that the agent if he could not resolve a doubt as to whether or not he should do an action, should always choose the 'safer side'.[55] But in one important respect, however, Grove differed from Price on the question whether an action done according to conscience, though from voluntary ignorance is culpable. Price, I have argued, seemed to think that it is only the ignorance that is culpable and not the action that proceeds from it. Grove is in no doubt, for him both the voluntary ignorance and the action that proceeds from it are culpable.[56]

Samuel Clarke was one of Price's heroes. In the third edition of *Review* (1787) he included as an appendix, 'A dissertation on the being and attributes of the Deity' in which he referred to Clarke (along with Sir Isaac Newton and Bishop Joseph Butler) as one of 'three of the greatest [names] this world has ever known'.[57] As far as I know, Clarke did not use the distinction between abstract virtue and practical virtue, neither did he enunciate the principle of the convinced conscience. Nor did he say that sincerity in thought and action is all that is required to render a man's conduct acceptable to God. Nonetheless, it would seem as though the intellectual framework of his thought would accommodate, and indeed require, these elements. In the introduction to *The Scripture Doctrine of the Trinity* (1712) there is a striking passage which could serve as a brief credo stating the fundamental principles of rationalist and individualist approach to the justification of faith: rationalist in the sense that a person's religious beliefs need to stand the tests of rational criticism, and individualist in the sense that a person must live by the light of his own understanding and not by anyone else's. As befitted a good Protestant, Clarke maintained that the foundation of all true faith is to be found in Scripture and that every person must work out for himself what it is that Scripture teaches.

---

[53] Grove, *System*, II, p. 29.

[54] Grove, *System*, II, p. 31.

[55] Grove, *System*, II, p. 42; Grotius, *De iure belli ac pacis*, Bk II, ch. 23, sect. 15, '*In dubiis, pars tutior est eligendaa*'.

[56] Grove, *System*, II, p. 31.

[57] Price, *Review*, 291n.

The *only Rule of faith* therefore to every Christian, is *the Doctrine of Christ*, and that Doctrine as applied to him by his own Understanding. In which matter, to preserve the Understanding from erring, he is obliged indeed, at his utmost peril, to lay aside all Vice and Prejudice, and to make use of the best assistances he can procure. But after he has done all that can be done, he must of necessity, at last understand with his own Understanding, and believe with his own, not another's Faith, for whatever has sometimes been absurdly pretended to the contrary 'tis evidently as *impossible* in Nature, that in these things any one Person should *submit* himself to another's that one man should *see* or *taste*, should *live* or *breathe* for another.[58]

In his earlier works on moral philosophy, the Boyle lectures, *A Demonstration of the Being and Attributes of God* (1704), and *A Discourse concerning the unchangeable Obligations of Natural Religion* (1705), Clarke does not deal explicitly with the problems of moral perplexity. He maintains that the one who sincerely strives to do his duty will find acceptance with God;[59] it is true, but he does not explicitly state that virtue lies in doing what one believes to be one's duty, whether or not the conscience be ill-informed. As far as his earlier work is concerned, he does not make clear what is involved in applying the principles he was later to enunciate in *The Scripture Doctrine of the Trinity* to moral philosophy. I suggest that the reasons why he does not focus on the problems of moral perplexity are to be found partly in the fact that in the earlier works he was mainly concerned to demonstrate the objectivity, rationality, and universality of moral principles, and partly by the fact that he believes that the great majority of men are prevented from apprehending the truth by want of attention, idleness and their depraved preoccupations with the lusts of the senses and self-interest. It is true that men can attain to the truth if they use their reason – then all things will become clear – but most men are disabled from pursuing the truth by their predispositions. In *A Discourse concerning the unchangeable Obligations of Natural Religion* Clarke gives a very pessimistic and extraordinarily comprehensive account of the psychological forces that hinder men from reaching the truth. We are far removed from the optimism of the Enlightenment and a belief in the capacity of mankind to attain to perfection. In this climate of opinion, the main concern is with the disabling effects of human wickedness, which tends to displace and leave little room for relying upon the individual to follow his own judgment.

There is naturally in the greater part of Mankind such a prodigious Carelessness, Inconsiderateness and Want of Attention; as not only hinders them from making

---

[58] Samuel Clarke (1675-1729) was appointed Rector of St James's, London, in 1709. See *The Works of Samuel Clarke*, D.D. 4 vols (London: 1738), IV.1.

[59] Cockburn, *Works*, II, 'It being evident that God in his infinite Bounty may reward the sincere obedience of his Creatures, as much beyond the Merit of their own weak and imperfect Works, as he himself pleases.'

use of their Reason, in such a manner as to discover these things clearly and effectually for themselves; but is the cause of the grossest and most stupid Ignorance imaginable. Some seem to have little or hardly any notion of God at all; and More take a little or no care to frame just and worthy Apprehensions concerning him, considering the Divine Attributes and Perfections of his Nature; and still many more are entirely negligent and heedless, to consider and discover what may be his Will. Few make a due use of their Natural Faculties to distinguish rightly the essential and unchangeable Difference between Good and Evil.[60]

Conclusion

Among moral philosophers of Price's persuasion, especially when their teaching is contrasted with that of Sanderson and Conybeare, there is a shift of focus to the judgement of the individual. What matters to thinkers like Clarke, Grove and Price is that a person does his best to find out what his obligations and duties are and that he acts according to his best judgement. There are several factors in the intellectual climate which helped to foster this viewpoint. First, there is the force of the Protestant commitment to concentrate attention on the Scriptures as the true foundation of Christian belief. William Chillingworth's promotion of the sufficiency of Scripture – *sola scriptura* – had a profound influence in two ways. In the first place it emphasized that all the Christian needed to know could be found within Scripture, and, secondly, that the individual could find the essential truths of Scripture for himself without being dependent on any other external agencies. The latter contention is vividly illustrated, as we have seen, in the thought of Samuel Clarke who maintained that the Scriptures are perspicuous to the intelligent and honest reader. Among Dissenters the concentration on Scripture is enhanced by the desire to move away from any beliefs in the Thirty-nine Articles that are not established by Scripture. The role of the Church is, in effect, substantially diminished. Thirdly, the belief that the essential truths of Christianity are perspicuous to the individual runs in tandem with the belief that the necessary truths in moral philosophy can be accessed by the exercise of reason, or particularly by the exercise of rational intuition. This concentration on the role of the individual was to give a powerful stimulus to the development of liberal and democratic movements in polities throughout the eighteenth century.

It has to be admitted, however, that this concentration on the role of the individual has its dangers. Among the rationalists and the individualists there is a tendency to downgrade the role of tradition in religious and moral thought. What any one person believes in any given context and at any given time is to a large extent the product of the culture into which he or she was born. This can be seen even in the fact that many of those who believe in the exalted and

---

[60] Cockburn, *Works*, II, pp. 682-83.

exclusive superiority of Scripture are induced to do so by the status accorded to Scripture by the education they received in their youth. To emphasize this is not to subscribe to an inescapable relativism in philosophical thought, for to do so does not rule out the powerful role of rational criticism in the development of beliefs, but to emphasize the dangers of neglecting the influence of the cultures in which we are reared.

CHAPTER 3

'Fear where no fear is': Some Reflections on Heterodox Notions of Christian Unity

Martin Fitzpatrick

Professor Alan Sell has, through his many publications, shed much new light on eighteenth-century Dissent. As someone who has worked on eighteenth century Dissent, I am one of the beneficiaries. I also learnt a good deal during his time in Aberystwyth when he conducted seminars on a wide range of subjects, always with great skill, wit and aplomb. I shall always remember his complimenting Dr. Boyd Schlenther for an excellent paper on the Countess of Huntingdon. He said that Boyd had so brought the good lady to life that he felt glad that he had never met her!

While thinking about this paper, I happened to come across some recollections of May Griffiths who grew up in Birkenhead, my home town, early in the twentieth century. Reminiscing about Sundays, when she attended a local chapel, she recalled that the time of their service was altered by quarter of an hour so that they would not meet local Anglicans going to and leaving church. Also, she recalled how her own congregation was divided over whether or not they should say 'Amen' at the end of the hymn.[1] I wondered whether there is no end to the dissidence of Dissent. I also wondered what Alan would make of that.[2] In his own work he concentrates on essentials, but always has time for those who view essentials in a different way. He is able to acknowledge the potential value of contributions from non-Christians today, and in his study of the past he is equally generous to those of widely differing views. In particular I have in mind the way he encompasses the contributions of Arians and Socinians to eighteenth-century theology. He concluded his

---

[1] Audrey Balsdon ed., *May's Story. Growing up in Birkenhead. Marriage and Motherhood in North Wales by May Griffiths* (printed and published by West Wales Arts, 1990.), pp. 18-19.

[2] I suspect that the solution will amuse him: 'in the end people who didn't want to say Amen sat down, and those who wanted Amen stayed on their feet and sang it.' *May's Story*, p. 19.

inaugural lecture at the Aberystwyth and Lampeter school of Theology by remarking: 'The challenge of exploring the Christian heritage with a view to seeing what it is which must be conserved, and of exploring the current intellectual and cultural environment with a view to addressing it relevantly is one which should engage and excite all Christians'.[3] I am not sure that I can meet even part of that challenge; in what follows I shall examine ideas about church unity in the thought of Joseph Priestley while making some comparisons with his Rational Dissenting contemporaries, and reflect in a rather unsystematic way on their significance, in part by casting an eye into the nineteenth century. Priestley himself was not a systematic thinker on Christian unity. He did not set out detailed schemes, but one can see him setting out conditions for its attainment as a result of his views on church-state relations, truth and progress.

In 1780 Joseph Priestley left the service of the Earl of Shelburne and became minister at New Meeting, Birmingham. Although he did not give up his scientific work, indeed he was given generous conditions of service so that in today's terms he was only a part-time minister, he remained deeply committed to his theological studies. In 1782 published his *History of the Corruptions of Christianity*, a substantial work in which he attempted to prove that the earliest Christians were Unitarians. Priestley became involved in highly contentious debated with defenders of orthodoxy, beginning with Samuel Horsley, then Archdeacon of St. Albans. Priestley was a pugnacious controversialist and he wore down his opponents. In 1786 Horsley vacated the field by refusing to read Priestley's *History of Early Opinions Concerning Christ*, published in that year. But others followed in his wake. In that year Dr. George Horne, dean of Canterbury and subsequently Bishop of Norwich, preached a sermon at the visitation of John Moore, Archbishop of Canterbury entitled 'a Duty of contending for the Faith'. Subjoined to the sermon was a 'Discourse on the trinity in unity', which, published separately, went into several editions, the last being in 1830. Priestley, indomitable as ever, replied to Horne, beginning insouciantly: 'The readers of this controversy concerning *the person of Christ* will, I doubt not, congratulate themselves on seeing it in new hands, and in those of persons who promise to conduct it both with better temper, and with more knowledge of the subject, than it was done by Dr. Horsley.'[4] It is not the purpose here to go into the controversy over the Trinity, rather it is to draw out various strands of Priestley's thinking about the best way for Christian truth to

---

[3] 'Conservation and Exploration in Christian Theology. An Inaugural Lecture from the Chair of Christian Doctrine', Aberystwyth and Lampeter University School of Theology, 1992, p. 22.

[4] *Letters to Dr. Horne, Dean of Canterbury; To the Young Men who are in the course of education for the Christian Ministry at the Universities of Oxford and Cambridge; To Dr. Price, and to Mr. Parkhurst; On the Subject of the Person of Christ* (Birmingham: 1787), p. iii.

be pursued and for Christian unity, as he believed, to be achieved.

Truth and Christian Progress

The first thing to note that is that Priestley's pursuit of Christian truth was conceived as a pursuit backwards through time. In his *History of the Corruptions of Christianity* Priestley declared that his aim was 'not a *progressive religion*, but a *progressive reformation* of a corrupted religion'.[5] Priestley's combination of primitivism with progress made him very much a man of his age, when political reform as well as religious reform was often based upon ancient ideal models. Oddly, given his associationist psychology, Priestley did not consider himself as a product of his own environment. As Margaret Canovan has remarked, Priestley assumed that 'his own interpretations, like the original gospel, were somehow exempt from the distorting influence of historicity'.[6] Despite the flaws in his outlook, his purpose was to create a new understanding of the scripture which would be enlightening to all Christians. He explained in one of the letters published with those to Dr. Horne

> The proper object of my work is to ascertain what must have been the sense of the books of scripture from the sense in which they were actually understood by those for whose use they were composed; and to determine what must have been the sentiments of the apostles, by means of the opinions of those who received their instruction from them only.
>
> This is a new, and certainly an important field of argumentation, open to the learned part of the christian world....[7]

However, Priestley's thinking about progress was not always backward looking even in his religious thought. Margaret Canovan suggests that Priestley could only have escaped from his paradoxical position had he adopted Lessing's view that church doctrines 'when they were revealed...were certainly no truths of reason, but they were revealed in order to become such'.[8] There are elements of such a view in Priestley's thought. For example he suggested that Jesus sometimes deliberately spoke enigmatically, from which one might come to the conclusion that aspects of his message would be more effectively

---

[5] *An History of the Corruptions of Christianity* (2 vols; London: 1782, Garland repr. 1974), vol. II, p. 483.
[6] Margaret Canovan, 'The Irony of History: Priestley's Rational Theology', *The Price-Priestley Newsletter* 4 (1979), pp. 16-25, at p. 21.
[7] *Letters to Horne,* p. 176. The letter was to 'Rev. Mr. Parkhurst'.
[8] Canovan, 'Irony of History', p. 23, citing G.F. Lessing, *The Education of the Human Race* (1780).

revealed to later ages.⁹ It thus becomes possible to think in terms of endless 'progress' in truth, either conceived as a reinterpretation of the Christian message appropriate to one's own age, or of a growing understanding of the Christian message and of an endless progress in divine truth.¹⁰ Priestley seems to be thinking in the latter terms in some of his writings — a view which can be found in Hartley's *Observations on Man, his Frame, his Duty, and his Expectations* (1749). Hartley believed that man could be restored to the paradisaical state. Priestley concurred. In an oft quoted passage from his Essay on the First Principles of Government (1768) he wrote: 'Thus, whatever was the beginning of this world, the end will be glorious and paridisaical, beyond what our imaginations can now conceive.'11 Although at times Priestley talks of mankind being in the 'infancy' of being, at other times he seems to think that the prospect of dramatic improvements was imminent, a view encouraged by the dramatic changes of the age in which he lived.12 It was an outlook which often made if difficult for him to maintain a measured response to both religious and political reform for he did not expect the existing institutions in church and state to survive millennial change.13 The notion of a world transformed was never far from his mind He concluded his Letters to Edmund Burke by looking forward to a world at peace with itself. He believed that

---

⁹ *Socrates and Jesus compared* (London: 1803), p. 35: 'He [Jesus] did not always wish to be understood at the time, but to have what he said to be remembered, and reflected upon afterwards.' It can be argued that Priestley is only referring to the hearers of Jesus, but his description of some parables as 'concise, figurative and enigmatical' does allow a wider interpretation, although it is important to note that Priestley did not draw out the implications of his statement.

¹⁰ These various aspects of his attitude to progress can be seen in his plan for a 'continually improving' translation of the Bible. As Marilyn Brooks has noted, 'Its distinguishing feature was that it should "always be in a state of improvement" rather than being definitely "improved".' See her 'Priestley's Plan for a "Continually Improving" translation of the Bible', *Enlightenment and Dissent* 15 (1996), pp. 89-106, at p. 91.

¹¹ *An Essay on the First Principles of Government* (1768; 2ⁿᵈ edn enlarged, London: 1771), pp. 4-5.

¹² I have discussed Priestley's ideas relating to progress in, '"Through the glass of history"; some reflections on historical knowledge in the thought of Joseph Priestley', *Enlightenment and Dissent*, 17 (1998), pp. 172-209.

¹³ For example, Priestley wrote to Theophilus Lindsey on 23 August 1771, 'To me everything looks like the approach of that dismal catastrophe described, I may say predicted, by Dr. Hartley, in the conclusion of his Essay, and I shall be looking for the downfall of Church and State together. I am really expecting some very calamitous, but finally glorious, events.' J.T. Rutt ed., *The Theological and Miscellaneous Works of Joseph Priestley* (25 vols, London: 1817-31), vol. I, Pt. I, pp. 144-47.

everything pointed to such a conclusion.[14] It was foretold in Isaiah 2.4 and Micah 4.3. But material improvements also indicated such a conclusion: 'This is a state of things which good sense, and the prevailing spirit of commerce, aided by Christianity, and true philosophy, cannot fail to effect in time.'[15]

Church, State and Christian liberty

Few shared Priestley's optimism in the co-operation of material progress with the dispensations of providence. His prescription for the emergence of truth was difficult for his own age to accept and continues to pose something of a challenge. One of the most enduring themes in his thought was for the need for civil liberty, of which religious liberty was a crucial constituent. He defined civil liberty as 'that power over their own actions, which the members of the state reserve to themselves, and which their officers must not infringe'.[16] Such liberty was imperfect so long as the state used religion as a test for citizenship and maintained a religious establishment: He argued that, 'human establishments, by calling off men's attention from the commandments of God to those of men, tend to defeat the great ends of religion. They are, therefore, incompatible with the genius of christianity'.[17]

Priestley was prepared to accept that some forms of establishments were better than others. He made four suggestions for improving the Church of England. It would be much improved by replacing the requirement for the clergy to subscribe to the Thirty-nine articles by a subscription to a belief 'in the religion of *Jesus Christ*, as it is set forth in the *New Testament*'; if the livings of the clergy were made more equal, and their remuneration made proportional to their duties; if the political role of the episcopate was abolished; if toleration was made complete by granting the right of citizenship to 'every member of the community' 'whether he chuse to conform to the established religion or not'.[18] The least objectionable form of establishment was that found in some American colonies where all citizens paid a tax for the support of the Christian religion and were able to choose the denomination to which it was paid. Rather like the Scandinavian model today, this was for Priestley still

---

[14] *Letters to the Right Honourable Edmund Burke* (2nd edition corrected, Birmingham: 1791), Letter XIV, p. 146.

[15] *Letters to Burke*, Letter XIV, p. 150.

[16] *Essay on the First Principles*, p. 9.

[17] Ibid., p. 141. In his introduction to this work (ix-x) Priestley had noted that 'violent opposition' to the 'modest' proposals of Francis Blackburne and John Jones for church reform was indicative of the way church establishments were harmful to the interests of religion. Jones's *Free and Candid Disquisitions Relating to the Church of England* (1749) and Blackburne's, *The Confessional* (1767) were key works in the mid-eighteenth century campaign for church reform.

[18] *Essay on the First Principles*, pp. 198-200.

inferior to the separation of church and state, but he thought that it might pave the way for 'unbounded liberty in matters of religion'.[19]

Many Enlightenment writers accepted the value of religion to society and were prepared to accept church establishments on an Erastian basis. Priestley also accepted that religion helped to reinforce the moral order: 'all the modes of religion....enforce the more essential parts...of that conduct which the good order of society requires'.[20] But whereas William Warburton had argued for the establishment of religion because it fortified the moral order,[21] Priestley argued the contrary, for under a regime of complete religious liberty the different religions would vie to prove to the magistrate their virtue and the value of civil protection.[22] There is no doubt that on his own principles, Priestley would have had to accept the notion of civil interference in religion if it could be proven to be useful. He refused to accept such a possibility. He believed that the best way to combat dangerous opinions was not to outlaw them and seek to repress them, but to allow them to be aired. In his optimistic way, he believed that subversive opinions 'must be evidently false, and easy to refute'.[23] Just as the free competition of religions would be for the general well-being, so too would the free contest of opinions further the cause of truth. Whereas for some even heterodox thinkers there was no necessary connection between freedom of opinion and complete religious equality, that was not true of Priestley.[24] If he had some elements of sympathy for those who wished to reform the established church, his preference was for the complete separation of church and state. In those circumstances church unity would not occur through an established church comprehending Dissent but by churches freely agreeing to worship together. And for him that would occur through progress in the doctrine of the churches. It certainly would not occur through the development or re-vamping of arguments for a broader more comprehensive national church on grounds of its usefulness to the state. Indeed, Dissenting campaigning for toleration, and maybe some of Priestley's own provocative ideas, helped to begin the process in which Anglicans began to question their dependence on the state.[25]

---

[19] *Essay on the First Principles*, pp. 201-202.
[20] Ibid., p. 117.
[21] William Warburton, *The Alliance between Church and State* (2nd edn, London: 1742), p. 16.
[22] *Essay on the First Principles*, p. 117.
[23] Ibid., p. 121.
[24] David William, an even more forthright proponent of intellectual liberty than Priestley favoured the creation of a Deist national church in the interest of public morality, although all those not wishing to join in would enjoy toleration. See my 'Toleration and the Enlightenment Movement', in Ole Peter Grell and Roy Porter eds, *Toleration in Enlightenment Europe* (Cambridge: Cambridge University Press, 2000), pp. 43-5.
[25] See G.M Ditchfield 'How Narrow will the limits of this Toleration Appear? Dissenting Petitions to Parliament 1772-1773', in Stephen Taylor and David L. Wykes,

Priestley's ideas may be regarded as the product of a time when Dissenters were second class citizens, technically disabled from serving on Corporations or from taking civil office, and when Dissent was still designated a crime in the authoritative *Commentaries on the Laws of England* (1765-9) of William Blackstone.[26] Admittedly the theory was contentious, the law was complicated, and practice was broadly tolerant,[27] but many Dissenters felt their situation to be dishonourable and disgraceful, amounting for some to persecution.[28] This situation did not change decisively until the repeal of the Test and Corporation Acts until 1828.[29] However, it can be suggested his ideas retain validity in a situation of greater religious equality. Priestley, like Voltaire, thought that the more numerous sects there were the better it was for the cause of toleration and Christian understanding.[30] But he went much further than the *philosophe* in believing that diversity ultimately furthered unity. He wrote to Burke

> You, Sir, seem to dread a *number of sects* among christians. But what serious inconvenience would arise from their being increased tenfold? It would be much better for the state, than if there were only two. Religious bigotry would also be diminished by this means, and the members of these sects would sooner learn to exercise charity for each other, distinguishing the great things in which all christians agree, from the comparatively smaller things in which any of them differ. In this way, also, they would sooner arrive at a *rational uniformity*, the

---

Parliament and Dissent (Edinburgh: Edinburgh University Press for the Parliamentary History Yearbook Trust, 2005), pp. 91-106, at pp. 105-106.

[26] Priestley immediately responded to Blackstone in his *Remarks on Some Paragraphs in the Fourth Volume of Dr. Blackstone's Commentaries* (1769) and a further public exchange of views then took place. Blackstone modified his position slightly but continued to insist that Dissent as such was a crime. J.C.D. Clark, *English Society 1688-1832. Ideology, Social Structure and Political Practice during the Ancien Regime* (Cambridge: Cambridge University Press, 1985), p. 208.

[27] See the authoritative account of complexities of the situation of Dissent in the late eighteenth century by G.M. Ditchfield, 'Ecclesiastical policy under Lord North', in John Walsh, Colin Haydon and Stephen Taylor, eds, *The Church of England, c.1689-c.1833. From Toleration to Tractarianism* (Cambridge: Cambridge University Press, 1993), pp. 228-46, esp. pp. 235-40. For a general account of the situation for all forms of Dissent see my 'Toleration' in Iain McCalman gen. ed., *An Oxford Companion to British Culture 1776-1832* (Oxford: Oxford University Press, 1999), pp. 729-31.

[28] Philip Furneaux, following Priestley, took Blackstone to task for his attitude to Dissent, arguing on the basis of general principles and detailed legal knowledge that Dissent had been legalized by the Toleration Act of 1689 and that to disadvantage citizens on the basis of their religious opinions amounted to persecution. Philip Furneaux, *Letters to the Hon. Mr. Justice Blackstone* (London: 1771), esp. pp. 164-65.

[29] J.C.D. Clark, *English Society 1688-1832*, p. 208, n. 28.

[30] See Leonard Tancock trans., *Voltaire: Letters on England* (Harmondsworth: Penguin Books, 1980), pp. 37-41.

points of difference being freely canvassed, and truth prevailing and establishing itself, as, no doubt, it will in the end.[31]

Christian Unity and National Churches

If we return to his *Letters to Dr. Horne* we can see how he relates his various concerns concerning liberty, free inquiry, and the progress of truth toward unity. Priestley begins his letters with the confident assertion that the discussion of the issue of the person of Christ between Unitarians and Trinitarians will result in the question being resolved and, naturally, he expected it to be resolved in his favour, believing that 'scripture, reason and antiquity' were on the Unitarian side.[32] Perhaps even more optimistically he thought that progress towards Unitarian truth would further the cause of Christian unity. Horne begged to differ, believing that a Unitarian national church would be exclusive. One would have thought that Horne had no cause for anxiety, but his traditional Anglican fear of ambitious Dissenters, who would take over national life unless they were kept firmly in their place, was compounded by the fact that heterodox Dissent was fortified by a small influx of distinguished Anglican clergy led by Theophilus Lindsey who established an influential Unitarian Chapel in Essex Street, London, in 1774. This had occurred as a result of the failure of the Feathers Tavern petitioning movement (1770-74) which had sought to create a more comprehensive established church by substituting subscription to the Thirty-Nine Articles with a profession of belief in the scriptures as the only rule of faith, and as sufficient for salvation. Priestley, as we have seen, had recommended such a reform, and knew the leading figures in the campaign, including Theophilus Lindsey and Archdeacon Francis Blackburne. But his attitude towards the petitioners had always been somewhat ambivalent. If they had been successful and the church would have become more comprehensive, it would still have remained established.[33] In his *Letters to Dr. Horne* he offered a different form of comprehension, one founded on a minimalist creed. Such a creed he thought would be inclusive. Horne had grumbled, 'An unitarian people, we are told, will not long be satisfied with a

---

[31] *Letters to Burke*, p. 136.
[32] *Letters to Dr. Horne,* pp. 16-17.
[33] Priestley's own proposals were more far-reaching than those of the petitioners, yet his basic position was one of hostility to civil involvement in religion. He wrote on 2 March 1772 to Theophilus Lindsey, 'You must permit us Dissenters ... who are not used to the idea even of *Spiritual Superiors*, to smile at your scheme, as an application to the *powers of this world* for a reformation in the business of religion.' Typically, in his next letter on 9 March to Lindsey, he apologised for the 'observations' he had made in his previous letter, said he would be delighted if the petitioners succeeded, but then repeated his essential point about applying for reform to 'temporal powers'. Dr Williams' Library, MS. 12.12, Letters of Joseph Priestley.

trinitarian establishment. Indeed, I suppose they will not. They will endeavour to overturn it, and it is our business to prevent them from so doing'.[34] Priestley assured Horne that far from excluding Anglicans, a Unitarian liturgy would 'contain nothing offensive to you, nothing in which you could not heartily join'. He argued that Unitarian prayers were scriptural and that Trinitarians could worship with them while placing their own meaning on Unitarian scriptural minimalism. Thus prayers would be addressed to *'the maker of heaven and earth, the God and our father of our Lord Jesus Christ, the one true God…'* Trinitarians willing to make their own sense of such prayers could worship alongside Unitarians: 'so long as you can accommodate to your notions this scripture language, and suppose Jesus Christ himself, and the Holy Spirit, to be in any manner included in this definition, or description of *the one true God*'.[35] Priestley noted that already Unitarians could join in much of the Anglican liturgy, and he could not see why Anglicans could not join in theirs. He prepared his own prayer for Easter Sunday 'for the sake of a peaceable accommodation'.[36] At the same time he accepted that such an accommodation was unlikely. Moreover, he did not think that reforms of an 'an intermediate kind' would occur or indeed work. Rather he thought that once reform began, Anglicans 'will never be able to agree … where to stop'.[37] Still, on his own analysis, the chances of reform were slim, since he believed that the religious establishment inhibited the progress of religious truth and that genuine reform could only be effected if the leading figures in church and state were excluded from the process.[38] Priestley drew attention to Horne's defence of the established church, and especially to his comment that the doctrine of the trinity 'requires, and demands the support of every state wishing to enjoy the favour and protection of that God, who for gracious purposes has revealed it'.[39] Priestley pointed to the fact that the early church was not established, and that it was Unitarian in doctrine. Civil interference in religion was for him always to the detriment of religion. It limited freedom of enquiry and conceded to the state powers which were illegitimate. It put religion under the protection of a power which 'may equally promote truth or falsehood' and conceded to it the right to decide which religion should be established.[40] Priestley was fond of asserting that in a free contest Unitarian truth would triumph. On occasion he sounded distinctly bullish about its rapid progress with the expectation that the

---

[34] *Letters to Horne,* p. 20.
[35] Ibid., pp. 20-21.
[36] Ibid., p. 22.
[37] Ibid.
[38] Ibid., pp. 22-24
[39] Ibid., p. 23.
[40] Ibid., p. 24. Priestley had been consistent in such matters: 'truth can never have a fair chance of being discovered, or propagated, without the most perfect freedom of inquiry and debate'. *Essay on First Principles,* p. 185.

Anglican church would not survive the contest.[41] Yet in his *Letters to Horne* he was more measured. While he looked forward to the day 'when a pure *Unitarian worship* will be universally adopted, and with universal consent', he refused to conjecture when the Anglican church would be reformed. Unitarian truth would no doubt prevail but 'in God's way, and his own time'. In the meantime, he asked Horne not to *'fear where no fear is*, or alarm others with apprehensions of our intolerance, which if you seriously reflect, cannot really entertain yourselves'.[42]

Priestley's Unitarian prescription for Christian unity was always likely to fail. By the time of the 1851 census some 50,000 attended their chapels on census Sunday, a reasonable number for the development of the movement but not for the creation of a broad church.[43] Nor is there any sign that Priestley's invitation to Anglicans to participate in their worship had any significant effect. This is hardly surprising. The real challenge to the Anglican church came from evangelical Dissent, and that arose in part from its failure to comprehend Methodists within its fold. Nonetheless, the development of Unitarianism signifies in part the failure of aspirations for comprehension. That failure and the dominance of the Anglican church in national life continued to cause deep problems, and calls for the separation of church and state would retain a radical complexion even in much more settled times than those of the late eighteenth century: '…everyone must be cognisant of the fact that the spirit of exclusiveness, born of the establishment system, and fed by the encouragement given to it by the sanction of law, permeates, more or less, the whole framework of society in this country'. So argued Edward Miall in the House of Commons on 9 May 1871.[44] Miall, a Congregational minister and an M.P., campaigned through the Liberation Society for the separation of church and state. He argued that establishment was politically unjust, socially divisive and harmful to Christianity. He did not argue, as Priestley did, for separation so that

---

[41] In *The Importance and Extent of Free Inquiry in Matters of Religion* (Birmingham: 1785), pp. 40-41, Priestley gained notoriety by suggesting that he was 'laying gunpowder, grain by grain, under the old building of error and superstition (the Anglican Church) which a single spark may hereafter ignite.' He had difficulty persuading his opponents that his gunpowder consisted of arguments.

[42] *Letters to Horne*, pp. 22-23.

[43] A.D. Gilbert, *Religion and Society in Industrial England. Church, Chapel and Social Change 1740-1914* (London and New York: Longman, 1976, 2nd impress., 1984), p. 41; see also Leonard Smith, 'The 1851 Religious Census and the Unitarian Home Missionary Board 1854', *Transactions of the Unitarian Historical Society*, vol. 23 no.3, April 2005, pp. 625-628, which offers alternative figures of attendance. He notes that the census revealed that religion was not reaching the working classes and that the Unitarians in response tried to develop a new kind of ministry.

[44] David Nicholls ed., *Church and State in Britain since 1820* (London: Routledge and Kegan Paul, 1967), p. 89. Miall's speech was republished as a pamphlet entitled, *Disestablishment*.

there would be free and open debate about the nature of Christianity, but he did feel that the state by interfering in religious opinions, 'has thrown the torch of discord into every corner of the kingdom, and, to an immense extent, has transmuted differences of belief into personal alienation of feeling'.[45] Dissent today may no longer have the feeling that it is 'everywhere spoken against' – indeed, the danger is that it is simply ignored – but it can still be suggested that unity in whatever form can only be attained on the basis of religious equality. So in a sense Priestley was correct to suggest that the pre-requisite of unity is diversity, and for all Christian (and non Christian groups) to be on equal terms with each other, and that does require the complete separation of church and state. Nonetheless, it is doubtful if Unitarians would ever be accepted as part of moves towards Christian unity, partly because many are much less obviously Christian than they were in Priestley's time, but much more so because it remains a heretical sect in the eyes of most of the orthodox. Their presence poses in acute form the problem of how different theological positions can be comprehended in a united church. What would such comprehension mean? Hopes for comprehension of orthodox denominations into a single national church did not end with the failure of the Feathers Tavern petitioners in 1774. Indeed some influential thinkers in the nineteenth century were anxious for greater unity in both church and state. They provide interesting variations on the old aspiration for comprehension.

The Anglican clergyman, Thomas Arnold, headmaster of Rugby school, believed that membership of the national church should be a condition for citizenship, but he also believed that the national church should be widened to embrace all Nonconformists. Indeed rather than separate church and state he wanted the power of the state and the wisdom of the church to be united: 'A Christian church ... should be a sovereign society'.[46] A feature of such a society would be that the 'principle of co-operation through the varied talents and habits of the several members of the society' would be encouraged. A national church would embrace the diverse traditions of Dissent while discouraging the special claims to distinctiveness. He was prepared to embrace even 'nominal Christians' in the hope the national church would gradually be 'raised gradually.... to as great a degree of purity as was ever attained by the smallest and most exclusive congregation'.[47]

Arnold's son, Matthew, developed the idea of a harmonious national church, although his views on Nonconformity were hardly complimentary. The

---

[45] Nicholls ed., *Church and State*, p. 89.
[46] Thomas Arnold, *Fragment on the Church* (1844) in Nicholls ed., *Church and State*, p. 35. Nicholls suggests that the church would be broadly comprehensive in Christian terms 'with the exception of recalcitrant unitarians'. All those who could not be comprehended, including Jews and atheists, would have no status as citizens (p.3).
[47] Thomas Arnold, Letter written to the *Hertford Reformer*, 1839, in Nicholls ed., *Church and State*, p. 38.

proliferation of denominations was an anathema to him. He believed that the Nonconformists lacked the 'more full and harmonious development of their humanity'. They were provincial and had failed to contribute at the highest level to 'literature, art and science' nor to 'religion itself'.[48] He ignored the contribution of a Priestley or a Faraday to science. His notion of unity based on cultural harmony would sweep away what he slightingly called '*hole-and-corner* forms of religion'.[49] This was very different from Priestley's notion of unity through diversity and the free exchange of ideas. For Matthew Arnold, contentious debate between the Nonconformist and Anglicans had merely encouraged and fortified the prejudices of the Nonconformists.[50]

In looking into the nineteenth century one can see that the question of church unity was not only different because of the failure of comprehension but also because the Nonconformists had become so much stronger that they presented a much more serious challenge to the establishment than old Dissent in the eighteenth century. Matthew Arnold's assertion of cultural superiority was one reaction to the challenge.[51] It embodies another claim which had been challenged in the late-eighteenth-century by Priestley, namely the superiority of the Anglican educational institutions. In his *Letters to Horne* he had addressed the students at Oxford and Cambridge who were intended for the church, in the hope that he could convert them to reform and appeal to those who may have had scruples about subscribing to the Thirty-nine Articles. But he should have expected the appeal to fall on deaf ears for he indicated his own disdain for the quality of university education in an open letter to the Prime Minister, William Pitt, published in 1787, the same year as his *Letters to Horne*.[52]

---

[48] *Culture and Anarchy* (1869) in Nicholls ed., *Church and State*, p. 137. Arnold spent much of his life working as an inspector of schools, including many tedious hours visiting Nonconformist schools. This helps to account for his low estimate of Nonconformist culture. See the entry on Matthew Arnold by Stefan Collini in the *Oxford Dictionary of National Biography*.

[49] *Culture and Anarchy*, p. 139.

[50] Ibid., p. 144.

[51] Gilbert, *Religion and Society*, p. 158, argues that Arnold's attention to Nonconformist culture 'was evidence of its emergence from the subcultural isolation of the early industrial age.'

[52] *A Letter to the Rt. Hon. William Pitt on the Subject of Toleration and Church Establishments* (1787) in Rutt ed. *Theological and Miscellaneous Works*, XIX, pp. 125 & 128. Priestley repeated his belief that free inquiry would produce uniformity of opinion and compared the stagnant backwaters of the universities with the living waters of the Dissenting academies. The *Letter to Pitt* was occasioned by his failure to support the motion for the repeal of the Test and Corporations Acts in the House of Commons on 28 March 1787.

A Clerisy: An Independent Establishment

Priestley's desire for education which was free from the control of both church and state was to a degree reflected in one of the most influential notions of a national church, that outlined by Samuel Taylor Coleridge in his *On the Constitution of Church and State according to the Idea of Each* (1830) A onetime admirer of Priestley, Coleridge argued that 'a permanent, nationalized, learned order, a national clerisy or Church is an essential element of a rightly constituted nation'.[53] For him, religion was 'the centre of gravity in a realm', but his idea of clerisy embraced not merely the clergy, 'the learned of all denominations', but also the professions. His church would include representatives of the liberal arts and sciences.[54] In many ways this was a heterodox notion of a national church, for it was independent of the state and of the established church. Its aim was 'to secure and improve that civilization, without which the nation could be neither permanent nor progressive'.[55] Given that such a national church would be independent of both the state and the established church, Priestley might well have had some sympathy with Coleridge's argument that a clerisy would be far more effective than the range of competing educational institutions which existed. Its purpose was not far removed from Priestley notion that the end of government was general happiness, given that he believed that true happiness was ultimately religious. However, if he would have found it attractive, it was a solution that he, in his time, would not have contemplated. Despite his altercation with Horne about Anglicans attending a Unitarian establishment, institutional church unity was not on his agenda. His emphasis is on the progress of truth and on 'every man' providing 'religion for himself' which arrived at 'after due enquiry and examination,' would turn men into 'good citizens, good friends and good neighbours in this world, as well as to fit them for another'.[56] That is his agenda for the elimination of prejudice, for harmonious religion, and for universal peace. Athough Coleridge repudiated much of his radical heritage and Priestley's materialism, his ideals continued to have strong resemblances to those whom he admired in his youth. As Richard Holmes has noted, he 'never quite ceased being a Pantisocrat, looking for his magic river', and his notion of truth being like a stream, which finds it way round obstacles and ever increases

---

[53] *On the Constitution of Church and State according to the Idea of Each* in Nicholls ed. *Church and State*, p. 32. Coleridge kept a permanent place in his ideals for natural philosophers like Priestley whose concerns embraced the arts and sciences. For him, Humphry Davy epitomised that tradition. See Richard Holmes, *Coleridge. Early Visions* (London, Sydney, Auckland and Toronto: Hodder and Stoughton, 1989), pp. 78, 81, and 245n.
[54] *Constitution of Church and State*, p. 30.
[55] Ibid., p. 29.
[56] *Letters to Burke*, Letter XIV, pp. 151-2.

its flow, is a poetic version of Priestley's providentialist notions.[57]

A Latitudinarian Approach

It is possible that Matthew Arnold's theological doubts,[58] which explain at least in part his emphasis on culture rather than doctrine, might have been encompassed within the old Latitudinarian tradition. Unfortunately the debates of the late eighteenth century on subscription to the Thirty-nine Article and the nature and coherence of the Articles themselves had weakened the appeal of Latitudinarians and had led groups within the church to find alternatives for binding the church together.[59] None entirely succeeded. The strength of the Latitudinarian tradition was its emphasis on scriptural truth and its willingness within certain parameters to accept differences of interpretation. William Chillingworth, the exemplar of such notions and mentor of subsequent Latitudinarians, believed that that the essential divine truths were clearly revealed in the Bible. But the Bible was not clear in all things and individual reason was needed to interpret its message.[60] From the beginning the liberal dimensions of the tradition came under attack. Chillingworth was accused by the Jesuit Edward Knott of Socinianism,[61] and there are parallels between his ideas and those of Socinians especially in relation to toleration. Even Priestley, a more advanced Socinian than the Socinian contemporaries of Chillingworth, was not entirely removed from that tradition, for he believed, as they did, that the simplest creed is the best and in the need to use reason to interpret revelation. However, his expectation of a progressive reformation and his belief

---

[57] Richard Holmes, *Coleridge* (Oxford: Oxford University Press, 1982), pp. 45-46.

[58] Arnold abandoned his belief in the Atonement and Resurrection while at Oxford, yet later in life he would defend a conservative position, in controversy with the Anglican bishop of Natal, Colenso, on the authority of the Pentateuch. He was not ordained, and his own beliefs are difficult to define. His main concern was to defend the cultural traditions of the Anglican Church. See Maurice Cowling, *Religion and Public Doctrine: volume III, Accommodations* (Cambridge: Cambridge University Press, 2001), p.76; George Watson, *The Literary Critics. A Study of English Descriptive Criticism* (Harmondsworth: Penguin Books; 1962, repr. 1963), p. 151; Collini, 'Matthew Arnold' *ODNB*.

[59] B.W. Young, *Religion and Enlightenment in Eighteenth-Century England. Theological Debate from Locke to Burke* (Oxford: Clarendon Press, 1998), pp. 76-80.

[60] Herschel Baker, *The Wars of Truth. Studies in the Decay of Christian Humanism in theEarly Seventeenth Century* (Gloucester, Mass: Peter Smith, 1969), pp. 222-23.

[61] Baker, *Wars of Truth,* p. 222, n. 105. Those of an Arminian persuasion and Latitudinarian outlook were often regarded as Socinians. Indeed, they were closely related. John McLachlan, *The Divine Image* (London: The Lindsey Press, 1972) pp. 136-37; Hugh Trevor-Roper, 'The Religious Origins of the Enlightenment', in his *The Religion, the Reformation and Social Change and Other Essays* (London: Macmillan, 1967), esp. pp. 215-217.

that everyone who was able to conduct his or her enquiries impartially would eventually come to the same conclusion were departures from the tradition. What was absent from his outlook was an element of genuine scepticism, for he was confident that it was 'a general law of nature' that truth only requires time to establish itself in place of error.[62] John McLachlan has remarked, 'once a grain of uncertainty or scepticism is introduced into the cauldron of theological controversy, its effect is usually cathartic and entirely wholesome'.[63] That was undoubtedly missing in most of controversies which Priestley fought. If Priestley's views on toleration were extremely liberal, his tolerance of rival viewpoints was limited. They were useful for encouraging debate but they were not to be accepted for what they were. Priestley not only urged his fellow Dissenters to stand up and be counted, but he also introduced a new element of combativeness into old Dissent, which fractured an eirenic tradition which existed in Dissent as well as Anglican Latitudinarianism, with many points of contact.[64] His impact on the Dissenting tradition can be compared to that of Francis Blackburne on the Latitudinarian tradition. Indeed, from the first there were Dissenters like William Enfield who were upset by his assertion of superiority over the established church and warned him of the danger of his recklessness in controversy. Enfield's warnings were prophetic. Priestley would pay the price for his lack of caution by having to flee Birmingham in the riots of July1791. Leading local Anglicans played a part in inciting the rioters.[65] Enfield's advice was not based entirely on prudence. He saw value in the establishment of religion and in the Anglican Church, and he was sceptical of the value of controversy as a means of furthering truth.[66] Yet even Richard Price, who took a much more vigorous view of candour than Enfield, and was

---

[62] Jean Bion, *An History of the Sufferings of Mr. Lewis De Marolles and Mr. Isaac Le Fevre upon the Revocation of the Edict of Nantz ... translated from the French about the beginning of this century. And now republished by Joseph Priestley* (Birmingham: 1788), p. xiii.

[63] McLachlan, *The Divine Image*, p. 136.

[64] See for example the way in which the Latitudinarian Bishop Richard Watson recommended the *Five Dissertations* of the heterodox Dissenter, Edward Harwood, in his six volume collection of theological tracts. Watson, like Harwood, believed that 'it is safer to continue in doubt than to decide amiss'. It was, however, a sign of changing time that Watson was criticised for including Dissenting works in his collection. *Anecdotes of the life of Richard Watson, Bishop of Llandaff* (2 vols; 2nd edn. London: 1818), vol. I, pp. 222-27.

[65] See my '"Rousing the Sleeping Lion": Joseph Priestley and the Constitution in Church and State', The Inaugural Leeds Library Priestley Lecture, Friday 1 November 1991, *Occasional Publications of the Leeds Library*, 3 (1993), esp. pp. 16-19.

[66] See my 'The Enlightenment, politics and providence: some Scottish and English comparisons', in Knud Haakonssen ed., *Enlightenment and Religion. Rational Dissent in Eighteenth-Century Britain* (Cambridge: Cambridge University Press, 1996), pp. 85-86.

as firm an advocate as Priestley of the need to separate church and state,[67] found himself in fundamental disagreement with Priestley over the purpose of controversy.

Appended to Priestley's letters to Dr. Horne, were letters to Price on his Arianism, in which he attempts to demonstrate that Price's ideas were wrong. Here one can see profound differences in their approach to truth. Priestley praises Price for his candour, as he had in a private letter telling him that he had written the letters in reply to Price's defence of Arianism in his *Sermons on the Christian Doctrine* (1786), but he objects to Price's diffidence about truth and attitude to proselytism.[68] He could not understand why Price, having rejected Calvinistic and Athanasian schemes, should hesitate in his views about the person of Christ. Price had written, 'I can in this instance, **as in most others**, with much more confidence say what is *not*, than what *is* the truth' [my bold].[69] Since Socinianism was the only clear alternative to Calvinism and Athanasianism, Priestley believed that he should embrace it, as he had 'from similar premises'.[70] But whatever Price's views, Priestley believed that he should seek to proselytise them. Price, who was as keen as he to promote liberal religion, nonetheless, with typical reticence, had confessed that he had 'no disposition to be very anxious about bringing you over to my opinion. The rage for proselytism is one of the curses of the world. I wish to make no proselytes except to candour, and charity, and honest enquiry'. Priestley found that hard to understand for his stance was the opposite; 'I profess to write with no other view than to make proselytes; nor indeed do I see that there can be any other rational object in writing at all.'[71]

Considering how much they were partners in religious and political radicalism of the late eighteenth century, it is remarkable how much they differed. Price was inclusive in his attitude to truth and was prepared to allow both broad definitions of theological positions, as for example of the Unitarian position, and also to allow for considerable differences with others. For him this was an imperfect world in which many things were unclear; 'one of the best proofs of wisdom is a sense of our want of wisdom; and he who knows

---

[67] *Observations on the Importance of the American Revolution (1785)* in D.O. Thomas ed., *Richard Price. Political Writings* (Cambridge: Cambridge University Press, 1991), pp. 130-35.

[68] W. Bernard Peach and D.O. Thomas eds, *The Correspondence of Richard Price* (3 vols, Durham N.C. and Cardiff: Duke University Press and University of Wales Press, 1983-1994), vol. III, pp. 108-110, Priestley to Price, 7 Jan. 1787; *Letters to Price* (see n.4 for full title), pp. 90-91.

[69] *Letters to Price*, p. 91.

[70] Ibid.

[71] Ibid., pp. 91-93; in the second edition of the *Sermons on the Christian Doctrine*, Price added an appendix summarizing Priestley's main criticism, but did not respond to them. *Correspondence of Price*, vol. II, p. 305 n. 3.

most possesses most of this sense.'[72] Although Priestley conceded that there were certain things which we did not understand, that did not deter his arguing that this is the best of all possible worlds, that understanding was constantly increasing, and that the issue between Price and himself would soon be resolved. The emphasis should be on our growing knowledge of the truth: on enlightenment not mystery, on certainty not doubt.[73] Whereas Price would modify statements which might appear dogmatic Priestley had no such hesitations, as clearly exemplified in this passage from his letters to Price

> Speaking of the socinian interpretation of scripture, you say... 'I must own to you, that I am inclined to wonder that good men can satisfy themselves with such explanations.' But you candidly add, 'But I correct myself. I know that christians, amidst their differences of opinion, are too apt to wonder at one another, and to forget the allowances that ought to be made for the darkness in which we are all involved.'
>
> You are too much of a philosopher to think that there can be any *effect* without an adequate *cause*; and you know that *wonder* is nothing more that the state of mind into which our ignorance of the causes of events throws us. And therefore whenever we think we can account for any appearance, all wonder ceases.[74]

The problem with Price's view is, as D. O. Thomas has noted, that 'it would seem as though the duties of candour have displaced the universally accepted elements of Christian belief as the fundamentals of faith'.[75] But such diffidence offers a healthy antidote to Priestley's assertiveness. Yet if Priestley was wrong to believe that unity needed agreement on doctrine, it did need a measure of agreement. At the same time, it is doubtful whether it could be achieved without a measure of Prices's modesty and diffidence about Christian truth.

Some Concluding Reflections

If Priestley did not assist church unity in the widest sense, he did further it in a narrower one. His controversy with Anglican clergymen over the doctrine of the Trinity helped to unite all orthodox Anglicans,[76] who for the most part

---

[72] See *Observations on the Importance of the American Revolution*, p.142.

[73] *Letters to Price*, p. 90. Priestley wrote that 'nothing is more painful and distressing' than 'a state of *doubt* '.

[74] *Letters to Price*, pp. 165-66.

[75] D.O. Thomas, *The Honest Mind: the Thought and Work of Richard Price* (Clarendon Press: Oxford, 1977), p. 36.

[76] This point has been made more circumspectly in relation to the whole Trinitarian controversy in the eighteenth century by John Walsh and Stephen Taylor, in 'Introduction: The Church and Anglicanism in the 'long' eighteenth century', in John Walsh, Colin Haydon and Stephen Taylor eds, *The Church of England, c.1689-c.1833. From Toleration to Tractarianism* (Cambridge: Cambridge University Press, 1993),

accepted it without qualification.[77] There were, of course, other factors at play, not least the perceived threat to Christianity of French Revolutionary philosophy and the threat to church and state from radicalism at home – a threat with which Priestley was associated. In due course the questions posed by liberal and heterodox Christianity faded, and new problems arose between the growing Evangelical Party in the church and the High Churchmen. These remained broadly contained within the Hanoverian Anglican consensus. It was the emergence of the Tractarians which would pose new problems for church unity and led to some of the new solutions to the question which we have noted. J. A. Froude, in his *History of England* (1856) looking back on the Hanoverian period with an element of nostalgia, suggested that the disappearance of 'theological doctrinalism' after the Glorious Revolution had enabled the church to have filled the 'wholesome functions of a religious establishment with moderate success'. He was pessimistic about unity in his own day. His prescription was not entirely different from those like Price and Priestley who had formerly argued for candour and equality between churches.[78] Nostalgia aside, the Anglican church in the Hanoverian period was perhaps closer to comprehension than at any time in its history, internally maintaining a 'dogmatic tolerance'.[79] Yet its privileged position meant that wider unity, embracing Dissenters as fellow Christians rather than seeking to comprehend them within their church, was always unlikely. The Anglican church felt no great need to develop its apologetics in relation to Dissenters over whom they retained a real sense of superiority.[80] In retrospect one might argue that Dissenters who very publicly stood up for their own values and who were critical of the special status of the Anglican church, that is Dissenters who pushed Anglicans into defending their status and theology, rendered the church a favour.

There were undoubtedly many flaws in Priestley's approach to Christian unity, but the central problem lay in his expectation that Christians would come to complete agreement on the nature of Christian truth. Yet he contributed more to Christian understanding than his orthodox opponents were willing to concede. One of the consequences of Priestley's heterodox views and dreadful reputation amongst the orthodox is that his contribution to biblical scholarship has not been recognised, except, naturally, by Unitarians and Universalists. Since minor denominations tend to claim too much for their own, that tends to

---

p. 47, but, as they have noted, Priestley being a Dissenter, and, one may add, deeply hostile to the church establishment, helped to close Anglican ranks.

[77] Walsh and Taylor, 'Introduction', pp. 47-8.

[78] Cowling, *Religion and Public Doctrine*, p. 23. Froude was in fact pessimist that one could convert those who 'believed it their highest duty to destroy each other' to 'respect each other's opinions'.

[79] Walsh and Taylor, 'Introduction', p. 59.

[80] Ibid., pp. 57-59.

provide a further reason for ignoring him. What is tend to be forgotten in all this is that the questions that Priestley posed could not be overlooked and that Trinitarians had to find their own answers. And that is what they did, though with a measure of hypocrisy. In 1818 Priestley's scholarship was plagiarised by Rev. Thomas Hartwell Horne in his *Introduction to the Critical Study and Knowledge of the Holy Scriptures* (1818), a work which became a 'standard work of reference for scriptural study'.[81] It went into many editions and was in print for most of the century. That can perhaps be regarded as a triumph by the backdoor for Priestley. But it would surely have been healthier for nineteenth century biblical scholarship if his work could have been examined, accepted and recognised where appropriate.

If we follow the example Alan Sell has set us, we should put aside our prejudices and acknowledge the work of those who conscientiously pursue truth, however much we may dislike their theology. In a recent paper he calls for calm consideration of the vexed question of the relationship between enlightenment and religion. He cites Henry Grove's view, 'Honest men that think for themselves, will value you the more for doing what they themselves have done, though the consequence should be your differing from them in some opinions.'[82] He also shows how Priestley stood foursquare in the tradition of honest Dissent, in which one's enquiries should be unconstrained by tests or articles of faith. This is the true tradition of Dissent, not that of silly squabbles about when to say 'Amen'. Unity, of whatever sort, will not be possible without acceptance of the valuable role of individual inquirers who pose extremely awkward questions to the faithful. For Priestley unity was his aspiration, diversity remained his location. That is a risk one always has to take, and it is one for which Alan Sell is prepared. In his own words

> No doubt nobody has ever been argued into faith, and I am not pleading that we try to imprison the Gospel within a new rationalism; but it is equally certain that some have had intellectual obstacles removed by careful apologetic discussion (and what is to prevent the Holy Spirit working through such discussion?); and it

---

[81] Robert E. Schofield, *The Enlightened Joseph Priestley. A Study of his Life and Work from 1773 to 1804* (University Park, Pennsylvania: Pennsylvania State University Press, 2004), p. 238.

[82] 'Some Theological Aspects of the English Enlightenment Calmly Consider'd', *Eighteenth-Century* 2 (2004), pp. 255-98 at p.275, citing Henry Grove, *Ethical and Theological Writings (1747)*, repr. with intro. by Alan P.F. Sell, 4 vols (Bristol: Thoemmes Press, 2000), vol. 4: p. 213. It may be of interest to note that in a much earlier paper Alan Sell drew attention to the way in which both Thomas Reid and Joseph Priestley were men of the Enlightenment. They belonged to an age 'in which the more 'respectable' thinkers sought to commend their faith by showing how eminently reasonable – even commonplace it was.' 'Priestley's Polemic against Reid', *The Price-Priestley Newsletter*, 3 (1979), pp. 41-52 at p. 49.

is utterly undeniable that to refuse a sincere question on grounds of theological policy represents a profound pastoral failure.[83]

---

[83] 'Conservation and Exploration in Christian Theology', p. 21.

CHAPTER 4

The Power of Christian Unity

Andrew D. MacRae

The search for Christian unity, which marked the twentieth century, received its initial impetus from a World Missions Conference in 1910, which contributed greatly to the development of inter-Denominational consultation and concern. The discovery that reconciliation was found in commitment to a common mission, played a significant part in drawing Christians together, and opening them to one another in new ways.

Interestingly, from all parts of the Christian church, from narrowly conservative fundamentalism to the very liberal, radical and self-professed postmodernism of some contemporary theologians, historians and churchpersons, a common appeal is made to the famous, 'High-Priestly' prayer of Jesus, 'My prayer is not for them alone. I pray also for those who will believe in me through their message, that all of them may be one, Father, just as you are in me and I am in you. May they also be in us so that the world may believe that you have sent me.'[1]

Alan Sell, who is the focus of this festschrift, began his Kaz Iwaasa Lecture on *Richard Baxter and the Unity of the Church* with words that set the tone and theme for this study. He argued that the concern for unity is as old as the Church itself. It is borne witness to both in the New Testament, with its multiple pleas for the people of God to recognise their oneness, and also in the ecumenical creeds of the early Church. He made a strong plea to recognise that 'The truth is that we do not create or concoct the unity of the Church at all. The Church's unity resides in the Church's Lord.'[2]

The power of Christian unity is that it has the potential to demonstrate the concept, the doctrine, and the reality of the Gospel's central message of reconciliation, as enunciated by St. Paul in his second letter to the Corinthians, when he writes, 'God was reconciling the world to himself in Christ, not

---

[1] John 17: 20-21 (TNIV).
[2] A. P. F. Sell, *Commemorations: Studies in Christian Thought and History* (Calgary: University of Calgary Press, 1993), p. 31.

counting people's sins against them. And he has committed to us the message of reconciliation. We are therefore Christ's ambassadors, as though God were making his appeal through us. We implore you on Christ's behalf: Be reconciled to God.'[3]

During the past century of ecumenical activity, several notable developments have taken place, three of which will occupy our attention in this study. Each of these developments has been an expression of Christian unity: the Ecumenical Movement, as it is represented in the World Council of Churches, the goal of which has always been the visible unity of the church and the churches; the Charismatic Renewal movement, expressed in a revitalised interest in the person and work of the Holy Spirit in the life of the Christian believer, the church and the churches, and especially in a widespread quest to rediscover the vitality of spiritual renewal through experiencing the 'gifts of the Holy Spirit'; and thirdly, the Evangelical Movement, with its emphasis on the spiritual unity of the people of God, expressed in the rapid growth of evangelical communities of faith, which have resulted in more rapid expansion of Christian mission in this time-frame than in any comparable period in the history of the church.

These three, though from rather different beginnings, have overcome the divisions of denominationalism to a remarkable degree, and have all touched the widest spectrum of denominational life. They are all evidences of growing Christian unity across the historic divisions of denominationalism. They have all faced the challenges of being, becoming or remaining true to a gospel of reconciliation, which lies at the very heart of the mission of Christ and of his church. The power of Christian unity to contribute positively to that mission will be evidenced if we are able to recognise the legitimacy of each of these quests, and if all three approaches and attempts lead to the acceptance of each by the others.

The Foundation of Christian Unity

Christian unity is of paramount importance, both in understanding the dominical intentions for the Church and in furthering its mission of reconciliation. At the opening of the twenty-first century, when the divisions in our world are so apparent, and when conflict among rival ideologies, ethnic groups, diverse cultures, and philosophical worldviews, are so evident, there is a critical need for Christians to go back to their source and re-learn the importance of unity in our common commitment and allegiance to Jesus Christ, whom all Christians acknowledge to be the Lord of the church, and of all life. I am persuaded that so long as we miss or ignore this one truly unifying element in our faith, no amount of ecclesiastical manoeuvring, structural engineering or theological persuasion will bring about the kind of unity which the Gospel of

---

[3] 2 Cor. 5:19, 20 (TNIV).

St. John indicates our Lord intended, and yield the power such unity has to persuade others to share our belief in Christ.

The early church, despite all the evidences of its fallible humanity, which are something of a comfort to us in our continuing frailty, found its unity, and its amazing power to impact society in its unshakeable conviction concerning Jesus and his significance. The principle of such unity is to be found in the person and the teaching of Jesus Christ, and is expressed most clearly in his prayer for the future of the church he established.

In the account of his 'High Priestly Prayer' in John 17, he prays first for himself as he dedicates himself to the task of bringing his heavenly Father's gift of eternal life to all who would believe in him and through him come to know God as Father. The full significance of his prayer needs to be grasped in the light of John's prologue to his Gospel, where he describes Jesus in the loftiest terms, and yet the most down to earth, when he calls him 'the Word', who was before creation, and both its life and light, and who, although his own Jewish kin did not recognize him when he came in the Incarnation, made God real and understandable. As John suggests, 'So the Word became flesh; he made his home among us, and we saw his glory, such glory as befits the Father's only son, full of grace and truth.'[4]

Jesus prays for his disciples, as he sends them into the world to continue his mission, that the Father will protect them by the power of His name, keep them from the evil one, and lead them to experience a unity that comes from their relationship to God in Christ, then and in coming days. John's words are of the greatest importance, as he records the prayer in words already cited from in verses 20,21, where the goal of unity is clearly desired in order to bring the world to faith.

In an exegetical comment on verses 20 – 23, Wilbert F. Howard writes

> After this exclusive prayer for the disciples Jesus prays for the church of the future, the whole company of the faithful won from the world by the apostolic preaching. He prays for its unity in God, that it may share that fellowship which the Son has with the Father. This spirit of unity in the church is to convince the world that Jesus was indeed commissioned by God (cf. vs. 3,8,18; 3:17; 5:36, 38; 6:29,38.57; 7:29; 8:42; 10:36; 11:42; 20:21; 1 John 4: 9-10,14). The incarnate life was a revelation of the nature of God (1:14), 'full of grace and truth', the shining forth of the filial love of the Logos. This the disciples had received from their Lord, and had shared in the unity of the divine fellowship, in the gift of eternal life (v.2). The unity is not that of a human organization, but is a gift of divine love. The unity of the Godhead demands the unity of the entire Christian

---

[4] John 1:14 (REB).

communion. This can be perfectly consummated only as its members have fellowship with the Father and with his Son Jesus Christ (1 John 1:3).[5]

To this exegetical explanation of the text, we may appropriately add this comment from William Temple, which has profound implications for all our ecumenical conversations

> ...we are reminded how transcendent is that theme which alone deserves the name of Christian unity. We meet in committees and construct our schemes of union; in face of the hideous fact of Christian divisions we are driven to this; but how paltry are our efforts compared with the call of God! The way to the union of Christendom does not lie through committee-rooms, though there is a task of formulation to be done there. It lies through personal union with the Lord so deep and real as to be comparable with His union with the Father. For the prayer is not directly that believers may be "one" in the Father and the Son, though by a natural error an early scribe introduced that thought. The prayer is that they may be in us. If we are in the Father and the Son, we shall certainly be one, and our unity will increase our effective influence in the world. But it is not our unity as such that has converting power; it is our incorporation into the true Vine as branches in which the divine life is flowing. When all believers are truly "in Christ", then our witness will have its destined effect – that the world may believe that thou didst send me.[6]

The continuing debate between those who conceive of Christian unity as entirely and exclusively spiritual in nature and those who argue that unity which is not visible is no unity, has its solution, surely, in the Dominical prayer, which looks and longs for a unity that is brought about by the relationship of believers to God in Christ.

This emphasis is not only foundational, in that it has its origin in the prayer of Jesus himself, but it is reinforced repeatedly in the apostolic writings, which, for the most part, preceded the writing of the Gospels, and certainly the writing of this Gospel. The fact that the latest of the canonical writings of the New Testament deals in such detail with a prayer attributed to Jesus comes as a reinforcement to the clear teaching of the New Testament letters, as, for example, the letter to the Ephesians, with its very practical appeal for unity

> As a prisoner for the Lord, then, I urge you to live a life worthy of the calling you have received. Be completely humble and gentle; be patient, bearing with one another in love. Make every effort to keep the unity of the Spirit through the bond of peace. There is one body and one Spirit–just as you were called to one hope when you were called–one Lord, one faith, one baptism; one God and Father of

---

[5] W.F. Howard, *The Interpreter's Bible, Vol. VIII* (Nashville: Abingdon Press, 1952), pp. 750, 751.
[6] William Temple, *Readings in St. John's Gospel* (London: MacMillan, 1945), p. 327.

all, who is over all and through all and in all.[7]

The emphasis is clear. Christians are called to a lifestyle modelled on the spirit of Christ, characterized by humility, gentleness, patience, mutual acceptance, unity and peace. These characteristics are the outcome of recognizing the supremacy of God in all of our life and all our relationships. The trinitarian formula, at least implied in these verses, is a reminder (as is Jesus' prayer) that Christian believers are what they are because of their relationship to the God who, through his Spirit, binds his people together in peace, uniting them in one body, with all their diversity. This body is united and enriched by its diversity, with a primary and ultimate allegiance to Christ, who has called its members to a life of discipleship and loyalty to the same Lord, to a life of faith in God's incarnate love, and to the God who is everywhere, and who, in all our relationships as Christians, is to be acknowledged as supreme.

In one of the most outspoken of the New Testament's letters, the apostle chides the church in Corinth for its divisions. In one of the severest passages of his first letter, he writes to them as 'worldly – mere infants in Christ'[8] He goes much further than that, however, in censuring this local church for its divisiveness. Early in the chapter, he complains that they are subject to jealousy and quarrelling, not on account of theological disagreement, but on account of their preferences for different, and perhaps even opposing styles of leadership, as represented in Paul, Apollos and Cephas. He describes the Christians in Corinth, collectively, as 'God's temple', and reminds them rather bluntly, 'God's Spirit lives in you. If anyone destroys God's temple, God will destroy him, for God's temple is sacred, and you are that temple.'[9] For the apostle the Christian community of faith was a temple for God to inhabit.

His concern was very much for the unity of the people of God. It is, I believe, appropriate to conclude that the early church, as represented in the apostolic teaching, concurred with our Lord's teaching of his disciples, and his recurring pleas that they 'love one another', in the well-known dictum attributed to him: 'I give you a new commandment: love one another; as I have loved you, so you are to love one another. If there is this love among you, then everyone will know that you are my disciples.'[10] This, together with his prayer for the unity of his people, is of supreme importance for the fulfilment of his mission to the world, in persuading the world to believe.

A similar idea is taken up in Ephesians 2, where the writer tells the Gentile Christians, who were sometimes in danger of feeling disenfranchised by the Jewish element, that they are now full citizens of the kingdom

---

[7] Eph. 4: 1-6 (NIV).
[8] 1 Cor. 3:1 (NIV).
[9] 1 Cor. 3: 16-17 (NIV).
[10] John 13:34-35 (REB).

...You are no longer foreigners and aliens, but fellow-citizens with God's people and members of God's household, built on the foundation of the apostles and prophets, with Christ Jesus himself as the chief cornerstone. In Him the whole building is joined together and rises to become a holy temple in the Lord. And in him you too are being built together to become a dwelling in which God lives by his Spirit.[11]

The inclusiveness of the dominical and apostolic ideal is a perpetual challenge to Christian division. Prior in importance to any re-alignment of our ecclesiastical or structural witness, is the centrality of Jesus Christ Himself, in the unity of the Godhead, which God intends to be reflected in the unity of the church.

The Development of the Ecumenical Movement

Any expression of ecumenism that has any hope of creating ever-stronger bonds of unity among Christians needs to be built on the only foundation that matters, which is Christ, known to us in the incarnation and reconciliation achieved in him, and, since Pentecost, mediated to us through the ministry of the Holy Spirit. This provides a foundation on which the mission of the church must always be established.

The early church wrestled with various heresies, virtually all centred on the person of Christ. The Apostles' Creed emphasized the true humanity of Jesus, which was denied by the Gnostics, the Marcionites, and the Manicheans. The fourth century Nicene Creed affirmed the Deity of Christ, in contrast to the Arians. The Chalcedonian Creed (451 AD) clearly asserted that Jesus Christ was perfect both in deity and in humanness. It spelled out the two natures of deity and humanity in Christ, by affirming him to be fully God and fully man

inconfuse, that is, without confusing the two natures;
immutabiliter, that is, without changing one nature into the other;
indivise, that is, without dividing them into two separate categories; and
inseparabiliter, that is, without tearing them apart, as if exclusive of each other.

A series of essays in christology was published in 1956 by a group of British theologians as a tribute to Karl Barth on his seventieth birthday. One striking essay was contributed by Dr. D.T. Jenkins, which began with these words

Those who have taken part in the discussion of the doctrine of the Church, which has been promoted by the Faith and Order department of the World Council of Churches, have come increasingly to see that questions of Christology are bound up with those which deal with the unity and disunity of the churches. The Lund Conference of 1952 affirmed: 'We believe in Jesus Christ our Lord, who loved the

---

[11] Eph. 2:19-22 (NIV).

Church and gave Himself for it, and has brought the Church into an abiding union with Himself. Because we believe in Christ, we believe also in the Church as the Body of Christ'...All who gathered together at Lund believed in the truth of the familiar words, *Ubi Christus, ibi ecclesia*. It was that common conviction which drew them together. At the same time, to the extent that they took it seriously, they had to acknowledge that it concealed differences as well as affirmed agreements between them, for it was manifest that they still remained divided in their understanding of the Church's nature and its limits.[12]

The ecumenical movement found its formal expression in 1948 in the creation of the World Council of Churches. At its beginning it cherished the christological base that had given the early church its foundation. Over the years, as in the early church, its quest for unity has been challenged by the re-emergence of some of the same old heresies, though in more modern and postmodern garb. These, too, have frequently called into question the person and nature of Christ. Its beginnings, however, without any reasonable doubt, were orthodox in theology and focused on the church's world mission of reconciliation, a mission that is always placed in jeopardy by disunity.

The World Missionary Conference for Evangelism in Edinburgh, Scotland in 1910 was a remarkable event, which marked both the culmination of nineteenth-century missions and the real beginning of modern ecumenism. Protestant denominations and missionary societies from around the world sent 1,200 representatives to Edinburgh, Scotland. John R. Mott, American Methodist and leader of the Student Volunteer Movement for foreign missions, was conference chair.

It is crucial to our understanding, both of the past history and the future potential of the Ecumenical Movement, to remember that it began, in part at least, as a missionary movement with a global perspective. In that awareness lies a significant indication that real unity among Christians is to be found, not in endless discussions of our divergent theologies and traditions, significant as these are, but in the commitment to a mission which embraces the world, and which has the power to bring together in real, relational unity, all those who confess Jesus Christ as Lord.

This view of the World Council of Churches has, from time to time, been reinforced by it leadership. For example, in a World Conference on Mission and Evangelism, held in Melbourne, Australia in May 1980, Dr. Philip Potter, then the General Secretary of the World Council of Churches, said

> The World Council of Churches is proud to be the inheritor of the great missionary movement which launched the decisive stage of the ecumenical movement at Edinburgh 1910. It was, therefore, natural that when the World Council was formed in 1948, the International Missionary Council was declared

---

[12] D.T. Jenkins, 'Christology, the Holy Spirit and the Ecumenical Movement,' *Essays in Christology for Karl Barth*, ed. T.H.L.Parker (London: Lutterworth, 1956), p. 229.

to be 'in association' with it. One of the functions of the World Council was, from the beginning, 'to support the churches in their task of evangelism'. Since the integration of the International Missionary Council with the World Council in 1961, this function has been expressed comprehensively as follows: 'to facilitate the common witness of the churches in each place and in all places', and 'to support the churches in their worldwide missionary and evangelistic task'. The nearly 300 member churches in over 100 countries are committed to this task, and the purpose of this conference is to deepen and further that commitment.[13]

The missionary and evangelical nature of the World Council of Churches, at its inception, is evident in a report submitted to the Assembly entitled *Definition and Description of the Concept of Evangelism*, which included the following statements

> The basis of Evangelism is the outgoing and redeeming love of God made known in Jesus Christ so that men are brought, through the power of the Holy Spirit, to put their trust in God, to accept Jesus Christ as their Saviour from the guilt and power of sin; and to follow and serve Him as their Lord with the fellowship of the Church in the vocations of the common life...

> We are convinced that the present situation in Europe and in the world constitutes an urgent call to the Church and to its members to realise that everyone who has been called by the living Christ is meant to be a joyful witness to God's love and grace and to proclaim the good news of Christ's lordship and salvation to his neighbour, that is to all with whom he is brought into relationship by the circumstances of daily life...Evangelism must proceed from the Church and must gather into the fellowship of the Church those who are evangelized. It is the work of the whole church but at the present time there is urgent need to recognise and to develop the special gifts of those to whom God has given the call to be evangelists as their particular vocation within the Church. We should pray for the awakening of these special gifts as well as for the awakening of the whole Church to its evangelistic responsibilities.[14]

It seems clear, then, that mission and evangelism were primary foci in the beginnings of the World Council of Churches. Colin Buchanan, writes

> The point of origin is usually taken to be the Edinburgh (Missionary) Conference in 1910. This was not primarily concerned with matters of Faith and Order, but with the co-operation of societies conducting missions to non-Christian peoples.

---

[13] Philip Potter, WCC General Secretary in *Your Kingdom Come. Mission Perspectives Report on the World Conference on Mission and Evangelism*, (Geneva: World Council of Churches, 1980), p.6.

[14] *Report on Evangelism to World Council of Churches Assembly* (Geneva: World Council of Churches, 1948).

The conference, however, led some to a vision of a united church, and this necessitated the facing of differences of belief through further forms of conference. Within weeks, movements were started which led to the formation of Faith and Order. World War I caused delay, and the first World Conference on Faith and Order met at Lausanne in 1927. The second was in Edinburgh in 1937, from which came a proposal (which was accepted) made by the Life and Work Movement to form a 'World Council of Churches'.[15]

The subsequent history of the World Council of Churches shows variations in emphasis, largely brought about by the growth of the Council in denominational breadth, and by its concerted effort to exercise a Christian presence in a rapidly changing world. Over the years, it became a more and more significant international expression of shared Christian reflection and conviction. The two founding movements particularly active in its formation, namely, Life and Work (L&W) and Faith and Order (F&O) united their voices at the first assembly. Although some of the founding documents and reports indicate a strong emphasis on mission and evangelism, it was in 1961 that the International Missionary Council (IMC), was integrated with the WCC, and a commitment to Christian education became part of the work of WCC through the 1971 merger with the World Council of Christian Education, whose roots went back to the 18th century Sunday School movement. In the most interesting way, many of the ecumenical agencies already in existence became contributory streams to the emerging and constantly developing movement represented and expressed in the World Council Of Churches.

One of the most significant endeavours of the World Council of Churches was in the production of the document on *Baptism, Eucharist and the Ministry*, (*BEM*) presented to the Lima meeting of the World Council of Churches in 1982. The statement represents years of ecumenical study and dialogue on the church's sacraments and offices of ministry. It explores what can be affirmed together by Christian churches of several (and historically separated) traditions—including churches of the Reformed, Lutheran, Methodist, Anglican and Orthodox families.

The Preface to the *BEM* document sets the tone of its concern thus

> ...the Faith and Order Commission of the World Council provides theological support for the efforts the churches are making towards unity...the stated aim of the Commission is 'to proclaim the oneness of the Church of Jesus Christ and to call the churches to the goal of visible unity in one faith and one eucharistic fellowship, expressed in worship and common life in Christ, in order that the world might believe' (By-Laws).

---

[15] Colin Buchanan, *The New International Dictionary of the Christian Church*, ed. J.D. Douglas (Grand Rapids: Zondervan 1979), p. 1061.

> If the divided churches are to achieve the visible unity they seek, one of the essential prerequisites is that they should be in basic agreement on baptism, eucharist and ministry... This Lima text represents the significant theological convergence which Faith and Order has discerned and formulated.[16]

This document revealed the remarkable degree of agreement across many, though not all, of the historic divisions in the church.

To review the major developments in the World Council of Churches, as a focal point of the ecumenical movement, would go far beyond the purpose of this discussion. Suffice it to say that, in diverse situations and circumstances, the World Council of Churches and its affiliated regional ecumenical organisations have engaged in considered, shared reflection not only on the theological issues still requiring resolution, if visible unity is to be achieved in the observation and the practice of the sacraments and the nature of ministry, but also on the priorities demanded by the day and the times, and in the encouragement of concerted action in the name of Christian witness and involvement. To illustrate this, the Conference of European Churches (CEC) became a significant ecumenical instrument in the complex culture of Europe, particularly during the period of the 'cold war'.

The website of CEC, in summarising the history of the Conference, states

> The Conference of European Churches (CEC) is a fellowship of 126 Orthodox, Protestant, Anglican and Old Catholic Churches along with 43 associated organisations from all countries on the European continent. CEC was founded in 1959 and has offices in Geneva, Brussels and Strasbourg.
>
> Christians from different confessions are committed to live and witness together in a spirit of ecumenism, sharing, understanding and mutual respect. All are committed in spite of the historic divides, many languages, geographical and economic barriers which exist on the European continent. Together, the churches work to promote the unity of the church and to present a common Christian witness to the people and the institutions of Europe...
>
> Born in the 1950s in the era of the 'cold war', CEC emerged into a fragmented and divided continent. Out of this experience, the churches of eastern and western Europe felt that one priority of their work would be to promote international understanding – to build bridges. CEC has consistently tried to do this over the years, insisting that no 'iron curtain' exist among the churches. This insistence led to the holding of CEC's 4th Assembly, in 1964, on board a ship in the Baltic Sea

---

[16] *Baptism, Eucharist and Ministry,* WCC Faith and Order Paper No. 111 (Geneva: World Council of Churches, 1982).

in order to overcome visa problems and ensure that all churches enjoyed representation.[17]

Thanks to the creative leadership of people like Dr. Glenn Garfield Williams and others in these difficult years, CEC worked hard to harmonise relationships between minority and majority churches, intergenerationally, between women and men, and between Christians of different confessions. In expressing the unity of the churches in their loyalty to their shared faith in Jesus Christ as Lord and Saviour, it also endeavoured to address the ideological, political and cultural changes of a rapidly and constantly changing world.

Despite the periodic pejorative criticisms of the World Council of Churches by well-meaning, devout people, with accusations of 'communist infiltration', political 'leftism', theological liberalism and ecclesiastical manipulation in efforts to achieve structural and organic union, the World Council of Churches, and its regional affiliates, have contributed much to the enrichment of mutual understanding among Christians and to the reduction of the image of a religion fragmented and hopelessly broken by conflict, and have done it by a constant insistence on a gospel of reconciliation as the heart of the universal Christian message. Alongside other discernible movements and developments, that has, I believe, contributed to the unity our Lord desires.

The Emergence and Influence of Charismatic Renewal

The second ecumenical agency in recent times, and particularly since the 1950s has been the charismatic renewal movement, with its challenge to all Christians, and particularly to those whose theology and practice have appeared to be dualistic more than trinitarian, to recognise, and in some cases to reinstate, the person and purpose of the Holy Spirit, not merely as a theological concept, but as a dynamic, divine reality. It has been characterised primarily by its strong and unapologetic emphasis on the ministry and the gifts of the Holy Spirit, which it insists are still relevant and operable.

It is without question a child of the Pentecostal movement, which, with its roots in the Azusa Street revival in Los Angeles in 1906, has become the fastest-growing expression of Christianity in America and throughout much of the world. A review by Dr. Albert Mohler Jr, the theologically conservative President of Southern Baptist Seminary, in a review of *Spirit Works: Charismatic Practices and the Bible* by Jerry Vines, makes this assessment

> The rise of the Charismatic movement is one of the most remarkable developments of the twentieth century. From modest beginnings in the Azusa Street revival, the modern-day Charismatic movement has been transformed into the fastest- growing segment of Christianity in America and throughout much of

---

[17] http://www.cec-kek.org/content/history.shtml

the world. Some experts estimate that the movement includes almost a half-billion adherents worldwide.

> The Charismatic movement now spans much of the globe, incorporating traditional Pentecostals, the Assemblies of God, the Vineyard movement, and new-wave phenomena including purported 'prophets' and 'apostles.' Central to the movement is the claim that a new visitation of the Holy Spirit has brought back the apostolic gifts and manifestations of the New Testament. With an emphasis on a 'second blessing' after conversion, the movement is calling all Christians to 'catch the wave'…the Charismatic influence has reached even into the most traditional denominations, including the Episcopalians in the United States and Anglicans throughout the world. A Roman Catholic Charismatic movement has thrived since the 1970s. More recently, questions of Charismatic influence within the Southern Baptist Convention have been raised.[18]

Now while the spread of charismatic interest and even renewal has been as extensive as Dr. Vines suggests, it should not be confused as being identical with Pentecostalism, than which it has a wider appeal across the Christian spectrum. To illustrate, in *the Statement of Fundamental and Essential Truths* of the Pentecostal Assemblies of Canada, the section on Baptism in the Holy Spirit reads

> The baptism in the Holy Spirit is an experience in which the believer yields control of himself to the Holy Spirit (Matt. 3:11; Acts 1:5; Eph. 5:18). Through this he comes to know Christ in a more intimate way, (John 16:13-15) and receives power to witness and grow spiritually (2 Cor. 3:18; Acts 1:8). Believers should earnestly seek the baptism in the Holy Spirit according to the command of our Lord Jesus Christ (Luke 24:49; Acts 1:4,8). The initial evidence of the baptism in the Holy Spirit is speaking in other tongues as the Spirit gives utterance (Acts 2:1-4,39; 9:17; 1 Cor. 14:18). This experience is distinct from, and subsequent to, the experience of the new birth (Acts 8:12-17; 10:44-46).[19]

Christians of many denominational affiliations, who are pleased to be aligned with charismatic renewal, do not hold a post-conversion, 'second-blessing' understanding of the working of the Holy Spirit in the life of the Christian or the church, believing that the bestowal of the Holy Spirit on the life of the Christian believer is part of God's saving initiative, actualised at the point of faith.

Certainly, some quite prominent voices from other denominations, who have embraced much of the charismatic renewal, and who recognize its roots in the Pentecostal movement, make little distinction between them. One of the

---

[18] Albert Mohler, Jr., Review of Jerry Vines, *Spirit Works: Charismatic Practices and the Bible*, in *SBC Life: Journal of the Southern Baptist Convention*, 4:4 (January 2000), p. 4.

[19] http://www.bible.ca/cr-PAOC.htm

strongest and clearest voices comes from Tom Smail, a Presbyterian charismatic, who argues strongly both against the 'second blessing' implication of the Pentecostal position, but also against the outright rejection of charismatic renewal: 'There could be nothing more ridiculous than for Pentecostals to insist on a single phrase as the one necessary description of the spiritual experience whose recovery they seek for the whole Church; or for non-Pentecostals to think, that in exposing the theological inadequacies of talk about spiritual baptism, they have somehow disposed of the whole charismatic challenge.'[20]

However, the amazing rise and spread of the Pentecostal movement during the twentieth century, with its blend of energetic, enthusiastic, expressive, empathetic and sometimes enigmatical spirituality is, to put it mildly, an astonishing religious phenomenon. As an expression of a movement which conceives of the Christian life as a life begun in conversion, and later enriched by a separate experience of God in the 'baptism in the Holy Spirit', the validity of which is demonstrated in 'the gift of tongues', Pentecostalism should not be identified with 'charismatic renewal' or the 'charismatic movement', as if they were one and the same.

Historically, the emergence of Pentecostalism in the early years of the twentieth century, marks a powerful, sometimes bizarre, spiritual movement, as the spring from which charismatic renewal emerged. The Pentecostal movement had its most dramatic early expression in the Azusa Street Revival in Los Angeles, California. The April 18, 1906, issue of the *Los Angeles Times* carried a story on the Azusa Street revival. It read that a bizarre new religious sect had started, with people

> breathing strange utterances and mouthing a creed which it would seem no sane mortal could understand.... devotees of the weird doctrine practice the most fanatical rites, preach the wildest theories, and work themselves into a state of mad excitement.... night is made hideous in the neighbourhood by the howlings of the worshippers who spend hours swaying forth and back in a nerve-racking attitude of prayer and supplication. They claim to have the 'gift of tongues,' and to be able to comprehend the babble.[21]

However we may feel about the extravagance of this outburst of Christian devotional fervour, many church historians and missiologists regard it as the most, or one of the most, significant indications of a renewed dependence on the Holy Spirit, who energises the Christian and the church for his witness in the world. The coming of the Holy Spirit in power is based on Luke's record of Jesus' last post-resurrection words: '…you will receive power when the Holy Spirit comes on you; and you will be my witnesses in Jerusalem, and in all

---

[20] T. A. Smail *Reflected Glory* (London: Hodder and Stoughton, 1975,) p. 139.
[21] http://dunamai.com/Azusa/asuza_pages/latimes.htm reprinted from the *Los Angeles Times*, April 18, 1906, p. 1.

Judea, and Samaria, and to the ends of the earth'.[22]

James Packer, in his book on the Holy Spirit, has a chapter entitled, 'Mapping the Spirit's Path: The Charismatic Life', in which he seeks to examine the charismatic movement carefully. Writing in 1984, he states

> Not yet a quarter of a century old, it boasts more than 20 million adherents and has significantly touched the entire world church – Roman Catholic, Orthodox, Anglican and nonepiscopal Protestant – at all levels of life and across a wide theological spectrum. Sometimes it is called neo-Pentecostalism because, like the older Pentecostalism that spread round the world at the start of this century, it affirms Spirit baptism as a distinct post-conversion, post-water-baptism experience, universally needed and universally available to those who seek it. The movement has grown, however, independently of the Pentecostal Denominations, whose suspicions of its nonseparatist inclusiveness have been (and in some quarters remain) deep, and charismatic renewal is its own preferred name for itself today.[23]

Packer's identification of the Pentecostal and charismatic movements with respect to the 'post-conversion' nature of Spirit baptism is not, by any means, shared by everyone within the movement. For example, the Rev. Gottfried Osei-Mensah, Pastor of the Nairobi Baptist Church in the 1970s, in a contribution to the reference volume of the International Congress on World Evangelization in Lausanne, Switzerland, entitled *The Holy Spirit in World Evangelization*, wrote

> The baptism with the Holy Spirit has been variously understood and interpreted by Christians. The Holiness Movement (late nineteenth century) identified it with 'entire sanctification' as a second blessing subsequent to conversion. The early Pentecostals understood it as a third distinctive experience – 'a gift of power upon the sanctified life'. Today, most people use the phrase to describe 'a second encounter with God (the first being conversion) in which the Christian begins to receive the supernatural power of the Holy Spirit into his life'…For most people who seek this experience, the undisputed sign of its fulfilment is to speak in tongues…However, there are other leaders in the movement who dismiss the sentiment as unnecessary, unbiblical and divisive.[24]

The Pentecostal movement, like the charismatic renewal movement as a whole, places central emphasis on the person and work of the Holy Spirit, but it has usually insisted on the gift of tongues as a *sine qua non* of the baptism in the Holy Spirit, thus dividing it firmly from many within the charismatic

---

[22] Acts 1:8 (NIV).

[23] J. I. Packer, *Keep in Step with the Spirit* (New Jersey: Revell, 1984), p. 170.

[24] Gottfried Osei-Mensah, 'The Holy Spirit in World Evangelization,' J.D. Douglas, (ed.), *Let the Earth Hear His Voice* (Minneapolis: World Wide Publications, 1975), p. 263.

movement, which has not often seriously disrupted those churches and denominations it has touched deeply, but has rather contributed to their vitality by emphasising the Holy Spirit's ministry as the one who empowers the Christian and the church by bestowing gifts needed to fulfil the dominical mission of the church, in 'making disciples of all peoples'. In fact, the movement has helped to infuse new life into many churches and Christian groups around the world, without regard for their affiliation, whether Roman Catholic, Orthodox, Anglican, Baptist, Presbyterian, or other Protestant Denominations. Although it grew out of Pentecostalism, they are not identical.

A major difference is that, whereas Pentecostalism separates itself from other Christian communions by the inflexibility of its understanding of the ministry of the Holy Spirit and of the nature of his special gifts, the charismatic movement usually avoids divisiveness on such an issue, contributing thereby to the unity of the church. Indeed, as Dr. John Stott states in a chapter on *Theological Foundations for Preaching*, '...largely as a result of the charismatic movement, the New Testament doctrine of the Body of Christ has been recovered, with its corollary that every member has a gift and therefore a ministry.'[25]

This understanding of the contribution of the charismatic movement to the unity of the church is strongly endorsed by Tom Smail, who writes

> ...the Spirit leads people out of their subjectivity into a new understanding of how the gifts of the Spirit have their significance only in terms of the upbuilding of Christ's Body for doing Christ's corporate work; out of their individualism to an exploration of Christian community, of how in very practical costly and down-to-earth ways Christians may share together the life that Christ puts in them by his Spirit, and to see that the only context in which the Spirit and his power have any meaning is in relation to our witness and evangelism.[26]

While recognising a significant difference between denominational Pentecostalism and interdenominational charismatic renewal, we ought not to dismiss the challenge from both concerning the renewing influence of the Holy Spirit, and the unifying potential of genuine charismatic awareness. J.I Packer refers to the analysis made by Lesslie Newbigin, who, as far back as 1953, when the charismatic movement was just beginning to be a world-wide influence, but before its significance was fully recognised, 'typecast the Protestant and Catholic views of the church as "the congregation of the faithful" and "the body of Christ",' respectively, and went on to describe the Christianity of the Pentecostal churches as an authentic third stream of Christian awareness, embodying a view of the church as 'the community of the Holy Spirit'. He saw it as necessary to fertilize and irrigate the other two views, and asked: 'May it not be that the great churches of the Catholic and Protestant

---

[25] John R.W. Stott, *Between Two Worlds* (Grand Rapids: Eerdmans, 1982), p. 116.
[26] Smail, *Reflected Glory*, pp. 20, 21.

traditions will have to be humble enough to receive [a new understanding of the Holy Spirit] in fellowship with their brethren in the various groups of the Pentecostal type with whom at present they have scarcely any fellowship at all.' And Packer suggests, Newbiggin's question is still an urgent one 'as we survey the pervasive phenomenon of charismatic renewal a quarter of a century later'.[27]

The Influence of Evangelicalism

The third unifying movement for many Christians is the evangelical movement. Around the world, evangelical Christianity has grown at an unprecedented pace through the twentieth century. It is often castigated in Western society as authoritarian, intolerant, fundamentalist, anti-social and obscurantist. Such negativism is a fairly clear sign that it is not understood, although it should be acknowledged that evangelicalism, like any significant movement, has its extreme fringes, which hinder its potentially positive influence, and which convey a serious misrepresentation of its core values, as does fundamentalism in any religion.

At the time of writing, the image of evangelicals is in danger of being distorted by the dominance of the so-called 'conservative right' in the USA. While that 'conservative right' upholds many basic Christian values, such as the sacredness of life and the sanctity of marriage, it is also characterised in the popular media as anti-social, anti-human rights, and counter-cultural.

In increasingly secular Western societies, which currently favour the description of 'postmodern', in an attempt to contrast themselves with the 'modern', one of the main features of the so-called postmodern world view is the absence of absolutes. The insistence on individual freedom from any external authority or accountability in the name of 'individual rights and freedoms' has led to the abandonment of any idea that religion carries moral or social authority. In such an environment, the concept of the separation of church and state frequently regards it as inadmissible for the church to interfere in what are now described as 'social issues', rather than moral issues. However, none of that is particularly new. In reality, postmodernism in the late twentieth/early twenty-first century has offered somewhat different configurations of old ideas, in the ideological mix of individualism, narcissism, hedonism, secularism, relativism, pluralism, syncretism, and materialism, as some of its main features. The current mood of Western culture may fairly be described as secular, since one of its most apparent impacts is the ease with which Western societies that embrace secularism as a worldview dispense with God, and the moral accountability that arises from an affirmation of his personal reality.

Although this has led to a tendency to marginalise evangelical Christianity

---

[27] Packer, *Keep In Step With the Spirit,* pp. 171, 172.

in such societies, the evangelical movement has continued to draw together Christians of all traditions world wide, and to bear effective witness to the gospel.

A most interesting review of evangelical Christianity in America was first published in 1975, just before the American bicentennial, the editors of which begin their introduction to a revised edition in 1980 by stating

> After a long period of painful eclipse, evangelicals have emerged as a powerful force in the nation's religious and political life. The keeper of the national pulse, George Gallup, reported in 1976 that a full 34% of all Americans over eighteen had had a 'born again' experience...To crown matters, Jimmy Carter was elected to the presidency despite his unabashed evangelical convictions...that all of this should be happening in the full blaze of secularism and when, only a few years ago, the demise of evangelicalism seemed complete, is all the more remarkable. Indeed, progressive interpretations of our history had assumed that once the decline of evangelical Christianity had been established, as it was in the early decades of this century, it could not be substantially reversed. The modern world would simply pass it by. But here is a movement that is slowly awakening to a new role in American life, vigorously and often creatively speaking to the needs of contemporary society and simply refusing to retire to its assigned oblivion.[28]

This review, however, includes in its list of contributors a wide range of writers, from dedicated evangelicals to outspoken critics, which makes for a remarkable overview of the 'movement', warts and all.

Evangelicalism and fundamentalism have been widely regarded as synonyms, not only in the secular media, but also in much mainline Protestantism. David Moberg writes

> One of the troublesome aspects of identifying and describing evangelicalism is how to differentiate it from fundamentalism. The complications of this are great because of subtleties of distinctions, so I prefer to view them as blending into and overlapping with each other instead of as absolutely distinct categories. A strictly doctrinal differentiation makes them fellow members of the same religious category. Both evangelicals and fundamentalists are committed to the basic fundamentals of the Christian faith – the deity and virgin birth of Jesus Christ his

---

[28] D. F. Wells and J. D. Woodridge (eds), *The Evangelicals: What They Believe, Who They Are, Where They Are Changing* (Grand Rapids: Baker, 1980), p. 9. A number of recent books on Evangelicalism also suggest themselves here. See for example James Packer and Thomas Oden, *One Faith* (Downers Grove: IVP, 2004); Robert Webber, *Ancient-Future Faith*, (Grand Rapids: Baker, 1999); Mark Noll, *The Rise of Evangelicalism* (Downers Grove: IVP, 2004); David Bebbington, *The Dominance of Evangelicalism* (Downers Grove: IVP, 2005). (I have avoided listing volumes that raise the specters of traditionalist and reformist Evangelicals, as persons like Roger Olson define them, which they see as threatening to destroy our theological consensus – although some of them are very interesting.)

vicarious atonement for sin, his bodily resurrection, his personal second coming, and the inspiration and authority of the Bible.[29]

Clearly, Moberg does not understand how different they are. Fundamentalism goes far beyond the parameters he describes, with its rigid demands. Similarly, it is important not to confuse the evangelical movement with the charismatic movement. While they undoubtedly share many common beliefs with one another, some of which are also held by many people within the ecumenical movement, they should not be confused, since evangelicalism, being broader in scope, includes some who are strongly committed to charismatic renewal, while others are adamant in believing that the 'sign gifts', including the gift of tongues, were withdrawn at the close of the apostolic period, and have not been restored.

Richard G. Hutcheson, Jr, whose work with the Presbyterian Church of the USA Office of Review and Evaluation involved him in examining 'general trends and indices affecting the health and work of the church',[30] was persuaded that the mainline churches were, for the most part, liberal in theology and pluralist in practice, to such an extent that he could write

> Mainline churches are pluralistic by design. They welcome to their membership diversity of faith, style and opinion. While doctrinal standards establish general parameters, they are seldom applied in a way excluding anyone. Even candidates for the clergy, in mainline denominations, are more likely to be rejected for excessive narrowness than for violation of confessional standards. As for the laity, one can hardly conceive a belief, idiosyncrasy, or variance which would disqualify a lay person conscientiously and sincerely seeking membership in a mainline church.[31]

Hutcheson describes the evangelical resurgence as 'probably the most significant development in American Christianity in the decade of the seventies'. The liberal-mainline churches did not know how seriously to take it, or how to explain the election of the evangelical Jimmy Carter to the Presidency and the persistence of Billy Graham and his ministry, despite the scorn of the theological liberals in the mainline denominations.

One of his most insightful assessments is in his description of the main features of the evangelical movement, which he describes as follows

> 1. The principle of the reliability of the Scriptures in matters of faith and practice is central for evangelicals...The liberal tends to approach the task from the

---

[29] Wells and Woodridge, *The Evangelicals*, pp. 164, 165.
[30] Richard G. Hutcheson Jr., *Mainline Churches and the Evangelicals* (Atlanta: John Knox Press, 1981), pp. 7, 8.
[31] Hutcheson, *Mainline Churches*, p. 21.

scientific side; criticism is a given, and the Liberal looks for the religious values still to be found in the Bible despite its human and historic conditioning. The evangelical approaches from the biblical side; the authority of Scripture is given, and the question is how criticism can help to understand it.

2. Evangelicals are united in giving a central place in their concept of Christianity to personal faith in Jesus Christ as Saviour from sin, and to commitment to him....

3. They believe in sanctification conceived as a distinctively Christian life following rebirth...

4. Many...are deeply involved in social concerns...Evangelicals want to combine evangelism with social action and insist on both...

5. Evangelicalism is marked by friendliness to science, which is no longer seen as the enemy...

6. Evangelicals insist on a rational faith and reject the anti-intellectualism of some fundamentalists.

7. While their attitude to ecumenism is ambivalent, it is not the unqualified rejection of fundamentalists...They are not primarily interested in conciliar ecumenism...They do, however, talk about and practice a functional ecumenism, and are often deeply involved in non-institutional ecumenical undertakings.

8. New evangelicals tend to reject dispensational premillennialism, particularly the dispensationalism associated with the Scofield Reference Bible...They do not reject the second coming of Christ.

9. Perhaps the greatest difference between evangelicals and fundamentalists is tone, style, or spirit...they reflect a more open, listening, and reconciling spirit than do their fellow conservatives of the extreme right.[32]

Writing from within contemporary evangelicalism, it is my judgment that it is not possible, legitimately, to treat evangelicalism and fundamentalism as homogeneous. Evangelicals represent a great deal of variety of emphasis and interpretation, even of Holy Scripture. However, in terms of fundamental theological or doctrinal agreement, it may be argued that contemporary evangelicals, from whatever denominational, racial or social background, affirm the importance of a decisive commitment to Christ, to evangelism, discipleship and service, which cannot be limited to any denominational label, but which is to be found in the other two expressions of Christian Unity. Many evangelicals have enjoyed the fellowship and service of other Christians within the ecumenical movement, as expressed in the World Council of Churches or its national or regional associates, and equally with Christians in the

---

[32] Hutcheson, *Mainline Churches,* pp. 33-35 (ellipses mine).

charismatic renewal movement.

It is often beneficial to listen to Christians whose theological orientation is different from our own, and to take seriously their assessment of our own position, and, having listened, to engage in constructive dialogue within the wider fellowship of the universal body of Christ. Evangelicals have contributed significantly to that dialogue.

The Next Steps

It is futile, in my view, to expect or even hope for these movements, which represent large areas of Christian unity, to be coalesced into any one of them, so that all agree on everything. That would be dangerously like uniformity, which is not an idea that sits well with the concept of the church as the body of Christ. However, each of them has a significant contribution to make to the unity of the church, which can empower it for its mission, for which Christ prayed.

The goal of the World Council of Churches is 'to proclaim the oneness of the Church of Jesus Christ and to call the churches to the goal of visible unity in one faith and one eucharistic fellowship, expressed in worship and common life in Christ, in order that the world might believe (By Laws).'[33]

The goal of the charismatic movement is that all Christians come to recognise the Holy Spirit as the common source and sustainer of the Christian life, and to depend on his enabling for the service of Jesus Christ.

The goal of the evangelical movement is to share the good news of God's grace, forgiveness and reconciliation through Christ for all humankind, and to acknowledge Christ as Lord through open commitment to him, and to the service of others for whom he died.

All three movements profess to acknowledge the centrality of Jesus Christ, fully God and fully human, and to share a common life in Him. The affirmation of that indispensable element, without diminution or reduction, is surely an important key to further progress.

If all three expressions of Christian unity can learn to love one another, to accept one another, and to forgive one another for the long record of past failure to live as loving, caring members of the same family, the gospel of reconciliation will be greatly enhanced, as Christ's prayer is answered, 'that all of them may be one, Father, just as you are in me and I am in you. May they also be in us so that the world may believe that you have sent me.'

---

[33] *WCC Faith and Order Commission* (Preface to *Baptism, Eucharist and Ministry*, p. 1).

Ecumenical and Eclectic: Reflections

CHAPTER 5

'A tradition handed on by preaching': The Allure of Broad Sermons – William Page Roberts of Vere Street[1]

Clyde Binfield

I

Christians who take worship seriously are constantly exercised by the tensions between continuity and change. Continuity may suggest movement but it must suggest tradition; it presupposes a long view. Change could suggest contrast but it more likely implies development; it too presupposes a long view. Christian worship might be described as doctrine expressed as ritual; it fuses belief, emotion, and intellect and it allows for physical activity. It is tempting, when considering worship, to focus on the ritual itself or on the ritualists, that is to say on the choreographers of worship, but since there is a priesthood of all believers a wider relationship might be entertained, of those who watch and share as well as those who lead and direct. Seen thus, each ritual act is unique. It cannot be replicated. Yet its power depends on the associations, the repetitions, the familiarity, which bind the participants. One such act, given that

---

[1] In the preparation of this paper I have been much indebted to Mrs. Betty Baker, Miss Melanie Barber and Lambeth Palace Library, Mrs. J. Chaplin, Mr. John Creasey and Dr. Williams's Library, Lady Dainton, Dr. Ian Dungavell, Christine Hughes and City of Westminster Archives, the Ven. Dr. W.W. Jacob, Margaret Mortimer, Mr. B.R. Martin, Mr. R. Morley Fletcher, Mr. Nevill Melland, Dr. Peter Nockles and Methodist Church Archives (the John Rylands University Library Manchester), Mr. G.F. Palmer, Kay Parrott and Liverpool Record Office, Dr. Alison Pears and St. John's College Cambridge, Miss Bessie Preston, Mr. Bernard Reeve, Mrs. Joy Rowe, Mrs. Margery Rowe and Devon Record Office, Mr. L. Skinner, Mr. H.O. Tester, the Revd. Dr. John Travell. The quotation in the title comes from W. Page Roberts, *Our Prayer Book: Conformity and Conscience* (London: 1899), p. 158.

Christianity is a tradition handed on by preaching as well as new life in each believer, is the sermon. In short, for the Christian as for any person, continuity and change are as inseparable as they are inevitable, and Christian worship celebrates this. Or so it seemed to a late-Victorian canon residentiary of Canterbury preaching in Marylebone on the Prayer of St. Chrysostom and calling a Harley Street scientist and a Liverpool Unitarian in aid

> It is disastrous to separate ourselves from the past suddenly and violently.... Sir William Grove declared that: 'All change to be healthy must be extremely slow, the defect struggling with the remedy through countless but infinitesimally minute gradations.' In a similar spirit a Unitarian minister has said: '....Even when the process of change in religious conviction is most rapidly and surely going on, it is fatal to emotion to break with the past too abruptly, too completely. Religion belongs to the conservative side of our nature; we pray best in familiar words....'
> ...There is a law of mental and spiritual continuity from which it is disastrous to break away.[2]

As will be seen, this quotation contains several clues as to the preacher's churchmanship and his hearers' social and educational standing. They indicate a certain type of late-Victorian Anglicanism. Perhaps they are even more representative than that. My aim is to explore the theme of change within continuity using two collections of this Marylebone preacher's sermons as a spine. Their immediate social and liturgical contexts, which in retrospect seem so rooted though in fact they were in constant reformation, have quite vanished. Their circumstances, indeed, were eccentric; they were a succession of exceptions to prove the rule. Their temper, therefore, may be regarded as representative of the comprehensiveness of the English National Church.

The metropolitan dimension of their social and liturgical contexts and its representative eccentricity can be introduced through a cartoonist's recollections. Successful cartoonists must be masters of caricature and the secret of caricature is accuracy. Sir Osbert Lancaster was a successful cartoonist, hence the value of his childhood recollections of St. John's, Notting Hill, well west of Marylebone and Paddington where furthest Bayswater has lapsed entirely into North Kensington. In 1911 St. John's was at its social peak. Here could still be Forsytes and here, after Morning Prayer

> ....was a mass of elaborate, pale-shaded millinery, great cart-wheels...decorated with monstrous roses and doves in flight, old-fashioned bonnets trimmed with parma-violets, among which the glittering top-hats, ceaselessly doffed and

---

[2] Ibid., pp. 274-5. Page Roberts was quoting from Sir William Grove FRS in *Nature* (26 April, 1886) and from Charles Beard's Hibbert Lecture, 'The Reformation in its Relation to Modern Thought' (1883, pp. 411-2). For Grove (1811-1896), 'man of science and judge', and Beard (1827-1888), 'unitarian divine and author', see *DNB* and *ODNB*.

replaced, provided the sharper, more definite accents....I had ample opportunity to study and recognise the principal notables of our little world....There was Sir Aston Webb, not yet president of the Royal Academy, cross-eyed and severe, resting on the seventh day from creating a new Buckingham Palace in the current Potsdam style; there was old Dr. Waldo, side-whiskered and benign, whose daughters I played with but the exact nature of whose functions as Chief Coroner for London no one would ever explain to me, albeit that the importance of this position was held to reflect great credit on the local community; there was Professor Perry who with his long hair, glasses and thick walrus moustache, was the very type of the stage scientist, whose researches in electro-physics were nevertheless to bear abundant fruit in the coming war...[3]

There are several things, none obvious yet each foundational, to note about this promiscuously respectable crowd. For a start, its status was new: two, perhaps three, generations at most, seldom more. Its ramifications were as much provincial as they were metropolitan, its spiritual formation was as likely to be Dissenting as it was Anglican, and it was Morning Prayer which had brought it together. For at St. John's, 'sermons were taken seriously and the congregation included many cognoscenti of fine preaching.'[4] Lancaster catches them as a phenomenon and explains their dispersal

> the old upper-middles, in so far as they possessed a definite culture and set of values of their own, are as extinct as the speakers of Cornish...However formal may have been the religion of this section of the community, the whole pattern of their life, anyhow in London, yet centred round the church, and once the cohesive force exercised by 'Morning Prayer' became weakened by the disruptive influence of the golf-links and the week-end cottage the whole social organism collapsed into its individual units.[5]

While what follows may corroborate and even explain both the primacy and the collapse of Morning Prayer and its adherents, Lancaster's own observations are capable of further exploration. Sir Aston Webb is a case in point. A decade later, and at a post-war St. John's, he had become a last pillar of an already past order, 'not a frock-coat in sight and only Sir Aston still sporting a top-hat.'[6] There was, however, more to Webb than met the eye for although he was born in Clapham with Piccadilly a generation behind him, his mother's family and his wife's were as much Essex and the West Midlands and the Welsh Borders so they were ever London and their formation was Congregational rather than Anglican. Webb's steady professional rise owed a great deal to their useful

---

[3] O. Lancaster, *All Done from Memory* (London: Murray, 1963), pp. 42-43.
[4] Ibid.
[5] Ibid., pp. 6-7: 'the coming of the motor-car made possible the "week-end", and the week-end spelt doom'.
[6] O. Lancaster, *With an Eye to the Future* (London: Murray, 1967), p. 11.

business networks.[7]

The ingrained provinciality of Britain's upper middles was seized on by Herbert Henry Asquith when he described an expedition to Earl's Court in search of the 'Kensington abode' of his rival Bonar Law, 'Pembroke Lodge - a rather suburban looking detached villa - with a small garden, and furnished and decorated....after the familiar fashion of Glasgow or Bradford or Altrincham.'[8] Like most Balliol men of his generation Asquith was unusually well-placed to know about such things even if, now that he had himself left Hampstead behind him, it was easy to discount the high-minded flair of contemporary Glasgow, Bradford, or Altrincham, to which, since it was in fact nearer to Asquith's home, he might have added Huddersfield. In January 1911 he wrote from Downing Street to his elder daughter who was en route for the Nile. He had been on family business to somewhere almost as outlandish as Cairo

> ....your grandfather Melland died, and I went down to Altrincham to Auntie Joe's on Friday night to attend the funeral. It turned out to be a cremation: the first at which I have ever been present. Rigby's brother Elkanah Armitage, who is a Professor at one of the Dissenting colleges and a very cultivated man, conducted the service and gave quite an admirable address.
>
> He had a difficult task - to explain why the old gentleman, who became more and more of a sceptic the longer he lived, was being buried (or burned) with Christian rites. He got through it with great skill and taste. The actual ceremony - the coffin gliding imperceptibly under a canopy of curtains, and being committed to the 'purifying fire' (which you don't see) - struck me as, on the whole, less repellent than the ordinary grave burial. I made the acquaintance of a number of sisters in law, two of whom have attractions - Mrs Norman, who makes £400 or £500 a year out of teaching singing, and Mrs. Charles, who is a young Australian.[9]

This too bears exploration. That service at Manchester Crematorium was conducted by a Unitarian minister and two Congregationalists (of whom Elkanah Armitage, who lived between Leeds and Bradford, was one), reflecting the balance of grandfather Melland's religious observance. The mourners also reflected that balance, a traditionary Congregationalism leavened in the

---

[7] For Sir Aston Webb (1849-1930) see *ODNB*. Webb's Dissenting business networks concentrated on Hill, Evans & Co. Ltd., the Worcester vinegar manufacturers, and Evans, Lescher & Webb Ltd., the Liverpool wholesale druggists: the Hills, Everetts, Lamings, Worthingtons, Evanses, and Edwardses were an exemplary and upwardly mobile tangle (personified in the name of Sir Laming Worthington Evans, the politician) of London and provincial business and professional usefulness.

[8] R. Jenkins, *Asquith* (London: Collins, 1964), p. 323.

[9] H.H. Asquith, 10 Downing Street, Whitehall, S.W., to Violet Asquith, 23 January 1911: M. Bonham Carter and M. Pottle eds., *Lantern Slides: the Diaries and Letters of Violet Bonham Carter 1904-1914* (London: Phoenix, 1996), pp. 255-6.

younger generation by Unitarianism, Christian Science, and Anthroposophy. Asquith's own observance by 1911, like that of others at the service, was Anglican. This describes their Sunday fare. Put in secular terms, Liberalism, sensible philanthropy, well-established business, and the better professions were out in force.[10]

Their spiritual and social temper, class and metropolis, class and cottonopolis, class and Establishment and Dissent, change rooted in continuity, might be tasted in sermons - two have already been quoted - preached between 1878 and 1907 in St. Peter's, Vere Street, a Marylebone proprietary chapel dog-legged between Cavendish Square and Oxford Street. St. Peter's had a suggestive hinterland. Quite apart from the medical men, superior retailers, and retired public servants who gathered in the area, there had been Gladstone, who left 73 Harley Street for Downing Street in 1880, and since 1894 there had been Asquith, who was to leave Cavendish Square for Downing Street in 1908. St. Peter's, so convenient for Harley Street, was the church nearest to Cavendish Square.

II

The heart of the matter lies in the sermons, the place in which they were preached, the people for whom they were preached, and the man who preached them.

The sermons are to be found in two of the five collections published for their

---

[10] The funeral is described in *Manchester Guardian*, 23 January 1911. Frederick Melland MRCS, LSA (1818-1911) was described in one obituary (*Manchester Guardian* 19 January 1911) as an amateur of old churches. The service was conducted by J. Kirk Maconachie, minister of Rusholme Congregational Church, where Melland had been a member for many years, and E.P. Barrow, minister of the famous Cross Street Unitarian Church. Elkanah Armitage (1844-1929), of Yorkshire United Independent College, Bradford, had been a family friend at least since the 1870s. On 3 September 1879 he had assisted at the wedding in Rusholme Congregational Church of Melland's daughter Josephine (Auntie Joe, d. 1933) to Samuel Rigby Armitage (1854-1939), cotton spinner of Warrington and Manchester; in August 1891 she had been called to the death bed, at Lamlash, Isle of Arran, of her sister Helen, Asquith's first wife. The Asquiths too had been married at Rusholme Congregational Church, 5 October, 1877. The Rigby Armitages were members of the influential Bowdon Downs Congregational Church, Altrincham. The Norman Mellands attended Withington Congregational Church and the Charles Mellands attended Platt Fields Unitarian Chapel. Norman Melland CBE (1865-1933), half-brother of Josephine and Helen, was a calico printer and champion tennis and lacrosse player (author of *How to Play Lacrosse* and *Some Impressions of West Africa*); his younger brother Charles Melland MD, FRCP (1872-1953), practised in Manchester with a specialism in the feeble-minded. Mrs. Charles Melland, born in Adelaide, would have been in her early thirties. Also at the funeral were Frederick's nephew William, who was a Christian Scientist, and his sister Mary Melland, a Congregationalist increasingly interested in Anthroposophy.

author between 1874 and 1929.[11] These two collections, however, were preached on consecutive Sundays to the same congregation at Morning Prayer, which was the chapel's most numerously attended service. The earlier collection is concerned with belief and the later one with worship. Their titles, *Liberalism and Religion* and *Our Prayer Book: Conformity and Conscience*, make that clear.

Liberalism and Religion consists of fifteen sermons and a memorial address. Its author, with nicely calculated impudence, sent a copy to Gladstone but he dedicated it 'to MY WIFE constant companion and best friend'.[12] Its preface proves to be characteristic: a touch of humour, a shrewd eye on Dissenters, and an up-to-date affirmation of churchmanship. The humour concludes the preface: 'The liberal deviseth liberal things, and by liberal things shall he stand'. (Isaiah XXXII v. 8). The weather eye on Dissent begins it: 'the sects which are supposed to be the backbone of political Liberalism are the most obstinately immoveable in religion; and men ever ready to catch the first breeze impelling to political change have remained stolid as stone to the impulses of spiritual progress.' The way is now clear for a stance to be avowed: 'Liberalism in religion is Conservatism *of* religion'.

> It is used to denote a party which exists in the Protestant Churches, and which has ever had its analogue in the Church Catholic. Its apostle is St. Paul, and the Church which is without it must have the same fate as the Church of Jerusalem.

And the preacher floats the idea of a second volume, 'intended to show how admirably the Church's Offices of Common Prayer and of the Holy Communion serve to express the worship of a Liberal in religion....If I may say so without levity, we are "Liberal Unionists", and the Prayer-Book is the bond which binds us all together.'[13]

It was fourteen years before that second volume appeared, this time with twenty-one sermons, dedicated to the Queen's son-in-law, the markedly Conservative Prince Christian of Schleswig-Holstein, and calculated 'to keep

---

[11] These are, in order, W. Page Roberts, *Law and God* (London: 1874), *Reasonable Service* (London: 1876), *Liberalism in Religion* (London: 1886), *Our Prayer Book: Conformity and Conscience* (London: 1899), *Religion* (London: 1929).

[12] Gladstone responded 3 December 1886. Ten years earlier (2 November 1876) Gladstone had written to the author from Hawarden, perhaps in acknowledgment of *Reasonable Service*. H.C.G. Matthew ed., *The Gladstone Diaries with Cabinet Minutes and Prime Ministerial Correspondence*, Vol. X, January 1875-December 1880, (Oxford: Clarendon Press, 1986), p.167; Vol XI, July 1883-December 1886, 1990.

[13] W. Page Roberts, *Liberalism in Religion* (London: 1886), pp. x, xii, xiii, ix. The preface is dated Brynygwin-Ucha, Dolgelly, September 1886. Roberts later called St. Paul 'the great agent of the unfettered catholicity of the Christian religion'. (*Our Prayer Book: Conformity and Conscience*, 1899, p. 42).

within the Church some who were in danger of dropping out of it.'[14]

They were sermons, not homilies or addresses. They explore the Word, to demonstrate its relevance for personal experience, its unfolding role in social development, and its intricate relationship with the Church and its formularies. They are of reasonable length (nine to a dozen pages each) and every word counts. Their author enjoys logic, is well travelled, is something of an anthropologist, and more of a historian. He is also a stylist. He is a preacher between generations, mannered without being either florid or convoluted, clear, indeed musical (and noted for his rich-toned voice), though still some way from the apparently effortless and plastic simplicity of the best younger pulpit practitioners. He is a master of the arresting opening statement, the relevant question, the carefully planted epigram, the occasional exercise of responsible emotion. This man knows his congregation and is fortunate in them. They are people of affairs with the mental energy to read serious reviews and subscribe to the quarterlies. He takes no liberties with them but he can expect to raise appreciative smiles as they break the Word together.

Those qualities of timely, crafted relevance are demonstrated in the first of two sermons on Revelation.[15] First, the baffling fact of the matter: there are some things 'about which one thing only is clear, that they never can become clear'. Next, the human condition, every bit as applicable in Wimpole Street as it was mirrored in Dickens

> The mother whose eyes are fastened on the dead child, the powerful and far-seeing mind unable to do its work because of physical disease, the man whose fortune has been destroyed by the faults of others, the philanthropist appalled at the amount of human misery and sin which no labour seems to diminish - all ask in vain Why? The question, Why is there any evil if God is good and God is omnipotent? and, How can I be free and responsible if all my future is certain and known to God so that nothing can alter it? and questions like these, which rise up from the poor cradle of the dead babe....attest the fact that there are things which, in this life at least, refuse to give up that secret.

That hopelessness is not dispelled by science - a conviction affording scope for a set piece which is both painterly and poetic, clearly directed to the libraries, drawing rooms, and consulting rooms of Harley Street and Wimpole

---

[14] W. Page Roberts, *Our Prayer Book: Conformity and Conscience* (London: 1899), p. vii. Prince Christian (1831-1917), whose wife, Helena Victoria (1846-1923), was Queen Victoria's third daughter, was Ranger of Windsor Great Park; the author's brother-in-law, Philip Frank Eliot (1835-1917), a Low Churchman, had been Dean of Windsor and Domestic Chaplain to the Queen since 1891, and the Hon. Mrs. Eliot (d. 1900) was a Maid of Honour to the Queen. Since the preface was written midway between Slough and Burnham Beeches, at East Burnham Grove, Farnham Royal, Bucks., these links may explain the dedication.

[15] *Liberalism in Religion*: 'Revelation. I' (Deuteronomy XXIX v. 29), pp. 28-37.

Street

> And if the long experience of the race tells us that for some things we cannot get explanations, that, whether we are patient or not, the mystery will still stand before us unmoved and unchanging, like the black cruel cliffs which throw back the ever-beating sea, so too declare the materialistic teachers of to-day. These carpenters of science seem to say, there is only one thing you can do, and that is cut up the world into positive planks; there is only thing you can look forward to doing in the future, and that is to doing the same thing, only doing it faster, now by steam, then by electricity, and then perhaps by something else; until knowledge becomes a vast timber yard of regulation planks all positively wooden, with no philosophy, metaphysics, nor theology about them...

The congregation is now ready for the preacher's attack: there are things which the materialist 'calls unknowable which I say are freely offered to our knowledge; things plain in this world, where so much is mysterious, which he says are obscure; and the text recognises alike the spirit of uninquiring reverence and of rational freedom'. And with the high ground seized, it is time for definition, scriptural application, and conclusion. Revelation is 'the giving of light or the removal of a veil'. In the Old and New Testaments that can be a variable process: 'Truths are intimated, suggested, pointed at, dimly outlined, like a mountain castle scarce seen through the mists of evening which fill the valley; but, inasmuch as they are not clear, to that extent they cannot be said to be revealed. They may be....suggestions of most certain truths; but until they are brought to light they are not revealed truths'. Save for 'the revelation which it has pleased Almighty God to make, and that is Himself. "Revelation" as Mr. Maurice says, "is always the unveiling of a person". It is Christ who is the revelation of God....God the Infinite Spirit is a mystery. God in the face of Jesus Christ, God as redeeming, saving love in the midst of men, is the Word of life which can be seen and handled'.

If that sermon's development teased its hearers as much as it comforted them, it was because a second was to follow.[16] If 'the Bible is not the sole medium of revelation,' what of the Church? 'The Church has been the minister of God in unveiling and drawing forth into dogmatic precision, truths, which have been but dimly suggested in Holy Scripture'. Yet, as the doctrines of the Trinity, Original Sin, Purgatory, the Atonement, and Justification by Faith all demonstrate, 'the knowledge of the Catholic faith has never yet been completed and perfect....And if the Christian Church shows us the evolution of dogma and the variation in dogma, the English Church shows the reversibility of dogma and the reformability of dogma....That was one work of the Reformation, and who shall say it is now complete? Certainly Holy Scripture does not....' So what is the medium of revelation? Is it miracle or man?

---

[16] Ibid., 'Revelation. II' (Deuteronomy, XXIX, v. 29), pp. 38-59.

Now I affirm that the Bible revelations have come through the mind of man....they were convictions, certainties, in some man's mind, which he declared to his fellows....Any man can try Christ's method of salvation, and find out for himself whether indeed it is the power of God and the wisdom of God. The humblest man can test it and prove whether it is true or not. But to prove whether or not some miracle took place is a very different thing indeed....revelation comes from the mind of man, it comes according to the mind and determination of God....Whatever portion of truth was revealed to any nation in times past, authenticated itself. If it was a revelation, it was a truth clear to those who received it....The one ever-speaking revelation of the mind of God in the history of man....the Great Bible, of which our Bible is the most precious part.

Those two sermons on Revelation are characteristic of all this preacher's sermons: the affirmation of the proper authority of Bible and Church; the insistence on submitting that authority to the liberating tests of logic, reason, and scholarship; the determination to do so from the inside, and the detached enjoyment which such commitment brings. Such relish infects 'Does it Matter What a Man Believes?', a sermon which begins by confronting the damnatory clauses of the Athanasian Creed ('He that keepeth not the Catholic "Faith whole and undefiled shall without doubt perish everlastingly".') and cutting them to size, and ends by confronting the Trinity and making it credible[17]

> these clauses, however objectionable their form, contain and proclaim a truth on which all creeds....take their stand - that what we believe becomes the texture of our mind and the law of our conduct - in a word, settles our state...I am amazed to find myself the apologist of phrases which I have always trembled to use....
>
> And yet there is truth in them....The more I think of it, the more I see that these clauses deal with conduct and the influence of belief upon conduct....in essence it is only what is declared by every reformer, revealer, and moral teacher....The damnatory clause is in essence - rude and misleading as is its form of expression - a statement of the law of cause and effect in morals.

There follow two demonstrations of belief. The first is of its importance, the second is of its impact

> belief is the potentiality of action...If you were a large shareholder or depositor in a bank, and were told by the directors, who knew all the secrets of its management, that it was really insolvent, and believed what you were told; if you believed that the child of your love was hanging from a window-ledge ready to drop - would your conduct be altogether uninfluenced by your belief?....Whether your beliefs are right beliefs or not...if they are real beliefs,...your conduct is decided by them. They may be madmen's beliefs, but they make the madman's life....A mistaken belief may make a very hell on earth...In the affairs of this life, whether you believe in God or not, you must have a right creed or suffer....If there

---

[17] Ibid., 'Does it Matter What a Man Believes?' (Romans X, v.10), pp. 75-88.

is no life after this, and if this life - the only life - be spoilt by a wrong belief, then in this case a wrong belief, a mistaken belief, has wrought irrevocable ruin.

Importance in belief is inseparable from impact and misbelief will have a deteriorating impact

> Each new belief which takes possession of the mind tends to rearrange its parts or to modify their colour and their quantity....belief is certitude....the grasp of the whole nature, of head and heart combined....A new belief makes a new creature....beliefs hang together, and are found in cliques....Millenarianism [will] probably be combined with strong opinions on the 'Ten Tribes' and a deep interest in 'Psychical phenomena' and in esoteric Buddhism.

With Buddhism on his mind - earlier in the sermon he has referred to Schopenhauer's 'Teutonic Buddhism' - the preacher turns to the Trinity. Is that a necessary doctrine? It is, if only in the sense that 'every doctrine, which reveals itself to a man as truth, is a necessary doctrine...In this sense the smallest truth which the mind perceives as truth is necessary to salvation - that is to salvation from some ignorance, and to salvation from untruthfulness of spirit. To turn away from a truth which commends itself to our acceptance is immoral, and so long as a man consciously turns away from a truth he is unsaved'. The Trinity is clearly commendable truth

> That doctrine through all its subtle explanations - explanations which are but human reflections of the Divine fact - declares to us the one Eternal Spirit and Eternal Law, in itself for ever inaccessible, the God who is called by some the Unknowable. It reveals to us God in man, intelligible and adorable and redeeming. And it reveals the reconciling and sanctifying Spirit proceeding from the Father and the Son - the Almighty Spirit which shall subdue all things unto itself that God may be all in all. If this be true, it is indeed a message of salvation....and he who will not accept it must lose the blessing it can convey.

> The doctrine of God's pardoning love to all mankind, which is the very essence of the doctrine of the Trinity...is absolutely necessary to bring peace and assurance to a mind burdened with a sense of sin.

A more historical and contextual logic is brought into play by the call of Abraham[18]

> The certainties for us are, that a family or small tribe migrates from Mesopotamia into Palestine, whose head or sheik was Abraham; that the impulse which moved it from its original dwelling-place was religious; and that from this family or tribe...the Jewish nation arose; that that which governed the small tribe became eventually the bond of a nation...and that bond was religious...you cannot rid the

---

[18] Ibid., 'The Calls of God' (Genesis XII, vv. 1-4), pp. 178-188.

Bible of religion. The history is steeped in religion. Its whole attitude is that of no other history. Its explanation is singular. Its power is undying. In a word, it is inspired. And so I am going to speak on the Call of Abraham because of its inspiration; and we shall find that it is a picture of God's method of dealing with each one of us.

This sermon certainly has direct personal application but Abraham's call from the religious world of polytheism and human sacrifice to another spiritual air also prompts a much longer perspective: 'how long is prophecy before it is fulfilled! Great thoughts are uttered, but it takes ages to assimilate them so that they become part of the mental tissue of a whole nation or age'. Direct personal application and the long perspective provide keys to this preacher's doctrinal method.

III

That he was a broad and liberal Churchman will by now be quite apparent. The address which prefaces Liberalism in Religion was delivered in memory of Frederick Denison Maurice. It allowed for a pointed and prolonged comparison with another notable nineteenth-century English Christian

> Maurice and Newman have had more shaping and controlling power over the mind of English Christianity than any other teachers the Church, this age, has produced. I have been honoured by the notice of one of them; and he who has once felt the fascination of Newman will keep its charm until he dies. But of the two, I venture to think that the influence of Maurice has been profounder, as it has been more far-reaching and cannot but be more lasting....He has revolutionised religious thought...The change which has come over the tone and temper and intelligence of religious teaching, during the last quarter of a century, is something marvellous....Newman was a priest, but Maurice was a prophet....Newman could never have stayed in the Church of England...it was not a wider Church he wanted. The great world alarmed him and he took sanctuary in the Roman Communion. He could not have stayed in the Church of England and Maurice could hardly have got out of it. Maurice had been called to enlarge her borders and make her wide as the love of God. He looked into the world with reverence and saw the Kingdom of Christ, and said, 'The earth is the Lord's and the fulness thereof'. The one was a cloister mind and the other the spirit of perfect freedom.[19]

---

[19] Ibid., 'Frederick Denison Maurice', pp. 1-14. This sermon was delivered 4 February 1883. Page Roberts returned to Newman's cloister mind in a later sermon: the cloister mind could conduce to decency, beauty, and fervour of worship, but when it turned to thought it became, in Newman's case, reactionary 'and that is Romanising and materialistic. But in the long run materialistic religion conduces to Atheism'. That was a standard Broad Church criticism. (*Our Prayer Book: Conformity and Conscience,* p. 29).

Hence no doubt the frequent references to Maurice, Mozley, Harvey Goodwin, Frederick Temple and *Lux Mundi*, the tender attention to Richard Hooker and Jeremy Taylor, the familiarity with Matthew Arnold, Tennyson, Browning, and Clough, and the occasional obeisance to the inevitable Ruskin. Evangelical writers are conspicuous by their absence, Dissenters tend to be Unitarian. High Churchmen, like Roman Catholics, are respected up to a point; Charles Gore is respected beyond that point; the secular prophets of the age are respected within reason. The enemy, chiefly Positivists, are saluted; the scholars, frequently German, are fellow travellers in truth.[20] And the truth, insistently reinterpreted for the current day, is no less insistently found in the deposits of old formularies. Thus, a sermon on 'Eternal Punishment' seems clear enough: 'one thing is certain, that there is no remission of the punishment of sin...You ask me, Do I believe in eternal punishment? I answer, I do....I cannot believe in anything else'.[21] The argument is crisp: sin is refusal to conform to the conditions of existence; punishment follows that refusal. The evidence is impartial: Genesis is called to witness ('And so the words spoken to primitive man - one of the earliest revelations made to him, a warning by which his life might be saved - were, "In the day thou eatest thereof thou shalt surely die." The Law is inexorable') and so is Leslie Stephen ('Nature has but one punishment, decay culminating in death or extirpation; and takes cognisance of but one evil, the weakness which leads to decay'.) There is a positive delight in putting the old divines (at least 'they did feel the awful solemnity of human conduct'. Their God was not 'like some feeble, profligate monarch, too old to do much harm himself, but who did not mind it in other people.') alongside the new scientists ('it is surprising how fierce some of the new teachers, who ignore Christianity, are becoming. They catch up the tones of the old threatening prophets....What we used to call perdition when we had the use of our tongue, they call "extirpation and natural elimination".); and, four years too soon, there is a prefiguring of Dorian Gray

> Every sin is a step to death...No single act can be lost. It is all marked into the being. It has been said that "In the living present the incorporate past is active"....;and as the Ninth Article declares "the infection of nature doth remain in them that are regenerate". ....*On the unseen face which stands behind thine eyes, every sin has marked its line; leaving a bewildering confusion, like the labyrinth*

---

[20] Thus there are references to Newman, Gladstone, James Martineau and Charles Beard, James Baldwin Brown (the Brixton Congregationalist), John Dryden, Burke, Carlyle, Tocqueville, Renan, Hagenbach, Auguste Comte, Leslie Stephen, Clifford, Frederic Harrison; the trouble with the Positivists was their deadly seriousness: 'If M. Comte had possessed the smallest sense of humour, much more attention would be paid to him than he has received'. (*Our Prayer Book: Conformity and Conscience*, p. 168).

[21] *Liberalism in Religion*: 'Eternal Punishment' (2 Corinthians V, v.11) pp. 123-136.

of veins and nerves and reticulations betrayed when the skin is removed[22] ....Remember, for God's sake, we can never make that to be undone which once we have done. Omnipotence cannot do it. The blood of Christ cannot do it. *It can wash out the guilty taint*, but the fact must remain a fact about us for evermore. Is not that a punishment? Is not that an eternal punishment?...a punishment for the saint and even for an apostle like St. Peter, that each sin we have committed will be a fact about us nor time nor eternity shall wash away....I have not said one word of hellish flames, or curses from sinful souls never to be silenced. We do not so much express ourselves in that way now. It is archaic, but facts are changeless....And now, whatever scepticism may say, and whatever sentimental religionism may say, this is what in her own way science says, and this is what the Bible says, 'Be not deceived, God is not mocked, for whatsoever a man soweth that shall he reap.'

Having recognised sin, there often remains spiritual depression, 'the fact that really good people may yet be enveloped in gloom.'[23] The sermon on this subject turns to illness (here is a word for those whose temperament might in a few years turn them to Christian Science), it turns to deathbeds, reconciliation with God, and conversion. It copes with the detritus of Evangelicalism. 'Now we must admit that there is wrong somewhere when the mind and soul are not in a state of peace and happiness. Pain is the alarm-bell which tells us something is wrong': the crux, of course, lies in the diagnosis. The sermon's concern is with good people, 'people who try to do God's will....In Bible words, *they are reconciled to God*'. There can be no doubt about that

Reconciliation with God can only mean union with God. He who takes God's will, as it becomes known to him, and makes it his own, is one with God, is reconciled to God. However dark or uncertain or apprehensive or distressed may be his spirit, that does not in the least interfere with his reconciliation with God, any more than the anguish of neuralgia shakes a man's credit with his banker.

Were such a man to die after a long illness, his last words ones of agitation and alarm, 'that would not in the very least interfere with his reconciliation....any more than the vapours and fogs of earth can destroy the sun'. So too with those who, 'especially in seasons of religious excitement', are troubled because 'they do not feel that they have been converted': 'Now in many cases no conversion whatever is needed. Already the life is simply and carefully ordered in the way of God's commandments....If you convert such a character you must make it bad, for conversion is turning a thing round into an opposite direction. Such people have not to be converted, they have to go straight on'.

This gives the preacher, at least in the published version of his sermon, room

---

[22] My italics. Oscar Wilde's *The Picture of Dorian Gray* was first published in *Lippincott's Monthly Magazine*, 20 June 1890.
[23] *Liberalism in Religion*: 'Spiritual Depression', (Isaiah I, v. 10), pp. 157-167.

for a rare direct criticism of a fellow Churchman, W.H. Aitken,[24] whom he characterises as 'a preacher of the school of irrational earnestness', a school fond of identifying people, usually 'in our morning congregations....who are leading outwardly decent, respectable, and even religious lives', while in fact living 'without any personal experience of the justifying grace of God'

> I should say that that is simply impossible. Justifying grace is the grace which makes a man just, the grace which puts him into his right place, which makes his will one with God, reconciles him to God. It is the grace which makes him decent, respectable and religious.....Do not allow your minds to be harassed and disturbed by irrationality, however earnest....Is not God your Father and Friend? Is not Christ your redeeming, saving Brother? Does not the Spirit bid you say Father?....Be sure that while you live seeking the will of God in all things, and praying daily that it may more and more abide in you, be sure that you are the child of God, every day be sure about it. Be sure, when sickness or sorrow or shame or ruin befall you, that you are the child of God; and when your last breath rises to your lips with the flitting spirit, let its last word be 'Father'.

These are not in fact the sermons of an explicitly Fatherhood-of-God and Brotherhood-of-Man preacher; there were more grateful places for that sort of rhetoric than the hinterland of Cavendish Square.[25] But their drift was clear enough and it was taking preacher and hearers into exhilarating waters. The man who in the 1880s found surprising truth in the Athanasian Creed's damnatory clauses found none at all - or at least no Gospel truth - in them in the 1890s and he devoted a sermon to the implications of his conclusion.[26] His

---

[24] William Hay Macdowell Hunter Aitken, curate at Everton, Liverpool 1871-5, later Canon of Norwich, was a pioneer proponent of evangelistic missions, an Evangelical with some appeal to such High Churchmen as G.H. Wilkinson (1833-1907), Bishop of Truro and, later, Primus of Scotland.

[25] Perhaps that fact allowed the perceptive reflection in another sermon, surely drawn from the preacher's own early pastoral experience, and certainly applicable to his upbringing and that of at least some in his present congregation: 'But in truth the Christian brotherhood as a realised fact scarcely exists. The bonds of fraternal affection are no tighter in a Christian congregation than in a concert room....It was not so in the early days of the Church....Some remnants of their brotherhood may be found among the nonconforming bodies of Christians, where the distinctions of class are not so marked as in the Church of England; and the humbler the sect the more is the brotherhood realised. I am sure that one reason why our agricultural labourers turn rather to the chapel than to the church is because at the chapel they are more "at home". There they have their socially religious evenings where a good deal of equality is maintained. While the humble are entertained at tea by rector or squire, they themselves cooperate in providing it and distributing it in the chapel'. It was similar in America - there, to quote James Bryce, '"A congregation....is the centre of a group of societies".' (*Our Prayer Book Conformity and Conscience*: 'Exhortation', pp. 61-63).

[26] *Our Prayer Book: Conformity and Conscience*: 'He that Believeth Not Shall Be Damned', pp. 225-236. In the preceding sermon, directly on the Athanasian Creed, he

argument turned on Matthew XVI v. 16: 'He that believeth not shall be damned'. That, whatever its authenticity, he could regard 'as a very solemn arresting truth' about belief in the Gospel. But one needed to realise, as the Revised Version had realised, that 'damn' should be read as 'condemn'

> The word 'damn' may just as properly be applied to a punishment of a week or a year as of an age, to a fatherly rebuke and chastisement as to a perpetual expulsion from home.

> But people nearly always look upon a damnation as necessarily an everlasting hell.

That was the sentiment of the Athanasian Creed; it was not the sentiment of Matthew's Gospel

> Now the Gospel and the Catholic Faith are not identical. And being damned and perishing everlastingly are not convertible terms. A man may be damned a thousand times and not perish everlastingly. The Gospel was the good news of a Father in Heaven....The Catholic faith is the product of centuries of logical analysis and deduction....There is as much difference between the Gospel of Christ and the Catholic faith as there is between the light of heaven and celestial mathematics, between nourishing food and its chemical analysis, between a father's and a mother's love and a theory of the emotions. You may have the light, you may have the food, and you may cherish the love, and be ignorant alike of mathematics, of chemistry, and of psychology. You may suffer if you are without the light, you may suffer if you are without the food, your life will be poorer without the love; but you may do perfectly well without the science.

The sermon's pursuit of its argument is almost relentlessly apposite. Marylebone's civic-minded Christians, city liverymen many of them, are set alongside those Corinthian Christians, cosmopolitans all, who 'ate and drank to their own damnation. They did not instantly fall into hell. But that instant they were damned, they were condemned as irreverent, and shameless, and sacrilegious. They saw their feast and they saw their office. They did not discern the Lord's Body'. There is a word for home-mission-minded Christians too

> The essence of the Gospel was that God is love. The disciples went forth to men who believed that God was hate, that God was cruel caprice, or One to be mollified by blood and human pain and slavish human etiquette. They told them that God was not these things, but that God was love. This was the Gospel. If they would not believe it; if they still held fast by their faith, that God was a Being,

---

had concluded: 'many will agree with Mr. Maurice that "It is impossible much longer to retain the Athanasian canticle as a part of our services".' (p. 224)

cruel, unrelenting, greedy, and degradingly punctilious, then they were damned; they were condemned to remain in a state of craven fear and unmanly prostration.

The conclusion is ineluctable. It is also daring

> Nearly all to whom Christ spake, nearly the whole Jewish race, refused to believe that Christ was the Divine Revealer. They died in their error, and in this sense died in their sins. But who can believe Christ meant that, because of their blunder, they should be tortured for evermore, or that at this moment they roll in the pit of unutterable anguish? It is impossible to make the words of the text attributed to Christ identical with the unqualified hopeless damnation pronounced by the Athanasian Creed on every one who does not *keep whole and undefiled* the Catholic faith. The Gospel and the Catholic faith are not identical; to be damned does not necessarily mean to perish everlastingly: the words of Christ are a solemn truth; and the damnatory clause of the Athanasian Creed is literally a misinterpretation of them.

That line and tone of argument is pursued in a sermon on the 'Apostolic Benediction'.[27]

> Wherever we see a man...subordinating in all things mere personal desire to the universal charity of God, we see a specimen of the grace of our Lord Jesus Christ. Who can deny that in Gautama the Buddha....there was something of the grace of Christ? His method by which human life might be rescued from evil was a mistaken one. It was the extinction of self. Christ's method is the realisation of self in accordance with the Eternal Order. But, like Christ, Buddha for the sake of others became poor, and gave his life to enrich them. Wherever this spirit exists, we see the grace of our Lord Jesus Christ.

> What is the love of God? No mere animal sentiment...Love of the unbounded....cannot be like that of a fellow creature.....It is the universal order which is the mind and law of God. The love of God is recognition of this order as the mind of God....He who in nature and in social life seeks this order....he has the love of God. Be he Atheist, Agnostic, Rationalist, or religious mystic, he has in a measure the love of God...

IV

These, on the whole, have been sermons which presuppose a rigorously intelligent auditory, professional rather than intellectual, conceivably attracted by Catholicism but more likely to step from orthodoxy entirely. Many of them, already part dislodged by their material prosperity, must have been Dissenters. *Our Prayer Book: Conformity and Conscience* has them especially in mind,

---

[27] Ibid., 'The Apostolic Benediction', pp. 278-290.

viewing them with a wry affection,[28] wooing them too. Must Dissenters 'go apart and create new church organisms for themselves, to be split up again and again into ever smaller fragments, until egotism has destroyed the highest of our social instincts?'[29] Could they not profitably use a Prayer Book which he is at pains to show is as innocent of unnecessary theological definition as it is scriptural? Given the tolerance of Calvin, Knox, and Baxter for set forms, how could Dissenters 'who sang pre-composed hymns, who used set forms of praise' be 'so strangely illogical as to condemn set forms of prayer?' And thus render their praying vulnerable to 'the individuality of the minister?'[30] How could they ignore the spirit which had composed it?

> Christian freedom - in other words, Protestantism - reconstructed the offices of public worship; and now what can we say is the most distinctive quality of our service of daily public prayer? I beg our Nonconforming brethren especially to regard this. The most striking feature in our service is that it is Scriptural, or, if I may coin a word, Scripture-ful. There is more of the Bible in our services than in the services of any other denomination of Christians....The very first words....are Bible words...The majority of sectarians, who almost deify the Bible, would not endure so much reading of the Bible in their services. The meagreness of the part they allot to it, compared to their extempore prayers and prolonged sermons, is striking and almost perplexing. In the English Church service the Bible has a pre-eminent place; not merely enthroned on a mighty cushion, but read, recited, and sung by ministers and people.[31]

It was much the same with hymns: 'but Nonconformists seem to like Watts and Wesley better than David, Simeon, Zacharias, and the Mother of Jesus....They do not make that constant use of the hymns of the Bible which distinguishes the public worship of the Church of England.'[32] And as for the psalms

> The Church of England has kept more closely to ancient customs as to the use of the Psalms in public worship than any of the other Protestant denominations. They may occasionally use a Psalm for a lesson, and then it is often smothered in a lengthy exposition; or they make use of rude paraphrases or poor metrical versions of the Psalms instead of hymns. They have no such constant use of the

---

[28] Thus he called C.H. Spurgeon 'the earthwork of Nonconformity' (ibid., p. 194)
[29] Ibid., 'Prayer Book', p. 12.
[30] Ibid., pp. 15, 16.
[31] Ibid., 'Opening Sentences', pp. 46-7. He adds: 'For this reason the Common Prayer of the Church of England is specially suited to the Christians we call Liberal'.
[32] Ibid., '*Venite - Te Deum - Benedicite*', p. 120.

Psalms as we have; and, partly on account of this, their services are not so rich in refining and ennobling influences as are our own.[33]

This allowed for a marvellously palpable hit from gloriously high ground

> Churchmen chiefly know the Psalms in the Prayer Book version, Nonconformists in the Bible version. Unlettered Dissenters look a little suspiciously upon our Prayer Book version, as though it were not quite the genuine article....The Prayer Book translation is...part of the most venerable gift of Protestantism to England, the first English Bible. The New Testament was translated by Tyndale....assisted by Miles Coverdale....a Nonconformist *in the Church*. Would that our ligatures of uniformity were relaxed in order that place might be found within the Church of their country for multitudes of Nonconformists![34]

The relationship with Nonconformity could be complex even though the preacher simplified it by putting current political issues to one side and by ignoring Old Dissent's inescapably political (because ecclesiological) antecedents. A sermon on confession inevitably brought Wesleyan Methodism, 'one of the most Protestant of the sects', into focus for what else was their weekly Class Meeting but a kind of confession? 'Under the presidency of a layman, a dozen or more religious persons meet together, and each in turn is asked by the chairman: "what has been your religious experience during the past week?"'[35] Like Monsieur Jourdain, the Wesleyans had been speaking prose without knowing it. And that sense of service and community had much to offer to the Church. Suppose, for instance, that in far-flung corners of its parishes the Church were to use laymen to exercise a preaching ministry, 'from time to time conducting their little flock to the parish church, there to join in the holy feast of brotherhood....If Dissenting laymen can do this work, and if in Wales they have done it with so much effect that every hamlet has been occupied, while the Church is often unrepresented, it is certain that laymen of the Church of England might be equally useful'.[36] Suppose, too, that the Church took absolution ('The whole work of the Church is a ministry of absolution', that 'voice of God speaking to the congregation, through human lips') with logical seriousness?

---

[33] Ibid., 'Psalter', pp. 140-141. Metrical psalms would not do because 'Hebrew poetry can scarcely be represented by rhyming metres. Its form, which has been called "thought rhythm", is as totally unlike our modern forms as it is unlike classical forms....'

[34] Ibid., pp. 141-142. 'What a day it must have been when these Psalms were first heard in English, in the very words of Our Prayer Book! If you feel more tenderly to the Bible of your childhood than to the Revised Version, you will understand that religious people could not tear themselves away from the old Psalms when a new translation appeared'. (pp. 142-143).

[35] Ibid., 'Confession II' pp. 81-82.

[36] Ibid., 'Exhortation'. pp. 58-59.

> Who then has power to declare absolution? Every....man, woman, and child who has grasped the saving law. The power and the duty of proclaiming the law of absolution is laid upon every Sunday-school teacher, and upon every district visitor, and every parent, and every master, and every faithful friend. It is one of the rights of women...But if it is the clerical and unchanging law, then it is just the same whoever says it, Methodist or Papist, Prelatist or Positivist. It is not the sayer who makes it true; the comfort comes from the truth, and the truth makes us free. It is said in the church by the priest. No one else has the privilege of saying it in the church except the priest; nor is it desirable that anyone else should say it when he is present. But it is a grievous pity and most misleading in its implications, that when a superior minister is absent, the absolution should not be pronounced by a deacon, nor pronounced at all. If a layman were to stand up and say it in the teeth of church order, it would be just as true. 'To save a soul,' said John Hales, 'every man is a priest'. The proclamation of absolution is as valid in the humble prayer meeting as in the stately church, from the lips of the artizan local preacher as from the supreme pontiff. All distinctions of such kind are of no account in the presence of the eternal law: 'They shall perish, but Thou remainest'.[37]

V

So far these sermons have been used as evidence for significantly changing belief within an established setting. Indeed they were advocating change as well as demonstrating it and they were doing so within worship: advocacy is an aspect of worship. But they also provide evidence of changing worship itself for most of them are specifically about worship

> I suppose we none of us think that by certain regulated formalities and ecclesiastical machinery we can manipulate the heavenly world, as the sails of a mill are managed from below. We do not think we come to church to work upon the Almighty by a prescribed ritual; nor, by a kind of celestial wizardry, to make heavenly spirits do our bidding. We do not think we came here to utter the mind and law of God...It is to express our own minds and souls and to alter our own minds and souls, we come here to draw nigh to God.[38]

Our preacher's prime medium for this was the sermon. That was the focal point of Morning Prayer for his congregation, that was where he excelled even if he were more conscious than they that the sermon was merely a means to a greater end

---

[37] Ibid., 'Absolution I', pp. 94, 100, 102-103.
[38] *Liberalism in Religion*: 'Devotionality' (Psalm CXIX, v. 38), pp. 169-70.

> Deeply do I feel the importance of the work which the pulpit is called to perform. If there is a divine order in the universe, which year by year becomes clearer, it is for the pulpit to declare it. But if the preaching does not make you pray...
>
> The one thing I wish my preaching and our singing to do for you is, to help you to go up to the high altar of worship...If I do this for you, then I need not be cast down because I am less various and eloquent and interesting than the popular lecturer, or because our music is that of a simple psalm and hymn, and not that of the mass, the oratorio, or the opera.[39]

The challenge was to commend, in Morning Prayer, the essence of that greater end, a sense of Church and Sacraments, to reasonable people, *fin-de-siècle*

> The Church is the highest of the agencies which exist for the evolution of man....When we eat Christ's flesh and drink His Blood it means that His very life is becoming our life, entering into us, until Christ lives in us and we are members of His body, of His flesh, and of His bones. There is no other blood of Christ than His Spirit. The grace of the Lord Jesus Christ is the same thing as His Body and Blood. If we ever keep in mind the fact that Christ's Body and Blood mean His life and Spirit and grace, we shall not think, when the eucharistic elements are declared to be his Body and Blood, that His Spirit and life and grace have been inducted into bread and wine, but we shall be sure that His Spirit and life and grace enter into our souls. Thus the Church is said, in Holy Scripture, to be the Body of Christ.[40]

That was politely powerful language for Marylebone's professional intelligentsia. He had already used language like it when ruminating on Commonplace Belief in God, a striking sermon which manipulated pulpit commonplaces (like national infidelity and apostasy) in an uncomfortable way ('why should not women speak of God and Christ as of any heathen God and Oriental wonder worker?'). One section turned inevitably to 'carelessness in the matter of religious observance', concentrating on the 'large neglect of that bond and symbol of Christian intention and brotherhood - the Sacrament of the Eucharist'.

> I know some are prevented from sharing in that sacrament by perplexing uncertainty as to its meaning and obligation. But I think that the most careless of us would say that, except for such impediments, every very religious man, every man of real piety, whose belief in God and Christ lived in his soul like a fire, warming and kindling his whole nature, would delight in loving thanksgiving for

---

[39] *Our Prayer Book: Conformity and Conscience*, p. 8; *Liberalism in Religion*, p. 170.
[40] *Our Prayer Book: Conformity and Conscience*, 'Apostolic Benediction', pp. 279, 282-83.

the truth which had brought salvation. You would say, I know, whatever be your practice, that a man who really loved God, and was devoted to Christ, would find His Holy Communion a high and exalted privilege. But is it not a fact, too evident for speech, that tens of thousands who are quite orthodox, and dread these German writers, and these Ritualists and Freethinkers...do pass by this ordinance of Christianity?[41]

That is careful rhetoric. It might be described as defused intensity. Words like 'privilege' and 'ordinance' would speak to drifting Congregationalists, some of whom would have heard of 'eucharist' and might in time warm to its use. The last of three sermons on the Prayer Book spoke not just to their condition but to that of uneasy Wesleyans and even of visiting Presbyterians.[42] Here was English comprehensiveness at its most alluring. The argument begins modestly. The English Church's forms of public worship came 'From the heart of the universal Church. The English Reformers endeavoured to separate, without complete success, what was primitive in the old service books from that which may be called Roman'. It follows that 'the religious spirit should be as free to-day as it was when Christianity was young'.[43]

> There is no form of Church liturgy, no order of ministry, no theological system which is absolutely essential....Presbyterians have as truly a ministry of God as Episcopalians. Nonconformists are as really parts of Christ's Holy Catholic Church as the Greek, the Roman, and the Anglican Communions. All the various Churches and sects attempt to realise the Spirit of Christ....They have no stain of illegitimacy upon them, for we are all one in Christ Jesus. Churchmen have been too haughty socially, and it is to be feared that during the past fifty years they have become narrower doctrinally.

This English Churchman clearly regretted his Church's refusal 'to acknowledge the true ministerial character of the ministers of the unepiscopal Churches', particularly those of the Church of Scotland, for 'No permanent and distinct orders of ministers were imposed by the command of Christ upon the Church....The only priesthood in the early Church was that of the whole Christian people...All were free to teach to whom a gift had been imparted, with the exception of women', and while 'It is now most desirable that there should be a distinct class of ministers....[for the] higher the organism the greater its differentiation...we should remember that ministers are but the delegates of the people...there is no Biblical authority for an exclusive priesthood'. But there was not yet mutual acceptance of ministries, even with the Church of Scotland, and so the Lord's Supper had to be skirted delicately. What could he say? Here

---

[41] *Liberalism in Religion*: 'Commonplace Belief in God. II' (Jeremiah V, v. 31), pp. 101-111 esp. pp. 108, 105-106.

[42] *Our Prayer Book: Conformity and Conscience:* 'Prayer Book III' pp. 27-41.

[43] 'Never was there a religious teacher so detached from ceremonial worship as was our Lord'. Ibid., p. 30.

was the Eucharist (he used the word), 'the only authoritative act of united Christian devotion, the only form of public worship instituted by Christ'; what a thing it would be if 'our Nonconforming brethren and their ministers were able to join in Communion with us at the parish church while maintaining their own separate ecclesiastical organisations bearing witness to our fundamental union and brotherly love and of their right to a place in the National Church...'. That, perhaps, looked back to an early Wesleyan golden age but it placed the centralities in proper perspective

> I am afraid that Evangelical and Liberal Protestants, whether in the Church or out of it, have not allowed that pre-eminence to the Eucharist which it claims as the one service of united devotion ordained by Christ himself....If we may say that any one form of Christian congregational service is obligatory, it is the celebration of the Lord's Supper. No Christian should pass it by.

That phrase, 'the Lord's Supper', is particularly suggestive. It has a decidedly Nonconformist tone, but it is deftly used, for a little earlier the congregation had been told how at first the eucharist was an evening act of worship and they had been initiated into a gentle use of symbol.

> The lights with which so many of our fellow Churchmen adorn the Holy Table are a relic of those days. There is nothing to object to in them. A Nonconformist might use them, as indeed a Lutheran does. No doctrine is insinuated by them. They remind us of those who were faithful to Christ while death was lurking at their doors, and they might be used as a suggestive and touching symbol in every church and chapel in our land.

Such comprehensiveness marks the whole of this Prayer Book expedition through conformity with conscience. The journey is punctuated with light relief and sharp observation and informed with a steady, engaged sense of development. The intention is explicit: to stay honourably and responsibly within the national church. It is a study in integrity as well as a celebration of 'that fervour of a throng which is essential to public worship': 'One could not have a Pentecost in private'.[44] Each step in worship is reasonable. At the opening sentences, 'Stand, as when a monarch enters, to hear a saving note of God'.[45] With the exhortation we encounter 'a liturgical creation of Protestantism...it is as rational as it is religious. It begins with a text, and then it preaches a sermon'.[46] Confession 'is God making something known to us; it is God revealing us to ourselves, and our cry out of pain at the discovery'

---

[44] Ibid., pp. 8,7.

[45] Ibid., p. 52. 'Do you know with what sentence this morning's service began? Ah! Some of us have forgotten. There came a divine message to our souls, and we did not notice it'.

[46] Ibid., p. 55

Some denominations of Christians begin their public services of worship with a hymn of thanksgiving....But with us who are sinful men, a sense of humiliation must be the first impression; kneeling down the instinctive attitude. And this is the posture of confession commanded by the Church...I would rather begin my service with the prostration of the Romanist than with the unbending self-satisfaction of the consciously elect.[47]

The sharpness continues. 'Pardon does not mean being "let off". There is no letting off in the universe....Pardon means being conformed to the will of God'.[48] With music, however, this preacher lets rip. He knows how music takes some to church 'and fashion lounges through the anthem, declares it such a lovely service, and retires *before* the offertory, and takes its Sunday concerts gratis'.[49] What was at best a 'caressing sentimentality' and at worst sheer 'physical erotics' had infected Protestant and Romanist hymnody alike, thanks to the 'misuse of the Song of Solomon'. An old Evangelical hymn like Watts's 'O God, our help in ages past' was without doubt a noble example of spiritual religion but 'who with gravity can sing "I was a wandering sheep"?' *'The Skylark and the Cloud,* by the side of the Jewish *Benedicite* and the Latin *Te Deum,* are like the little French restaurant beneath the shadow of the great pyramid'.[50]

None of this was new. Devotion had seen it all before. In the long course of liturgical history the 'Salvationists are not the first enthusiasts who have made the streets disorderly and discordant with their processions. The occasions are rare when ecclesiastical processions are solemnizing'.[51] That comment came while tracing the development of supplicatory processions or litanies. The phrase *semper reformanda* nowhere appears in these sermons but its spirit is incessant and it was instructively enjoyable to tease out such developments. Thus, 'It was a grand day for the Christian Church when it disengaged itself from its parent Judaism', but with that Greek liberation 'old gods came back again and submitted to baptism - and the statues were crowned, and the sacrifice was offered, and the mysteries re-enacted'. Judaism was escaped at Antioch and paganism at Spires, 'And the first gift of Protestantism to our country was the English Book of Common Prayer. Not that it was a new creation. The English Reformation was not a revolution. It did not renounce the past. It adapted it to the wants and knowledge of the present....The Church again was free - free as when she made creeds and ministries in early times'.[52]

The long view allowed for the liberal view, understanding and

---

[47] Ibid., pp. 67, 69, 71.
[48] Ibid., p. 97.
[49] Ibid., p.9
[50] Ibid., pp. 120-28. 'Better the silent gravity of the Quaker meeting...than the feverish rhapsodies of the Revival and the Mission'. (pp. 120-1)
[51] Ibid., p. 241.
[52] Ibid., pp. 43, 45, 46.

discriminating rather than resigned. The sermons' historical excursions all tended to that end. Two sermons on the Lessons allowed the Bible to be given its proper place as 'the most precious book in the world...to be understood and not to be adored'. It was a vexed (though the preacher was not vexed by it) question of inspiration

> When the writers of the New Testament speak of the Scriptures, they mean the Jewish Scriptures. The primitive Church presents what seems to us a strange spectacle - a Church without a New Testament, and having only the sacred books of a discarded religion. The Old Testament thus acquired a pre-eminence in the Christian Church to which it had no just claim...But it may be affirmed that the Church has suffered from the superstitious use which has been made of the Old Testament. To the present day Christian theology is entangled in Jewish association and bonds which impede its progress....If it had not been for the superstitious regard for the Old Testament, the conflict between science and faith which has been so fierce, and which only subsides in the contemptuous *congé*, of physical science to religion, would never have existed.....Verbal inspiration is one of the remnants of Judaism, just as Sabbatarianism is, and the old crude doctrine of atonement....

But what of the New Testament's inspiration? 'The early Christians were not dependent on a book for their knowledge of Christ. Apostolic missionaries went everywhere telling about Christ. The question never occurred to their hearers whether they were inspired....Christianity was a tradition handed on by preaching', and the New Testament cannot consequently be seen as a system of doctrine or discipline. 'There is no system in it'

> Some of the most important doctrines of Christianity are not clearly or conclusively affirmed in the New Testament. We owe them to the spirit of Christ acting within the Church, but acting through fallible agents...Whether the developments be true developments, or in certain cases corruptions, we owe them to the Church....Little do many of the members of the humble and unlettered sects, who say they 'have the Bible and do not care about churches', know that it is to the tact, faith, courage, and spiritual discernment of the early Church they owe their New Testament.[53]

Our Prayer Book: Conformity and Conscience has one over-arching theme: the inclusiveness of the Prayer Book. Athanasian Creed apart, and the future of that was clear, a liberal churchman had nothing to fear from it; he need feel no embarrasment over creeds nor even such apparently illiberal words as 'dogma': 'creeds we must have and dogmas are indispensable....A dogma is something which is clearly seen and generally affirmed. Is there nothing in Christianity

---

[53] Ibid., 'Lessons I', pp. 150-63, 'Lessons II', pp. 164-80, esp. pp. 162, 153-55, 157-59, 161.

'A Tradition Handed on by Preaching'

which can be clearly seen and may be generally affirmed?'[54] That, as far as the Apostles' Creed was concerned, was a rhetorical question

> how very little of theological deduction it contains!...there is no theory of atonement in it, no law of Episcopacy, or of Presbytery, and not a word as to an everlasting pit of evil and burning torture. There is no intimation of the existence of a devil in it, but it confers on Pontius Pilate an infamous immortality...The Apostles' Creed is a creed of inclusion....All later creeds are creeds of exclusion, they ever grew more repellent.[55]

That was the spirit of the Prayer Book; of its prayers ('Prayers are not theological essays. If you thrust such things into your prayer, their influence becomes schismatical; they shut out from the communion of prayer all who hold the opposite opinions'), its General Confession (which does 'not intrude unnecessary theological distinctions and definitions....nothing about Adam's fall or original sin...no reference to imputed sin. It confesses real sin'), its Absolution ('absolutely free from theological exclusiveness...the best human utterance ever made in the Church. However narrow any of the clergy...may be in doctrinal perception....they cannot help declaring the Gospel of Christ'), the *Te Deum* ('It is simple, dealing with large facts which may be firmly grasped by all...[F]or the united worship of the multitude, great facts, which all can distinctly see, must be set before the mind'), and the Psalms ('what a treasury of....experience, and not theology! .....no intimation of the Triune nature of God...none of Adam's sin, none of the atonement as interpreted by Christian theologians, no trace of....Satan.... But to tell out the needs and desires and delights and despairs of our spirits, where else do we go....?')[56]

The moral was clear. An inclusive Church was the Church in which to be included. It was the Church for the nation. 'Each good man who leaves the Church because of some imperfection in it endows that imperfection with larger life, and weakens the men who live to remove it.'[57] The preacher's affection is palpable

> Some of our Church prayers are scarcely heeded at all - for instance, the State prayers. They are often regarded as a tiresome formality, like the report of a missionary society, which might be 'taken as read'. What is there more depressing and anaemic than official prayers - public meeting prayers and foundation-stone prayers and consecrations and State unveilings - when the King of all the earth is addressed by some honoured ecclesiastic, while all around is bustle and nods of recognition and cool indifference? The prayer is as soon forgotten as the penny paper and the infinitesimal coin buried with the foundation stone, while the ornate graces performed at civic feasts elicit the response of a sceptic smile.

---

[54] Ibid., pp. 181-82.
[55] Ibid., pp. 201, 205.
[56] Ibid., pp. 25, 89, 117, 130-31, 146.
[57] Ibid., p. 23.

> We have prayers in church for kings and for all in authority. But what good are they? They might be an enormous good. They might help to create a righteous and religious public opinion.[58]

That was not pious talk. There was argument behind it, a weighty sense of political responsibility. The preacher seized on the phrase in the prayer for the monarch which called God 'King of Kings and Lord of Lords, the only Ruler of princes': 'But Parliament is the ruler of princes, and the masses rather than the classes, are becoming the rulers of Parliament....Then it is all important that the mandate given be a good one....The motto of the King of Denmark is, "The love of the people is my strength". A Government may take for its motto, "The prayer of the people is my righteousness".'[59] This preacher knew his people and their neighbourhoods. After all, when he came to Marylebone Gladstone, seismically in opposition, had just moved into Harley Street; when he left, Asquith, still Chancellor of the Exchequer, lived in Cavendish Square. Men of affairs were parsimonious of time; they counted the minutes, grudged the words, weighed each concept. They had to be wooed, pampered even, then braced

> We are floating on a soft cloud, and all is hushed and indistinct, when with a little start we come to ourselves and to the thought that it is all over, with the words 'Almighty God, who hast given us grace at this time'. Perhaps we think, if we do not say, How long these prayers are! Yes, actually an hour of reading religious books and making prayer and praise to God. Actually an hour engaged in the very highest occupation which can enthral the mind of man! An hour is not long at a brilliant concert or a favourite play. For such pleasures high prices are paid, and people cannot afford to go to sleep. But who can help getting sleepy when a whole hour is spent in the presence chamber of the King of Kings and Lord of Lords? If we have had a little slumber in the hour of worship, at last we come to ourselves with the prayer of St. Chrysostom.[60]

Our preacher's mellow voice had, however, its trumpet tone

> Once at a celebration of the Mass in a foreign church I felt a thrill of exaltation when the Host was uplifted and the soldiers who lined the aisles presented arms; while the officers who stood at either end of the altar, within the sanctuary, saluted with their swords, and the trumpets made the church to resound with their

---

[58] Ibid., p. 244.

[59] Ibid., pp. 244-46. Gladstonians would have caught the reference to masses and classes but the reference to the King of Denmark was perhaps tactless, given the volume's dedication to Prince Christian of Schleswig-Holstein: in 1863 his Augustenburg branch of the Danish royal family had been forced to cede precedence to the Glucksburg branch - represented in Britain, of course by his sister-in-law, the Princess of Wales.

[60] Ibid., pp. 266-67.

stormy music. Our faith should be an enthusiasm. I think our creeds should always be sung....to confident, daring, triumphant tones, like a National Anthem.[61]

His was, after all, an imperial Church for people of liberal mind; 'the unity of the Spirit exists; the Catholic Christ is the "blessed company of *all faithful people*", as the Prayer Book says.'[62]

VI

The sermons have been considered. It may be felt that they are remarkably consistent in thrust and quality. They may be taken to exemplify the views of a significant section of the late Victorian Church of England and they merit attention because of their coherence. On all these grounds their interest is patent. So far, however, little has been said, although a certain amount has been suggested and perhaps assumed, about the preacher, his pulpit, and his people: yet the representativeness of the sermons, as opposed to their quality, depends largely on such factors.

The preacher's pulpit was in St. Peter's, Vere Street.[63] This suggestive survival was a proprietary chapel built by the 2nd Earl of Oxford between 1721 and 1724 when he was developing his Marylebone properties; hence its original name, Oxford Chapel. It was a brick building of architectural importance, since its architect was James Gibbs, and it was the purest distillation of Augustan religion: tiers of boxes, discreetly entered and serviced by retiring rooms for the use of Lord Oxford's family, still flanked the altar.[64] It remained obstinately ungothicised. In 1832, however, by which time it was under Crown patronage, Oxford Chapel became St. Peter's and was repaired accordingly. In the next seventy years the church was judiciously maintained. It was repewed in 1881, four windows by Morris and Co., three of them to designs by Burne-Jones, the fourth perhaps by Henry Holiday, were inserted between 1880 and 1903 and the sanctuary floor was repaired in marble. This, it was felt, transformed 'the whole interior of a somewhat dreary and dismal building.' There was also a painting, Burne-Jones's 'The Morning of the Resurrection', depicting Mary at the empty tomb, presented as an altar-piece in memory of F.D. Maurice 'by a few loving disciples'. This provided the occasion for *Liberalism in Religion*'s opening address, delivered on Sunday, 4 February 1883.[65]

---

[61] Ibid., pp. 190-91.

[62] Ibid., p. 287.

[63] This section is based on G. Hennessy (comp), *Novum Repertorium Ecclesiasticum Parochiali Londiniense* (London: 1898), p. 328; A. Leveson-Gower, *St. Peter's Vere Street 1722-1922* (London: 1922).

[64] For James Gibbs (1682-1754) see B. Little, *The Life and Work of James Gibbs 1682-1754* (London: B.T. Batsford, 1955).

[65] W. Page Roberts, *Liberalism in Religion*: 'Frederick Denison Maurice', pp. 1-14. The painting was sold in 1982 to pay for the church's restoration. The Burne-Jones windows

At the time of the altar-piece's presentation St. Peter's incumbent noted that 'It is the only monument to any of her ministers which this church possesses; and this will not surprise those for whom the name of Mr. Maurice alone reclaims it from obscurity'.[66] That name, of course, was enough. From 1860 to 1869 F.D. Maurice had held the appointment to St. Peter's, braving the protest of twenty clergy; two short incumbencies had followed, succeeded in 1878 by that of William Page Roberts, the most self-consciously Maurician of all the great man's successors. It was Page Roberts, whose sermons have fuelled this study, who repewed, rewindowed, and refloored the church. He had made it a place which could be appreciated almost despite itself. It was certainly one to be experienced, its worship 'devotional rather than ornate, congregational rather than processional', ideal for 'a Broad Churchman to whom a hearty service and simple, well-rendered music were more necessary than any points of ritual.'[67]

A proprietary chapel was a curious charge for a man who took churchmanship seriously. It had no parish and St. Peter's had no endowments. It was not a place for weddings and St. Peter's had no font. Its minister's income depended entirely on his ability to fill the building with people prepared to pay for their pews. In fact, it expressed Independency of purest essence unencumbered by Congregational ecclesiology, and to all intents it was just as free of episcopalianism. Its minister, indeed, was freer than that of a Unitarian chapel. It was doubtless ideal for a party man. It was also ideal for a man with no great ambition for further preferment. Page Roberts professed to like the relationship between pastor and people which it necessitated

> the bond which unites the minister and the members of his congregation in this church is more than usually close. No parochial obligation constrains them; no what I may call organic cohesion holds them together. Gathered from far and wide by a kind of natural selection, it is to the minister rather than to the church or to each other they are attached.[68]

In Page Roberts's case the attachment was numerous and prolonged: 'he

---

are the East Window (Christ and the Woman at the Well, presented in 1880 in memory of Baron de Blacquière), the South Window (Christ's Entry into Jerusalem, and the Reception of Souls into Paradise, presented in 1883 in memory of one of the retailing Snelgroves); and a North Window of 1892 (in memory of W.L. Dalrymple). A North Window of 1903, in memory of another Snelgrove, is thought to be by Henry Holiday.

[66] *Liberalism in Religion*: 'Frederick Denison Maurice', p.1.

[67] Leveson-Gower, *St. Peter's Vere Street,* p. 11. The text says 'professional', surely a misprint for 'processional'; also undated obituary cutting, Westminster City Archives.

[68] *Liberalism in Religion*: 'Frederick Denison Maurice', p.1. His reference to his predecessor, J.C. Coghlan (1874-8), who left a depleted congregation, speaks however, for itself: 'in those whom he found congenial he stirred a deep affection'. (p.2). Surely pastors - and preachers - have a responsibility beyond those whom they find congenial?

attracted many who would not ordinarily be present'.

> He said of himself that he was not an ecclesiastic, and he was very little associated with the Church's activities, but this doubtless gave him an influence with the type of worshippers at Vere Street. They were attracted to him personally rather than to the Church, as was manifest by the rapid falling off in attendance when he left.[69]

Attendance certainly grew while he was there. In 1878 things were 'at their lowest ebb' at St. Peter's. By 1883 congregations averaged 600 and by 1900 they stood at 850 in the morning and 550 at night.[70] That picture is corroborated by the *Daily News* survey of 1886 and the Mudie-Smith survey of 1902-3. Between thsoe dates aggregate attendances at St. Peter's rose from 1342, which made it the eighth best attended Anglican church in Marylebone, to 1607, when it came second only to Holy Trinity. In fact its ranking was higher than the aggregates suggest because the congregation was overwhelmingly adult. In 1902 its morning adults were the most numerous in Marylebone (691 women and 281 men); in the evening five Anglican congregations had more women and three had more men, and among Nonconformists only the Abbey Road Baptists and Upper George Street Presbyterians had more.[71]

The congregation's adult predominance and the relative - if trailing - strength of men in it bear out contemporary recollections: 'standing as it did in a neighbourhood inhabited by medical men of eminence and by those who stand high in other professions, the church was sure of a distinguished congregation, so long as the pulpit provided the careful and considered instruction that such men have the right to expect.'[72] Page Roberts's sermons

---

[69] 'Obituary, Dean Page Roberts', *Salisbury Diocesan Gazette*, August and September 1928, p. 97.

[70] Ibid., Lambeth Palace Archives: London Visitation Returns, 1883 and 1900 (Jackson 1/216; Creighton 2/152).

[71] R. Mudie-Smith (ed.), *The Religious Life of London* (London: Hodder and Stoughton, 1904), pp. 97, 98, 284. In 1902-3 only 122 children attended morning and evening worship at Vere Street (sixty-one at each service); the evening congregation mustered 336 women and 177 men. The Nonconformist attendances are instructive. The Congregational Paddington Chapel, the Wesleyan Hinde Street, and the Unitarian Little Portland Street all had had notable nineteenth-century histories; between 1886 and 1902 attendances at Abbey Road dropped but those at Paddington Chapel and Hinde Street had risen. Little Portland Street's relative strength was in the morning; Paddington Chapel's and Hinde Street's were in the evening.

[72] Undated cutting, Westminster City Archives. Dean Inge of St. Paul's, unveiling a memorial tablet to Page Roberts in Vere Street remarked: 'Dr. Page Roberts first had made St. Peter's pre-eminently the doctors' church and himself the doctors' clergyman. That was a great and proud thing to be. It was not so in every country, but in this the great doctors were, for the most part, the most deeply religious of men, the Dean added'.

reflect that. He was fond of words like 'ligature'; his themes encompassed the psychology of pain. They also reflect a shrewd sense of the social realities which held fast the Forsytes seated in front of him. A sentence of Arthur Hugh Clough's provoked a sermon from him. He could not believe that Clough, whom he liked to quote, was right: 'The belief that religion is, or in any way requires, devotionality, is, if not the most noxious, at least the most obstinate form of irreligion

> is this a danger against which the generality of Englishmen need to be particularly guarded? Are you afraid, you men of high position and active profession and crowded affairs, that you are really in danger of becoming too religious? Do you feel that you need plucking up from your knees, lest you should forget to go down to the House, or to be in Court, or Chambers, or society, because you are absorbed in devotion? Do you think you will lose many fees, or dinners, or dances, because you are so entranced by heavenly ecstacy that the world is an alien and forgotten thing?...No, that is not the danger...The danger is the hurrying life of business or of society - dressing and dining, talking about the same things until we are tired to death of them, and pushing into new places which soon become as monotonous as the old, working and worrying year after year, trying to look young when unkind age is scoring his lines upon us....I know you are not afraid of becoming too prayerful. There is no need to guard you against an encroaching devotionality. I would we had a little more of this Catholic spirit. It is a rational spirit and a becoming spirit. It is the only reasonable response to the greatest of facts...[73]

Those driven men of professional eminence were more and more likely to find their devotionality in the country. Roberts used a sermon on 'Commonplace Belief in God' to reflect on the predominance of women in Christian congregations, especially Catholic ones, and the depressing implications which that must eventually have for family solidarity and mutual respect in belief. How many men already protested: '"Oh, I always go to church when I am in the country or at the seaside". In other words, there is nothing else to do, and you see everybody at church, and it gives you something to talk about, and it has not yet become quite the thing for ladies and gentlemen to fix their tennis "tournaments" for Sunday mornings...."And in the country we go to church; one ought to set a good example to one's tenants and the labourers, and back up the clergyman a little, who, after all, is a poor creature unless we stand by him - lay assistance is so very important you know. But it is quite different in London".'[74]

Osbert Lancaster, reflecting in the 1950s on the dispersal of the affluent morning church parade at the rather low Edwardian St. John's Notting Hill, is

---

('"The Doctors' Church": Tribute by Dean Inge', undated cutting, Westminster City Archives).

[73] *Liberalism in Religion*: 'Devotionality' (Psalm cxix, v. 38), esp. pp. 170-71, 173-74.

[74] Ibid., 'Commonplace Belief in God II' (Jeremiah V, v. 31), p. 107.

prefigured in this glimpse of the decidedly Broad late-Victorian St. Peter's Vere Street, upper-middles all. So who was this man who knew his Marylebone upper-middles so well?

William Page Roberts could not have been more suitable. He was forty-three and newly married.[75] He was a man of proven spiritual, intellectual, administrative, and gentlemanly qualities. His career had so far been concentrated in East Anglia but he had mixed with men of affairs. He was a Cambridge man whose time at St. John's reflected more depth than distinction. The obituaries are agreed that he immersed himself in philosophy and literature. One tribute notes, incorrectly if logically, that since there was then no Moral Science Tripos he was unable to read for it and consequently 'took only a poll degree'.[76] He served a curacy at St. Thomas's Stockport between 1861 and 1864 and was ordained by Bishop Graham of Chester, 'taking the first place both in the Deacons' and Priests' Examination for Holy Orders'.[77] In 1864 he was presented to the living of Eye, Suffolk.

His ecclesiastical future was now assured. Eye was a compact market town with a well-established Baptist church, a magnificent parish church and a particularly rambling vicarage. As a directory noted in 1875, the living was worth £438p.a., and it was in the gift of Sir Edward Kerrison Bt., who had restored the chancel. The parishioners had restored the nave and a handsome Caen stone pulpit came from the vicar.[78] Although the pulpit has been replaced and present-day visitors are more likely to remark on the work of Sir Ninian Comper, Page Roberts's restoration of 1869 has left its mark on the famous roof and in 'the handsome oak benches which replaced the old lofty deal seats'.[79] Vicar Page Roberts left his mark on Eye as well as its church, for he enlarged its ancient grammar school and built and furnished a working-men's

---

[75] Most sources give 1878 as the commencement of his incumbency. It may have been so in practice but it was not strictly so. His predecessor, John Cole Coghlan, died 24 October 1878 (Leveson-Gower, *St. Peter's Vere Street*, p.6) and Page Roberts was appointed 13 February 1879 (Hennessy, p. 328).

[76] Leveson-Gower, *St. Peter's Vere Street*, pp. 6, 9; undated cutting, Westminster City Archives. A poll degree is a pass degree. In fact, the Moral Science Tripos was instituted in 1848 and Page Roberts was at St. John's 1858-1861; his tutor was Revd. Joseph Bickersteth Mayor (1828-1916).

[77] Leveson-Gower, *St. Peter's Vere Street*, p. 9. John Graham (1794-1865) was a congenial bishop. Politically Liberal and well-disposed to Dissenters, he 'enjoyed the friendship of the Prince Consort and the respect of the Queen'. Bishop of Chester 1848-65, he had been Master of Christ's 1830-48, and Vice-Chancellor in 1831 and 1840, and he had chaired the Prince Consort's committee in the contest for the Chancellorship in February 1847; it was under the Prince Consort's impetus that the University's statutes were reformed and, *inter alia*, the Moral Science Tripos instituted (*DNB* and *ODNB*).

[78] Kelly's Post Office Directory, Norfolk, Suffolk and Cambridgeshire, 1875.

[79] Undated cutting, St. John's College Archives: it correctly describes his restoration of its 'glorious' roof as sympathetic.

club.⁸⁰

If this suggests an already Maurician Broad Churchmanship, it also testifies to deft politics for the Kerrisons, to whom Page Roberts owed his fourteen years in Eye, were Tories. Sir Edward and his father were MPs for Eye from 1824 to 1866 and Sir Edward, his brother-in-law Lord Henniker, and his nephews J.M. Henniker and Lord Mahon, between them represented East Suffolk for thirty-four years.⁸¹ Theirs was a firm if provincial - and in Mahon's case quirky - Toryism. It is not clear how Page Roberts attracted the Kerrison patronage but one suspects a Cambridge and especially a Johnian network; Sir Edward's brother-in-law, the 4th Lord Henniker, was a John's man as well as patron of seven livings.⁸²

And it was Tory patronage which took Page Roberts to Vere Street. He published two volumes of sermons while at Eye, *Law and God* (1874) and *Reasonable Service* (1876). The former, which attracted notices in *The Times*, *The Spectator*, 'and the foremost Church and Nonconformist Papers', brought him to the notice of Disraeli who in November 1878 recommended him for St. Peter's Vere Street.⁸³ In that month he married.

The Hon. Margaret Grace Pitt-Rivers was agreeably, even surprisingly, well-connected for a parson's wife. Had her husband been set on preferment with his sights on Barchester, he could not have done better. Her father, the 4th Baron Rivers (1810-1866), 'an energetic man of business and an eminently practical agriculturalist', had done much to restore the reputation of a curiously rackety peerage.⁸⁴ He was a Peelite turned Liberal who had held office under Lords Aberdeen, Palmerston, and John Russell. Margaret was one of three surviving daughters and since three of her four brothers had predeceased their father and the fourth only survived him by a year she could be considered an

---

⁸⁰ Ibid., Leveson-Gower, *St. Peter's Vere Street*, p. 10.

⁸¹ Sir Edward Kerrison, 1st Bt. (1776-1853) was MP Eye 1824-52; Sir Edward Kerrison 2nd Bt. (1821-1886) was MP Eye 1852-66 and East Suffolk 1866-7; the 4th Baron Henniker (1801-1870), married to Anna Kerrison, was MP East Suffolk (his was an Irish peerage, which did not preclude him from a seat in the House of Commons) 1832-47, 1856-66, and his son, the Hon. J.M. Henniker, was MP 1866-70. Viscount Mahon, later 6th Earl Stanhope, whose mother was Emily Kerrison, was MP 1870-75.

⁸² M. Stenton, *Who's Who of British Members of Parliament*, Vol. I, 1832-1885 (Hassocks: The Harvester Press, 1976), pp. 188, 220, 256-57.

⁸³ Leveson-Gower, *St. Peter's Vere Street*, p. 9; 'Mr. Delane had heard him preach, and a striking review of a small volume of his sermons...appeared in *The Times*, undated cutting, St. John's College Archives; *The Eagle*, A Magazine Supported by Members of St. John's College, Vol. XLV, Nos. 199-204, 1929, p. 225.

⁸⁴ G.E.C. and G.H. White, *The Complete Peerage*, Vol. XI, 1949, pp. 32-34. The 4th Baron left £90,000; his father, the 3rd Baron drowned in the Serpentine in 1831, fearing ruin after gaming losses; his younger brother, the 6th Baron (1814-1880), married 'a notorious woman of the town, commonly known as Nellie Holmes', whose niece's death in 1877 'led to a famous murder-trial'. But that is another story.

heiress. There was, however, no land. The large estates in Dorset and Wiltshire passed with the title from her brother to an uncle and thence to a second cousin.[85] As for her sisters, Mary Emma was to marry the future Dean Eliot of Windsor and became Maid of Honour to the Queen, Frances had married the 9th Duke of Leeds and was Lady of the Bedchamber to the Princess of Wales. These were Tory connexions; Dean Eliot was an Irish Tory MP's grandson and the Duke was a Tory peer. There were, however, impeccably Whig connexions. 'Pussy' Granville (1815-1891), Gladstone's Foreign Secretary and troubleshooter in the House of Lords, loyal beyond the call of duty, was Margaret's uncle and George Leveson-Gower (1858-1951), Gladstone's private secretary from 1880 to 1885, was her first cousin.

Page Roberts may not have sought preferment but it came to him nonetheless and so did recognition, which is not quite the same thing. His published sermons ran to several editions, Glasgow awarded him an honorary doctorate (which perhaps has a bearing on the courteous reference in his sermons to Presbyterianism and the Church of Scotland), and in 1895 he became a canon residentiary of Canterbury Cathedral, a position which could be held in tandem with Vere Street. It entailed two months in Canterbury each year, preaching to congregations 'not of the intellectual calibre of the Verestreet seatholders'; his reward was to become the cathedral chapter's Proctor in Convocation and senior canon.[86]

The Canterbury appointment was a mark of Liberal patronage; it was on Lord Rosebery's recommendation. His next appointment was also a mark of Liberal patronage. In July 1907, the year of his Glasgow DD, and on the recommendation of Sir Henry Campbell-Bannerman, William Page Roberts became Dean of Salisbury.[87]

This was both gratifying and surprising. He was now seventy-two. He had never hidden his Liberal churchmanship but he had played no part in Church politics and his party politics were in fact by no means clear.[88] A deanery was a good place for an ecclesiastical man of affairs but it was not necessarily a good place in which to put even an ecclesiastical war-horse out to grass let alone a

---

[85] The family, originally seated at Stratfieldsaye, Hants, was now at Rushmore, Tollard Royal, near Salisbury. In 1880 the estates passed from the 6th Baron to his second cousin, General Augustus Lane-Fox. In 1883 they amounted to 24,942 Dorset acres, and 2,762 Wiltshire acres worth £35,396 a year.

[86] *Who Was Who 1916-1928*, p. 897; undated cutting, St. John's College Archives: A. Leveson-Gower, *St. Peter's Vere Street*, p. 10.

[87] 'Obituary: Dean Page Roberts', Salisbury Diocesan Gazette, August and September 1928, p. 97. Interestingly this obituary says the appointment was 'upon the recommendation of Mr. Asquith'. Asquith may well have approved but the recommendation lay with the Prime Minister, Campbell-Bannerman.

[88] 'In his earliest speech at Salisbury he said that he was supposed to be a Radical. As a matter of fact he had only once voted for a Liberal, and that was for the man rather than for the party; his second vote on that occasion was given to a Conservative'. Ibid.

hitherto unencumbered preacher. Page Roberts rose to the occasion. He was to be in Salisbury for almost as long as he had been in Eye. His deanery became a centre of hospitality and if he seldom showed undue enthusiasm for the practical duties of his post ('He was not fond of meetings - he had never been used to them - but he was always glad to hear of progress'), he made it clear that he still liked to preach and during the Great War he instituted Sunday evening preaching services which filled the cathedral nave, preaching frequently himself and reading 'the special prayers in a mellow voice which took the note of the building.'[89]

And indeed his first sermon in his new cathedral, delivered on 22 September 1907 as 'a pastor's prayer for his people', contained all the Vere Street notes attuned to cathedral dimensions.[90] Salisbury's new dean put status and ceremony in its place: 'It is not when we sound a trumpet before us that the essential character is most truly displayed, although self-trumpeting may safely be said to proceed from a brazen instrument'. He queried the certainties of those inclined to doze at the onset of cliché,: 'The first question which starts up at once in many minds when something new invites them is not: Is this really excellent, is this a new view of or nearer approach to truth, but is it catholic, is it Protestant, is it pleasant, is it fashionable, is it safe to attempt it, is it cheap, is it quite convenient, will it pay, is it what we have always thought, practised and supported?' Nothing could quite be taken for granted about anything he said: 'I have no leanings whatever to Socialism, even when it is lubricated with ecclesiastical sentimentalism, and described as Christian Socialism. The word Christian is here as much misapplied as it is when it is used by Christian Science. But the fact that Socialism exists and daily extends in Europe, so much so that it is becoming a kind of religion, inflaming men with missionary zeal, like that of the early Christians, this is enough to prove that modern life is not satisfactory.' It was the same when he turned to his Church, and, by implication, to the role of a cathedral in its community

> Is it not for the Church of England - the most spacious sanctuary of religious freedom the world has ever seen - to be eager to honour the presence of Christ, and the inspiration of His Spirit, in whatever denomination they are to be seen? And is it not for the various Christian denominations to regard with loving reverence the Church of England as their Mother church, and disdain to be jealous of her parental preeminence[?].

He ended by gently probing – 'My people - as such let me address you, for to you I have been sent as a pastor - let the first service I am permitted to render you be, if possible to make you dissatisfied with yourselves'; and then, as he had begun, in healing prayer: 'Prayer is one of the great laws of the spiritual world - the law of attraction. It is the drawing near of the mind of Man to the

---

[89] Ibid., undated cutting, St. John's College Archives;
[90] 'Sermon by the Dean', *Salisbury Diocesan Gazette*, October 1907, pp. 188-190.

mind of God, until at length they blend, the imperfect being lost in the perfect.'

Page Roberts retired to the Isle of Wight in 1919. He died 17 August 1928, two years after the wife on whom 'he had leaned to a quite unusual extent'. He was buried with her and their two young sons in W.E. Nesfield's high-Victorian Morris & Co-windowed church at Farnham Royal, an old Godolphin property of the Dukes of Leeds.[91] There is, however, more to be said about Dean Page Roberts. It concerns his first twenty-two years.

William Page Roberts was a Liverpudlian, probably Liverpool Welsh, certainly Liverpool Wesleyan. The information is fragmentary, gleaned from the records of Liverpool College and St John's College, Cambridge. His parents, William and Prudence Roberts, were of 23 Church Street, Liverpool, in the 1840s and of Elm Vale, Birchfield, by 1858.[92] In 1849 William Roberts was a hairdresser; in his Birchfield days he was apparently in the furniture trade. The son's schooling was more suggestive than sustained. He was in the Lower School of Liverpool College from 1844 to 1845 and in the Middle School in 1849. There is no reference to him between 1845 and 1849, or from 1850, and he seems to have won no prizes or distinctions.[93] Liverpool College was then in its first decade and its future was not yet wholly assured. Its principal, however, W.J. Conybeare, was already a name to conjure with. He was the man who in 1853 captured for posterity in the *Edinburgh Review* the name and concept of 'Broad Church'.[94]

The Robertses, however, were not Broad Church, even before its time. They were Great Homer Street Wesleyans, their chapel a little older than Liverpool College but already in its glory days as a carriage-trade church, and whatever William Page Roberts's occupation from 1850 - one supposes 'business' - he was intended for the Wesleyan ministry. From 1856 to 1858 he was a student at Richmond College, one of the Connexion's theological colleges; in its register, in the column headed 'subsequent career', which in most cases is full of useful information, there is the pencilled comment, 'no trace'.[95] Such Wesleyan

---

[91] 'Obituary. Dean Page Roberts, *Salisbury Diocesan Gazette*, August and September 1928, p.97.

[92] I am particularly indebted to Mr. B.R. Martin for information from the College Register of Liverpool College and to the late Revd. Dr. Ian Sellers for trawling through his encyclopaedic knowledge of Liverpool Nonconformity. All the sources, including the records of St. John's College, Cambridge, give the Roberts home as Brookfield; that is a misprint for Birchfield.

[93] Liverpool College Register.

[94] For William John Conybeare (1815-1857), whose *Edinburgh Review* article on 'Church Parties' reached a wider public in his collected essays of 1856, see *DNB*. Conybeare's successor as principal, J.S. Howson (1814-1887), who was in post in 1849, also became a notable ecclesiatic.

[95] Dr. Sellers provided the information about Great Homer Street and he and Dr. Peter Nockles confirmed the information from Richmond College Register, Vol. 1, (1834 -

ignorance - and lack of curiosity - is instructive. He had, in fact, proceeded to Cambridge where first degrees were now open to Dissenters, but he was no longer a Dissenter and perhaps as a Wesleyan he had never regarded himself as such: he had the National Church's ministry in mind. He was, indeed, taking a not dissimilar path to that of his future hero, F.D. Maurice.

His Wesleyan and Liverpudlian associations, however, were not wholly over, for on 13 December 1865, just into his second year as Vicar of Eye, his first wife, Mary Elizabeth Beynon, died; she was twenty-six.[96] The Beynons, like the Robertses, were Great Homer Street Wesleyans; John Beynon, of Grove Road, Fairfield, not far from Elm Vale, Birchfield, was a tea dealer, grocer, and Italian warehouseman; Mary Elizabeth died at his house. Had William and Mary been youthful sweethearts? Had William been employed at Beynon's? Here is certainly the *mise-en-scène* for a novel. It was thirteen years before William remarried. By then his formative years, though no secret, were firmly buried.

The cynical observer might feel that the rise of this Methodist hairdresser's son from Liverpool to be Dean of Salisbury and brother-in-law to a duchess is Trollopian beyond compare; Barchester could not better it.[97] That, however, is to reckon without the tenor of his ministry or the tone of his sermons. It is to ignore his insight into non-episcopalian Christianity and his respect for it. That would have stood him in good stead in Eye where Baptists were strong and where Methodists of all sorts abounded, especially as Norfolk came into view. It did him no harm in Salisbury which, like many cathedral cities, had its persistently conscientious Dissenters. And the example of such an ecclesiastical journey as his, taken with such integrity, informed the strength of his London ministry. It made him and his Church credible.

VII

A degree of proof, admittedly circumstantial rather than definitive, might be found in one particular family of Vere Street seatholders, the Willanses of 23 Holland Park and High Clyffe, Seaton, Devon, husband, wife, two sons and two daughters. The head of the family, William Henry Willans (1832-1904), died at High Clyffe, as commandingly placed on the cliffs between Beer and Seaton as its name suggested, on Monday 26 September 1904. The funeral service,

---

72), entry no. 282 (Methodist Church Archives, The John Rylands University Library, Manchester).

[96] St. John's College, Cambridge, biographical file, quoting *Gentleman's Magazine*, 1866, No. 1, p. 155.

[97] Or, perhaps, more appositely, Howatchian rather than Trollopian, bearing in mind the 'Starminster' novels of Susan Howatch, inspired by Salisbury and transposed from the political career of H.H. Asquith to a rather later ecclesiastical, yet no less political, setting.

however, was at St. Peter's the following Friday, conducted by Canon Page Roberts before interment at Kensal Green. There Willans was to be commemorated by an impressive memorial but there had been a no less impressive commemoration at the funeral service. The dead man had for years been Treasurer of the Homes for Little Boys at Farningham in North Kent. He had been one of their founders in 1863. Over the years he had conducted services in their chapel and umpired matches in their playing fields and when ill health kept him increasingly away, his Old Harrovian elder son and namesake joined their committee. Now, 'As the cortège arrived at the Church, the entrance was lined by several members of the Committee, and a detachment of boys from the Farningham and Swanley Homes'.[98]

This philanthropist had been in all respects an exemplary seatholder. While his country house was by the Devon coast, where he liked to spend his autumns, enjoying the view, the carriage drives, and the round of tennis and cricket tournaments, his town house was in that upper-middle-class parade, Holland Park, where he had lived, spaciously close-packed in the prosperous London way, since 1878 and where his son was to follow him. He had been one of the earlier residents of that grand development of identical double-fronted Italianate villas, complete with stables, coach-houses, ornamental canopies, and staffs of at least six servants.[99]

Like many of his neighbours Willans was in the City.[100] He was senior partner in a solid firm of woolbrokers (Copthall Buildings, Basinghall Street and Moorgate Street) but he had other irons in the commercial fire: director of the Notting Hill Electric Light Co. Ltd, director of Pawson and Leaf Ltd. (and its chairman from 1880), director of the National Provident Institution (and its chairman from 1896). His thirty-year association with the National Provident made him one of the city's more public faces (several MPs were among his fellow directors) and that public aspect was increasingly reflected in the 1890s: he served on committees for commercial exhibitions in Antwerp, Brussels, Paris and Glasgow; he chaired London's Chamber of Commerce. He was, of course, a JP (for London, Westminster, Middlesex, and Devon) and he was a Deputy Lieutenant (for Middlesex); and he played his part in Liberal politics. In the 1890s he sat on Middlesex County Council and became an alderman in 1892; and back in 1874 he had been persuaded to stand at the last minute as Liberal candidate for Frome.[101] He had not been elected and there is no further

---

[98] *The H.L.B. Old Boys' Journal*, January 1905, p. 3.
[99] F.D.W. Sheppard ed., *Survey of London*, Vol. XXXVII (Northern Kensington, London: 1973), pp. 118, 122-4.
[100] *Who Was Who 1897-1916,* p. 764; *The Times*, 28 September 1904; cutting, 1 October 1904 in volume of Obituary Cuttings 1893-1916, Huddersfield Central Library.
[101] See C. Binfield, 'The Acceptable Face of Carpet Baggery? W.H. Willans and Frome's Reformers', M. Turner ed., *Reform and Reformers in Nineteenth-Century Britain* (Sunderland: University of Sunderland Press, 2004), pp. 137-56.

evidence of parliamentary ambitions but a barrister nephew had been a Liberal Home Secretary and his youngest brother's barrister brother-in-law had been a useful Liberal back-bencher until becoming a High Court Judge and Master of the Rolls. Willans was thus professionally as well as commercially and philanthropically well-connected. Indeed, he could be woven into Vere Street's particular professional mainstay for his son-in-law was a highly regarded medical man, en route to a knighthood.[102]

One other factor makes him suggestively exemplary as one of Canon Page Roberts's seatholders. Like his minister Willans had been reared in Nonconformity. Indeed he had been a prominent as well as an active Nonconformist. His grandparents, parents, and each of his brothers and sisters, all of them Congregationalists, had been similarly active in the West Riding and his wife's family, the Wrights, were well-known in London Congregationalism, especially in Islington.

Willans's own church membership had been in denominationally notable Congregational churches: Ramsden Street, Huddersfield, in early manhood; Union Chapel, Islington, from 1858 to 1879; Kensington Chapel (Allen Street) from 1879, to which he transferred with his wife and daughters.[103] There was nothing nominal about this membership. In the 1870s he was a personal member of the Congregational Union of England and Wales and in the early 1870s he sat on its London Committee. In 1873 he read a paper at its annual meetings and in the same year he joined the committee formed to build Memorial Hall, the denomination's new national headquarters near Ludgate Circus. He was an active committee member, frequently called on to open its meetings in prayer. When Union Chapel was rebuilt in the same decade Willans contributed £500, with a further fifteen guineas from his wife and elder daughter. Such commitment was not to be compartmentalised. When leading Nonconformists spoke and preached at Farningham's anniversaries, they were clearly Willans's personal friends and when he stood for Parliament in 1874 however much he played up his Gladstonianism and played down his Dissent the fact remains that his platform was filled with Frome's Dissenting ministers and their lay officeholders. It could not easily have been otherwise in a town whose churchgoers had so recently been polarised by the alluring excesses of Father Bennett, the famous ritualist.[104]

---

[102] The nephew was H.H. Asquith; the brother's brother-in-law was H.H. Cozens-Hardy (1838-1920) MP. N. Norfolk 1885-1899; Judge in Chancery 1899, Lord Justice of Appeal 1901, Master of the Rolls 1907-1918. The son-in-law was Sir Robert Michael Simon (1850 -1914), in Birmingham from 1879, prominent in Midland medical circles, latterly Professor of Therapeutics at Birmingham University.

[103] This information is drawn from the records of Union Chapel, Minute Book 1856-1858; Index of Members 1874-1880, in the possession of Union Chapel when consulted.

[104] This information is drawn from *Congregational Year Book*s; Memorial Hall Trustees' Minutes; Union Chapel *Annual Reports*, passim. For Frome see Binfield, *Carpet Baggery*; for Revd. William James Early Bennett (1804-1886) see *ODNB*.

And then he changed course. It is not entirely clear when or why. The relevant membership lists for Kensington Chapel and seatholders' lists for Vere Street have not survived. Perhaps his daughter Maud's marriage at Christ Church, Lancaster Gate, in January 1887, was a marker. A more conclusive marker comes from Memorial Hall's Trustees' Minutes for 1894: 'The Treasurer, Mr. George F. White JP, Sir W.H. Wills, JP, DL., and Mr. W.H. Willans JP DL., have intimated their retirement from the Trust in consequence of their not continuing to hold all the necessary qualifications for Trustees, a point which had hitherto been overlooked.'[105]

This was a bombshell. White, Wills, and Willans were lay grandees. Willans was a rich man but White, the Portland Cement manufacturer, and Wills, the cigarette manufacturer (and future Lord Winterstoke), were very rich men indeed. One of the requirements likely to have been overlooked was membership (as opposed to attendance) of a Congregational church.

The Willanses had transferred their membership from Islington to Kensington in 1879. Their name does not appear in the list of members which survives for 1898-1950, and it does not figure in surviving lists of donors to the Chapel's Notting Hill Mission from 1893. At some point between 1880 and 1893-4 they had transferred their allegiance from Allen Street to Vere Street.[106]

Why? It cannot have been distance; Vere Street was no easier to reach from Holland Park than Allen Street. The perils of upward social mobility are not wholly convincing; Union Chapel and Kensington Chapel were certainly more socially eclectic than Vere Street but the Vere Street type was prominent in their pews. Henry Wright, a layman on a par with White, Wills, and Willans, was a Kensington man. Herbert Hardy Cozens-Hardy, the successful barrister, two of whose sisters in succession were married to Willans's youngest brother James Edward, had been a member since 1868. Perhaps the quality of ministry had something to do with it. In 1879 Kensington's minister was Alexander Raleigh, one of Victorian Congregationalism's most attractive pulpiteers, whom Willans had known in Islington and who had preached to the Farningham boys and their supporters.[107] He died in 1880 and his successor,

---

[105] I am indebted to Mr. R. Morley-Fletcher for details of Emily Maud Willans's marriage, 26 January 1887 and to Mr. B.J. Reeve for the transcript of the May 1894 entry.

[106] Kensington Chapel's records before 1898 are frustratingly sparse. Information about membership and adherents before 1898 had to be deduced from List of Church Members, October 1898-1950; Register of Baptisms 1865; and Annual Reports from 1893 (in possession of Kensington United Reformed Church when consulted).

[107] For Alexander Raleigh (1817-1880) father of the scholar and man of letters, Sir Walter Raleigh, see Mary Raleigh ed., *Alexander Raleigh: Records of His Life*, Edinburgh, 1881. Raleigh's principal pastorate had been at Hare Court, Canonbury (1858-1875); he and his congregation provided one of Farningham's Cottage Homes, 'Quiet Resting Place'; Willans himself funded 'Alexander House'. I am indebted to Mr. L. Skinner for this information; a list of preachers and speakers can be found in the eight

Colmer Symes, seems not to have had Raleigh's drawing power.[108] Indeed, from 1887 to 1889 Kensington chapel marked time. The church had called a promising young man, Charles Silvester Horne, but he was still at Oxford and until he was ready the veteran proponent of conditional immortality, Edward White, George White's brother, held the fort.[109] Horne turned out to be an inspired choice. He became an outstanding figure in Edwardian Congregationalism; in 1892 he married H.H. Cozens-Hardy's daughter Katharine; and he was on the friendliest terms with the James Willanses of Huddersfield. So he should have suited the William Willanses, but he was certainly very young. Was it that? Were there family tensions? Or had something happened in the Colmer Symes years? One cannot now know.[110]

Perhaps, however, it was more content than circumstances. Willans's upbringing had been Congregationally orthodox. Richard Skinner, the family's minister in Huddersfield, had been a man of the old school, powerfully and intelligently evangelical. Willans's earlier London associations had been along similar lines - his support for both Islington and London YMCAs, for example, and his involvement with Farningham where his fellow enthusiasts had included (Sir) Francis Lycett, the Wesleyan glovemaker, and Robert Hanbury, the Evangelical brewer (and Palmerstonian Liberal MP).[111] Union Chapel itself had been a product of the Evangelical Revival, seeking to unite evangelical

---

page (but unpaginated) advertisement for the Homes placed at the end of *Congregational Year Book* 1886.

[108] Such might be deduced from C.S. Horne, *A Century of Christian Service: Kensington Congregational Church, 1793-1893* (London: 1893), pp. 122-29. But Symes's years also saw the building of the ambitious West Kensington Congregational Church, primarily financed and peopled by Kensington Chapel.

[109] For Edward White (1819-1898) see F.A. Freer, *Edward White* (London: 1902). For Charles Silvester Horne (1865-1914) see *ODNB*.

[110] The late Basil Cozens-Hardy told the writer that his uncle, H.H. Cozens-Hardy, could not condone marriage of a deceased wife's sister, in part because of his duty to uphold the law, in part because of pressures that there might be for him to marry his own deceased wife's sister who kept house for him. This might have made for strained relations with J.E. Willans (whose Cozens-Hardy wives had died in 1879 and 1894) and therefore with W.H. Willans, but J.E. Willans was a naturally conciliatory man, and C.S. Horne was to officiate at the marriage in Huddersfield of his son Gerald Cozens-Hardy Willans.

[111] For Richard Skinner (1806-1885) see *Congregational Year Book 1886*, p. 211; I am indebted to Mr. G.F. Palmer for confirmation of Willans's YMCA activities.

For Robert Culling Hanbury (1823-1867) see *Who's Who MPs*, Vol 1, 1832-1886, p. 177

For Sir Francis Lycett (1803-1880) see J.A. Vickers ed., *A Dictionary of Methodism in Britain and Ireland* (Peterborough: Epworth Press, 2000), p. 215.

For further evidence of Farningham's Evangelical origins see Kathleen Heasman, *Evangelicals in Action*, London 1962, pp. 98, 117-8, 185. I am indebted to Mr. H.O. Tester for a copy of the founding minute of the Homes.

Anglicans and Dissenters.

But the structure of orthodoxy, and therefore the focus of its content, can change. Willans's paper to the Congregational Union in 1873 might be regarded as a case in point. His theme was "Attendance at Public Worship", by which he meant declining attendance at public worship. He took Berlin as a shocking example (Willans's business took him to Germany; that was where he was fired by the idea of cottage homes for little boys), and he worried at the high proportion of once-a-Sunday worshippers, the peripatetic sermon-tasters, and the general vulnerability of the English sabbath: 'Fashionable life in the form of late dinners and Sunday visiting, is insidiously attacking this last stronghold of Christian England'. So he posed a series of questions - were sermons too long? too philosophical? with too little of Christ about them? were services too wearysome to children? too old-fashioned and inflexible in structure? - which presupposed a predictable enough answer: make services more attractive by giving congregations more to do and their pastors less to do. The Congregational Union might consider issuing a permissive order of worship, for a more liturgical form would keep the young; sermons should be shorter (attention notoriously waned after thirty-five minutes); there might even be a monthly interdenominational exchange of pulpits.[112]

Some of this made sense in the wash of the new world of Moody and Sankey's first mission, but the references to late dinners and Sunday visits and keeping the young suggested a more socially elevated domestic agenda. Much of it propounded no more than was already practised at Union Chapel whose formidable minister Henry Allon had accustomed his growing congregation to a demanding quality of music and common worship, as his rebuilt chapel boldly celebrated.[113]

That was in the 1870s. In the 1880s a different sort of attractiveness hit the Willanses between wind and water. Ramsden Street, the church in Huddersfield which three generations of Willanses had done so much to shape, was at a parting of ways. Richard Skinner had been succeeded by John Turner Stannard, a young and brilliant preacher whose theological liberalism was not to be hidden. Huddersfield Congregationalism, a success story which prided itself that it had never multiplied by division, was now sharply divided. Leading trustees took action. Families were split. Willans's youngest brother, James Edward Willans, who maintained the family's woolbroking interests in Huddersfield, was a leading supporter of Stannard's and a prime mover in building a fine new chapel for him, bravely called Milton, and in getting Herbert Cozens-Hardy up from London to represent them in the lawsuit. Poor Stannard died soon after, in circumstances which suggested suicide, but Milton

---

[112] W.H. Willans, 'Attendance at Public Worship', *Congregational Year Book, 1874*, p. 8.
[113] See C. Binfield, *The Contexting of a Chapel Architect: James Cubitt 1836-1912* (London: The Chapels Society, Occasional Publication 2, 2001), pp. 45-64.

flourished for the next fifty years.[114]

The Stannard affair was unusually bitter but it was symptomatic of considerable tension in late Victorian Congregationalism. There was, for example, the case of William Wooding, a Congregational minister of some academic ability, advanced views, but mixed pastoral success. He was married to Willans's niece, Evelyn Asquith, daughter of his older sister Emily. The Woodings lived in Holloway and Canonbury, at first with Evelyn's mother, who was a member of Henry Allon's Union Chapel. After Emily Asquith's death William Wooding's name slipped from the roll of Congregational ministers. He now combined teaching mathematics at City of London School with what proved to be his most successful pastorate - that of the historic Unitarian chapel at Newington Green.[115] Perhaps in all the circumstances it was understandable that an ageing if public-spirited man like William Henry Willans, whose commercial and civic commitments pressed against the standards he had set himself as a Congregational layman, should turn to the elegantly restrained but judiciously enriched atmosphere of St. Peter's, Vere Street, with its dignified congregational worship and its undemanding, indeed virtually non-existent, eccclesiology. When allied to the pulpit ministry of William Page Roberts, every word of *Conformity and Conscience* striking home within a thirty-five minute span, it would have been powerfully attractive.[116]

The facts, though fragmentary, are reasonably clear. The conclusions to be drawn from them can only be conjectured. A postscript in two parts might strengthen the suggestion that there was more to Willans and Page Roberts than two notable examples of that numerous tribe which the Cambridge historian and Congregationalist Bernard Lord Manning was later to characterise as

---

[114] See C. Binfield, *So Down to Prayers. Studies in English Nonconformity 1780-1920* (London: J. M. Dent & Sons, 1977), pp 158-161; see M.D. Johnson, *The Dissolution of Dissent, 1850-1918* (London: Garland Publishing, 1987), pp. 146-8, 158-163.

[115] For William Wooding (1840-1918) see W. Wooding, 'From Congregationalism to Unitarianism', *Types of Religious Experience* (London: 1903), pp. 25-41; *The Christian Life*, 19 January 1918, pp. 22-3; *Essex Hall Year Book, 1919*, p 110. See also *Congregational Year Books* 1867-1889.

[116] It is tempting to speculate on relations between Asquith and the W.H. Willanses; William, with his elder brother John Wrigley Willans (1832-1910) who had also lived in Islington and been active at Union Chapel, paid for the education at City of London School of his Asquith nephews after their father's death. On at least two occasions (15 February 1898 and 6 February 1903), when Asquith was guest of honour at an '80' Club dinner, W.H. Willans was present, and his widow and elder daughter were at Asquith's Memorial Service in Westminster Abbey (21 February 1928) and, with his elder son, at Lincoln's Inn the previous day; that was to be expected - but was Asquith, once he left Hampstead, an attender at Vere Street, which was very close to his houses in Mount Street and Cavendish Square, Page Roberts would certainly have met his sermon-tasting standards.

'lapsed Dissenters'.[117]

The first part concerns Willans's will, dated 17 July 1903, and a proof of friendship. The will names three executors: Willans's wife, his solicitor, and a Bishopsgate shipbroker.[118] The last named, Sir John Glover, was an old friend of over forty years standing. The Glovers were from South Shields, as pervasive in their way as the Willanses from Huddersfield. John Glover had been associated with Willans in founding the Homes for Little Boys. In 1874 he had campaigned for Willans in Frome and in 1885 he had himself stood, with similar lack of success, for Scarborough. He too had been a Union Chapel man, with two of his brothers, Septimus who was in the family shipping business, and James who was a doctor. Here were more rising Upper Middles. Unlike Willans Glover had left Gladstonian Liberalism for Liberal Unionism, but also unlike Willans he had remained in membership of a Congregational church, leaving Islington for Highgate not long before Willans left for Kensington, and the next generation of Glovers maintained the tradition.[119]

So, to a degree, did the next generation of Willanses, and the second part of this postscript illustrates the ongoing themes of continuity, change, and comprehensiveness. The nearest Congregational church to St. Peter's, Vere Street, was the King's Weigh House, south of Oxford Street and a stone's throw from Grosvenor Square. The late-Victorian-turned-Edwardian Weigh House was a sport, transplanted from the City to the West End in Alfred Waterhouse's most idiomatic Gothic. Its records include a members' list of 1928 incorporating an earlier, amended, printed list of seatholders and members. Among several notable names, four stand out for the present study: they are Mrs. W.H. Willans of 23 Holland Park, her daughter Marian Isabel Willans, Miss H.M. Willans of 32 Cartwright Gardens WC1, who is almost certainly Marian's cousin, James Edward Willans's daughter, and the Hon. Mrs. Silvester Horne of 9 Campden Hill Gardens, the widow of Charles Silvester Horne, formerly minister of Kensington Chapel.[120] Mrs. Willans was a seatholder but Marian had been a member since January 1915. If that was when she and her mother first crossed Oxford Street for their Sunday worship, it was

---

[117] For Manning (1892-1941) see F.L. Brittain, *Bernard Lord Manning, A Memoir*, Cambridge: W. Heffer and Sons, 1942. "Some Lapsed Dissenters", the title of an address to Cambridge University Congregational Society, assumed a mythical status, and typed samizdat copies were handed down from generation to generation.

[118] Will dated 27 July 1903. Probate granted 1 December 1904; proved at £49,997. 5s. 5d.

[119] For Sir John Glover (1829-1920) see *Who Was Who, 1916-1928*, p. 417. On Census Sunday 1881, Willans's daughters Maud and Marian, their name transcribed as Williams, were staying with the John Glovers at Merton Lodge, Highgate (1881 British Census).

[120] King's Weigh House Congregational Church Members List 1928, (Congregational Library MSS, Dr. Williams's Library, 14 Gordon Square, London WC1). Mrs. W.H. Willans (born Mary Ann Jane Wright) died 1 December 1934, aged ninety-five.

towards the end of the incumbency at St. Peter's of Robert Burnaby, Page Roberts's successor, and at the beginning of the pastorate at the Weigh House of W.E. Orchard whose preaching had already restored that church to its flagship position for discerning metropolitan Nonconformists and whose liturgical practices, though already pronounced, had yet to become notorious. Orchard's sermons, warmed by his personality, had a crisp, compelling, and persuasive logic which would have spoken to hearers accustomed to Page Roberts. They were, moreover, responsibly enlivened by political radicalism and wholly free of war-time sentiment. His churchmanship, no doubt, was another matter for it was to carry him into the Church of Rome.[121] That particular essay in continuity, change, social class, ecclesiastical comprehensiveness confounded in division, of conformity and conscience reconciled by liberalism in religion, is almost rivalled by St. Peter's later transition to the supervisory evangelical care of All Souls' Langham Place. It is however quite beyond the scope of the present study.

---

[121] For William Edwin Orchard (1877-1955), minister at King's Weigh House 1914-1932 see Elaine Kaye and R. Mackenzie, *W.E. Orchard, A Study in Christian Exploration* (Oxford: Education Services, 1990).

CHAPTER 6

The Theological Legacy of Lesslie Newbigin

David R. Peel

Alan Sell and I are members of the United Reformed Church, the church to which Lesslie Newbigin belonged when he retired from his work in South India. Newbigin was an outstanding Christian: missionary, ecumenist, bishop, theologian and pastor. None who knew him either closely or distantly can have failed 'to recognize and respect the nobility of [his] character, the quality of his mind, and the depth of his devotion'.[1] It is not surprising, therefore, that, following his death in 1998, there should be a bourgeoning literature about him. Geoffrey Wainwright has provided us with a fine biography which admirably fulfils its intention 'to show Newbigin's theology as it emerged in the varied contexts of his life and work'.[2] It also reflects the importance which he, George R. Hunsberger and others attribute to Newbigin's theology.[3] While Wainwright describes that theology as 'an *authentic* representation of the scriptural Gospel and the *classic* Christian faith',[4] Hunsberger opines that Newbigin bequeathed to the world church 'a legacy of profound proportion'.[5] Others have been less hagiographical and more critical in their appraisals of Newbigin's theology; some of the contributions to the 'After Newbigin' international conference in Birmingham during 1998 belong to that genre.[6] I will seek to honour the Newbigin legacy by underscoring some important themes in his theology, while

---
[1] C.S. Rodd, Review of G. Wainwright, *Lesslie Newbigin: A Theological Life* in *The Expository Times*, 112, No.11, (August, 2001), p. 365.
[2] G. Wainwright, *Lesslie Newbigin: A Theological Life* (Oxford: Oxford University Press, 2000), p.vii.
[3] See G.R. Hunsberger, *Bearing the Witness of the Spirit: Lesslie Newbigin's Theology of Cultural Plurality* (Grand Rapids, Michigan and Cambridge, UK:. Eerdmans, 1998).
[4] Wainwright, *Lesslie Newbigin: A Theological Life*, p. vii. (Italics mine).
[5] Hunsberger, *Bearing the Witness of the Spirit*, p. ix.
[6] See T.F. Foust, G.R. Hunsberger, J.A. Kirk and W. Ustorf (eds), *A Scandalous Prophet: The Way of Mission after Newbigin* (Grand Rapids, Michigan and Cambridge, U.K.: Eerdmans, 2002).

also showing that his thinking was deficient at crucial points. Hopefully, a critical overview of the theology of a fellow member of the United Reformed Church will serve as a fitting tribute to Alan, from whose work I have learned a great deal and whose ongoing support I appreciate enormously.

A Brief Outline of Newbigin's Theology

Newbigin was 'a theologian by habit and a lifelong missionary by trade'.[7] His 'trade' set down the parameters for his 'habit' with the result that his theology is both evangelical as well as orthodox. He attempted to present an account of the Christian witness that does justice to the Christian story's power to change the lives of individuals and societies. Newbigin's theology was spoken from the church to the world: 'Christian theology is a form of rational discourse developed within the community which accepts the primacy of this story and seeks actively to live in the world in accordance with the story.'[8] Unlike many evangelicals, however, Newbigin possessed a healthy and forthright approach to social and political affairs. He recognized that the church's vocation is to call and equip men and women to be signs and agents of God's justice in all human affairs as well as to bring them into a personal relationship with Jesus Christ: 'An evangelism that invites men and women to accept the name of Christ but fails to call them to this real encounter must be rejected as false.'[9] It was hardly surprising that one who sat under John Maynard Keynes' feet at Cambridge (1930-31) later presented a powerful critique of unbridled capitalism.[10] More than many, Newbigin was aware of the need to do justice to both the vertical and horizontal dimensions of the Christian gospel: 'Evangelism which is politically and ideologically naive, and social action which does not recognize the need for conversion from false gods to the living God, both fall short of what is required.'[11]

Others have already pointed out how remarkably consistent Newbigin's theology was throughout his long career.[12] Only for the brief period surrounding the publication of *Honest Religion for Secular Man* was there any departure from the christocentric trinitarianism for which he became noted. His orthodoxy was underpinned by his grasp of what he called 'the central verities

---

[7] Hunsberger, *Bearing the Witness of the Spirit*, p. 33.
[8] J.E.L. Newbigin, *The Gospel in a Pluralist Society* (London: SPCK, 1989), p.152.
[9] J.E.L. Newbigin, *Foolishness to the Greeks: The Gospel and Western Culture* (Grand Rapids, Michigan, London and Geneva: Eerdmans, SPCK and WCC, 1986), p. 133.
[10] See Newbigin, *Foolishness to the Greeks*, pp. 95-123 and Newbigin, *The Gospel in a Pluralist Society*, pp. 198-210.
[11] Newbigin, *The Gospel in a Pluralist Society*, p. 210.
[12] See Wainwright, *Lesslie Newbigin: A Theological Life*, pp. 26, 50, and Hunsberger, *Bearing the Witness of the Spirit*, p. 37.

of the gospel' discernable from the canonical scriptures and the classical creeds.[13] Newbigin's theology, therefore, rests upon what amounts to a 'canon within the canon' or something akin to the Irenaen 'rule of faith' – a 'story' which is read out of the Bible.[14] The Bible is authoritative for Newbigin because it is the source of *this* story. The story provides us with the 'plausibility structure' (Kuhn) or 'fiduciary framework' (Polanyi) upon which we can base our lives; it presents 'a universal history' or 'an outline of world history' for which the life, teaching, death and resurrection of Jesus is the interpretive clue;[15] and it provides us with the unchanging heart of the Christian gospel. Familiar themes are covered by the story: creation, fall, election, redemption and consummation. It concerns God's inexhaustible graciousness with men and women as well as human disobedience and intransigence. At its centre is 'the absolute sovereignty of Jesus Christ'[16] and 'the total fact of Jesus Christ'.[17] This story is gospel: ' . . . the announcement that in the series of events that have their center in the life, ministry, death, and resurrection of Jesus Christ something has happened that alters the total human situation and must therefore call into question every human culture'.[18] While Christianity may change through time, the gospel's substance remains unchanging. It is a dogma to be advanced and lived out.

Christian discipleship, for Newbigin, therefore, is completely bound up with people 'indwelling' this authoritative story.[19] Its starting point is 'God's revelation of himself in Jesus Christ as this is testified in the Bible' rather than what contemporary culture might dictate.[20] With clear echoes of Karl Barth, Newbigin thus grounds his theology in a revelation that interprets the meaning, purpose and destiny of life. Hence, 'the gospel accepted in faith . . . enables us to experience all reality in a new way and to find that all reality does indeed reflect the glory of God'.[21] This does not entail setting reason against

---

[13] Newbigin, *The Gospel in a Pluralist Society*, p. 139.

[14] Ibid., p. 12.

[15] See J.E.L. Newbigin, *A Faith for this One World?* (London: SCM Press, 1961), pp. 46-53, and J.E.L. Newbigin, *The Finality of Christ*, (London: SCM Press, 1969), pp. 65-87.

[16] Newbigin, *The Gospel in a Pluralist Society*, p. 169.

[17] See Newbigin, *A Faith for this One World?*, pp. 57, 60, and Newbigin, *Foolishness to the Greeks*, p. 41. See also J.E.L. Newbigin, *The Open Secret: Sketches for a Missionary Theology* (Grand Rapids, Michigan: William B. Eerdmans Publishing Company, 1978) where Newbigin speaks of 'a single happening...of decisive significance to all' (p. 57).

[18] Newbigin, *Foolishness to the Greeks*, pp. 3-4.

[19] See Newbigin, *The Gospel in a Pluralist Society*, pp. 97-99. See also J.E.L. Newbigin, *Truth to Tell: The Gospel as Public Truth* (London: SPCK, 1991), pp. 41-54 and J.E.L. Newbigin, *Proper Confidence: Faith, Doubt and Certainty in Christian Discipleship* (London: SPCK, 1995), pp. 86-89.

[20] J.E.L. Newbigin, *Honest Religion for Secular Man* (London: SCM Press, 1966), p. 42.

[21] Newbigin, *Proper Confidence*, pp. 96-97.

revelation, but it does favour one 'tradition of rational argument', namely, the gospel, over and against the tradition of rational argument belonging to the contemporary secular spirit.[22]

Upon his return to England from India in 1974, Newbigin believed that he was encountering a terminally ill post-Christian culture: 'Apart from those whose lives are shaped by the Christian hope founded on the resurrection of Jesus as the pledge of a new creation, there is little sign among the citizens of this country of the sort of confidence in the future which was certainly present in the earliest years of this century.'[23] Later he was to lament: 'In the closing decades of this century it is difficult to find Europeans who have any belief in a significant future which is worth working for and investing in.'[24] Newbigin believed that he had encountered a society controlled by materialistic and utilitarian values, one that had lost a clear sense of purpose – a culture that 'has proved bankrupt'.[25] With the zeal of a latter-day Jeremiah he pointed to 'a collapse of confidence in our culture' which reveals that we are facing nothing less than the death of 'Western post-Enlightenment culture'.[26] The philosophy of the Enlightenment has not proved capable of producing a worldview which holds culture together. All Newbigin experienced was shot through with fragmentation, with the twin evils of individualism and relativism rampant.

The plausibility structure of this ailing culture 'is more than a body of ideas', Newbigin claims, since it is 'a whole way of organizing human life that both rests on and in turn supports and validates the ideas' upon which Newtonian science came to be built, namely, nature understood in terms of the laws of cause and effect, with a utilitarian outlook squeezing out teleological concerns.[27] The power of reason in this philosophy can hardly be exaggerated: 'No alleged divine revelation, no tradition however ancient, and no dogma however hallowed has the right to veto its exercise.'[28] According to Newbigin, the resulting vision of the universe has no place for God. An atheistic outlook produces a pagan society which possesses a number of clearly discernable features due to its utilitarian emphasis. Newbigin points firstly to the way in which Western culture separates reality into 'private' and 'public' worlds, with religion belonging to the private domain and possessing no credibility when it enters the public realm in which Enlightenment pre-suppositions and thought hold sway. It follows secondly that religion trades in 'values', while outside religion one enters the world of 'facts': 'The public world is a world of facts

---

[22] Newbigin, *The Gospel in a Pluralist Society*, p. 62.
[23] J.E.L. Newbigin, *The Other Side of 1984: Questions for the Churches* (Geneva: WCC, 1984), p. 1.
[24] Newbigin, *The Gospel in a Pluralist Society*, p. 96.
[25] Ibid., p. 191.
[26] Ibid..
[27] Newbigin, *Foolishness to the Greeks*, p.29.
[28] Ibid., p. 25.

that are the same for everyone, whatever his values may be; the private world is a world of values where all are free to choose their own values and therefore to pursue such courses of action as will correspond with them.'[29] The collective result of living on the basis of such dichotomies, Newbigin suggests, is that Western culture doesn't produce 'enough nourishment for the human spirit' because it possesses no credible answers to the fundamentally important questions which are rooted in teleology and, therefore cannot answer 'the question, "Why?" '[30]

Newbigin urges a return, first, to the vision of the Christian gospel as that is provided by the Bible, and, secondly, to a religious outlook whose claims belong to the public domain. He calls us to live on the basis of God's self-revelation in Jesus, a story which not only brought the church into being but is to be shared with others. Western society needs converting – moving from living on the basis of a rationalistic frame of reference which has no place for the transcendent realm to living inside the Christian fiduciary framework. The church has been given a tradition of understanding which, once indwelt, leads to life in all its fullness. While truth will therefore be discovered from inside the church, it will only fully be known eschatologically when the promises contained within the normative story are made good. Christian truth cannot be demonstrated *a priori*. We are invited to place our faith in it, and then make it the foundation on which we understand and live out our lives. This act of faith, however, is not based simply upon personal opinion and, hence, merely subjective; rather, claims Newbigin, we make our act of faith with what Michael Polanyi calls 'universal intent'.[31] This carries with it the conviction that, 'as the truth which is true for all', it must 'be publicly affirmed, and opened to public interrogation and debate'.[32]

With the grounds for evangelism thus established Newbigin invites us to live in Christian community confident that the Holy Spirit will give us a true understanding of history. That understanding, as we have seen, is rooted in a series of events concerning Jesus that make up the memory of which the church is the custodian. God has chosen and set apart the church 'to be the messengers of his truth and bearers of his love for all people'.[33] To use Newbigin's typical expressions, the church is called to be a 'sign, instrument, and foretaste of God's purpose for all human culture'[34] and 'a servant, witness, and sign of the kingdom',[35] as well as 'that community which bears the secret of the meaning

---

[29] Newbigin, *Foolishness to the Greeks*, p. 36.
[30] Newbigin, *The Gospel in a Pluralist Society*, p. 213.
[31] See M. Polanyi, *Personal Knowledge: Towards a Post-Critical Philosophy* (London, Melbourne and Henley: Routledge & Kegan Paul, 1958).
[32] Newbigin, *The Gospel in a Pluralist Society*, p. 50.
[33] Ibid., p. 85.
[34] Newbigin, *The Open Secret*, p. 163. See also *Foolishness to the Greeks*, p. 124.
[35] Newbigin, *Foolishness to the Greeks*, p. 117.

of history through history'.[36] But, as Newbigin never tires of making clear, this is an election to service rather than privileged status.[37] Christians are called to be 'the bearers of the secret of his saving work for the sake of *all*'.[38] No limits must be set to God's saving grace!

II

Interpreting Newbigin's Theological Legacy

Newbigin argues his position with remorseless vigour and absolute conviction. He writes with passion and lucidity. But what is the legacy of his theology? And where in the legacy is our contemporary theological understanding hindered rather than helped?

Ecclesiology

At a time when the Western mainstream churches are in numerical decline, and when many congregations lack vitality and a clear sense of their *raison d'être*, it is pertinent that we take to heart Newbigin's ecclesiology.

THE MISSIONARY CHURCH

The following is a typical snapshot of Newbigin's ecclesial vision:

> The Church . . . has listened to the words 'Come unto me', but not listened to the words 'Go – and I am with you'. It has interpreted election as if it meant being chosen for special privilege in relation to God, instead of being chosen for special responsibility before God for other men. It has interpreted conversion as if it was simply a turning towards God for purposes of one's own private inner religious life, instead of seeing conversion as it is in the Bible, a turning towards God for the doing of his will in the secular world. It has understood itself more as an institution than as an exhibition. Its typical shape in the eyes of its own members as well as of those outside has been not a band of pilgrims who have heard the word 'Go', but a large and solid building which, at its best, can only say 'Come', and at its worst says, all too clearly, 'Stay away'.[39]

Running throughout Newbigin's ecclesiology is the missionary context which provides the church with its proper shape. Like David J. Bosch, Newbigin knew that 'Christianity is missionary by its very nature, or it denies its very *raison*

---

[36] Newbigin, *The Gospel in a Pluralist Society*, p. 77.
[37] See Ibid., pp. 80-88.
[38] Ibid., p. 86. (Italics mine).
[39] Newbigin, *Honest Religion for Secular Man*, pp. 101-102.

d'être'.[40] At a time when the word 'mission' has been stolen by the secular world to enable organisations have a clear understanding of what they stand for, it is somewhat ironic that contemporary congregations by and large seem to have lost a clear sense of why they exist and what they are here to do. Instead of displaying evidence of being a sign and sacrament of God's love for the world they have come to resemble inward-looking, self-serving groups.

Part of Newbigin's legacy is that he has provided a mission statement for congregations who have lost their way and largely forgotten that they are chosen and sent to re-present God's way to people beyond their fellowships. So, in forthright fashion, Newbigin reminds us that 'the Church is a movement launched into the life of the world to bear in its own life God's gift of peace for the life of the world', and therefore that 'it is sent . . . not only to proclaim the kingdom, but to bear in its own life the presence of the kingdom'.[41] The primary task of the Church is to engage in God's mission in, for and with the world. This means that 'the Church is not the source of the witness; rather, it is the locus of witness.'[42] Newbigin was as dismissive of Churches which totally involve themselves with this-worldly activities, as he was of those which exist solely for soul-saving. He believed that the Church's essential activity centred upon channeling God's redeeming and emancipating love to individuals and society. The Church, therefore, has been bequeathed an awesome task. What Jesus brought into the world was meant to continue through history in the shape of a community. The Church exists, therefore, to make history.[43]

Crucial to Newbigin's ecclesiology is the local congregation, the gathered out-cropping of the Church which, in its place and time, is called to be the sign and sacrament of God's reign over all things. When true to itself, the gathered Church 'derives its character not from its membership but from its Head, not from those who join it but from Him who calls it into being'.[44] But since, like individuals, the Church often falls short of its proper calling, Newbigin accepts that 'it is at once holy and sinful'[45] and, hence, *simul justus et peccator* (both justified and sinner).[46] He recognizes the divine vulnerability and risk involved in God choosing 'a sinful community..., a weak, divided, and unsuccessful community', to be the sign, embodiment and foretaste of the Kingdom.[47] And the church clearly has no grounds for boasting, since repeatedly she has failed to live up to her calling; yet she retains that great calling and continues to have

---

[40] D.J. Bosch, *Transforming Mission: Paradigm Shifts in Theology of Mission* (Maryknoll, New York: Orbis Books, 1991), p. 9.
[41] Newbigin, *The Open Secret*, p. 54.
[42] Newbigin, *The Gospel in a Pluralist Society*, p. 41.
[43] See Ibid., p. 131.
[44] J.E.L. Newbigin, *The Household of God: Lectures on the Nature of the Church* (London: SCM Press, 1953), pp. 27-28.
[45] Ibid., p. 56.
[46] Ibid., p. 29.
[47] Newbigin, *The Open Secret*, pp. 59-60.

responsibilities through her often weak local gatherings.

Newbigin stressed the importance of the local gathered church at precisely the time when, in Britain at least, the congregation is under great threat. In the era of 'believing without belonging',[48] placing our faith and hope in local congregations might seem akin to Jeremiah's mid-summer missionary madness in buying the field at Anathoth (Jer.32), but it is difficult to envisage a future for Christianity without the 'local...public and shared Christianity' which they represent.[49] In a way that Newbigin would have endorsed, Haddon Willmer has made an invigorating plea that the significance of the local congregation should not be underestimated. As he says, 'In an increasingly punitively minded culture, divided between self-affirming people and those who are "taken out of society", congregations are places where we learn and witness to the saving and fragile way of being our true selves, in confessing sin and living by undeserved gift.'[50] Nevertheless, congregations often are parochial places where the vitality of the world church hardly ever penetrates and a close group of like-minded people become isolated through their independency. It was to Newbigin's credit that he had the insight to recognize that a sound ecclesiology required not only a Protestant stress on the true church always being present in the local, covenanting community gathered around Word and Sacraments, but also the more Catholic emphases upon the church as a continuing historical institution. The idea that the church is a recurrently, repeated event constituted ever anew when local congregations assemble under Word and around the Table requires a further ecclesial vision which gives due attention to 'the continuing life of the Church as one fellowship binding the generations together in Christ'.[51] Newbigin's ecclesiology was commendably balanced, spanning different traditions and emphases in ecumenically helpful ways.

THE ECUMENICAL CHURCH

Newbigin's ecumenical convictions were central to his theological vision and rooted in his belief that a divided church cannot heal a divided world. In *The Household of God* he laid out a principle which he followed throughout his life: '...we cannot be [Christ's] ambassadors reconciling the world to God, if we have not ourselves been willing to be reconciled to one another'.[52] Everything hinges, of course, on what we mean by 'to be reconciled to one another'. Newbigin was forthright and clear: it meant visible unity. A divided church is 'a direct and public contradiction of the Gospel' and the substitution of 'some partial and sectional message' instead of 'the good news of the one final and

---

[48] See G. Davie, *Religion in Britain since 1945: Believing without Belonging* (Oxford, UK and Cambridge USA: Blackwell, 1994).

[49] See H. Willmer, 'The Collapse of Congregations', *Anvil*, 18, 4 (2001), pp. 258-59.

[50] Willmer, 'The Collapse of Congregations', p. 260.

[51] Newbigin, *The Household of God*, p. 50.

[52] Ibid., p. 18.

sufficient atoning act wrought in Christ for the whole human race'.[53]

The quest for church unity thus became a passion for Newbigin who argued that faithfulness to Christ required Christians to seek unity with each other. There can only ever be one body of Christians if the New Testament view of the church as 'the body of Christ' is taken with absolute seriousness. It is a matter of the greatest priority, therefore, that the church recovers its 'true nature and quality of...life as the visible fellowship of all who in every place call upon the name of the Lord Jesus'.[54] Newbigin was as unhappy about divided denominations as he was about models of church unity which remain content with the 'reconciled diversity' strategy of federalism.[55] Nevertheless, he did not strive for any bland, monochrome uniformity. The following statement, written before the era of inclusive language, is typical of Newbigin's position

> Properly speaking, the Church . . . should therefore have as much variety as the human race itself. Nothing human should be alien to it save sin. The very vastness of its diversity held together by the single fact of Christ's atonement for the whole human race should be the witness to the sufficiency of that atonement. It should confront man with no sectional or local society, no segregation of people having similar tastes and temperaments and traditions, but simply as the congregation of humanity redeemed, as the family to which every man rightly belongs and from which only sin can sever him.[56]

As 'a home for people of all nations and a sign of the unity of all' the church will only possess complete credibility when, amidst a healthy diversity, it speaks and acts in unison.[57] Newbigin knew that full well: 'Splintered, confused, and compromised, the church seldom sounds worth listening to'.[58] His ecumenical commitment arose from his missionary mandate.

THE VOCATION OF THE WHOLE PEOPLE OF GOD

Finally, Newbigin very helpfully saw the church's role as equipping its members for their vocations in society (Eph. 4: 12). He affirmed the laity, maintaining that it is the job of ministers to enable and empower lay-people in their responsibilities in and for society. He never lost sight of the fact that the primary missionary location is daily life. The emphasis in his ecclesiology upon the gathered church is matched therefore by an equal stress upon the dispersed church. Believers must be prepared to live as a Christian counter-culture in the secular world, making heard what they stand for publicly, and revealing a Christ-like disposition in their commitments and actions. This led Newbigin to

---

[53] Newbigin, *The Household of God*, pp. 149-50.
[54] Ibid., p. 107.
[55] See Newbigin, *Foolishness to the Greeks*, pp. 144-46.
[56] Newbigin, *A Faith for this One World?*, p. 82.
[57] Newbigin, *The Gospel in a Pluralist Society*, p. 124.
[58] Newbigin, *Truth to Tell*, p. 90.

a healthy view of lay-ministry, in general, and non-stipendiary ministry, in particular – 'exercised by men (*sic.*) who continued to fulfil their secular callings' not because there might be a shortage of paid ministers but 'out of respect to the missionary character of the Church'.[59] In a typically Reformed fashion, Newbigin consequently expected lay-people to have an uncommon degree of theological literacy[60] to equip them to fulfil their 'subversive' role as Christ's 'undercover agents' in society.[61] Meanwhile, Newbigin rightly bemoaned the way professional ministers are often prepared for their work, maintaining that it involves 'far too much training for the pastoral care of existing congregations' and too little orientation 'toward the missionary calling to claim the whole of public life for Christ and his kingdom'.[62] It would be interesting to know whether the more recent contextual approaches to ministerial preparation have adequately addressed his concerns.

Missiology

A further aspect of Newbigin's theological legacy is found in his missiological proposals. These cut across those approaches which appear modelled on commercial sales drives or military campaigns. In particular, he is sharply critical of the Pelagian tendency that regards conversion as a human achievement. A great deal of contemporary mission focuses so much on strategies, techniques and head-counting that Newbigin fears it is not sufficiently directed by 'the greatness and majesty and sufficiency of God'.[63] Authentic mission arises out of a spontaneous response of joy and gratitude for what God has achieved in the Christ event. At its heart is 'thanksgiving and praise',[64] a natural outpouring 'that cannot possibly be suppressed';[65] it is distorted when reduced to outreach activities aimed at prolonging the church's existence.[66] Not surprisingly, Newbigin provides us with a significant and perceptive critique of the Church Growth Movement.[67]

Central to Newbigin's missiology is the free and unpredictable activity of the Holy Spirit. It follows that the church must never suppose that it is the *agent* of mission. The church's responsibility is to tell the Christian story faithfully, forthrightly and attractively; whether people respond is out of its hands. As Newbigin insists, 'It is the Spirit who brings about conversion, the

---

[59] Newbigin, *Honest Religion for Secular Man*, p. 114.
[60] Newbigin, *Foolishness to the Greeks*, p. 143.
[61] Newbigin, *Truth to Tell*, pp. 82-83.
[62] Newbigin, *The Gospel in a Pluralist Society*, p. 231.
[63] Ibid., pp. 224, 243.
[64] Ibid., p. 127.
[65] Ibid., p. 116.
[66] Newbign, *The Open Secret*, p. 66.
[67] See Ibid., pp. 135-80.

Spirit who equips those who are called with the gifts needed for all the varied forms of ministry, and the Spirit who guides the church into all the truth.'[68] The individual who encounters the gospel must be allowed the opportunity to say, 'No!' Coercion corrupts the message it seeks to propagate; human glory then usurps mission's proper goal: the glory of God.[69]

Newbigin believes that mission is 'the entire task for which the Church is sent into the world'.[70] In so far as the church has been chosen to live out as well as tell the Christian story, mission involves both performance and declaration. It is dialogical in nature, thus carrying with it the likelihood that the missionary church may learn things from the culture within which it operates. It is even possible that the missionary encounter will enable the church to get a firmer grasp of the gospel's richness. So Newbigin wisely challenges the arrogance and dogmatism of many missionary approaches when he warns that 'mission will not only be a matter of preaching and teaching but also of learning'.[71] But however hard he tries to paper over the cracks opened up by some of the ruthless destruction of indigenous cultures by past missionary work, Newbigin on occasions still uses language which undermines the sensitive approach to mission he elsewhere advocates, e.g. 'the invading culture'[72] as well as 'assault' and 'warfare'.[73] 'Dialogue' or 'conversation' is a more helpful model for understanding mission.

Newbigin is at his best, though, when he defines 'the Christian mission' as 'an acting out of a fundamental belief and, at the same time, a process in which this belief is being constantly reconsidered in the light of the experience of acting it out in every sector of human affairs and in dialogue with every other pattern of thought by which men and women seek to make sense of their lives'.[74] But it is a moot point to what extent he is open in practice to genuine two-way conversation given the virtually non-negotiable understanding he has of Christian believing and his abhorrence of anything which even hints at syncretism. The sole reason why he seems to urge us to share the gospel in the language and idioms of our working context would appear to involve making its challenge to that context relevant. What he calls 'dialogue' often seems to be little more than monologue.

Newbigin's understanding of the church's mission contains three elements: bearing witness to Christ and possessing the Christ-like shape befitting the Christian counter-culture; corporate witness to society in service and evangelism; and the exercise by church members of their individual vocations

---

[68] Newbigin, *The Open Secret*, p. 146.
[69] Newbigin, *The Gospel in a Pluralist Society*, p. 180.
[70] Ibid., p. 121.
[71] Ibid., p. 118.
[72] Newbigin, *The Open Secret*, p. 166.
[73] Newbigin, *The Gospel in a Pluralist Society*, p. 238.
[74] Newbigin, *The Open Secret*, p. 31.

in society. It is a holistic view which helpfully holds together not only the individual and corporate dimensions of the Christian task but also the so-called 'horizontal' and 'vertical' planes of Christian discipleship. The contemporary church would be wise to use it as the yardstick by which to judge its own endeavours.

Epistemology

If the social and political dimension of individualism is what Francis Maude has described as 'weakest to the wall, law of the jungle, everyone for himself, no such thing as society',[75] its religious aspect involves the assumption that all religions are similar, culture-bound means by which people deal with their personal awareness of transcendence. As such, the various Faiths are equally valid, each putting forward claims granted truth status within their particular religious circle. But since religions deal solely with transcendence they should not be involved in public debates concerning the temporal affairs. The faith-claims of religion thus belong to the private rather than the public realm.

Newbigin's critique of the privatization of religion takes him back to Cartesian dualism and the bifurcation of reality into facts and values. While he hardly gives full credit for what this philosophical revolution bequeathed to the West, Newbigin correctly objects to religious claims being deposited in the private domain of values rather than the public arena of facts. Individualism's consignment of faith-claims and religious values to the private realm neither does justice to their metaphysical dimension nor to the way they claim universal intent

> The Church witnesses to that true end for which all creation and all human beings exist, the truth by which all alleged values are to be judged. And truth must be public truth, truth for all. A private truth for a limited circle of believers is no truth at all. Even the most devout faith will sooner or later falter and fail unless those who hold it are willing to bring it into public debate and to test it against experience in every area of life.[76]

In so far as Christianity makes universal claims in its proclamation of Jesus Christ as the Saviour of the world, and views the life, witness, death and resurrection of Jesus as having cosmic significance, Newbigin's opposition to Western society's demotion of religion to the world of opinion is valid and welcome.

It is very easy, though, to see why Western society wishes to consign religions to the private domain when we consider the damage they have wrought in the public sphere. Polly Toynbee, for example, not only thinks that we are often the victims of 'the over-valuation of religion', but she also

---

[75] *The Daily Telegraph*, 8 October 2002.
[76] Newbigin, *Foolishness to the Greeks*, p. 117.

maintains that 'religion is not nice, it kills: it is toxic in the places where people really believe it'.[77] Indeed, she passionately believes that 'religion belongs to the personal, never in the public sphere' and, on the basis of a horrendous bill of indictment, presses us to confront religion – the very opposite of Newbigin's strategy of confronting Western culture with the Christian gospel. Faced with such a powerful argument, Newbigin's commitment to 'going public' with Christianity will only be carried through credibly if we recognize the evils which have emanated from past missionary activity. While Newbigin correctly reminds Christianity's critics that the church is no different to individuals in being both justified as well as sinner this side of eternity, and is also right to point out that at its best the spread of Christianity brought with it recognizable benefits, we never really sense that he owned the less wholesome results of missionary endeavour and Christian activity. Three points emerge from this observation. First, Newbigin's argument concerning the public nature of the Christian gospel is in danger of becoming a fresh form of Christian imperialism. Secondly, in the midst of shocking historical evidence, all future Christian mission needs to start not only by recognizing its past errors and asking God's forgiveness for them but also with what Michael Taylor has called a 'degree of astonishment that, if the gospel is as strong as a prophet like Newbigin suggests, after two thousand years of missionary endeavour, after Christendom, the Enlightenment, and modernity, it still leaves a divided, violent, and ambiguous world at much the same moral and spiritual level as it was'.[78] If 'by your fruits you will be known' is as reliable a criterion for Christian adequacy as the Bible makes out, it could be that the roots of the West's current disillusionment with mainline Christianity have less to do with the atheistic machinations of Descartes and Enlightenment thinking but rather more to do with the gap which has opened up between theory and practice in Christianity. We must do justice to the crucial sense in which going public with Christianity is not just a declaratory but also a performatory matter. A recognition of the requirement 'to do the truth' is crucial in our society if those commentators are correct who tell us that contemporary people are not just looking for a rational case for believing so much as evidence that belief positively alters people's lives and leads to the world being a much better place. Thirdly, if our attempt to make the gospel public in our plural society is to gain a positive hearing, then it will necessitate what Lynne Price has called 'a more reciprocal, dialogical relationship with the life of the world'.[79] However much Newbigin claimed to be open to new truth and fresh insights,[80] his public utterances and many writings increasingly revealed an exceedingly dogmatic

---

[77] *The Guardian*, 6 September 2002.
[78] M. H. Taylor, 'Afterward' in Foust et. al. (eds), *A Scandalous Prophet*, p. 242.
[79] L. Price, 'Churches and Postmodernity: Opportunity for an Attitude Shift' in Foust et. al. (eds), A *Scandalous Prophet*, p. 109.
[80] See Newbigin, *Truth to Tell*, pp. 34-35.

disposition. Indeed, he often showed precious little evidence of his position being open to modification in any way.

Newbigin adopts the Augustinian slogan *'credo ut intelligam'* ('I believe in order to understand') and follows Polanyi's thesis that all knowledge is irreducibly personal, to argue that the starting point of all enquiry lies in affirmations which cannot be questioned but must be held in faith. All investigation has to start on the basis of things which have to be taken as read. It follows that our critical facilities are not primary. They only ever become active on the basis of what we hold on trust: 'What is primary is the act of attending and receiving, and this is an action of faith'.[81] As far as Newbigin is concerned, therefore, '...the active principle in the advance of knowledge...is faith'.[82] In the process of knowing validation only comes at the end, so Newbigin's position not only involves the claim that 'our most fundamental beliefs cannot be demonstrated but are held by faith'[83] but also necessitates a direct recourse to a kind of eschatological verification when those beliefs are questioned. Validation, he tells us, can only ever arrive 'as the outcome of this process of exploration'.[84] Needless to say, Newbigin is confident that the Christian 'fiduciary framework' which is the basis for the Christian pilgrimage will not be found wanting: '...we expect to find, and we do find, that the initial faith is confirmed, strengthened, and enlarged as we go on through life'.[85]

But what is the content of the fiduciary framework which Newbigin invites us to take on trust? He is quite clear that it is not 'a set of beliefs that arise, or could arise, from empirical observation of the whole human experience'.[86] What has to be taken on faith is 'the announcement of a name and a fact that offer the starting point for a new and life-long enterprise of understanding and coping with experience',[87] nothing less than 'the revelation of God in Jesus Christ'.[88] Christian theology can proceed rationally then only on the basis that this revelation is received in faith. It follows that 'commitment to Jesus Christ' is Newbigin's 'point of entry' into a theological investigation.[89]

Few would want to deny that all investigations proceed upon the basis of things taken for granted. It is rather difficult, for example, to conceive how science could operate without the prior assumption that the universe is both contingent and rational. However, Newbigin puts matters on a somewhat different plane when he argues that people should take as read the fiduciary

---

[81] Newbigin, *The Other Side of 1984*, p. 20.
[82] Newbigin, *Honest Religion for Secular Man*, p. 84. See also Newbigin, *The Gospel in a Pluralist Society*, p. 243.
[83] Newbigin, *The Other Side of 1984*, p. 27
[84] Newbigin, *The Finality of Christ*, p. 63.
[85] Newbigin, *The Gospel in a Pluralist Society*, p. 243.
[86] Newbigin, *Foolishness to the Greeks*, p. 148
[87] Ibid., p. 148.
[88] Newbigin, *The Finality of Christ*, p. 22.
[89] Ibid., p. 21.

framework of the church, making that the lens through which to observe and understand reality. This quickly becomes obvious when one compares the content of what he regards as the given fiduciary framework with, say, the 'faith' that is presupposed by all scientific endeavour. The following is a list of beliefs which Newbigin would have us accept on the basis of the testimony of others: (i) Jesus as the Word of God incarnate;[90] (ii) the bodily resurrection of Jesus from the tomb on the first Easter morning;[91] (iii) the Ascension;[92] (iv) the Second Coming;[93] (v) an objective atonement wrought in the Cross of Christ;[94] (vi) a consummation of history which reveals the proper meaning of salvation in history's goal[95] and will involve the Millennium;[96] and by no means least (vii) the doctrine of the Trinity.[97] In other words, Newbigin expects people to take as given or accept in faith just about the entire pattern of orthodox Christian believing. That particular expectation is of a different order, say, to the scientists' trust in the contingency and rationality of the universe. It involves accepting several doctrines which, on reasonable grounds, other Christians have decided to jettison. Newbigin's strategy thus turns out to be little less than putting his own chosen understanding of the content of Christian believing beyond debate. In spite of all his talk about processes of investigation or journeys of exploration his theology is rooted in rather take it or leave it dogmas.

The question thus arises concerning the grounds that people have for adopting the Christian fiduciary framework. Many of the beliefs Newbigin views as essential 'givens' only ought to be accepted after reasonable consideration has been given to them. What has happened is that, conveniently

---

[90] See Newbigin, *The Household of God*, p. 113; Newbigin, *The Open Secret*, p. 17; and Newbigin, *Foolishness to the Greeks*, p. 90.

[91] Time and again, Newbigin asserts belief in the empty tomb as the fulcrum of the Christian world-view. See Newbigin, *The Household of God*, pp .114, 119, 136; Newbigin, *A Faith for this One World?*, pp. 44, 56-63; Newbigin, *The Gospel in a Pluralist Society*, pp. 11-12 , 108; Newbigin, *Truth to Tell*, pp. 10-11; and Newbigin, *Proper Confidence*, p. 77.

[92] Newbigin, *The Household of God*, p. 114.

[93] Newbigin opines that no theology which is bound to the Scriptures and the Creeds can formally deny faith in Christ's coming again. See Newbigin, *The Household of God*, pp. 82, 126, 129-134; and Newbigin, *The Gospel in a Pluralist Society*, pp. 102, 121.

[94] See Newbigin, *The Household of God*, pp. 115-118, 150; Newbigin, *A Faith for this One World?*, pp. 54, 70-71; Newbigin, *The Open Secret*, pp. 27, 56; and Newbigin, *Foolishness to the Greeks*, pp.123, 126.

[95] See Newbigin, *The Household of God*, p. 137; Newbigin, *The Finality of Christ*, pp. 60-61; Newbigin, *The Open Secret*, pp. 118-119; and Newbigin, *The Gospel in a Pluralist Society*, pp.87, 101, 110.

[96] See Newbigin, *The Finality of Christ*, p. 86

[97] See Newbigin, *The Open Secret*, pp. 28-30; Newbigin, *Foolishness to the Greeks*, p. 90; and Newbigin, *Truth to Tell*, p. 17.

for his theological methodology, Newbigin has turned Polanyi's understanding of faith (*viz* accepted understandings that constitute what he calls 'tacit' knowing) into his particular biblical understanding of faith. As Thomas F. Foust has argued, faith thus becomes 'a misnomer', since it means different things for Polanyi and Newbigin.[98] Nor will it do for Newbigin to make out that Augustine is the out and out fideist he would like him to be. Foust continues

> ...not only is there difficulty between Polanyi's and Newbigin's concepts of faith, but Newbigin and Polanyi are also presenting an incomplete understanding of Augustine on this point. Augustine did not assert that there is no knowledge without faith. He held that a certain amount of rational evidence for Christ is necessary before one believes, but after one believes it, one can go on to find new reasons to believe. Augustine is a moderate fideist and not a fideist as Newbigin and Polanyi suggest.[99]

In short, Newbigin's view is based upon a significant misunderstanding of Augustine, an error shared by Michael Polanyi, the philosopher of science to whom Newbigin turns when advocating his brand of fideism. Reason has a more fundamental part to play in Christian theology than Newbigin ever allows. While, to some extent, all verification must look to the end of the adventure of knowledge, waiting the time when any falsification of our ideas and theories has finally emerged, it is important that our substantive ideas and theories are based upon more than blind faith at the outset of our explorations. Otherwise we provide folk with a license to believe anything, however fanciful it might be.

Newbigin's confidence in Christianity's fiduciary framework was ultimately unshakeable – even if in a plural world we might have expected Christian attitudes to involve what Price calls 'faithful uncertainty'[100] or David Tracy describes as knowing with 'relative adequacy'.[101] Such intellectual hesitancy was dismissed by Newbigin since, for him, it represented the weakness of liberal theology: 'The mind open at both ends admits everything but finally holds nothing.'[102] But living in a dialogical engagement with fellow Christians and those of other Faiths or none does not necessitate total agnosticism. Contrary to Newbigin's fears, '...a pluralist or relativist...can have firm

---

[98] See T.F. Foust, 'Lesslie Newbigin's Epistemology: A Duel Discourse?' in Foust et. al. (eds), *A Scandalous Prophet*, p.155.

[99] See Foust, 'Lesslie Newbigin's Epistemology: A Duel Discourse?' in Foust et. al. (eds), *A Scandalous Prophet*, p. 156-157.

[100] Price, 'Churches and Postmodernity: Opportunity for an Attitude Shift' in Foust et. al. (eds), *A Scandalous Prophet*, p. 110.

[101] D. Tracy, *Plurality and Ambiguity: Hermeneutics, Religion and Hope* (London: SCM Press, 1987), p. 28.

[102] J.E.L. Newbigin, '"A Decent Debate about Doctrine": Faith, Doubt and Certainty'. Pamphlet. (Plymouth, Devon: GEAR, 1993), p. 12.

The Theological Legacy of Lesslie Newbigin

convictions and commitment;' hence everything is never up for grabs.[103]

Gospel and Culture

A fourth area in Newbigin's theological legacy concerns the impetus he provided for a radical discussion concerning the relationship between the Christian gospel and contemporary Western culture.

THE CURSE OF ENLIGHTENMENT?

Newbigin's analysis of Western culture is overtly simplistic, arguably based rather more upon his prior theological predilection than a convincing understanding of the empirical realities on display. His depiction of the West, shaped has it has been by the Enlightenment and moving through its modernist to postmodernist phase, is nothing short of apocalyptic. He argues that there has been a 'collapse of confidence in the great project of the Enlightenment'.[104] As early as *A Faith for this One World* he was announcing the disintegration of Western culture,[105] a theme that became ever more pronounced in his later writings.[106] Newbigin believed that there are signs that Western culture is heading for 'impending death';[107] he observed what he believed was 'systematic scepticism';[108] and he concurred with a Chinese philosopher who could only find 'bleak nihilism and hopelessness . . . reflected in the literature, art, and drama of our society'.[109] Words like 'relativism', 'pluralism', 'individualism' and 'narcissism' were regularly used by Newbigin to describe Western culture's plight as he advanced a case for a Christian missionary encounter with the West. He believed that we have lost a sense of direction, a pattern of purposefulness which can only be provided by Christian eschatology. A utilitarian outlook has now largely robbed the West of any worthwhile teleological frame of reference,[110] and only hope generated by the fact that 'the crucified Lord of history has risen from the dead and will come in glory' will restore confidence to our culture.[111] As he put in *The Household of God*

> Hope in the Christian sense is no mere human longing for an uncertain future. It is rooted in the life of God himself and founded on His own promises. It is the echo in our hearts, given to us by the Spirit, of that mind which was in Jesus who for

---

[103] Taylor, 'Postscript' in Foust et. al. (eds) *A Scandalous Prophet*, p. 241.
[104] Newbigin, *Proper Confidence*, p. 33.
[105] Newbigin, *A Faith for this One World?*, p. 15.
[106] See Newbigin, *Proper Confidence*, p. 102.
[107] Ibid., p. 35.
[108] Newbigin, *The Gospel in a Pluralist Society*, p. 28. See also Newbigin, *Proper Confidence*, p. 76.
[109] Newbigin, *Proper Confidence*, p. 47.
[110] Newbigin, *Foolishness to the Greeks*, pp. 34-41.
[111] Newbigin, *The Gospel in a Pluralist Society*, p. 101.

the joy that was set before Him endured the Cross, despising the shame. It is an anchor of the soul, a hope sure and steadfast and entering into that which is within the veil. The future is really future, and we long for it.[112]

But, given Newbigin's theological presuppositions, *whatever* world we might happen to live in this side of eternity is bound to 'lieth in the evil one'.[113]

The impression sometimes given is that Newbigin, a saintly and theologically wise Bishop, returned to Britain upon his retirement, where, reading 'the signs of the times', he prophetically announced that Western culture was terminally ill on the basis of what he saw. But that might claim too much for the man's insight, while it hardly does justice to the way Newbigin's theological standpoint led him to a pejorative view of the empirical evidence. One of the major reasons why he came to such a negative view about Western culture lies in the theology clearly displayed in *The Household of God* (1953). This thinking provides him with the lens with which to view the British scene. He adheres to the Augustinian – Calvinist – Barthian wing of Reformed theology, thus holding a perception of salvation rooted in the world's absolute need for an atoning act by which God can forgive a fallen race. Great stress in this theological scheme is placed on the total depravity of human beings, with a resulting scepticism about all human worth and achievement becoming rather inevitable. 'Hope', in this outlook, is essentially otherworldly since nothing in this world is of *real* worth. But what if we use as our lens another theological outlook, one which has its origins in Irenaeus (and, interestingly, partly shaped the theological outlook of John Oman, Newbigin's College Principal and one of his theological teachers)? What if the human predicament is not so much a fall from perfection to a state of alienation from God but is alternatively conceived as being concerned with the ups and downs of immature people, who born in 'the image of God' are on a journey towards becoming in 'the likeness of God'? Salvation could then be envisaged as a gradual transformation of life which can occur when people make an ongoing response to God's graciousness towards them. Lest this alternative view is seen to involve a doctrine of necessary and inevitable progress for individuals and the human race, we ought to emphasise that on the earthly pilgrimage we can process to hell as much as to heaven. Affirming the possibilities of being human and the value of the temporal order need not entail going soft on sin. But the point to be made is this: Newbigin's understanding of Western culture is arguably largely dependent upon the theological framework he brings with him. Adopt a different framework and one need not arrive at the unnecessarily pessimistic and apocalyptic assessment of modern culture for which Newbigin became somewhat notorious.

Newbigin's obituary note on Western culture seems somewhat premature,

---

[112] Newbigin, *The Household of God*, pp. 122-23.

[113] Ibid., p. 79.

even after the world-shaping implications of 9/11. Was he hankering after a bygone age which was actually less wholesome than is usually painted? Perhaps, unwittingly, he never totally liberated himself from the Christendom mentality which fuelled so much missionary activity? We will perhaps never fully know why he presented such an unnuanced account of Western culture and left himself open to criticism by those who came to regard him as a backwoodsman intent on affirming a plausibility structure that had its less wholesome elements and turned out to be oppressive for millions. I read The *Other Side of 1984* in one sitting after visiting two church members in hospital. Both had one thing in common, namely, they were still alive due to the medical science made possible by the same Enlightenment so savagely under attack in what I was reading. In fairness to Newbigin, he was prepared to acknowledge our indebtedness to the fruits of the Enlightenment.[114] He gratuitously admits that 'the "light" in the Enlightenment was real light'[115] as well as opines that 'no one, surely, can fail to acknowledge with gratitude the achievements of this period of human history'.[116] He also displays a willingness to acknowledge that God may actually be at work in 'secularist and anti-religious movements'.[117] But it is actually very difficult to believe all this when wading through his exceedingly anti-Enlightenment and anti-science and technology polemics. Whatever happened to the even-handedness which accepted that 'the triumph of secularization is certainly not the triumph of the Kingdom of God; but neither is it simply the work of the devil'?[118] Only a very narrow and otherworldly eschatology can prompt the following claim: 'Almost everything in the 'plausibility structure' which is the habitation of our society seems to contradict . . . Christian hope.'[119] Perhaps the qualifier 'almost' provides some room to contain the celebrations of my two church members concerning the success of their medical treatment? Be that as it may, Newbigin repeatedly failed to recognize fully that however much the Enlightenment (and, hence, science) is responsible for many of our contemporary ills, we will most certainly need it to provide some of the resources to achieve their healing.

Contrary to Newbigin, the ethos ushered in by the Enlightenment still has a great deal of life in it. As Michael Goheen has suggested, its view of freedom is a gain that must not be lost – although it is not scriptural.[120] Far from being a 'wicked witch' seeking to undermine Christianity an argument can be put forward to suggest the reverse. Andrew Walls, for example, maintains that

---

[114] Newbigin, *The Other Side of 1984*, p. 16.

[115] Newbigin, *Foolishness to the Greeks*, p. 43.

[116] Newbigin, *The Gospel in a Pluralist Society*, p. 223.

[117] Newbigin, *A Faith for this One World*, p. 46.

[118] Newbigin, *Honest Religion for Secular Man*, p. 29.

[119] Newbigin, *The Gospel in a Pluralist Society*, p. 232.

[120] M. Goheen, 'The Missional Calling of Believers in the World: Lesslie Newbigin's Contribution' in Foust et. al. (eds), *A Scandalous Prophet*, p. 48.

'there was a Christian appropriation of the Enlightenment which was not all a betrayal of Christian faith'.[121] The Enlightenment actually provided the 'world' in which Western Christianity became indigenized, thereby enabling Christianity to be credible in that world. While Newbigin untiringly insisted that theology must be appropriate to the biblical story, he was opposed to finding the kind of rapprochement with culture that often enables the gospel to be heard credibly. Rather ironically, it is only through the very process of syncretism he loathed that Christianity has repeatedly re-invented itself and thus remained alive.

III

Conclusion

The purpose of this essay has been to explore the theological legacy that Lesslie Newbigin has bequeathed to us. Whichever way readers feel the balance of judgement needs to fall on Newbigin's theology, it is a sign of a thinker's greatness that they leave behind a significant debate about issues that were a lifetime concern. Whether we are one of Lesslie's doting disciples or a member of the extensive group of his critical interlocutors really does not ultimately matter. The *real* Newbigin legacy has been that he has made us all think theologically about confessing Christ in the modern world. For that we can be most thankful.

---

[121] A. Walls, 'Enlightenment, Postmodernity and Mission' in Foust et. al. (eds), *A Scandalous Prophet*, p. 158.

CHAPTER 7

Olive Wyon: Prayer, Vocation and Ecumenism

David Cornick

Few people now know the name of Olive Wyon (1881-1996). She was born in 1881, in the heartlands of Hampstead Congregationalism. Olive's father, Alan (1843-1907) 'Her Majesty's Chief Engraver of Seals',[1] attended Lyndhurst Road Congregational Church. Olive, her brother Alan, and her sisters Dorothy and Hetty were all brought up at Lyndhurst Road. The family was determinedly Congregational. Alfred, brother of the senior Alan, was married to Kate Hitchcock, whose half-sister Helen married Sir George Williams, the founder of the YMCA, and a network of cousinhoods reveal many links to the London Missionary Society. The Wyons were well-connected.[2]

Her sister Dorothy (1888-1970) trained as a missionary at Carey Hall and served as a missionary in China before returning to Cheshunt College in 1948, eventually ministering at Duxford and Little Shelford, villages to the south of Cambridge.[3] It was unsurprising, therefore, that Olive too felt the call. She applied to the London Missionary Society in 1904, and with their encouragement went to study at the United Free Church Missionary Institute in Edinburgh. This was to become St Colm's Missionary College, and Olive was to serve with distinction as its Principal between 1951-54. Dorothy was the Congregational sheet-anchor of the family. Brother Alan, a seriously good professional sculptor, became an Anglican, and eventually vicar of Newlyn, via membership of W.E.Orchard's King's Weigh House. Sister Hetty ended her days as an Anglican deaconess in Chatham, and Olive herself was a citizen of the world church.

Ill-health, a recurring reality in her life, prevented her finishing her missionary training. She went instead to Switzerland for nine months of recuperation. Already a skilled linguist, she perfected her French and German

---

[1] Naomi Oates and Jean Foster, *Olive Wyon, D.D. 1881-1966. A Chronicle* (privately printed for St Colm's by J. & G. Innes, Cupar, Fife nd).
[2] I am grateful to Professor Clyde Binfield for this information, letter 14.10.2003.
[3] Information from Elaine Kaye, letter 1.6.2001.

there and produced her first translation, of Paul Sieppel's *Life of Adele Kamm* (1910). In 1908 she joined the staff of the Birmingham YMCA as Assistant Warden, and two years later went to Woodbrooke, the Quaker foundation at Selly Oak, to study theology. She then worked for the Friends amongst the Bretons and with students in Geneva before returning to England when war broke out in 1914. After the war she joined the World Dominion Press under J.H. Oldham, and that opened doors for her into the wider ecumenical world. She became Secretary to the World Dominion Prayer Fellowship in 1925. Her life was spent in a variety of posts within the ecumenical movement and the world church, and she rejoiced in the enrichment which this brought her. She was deeply involved in the heady early days of planning for and creating the World Council of Churches, and was on the administrative staff of J.H. Oldham's Edinburgh House office in the build-up to the 1937 world conference on 'Church, Community and State' in Oxford.[4] She attended the 1948 Amsterdam Assembly of the World Council as a delegate of the Presbyterian Church of England.

However, her reputation, and such financial stability as she enjoyed came from her remarkable work as a translator, and later as a writer on spirituality. Visser't Hooft judged her translation of Ernst Troeltsch's *Social Teaching of the Christian Churches* (1929) as 'one of the most difficult translations ever made'. Emil Brunner used to say his theology was better in her English than his German.[5] The University of Aberdeen honoured her work as a translator with the award of a D.D.

She travelled the world, but Geneva made a great impression on her. She was particularly influenced by her contact with the Community of Grandchamp, founded by a group of Reformed women in 1931 as a centre for prayer, silence and meditation, but which developed into a Women's Religious Order that worshipped according to the Taizé Office. That experience convinced her of the value of Christian community where '…men and women find each other in Christ and begin to pray and work as never before for the extension of the spirit of unity.'[6] She valued her Reformed roots deeply, but they rooted her in Scripture and therefore in the experience of all Christians, and she drank deeply and with delight from other wells. It is that combination of roots and generous openness that make her still a compelling guide to the spiritual life. We will consider three dimensions of her exploration of prayer - its relation to Scripture, to vocation, and to ecumenism.

The School of Prayer was published in 1943, so it is unsurprising that Wyon

---

[4] Keith Clements, *Faith on the Frontier: A Life of J.H. Oldham* (Edinburgh: T & T Clark, 1999), p. 311. She is also in the photograph of the preparatory group meeting at Bishopthorpe on p. 323, standing next to Reinhold Niebuhr.
[5] This paragraph relies on Oates and Foster, Chronicle, pp. 1-17.
[6] Stuart Louden, 'Wyon, Olive' in Gordon Wakefield ed., *A Dictionary of Christian Spirituality* (London: SCM Press, 1983).

begins her exploration of the relationship between prayer and Scripture with the Barmen Declaration - 'The Bible deals with God, and with nothing apart from God. Whoever seeks God in the Bible will find God there; for God comes to seek and find us in His Word...'[7] That is the heart of the relationship between the Bible and prayer. It has been the place of encounter between God and 'millions' of people. Being alone with Scripture and taking it seriously is a dangerous business, for we meet with Christ there. In his light we find ourselves judged and can 'suddenly we find that Christ steps out of the pages and confronts us with an absolute demand'. Being alone with the Bible means risking a revolution in one's life. That sounds austere and frightening, but judgement is merely the obverse of salvation; so Scripture also leads us to a knowledge of the trustworthiness of God, of forgiveness and mercy and 'infinite support'. Scripture is the '...springboard from which we may dive into the fathomless ocean of the love of God.'

Her prescription for meeting God in Scripture is uncomplicated and sensible. She echoes Richard Baxter's advice, 'Get thy heart as clear from the world as thou canst. Wholly lay by the thoughts of thy business, troubles, enjoyments, and everything that may take up any room in thy heart. Get it as empty as thou possibly canst, that it may be the more capable of being filled with God.' Quietness of soul and concentration should be followed by a variety of ways of encountering the text itself. This is not Bible study surrounded by commentaries and textbooks, but a gentle, expectant relationship with the Word of God. She recommends a variety of well-known techniques. Let one verse be yours for the day - learn it, repeat, let it roll around your mind. Or read slowly until a word or a phrase hits you. Or paraphrase what you have read. Or, using a concordance, follow a theme like God's will, or God's call to various characters in the Bible. Then she moves on to a consideration of the methods of meditation on Scripture - living in and with an incident in the gospel, trying to live in the minds of each of the characters, then writing down what it teaches about God, the self and God's will. An alternative is to take a psalm, meditate on the situation that produced it, and turn that into a prayer.[8]

However, it is in the Lord's Prayer that she finds the model of all prayer: 'Christ teaches us, in this wonderful guide to prayer, that the object of prayer is that God's will should be done, in and through and by us. GOD comes first. He is the supreme Object; His Name, His Character, His Glory, His Kingdom, His Will: for this we are to pray. Sinful, ignorant, imperfect as we are, He yet tells us that God is waiting to use us.'[9]

Prayer and the will of God are inseparable for Wyon. The end result of prayer is not self-satisfaction, but union with God. She is impeccably Reformed in her understanding of how the will of God can be discerned. The study of

---

[7] Olive Wyon, *The School of Prayer* (London: SCM, 1943), p. 75.
[8] All quotations from Wyon, *School of Prayer*, pp. 75-85.
[9] Ibid., p. 20.

Scripture reveals that it is God's will for men and women to be in a relationship with him, living as his children '...forgiven, reconciled, trustful, courageous in the face of every possible temptation to be the opposite.'[10] The focus of that community is the church, which nurtures vocation. The tragedy of modern 'civilisation' is that vocation has become an empty word. Recovery of the sense of call and obedience (her variation on the theme of election), is central to a healthy spiritual life. That means shifting our focus from ourselves (the most prevalent form of idolatry) to God, and learning to let go. 'A girl of nineteen once said to me: "I am trying to find where I can use my influence best!" "*My* influence...." "*My* gifts...:" we have only to repeat these short phrases to see what is wrong. Such a habit (she continues wryly) is particularly common amongst "intellectuals".' Her remedy is the life of prayer, for it is those who habitually practice the presence of God who will be most capable of discerning his will.

Wyon found de Caussade's sacrament of the present moment (waiting on and co-operating with God moment by moment) deeply appealing, and quotes him with alacrity. Christians should have but one desire, '...always to have our eyes fixed upon the Master, to whom we have given ourselves, and to be unceasingly upon the alert to divine and understand His will and carry it out immediately.'[11] God, she suggests, guides people in different ways, for individuals have different temperaments and psychologies. She illustrates this from Quaker history. Stephen Grellet, a French aristocrat who fled to America during the revolution and became a Friend, was continually aware of the prompting of God. He knew the hand of God upon his life, leading him to particular individuals at vital moments in their lives. He speaks continually of being 'sent' - and one of the people to whom he was 'sent' was Elizabeth Fry. Grellet went to see her after he had visited Newgate prison and asked her if she could provide some clothes for the babies of the women prisoners. Elizabeth, a practical, pragmatic woman knew nothing in her own life of such supernatural promptings, yet her devotion to God's will shone through her selfless work in prison reform. What matters, Wyon concludes, is hearts set on obedience to God's will. That is vocation.

The will of God is known in the rule of life - love God and your neighbour as yourself. It is known in vocation, in the special calling and leading, but more importantly and profoundly, 'God makes His will known to us through the things that happen every day.' What follows is her own profound exploration of the sacrament of the present moment. We receive God in all of life's encounters. The duties that face us, the trials to be endured, the joys to be delighted in, are all sacraments. God offers himself to us in each moment. Understanding life like this means that even dealing with evil and sin can becomes ways of '...releas[ing] the power of Christ into the life of the world.'

---

[10] Ibid., p. 31.
[11] Ibid., pp. 32-33.

And she offers the model of Jesus walking through the crowds, dealing with the heat, hassle and aggravation, all the time with the word or touch of healing for the hurt and excluded. Doing God's will in the present moment doesn't mean that we can see the way ahead at all clearly. Wyon resorts to another of her favourite guides, Dom John Chapman, Abbot of Downside

> One lives in perpetual doubt and ignorance what God's will is going to be, but not what it is *at this individual moment*: that we always know *because it is*. Therefore the whole point of the 'sacrament of the present moment' is that it is a (covering yet revealing) sacrament; it is God's action, God's will or 'it is God'. All my duty is to keep in touch with Him as this moment passes into the next. My obvious duty may be *at this moment* to consider what comes next - and not to know.[12]

One of the preconditions of being human is that the future is unknown. All we can do is abandon ourselves to God. The demands of such a life-style, says Wyon, are balanced by a sense of expansion and relief, for it is the way of love, the true way of being human. 'To live in quiet dependence upon God, finding him in every person who comes across our path, in every experience, will gradually impart to our lives a strange unconscious power.' That power is God turning all things to good, to quote de Caussade again, 'Your sufferings, your actions, your attractions, are the species within which God gives you Himself.' The world needs vocation.

That vocation was ecumenical for Olive Wyon. She was a woman of the world church who sought the wholeness of Christ through her encounters with Christians of all denominations. She drank deeply and joyfully of the living Christ from countless sources. *The School of Prayer* shows her appreciation of her own Reformed roots - she has read Bunyan and Anderson Scott and Maritain, but she rejoices too in the sense of God that breathes through the Anglican and Roman traditions. So it is that John Donne, Jeremy Taylor, William Temple and Evelyn Underhill sit happily alongside St Teresa, St John of the Cross, von Hügel, Cuthbert Butler and Dom John Chapman. Her range of reference is prodigious, and her sense of delight in belonging to such a large, varied Christian family almost tangible. Prayer, she knows, although it may be solitary, is never individualistic, for it is prayer '...in and with and for the Church, the "blessed company of all faithful people."'[13]

Prayer draws us out of ourselves into the worship and prayer of the whole Christian family for the whole family of humanity. Prayer is an expression of a unity which already exists in Christ, for prayer is a sharing in the life of the one Christ in the power of the Spirit. She understands that unity as focused in the eucharist, and sees that as the reality which judges the divisive disunity of the church. She has a profound sense of the vocation of the church: 'The world is

---

[12] Wyon, *School of Prayer*, pp. 39-40, quoting *The Spiritual Letters*, p. 83.
[13] Wyon, *School of Prayer*, p. 120.

waiting for a "revelation" of God in community. The church is called to be this living community, in which all barriers between man and man, class and class, race and race, are down for ever.' That, she rightly comments, is not something which we can achieve. It must be the work of God. She was writing during wartime, yet also in the childhood of world ecumenism when all seemed possible, and she pointed with excitement to the experience of the Week of Prayer for Christian Unity in Lyons in 1939 in bringing Protestants and Catholics together in prayer. She saw a close connection between the quest for unity and the struggle for justice because the love of Christ which draws the people of God towards unity moves us 'to an ever more urgent desire for the righting of human wrongs.'[14] It was, indeed it still is, a compelling vision. On it, she was bold enough to conclude, rests the hope of our world.

'Prayer', said P. T. Forsyth, 'is a gift and sacrifice that God makes…In prayer we go to God, in Sacrament He comes to us.'[15] It was apt then, that towards the end of her career at St Colm's, Olive Wyon should balance her books on prayer with *The Altar Fire: Reflections on the Sacrament of the Eucharist*. It is a beautiful little study. Her starting point is, as ever, thoroughly Reformed

> …the service begins with the revealed Word. That is: the first note struck in this rite is not the need of the worshippers, but the fact of revelation. From the very first the Christian Church realised that all worship must begin with God Transcendent. It is from such a God that we receive the revelation of His Being and His purpose. We begin with God, the high and Holy One, 'who inhabiteth eternity'. We listen, first of all, to His Word.[16]

Yet, she is deeply sensitive to the fact that the eucharist predates the earliest New Testament writings by at least twenty years, that in a sense the eucharistic tradition defines what the church is. She picks her way sure-footedly through contemporary liturgical scholarship, relying (as did all) on Gregory Dix's magisterial *The shape of the liturgy*. She also showed particular fondness for her Anglican friend Evelyn Underhill's wonderful book *Worship*, whose six-fold analysis of the eucharist she adopts as the framework for her study: adoration and thanksgiving, memorial of the passion, sacrificial centre, royal priesthood, heavenly food and the mystery of the Presence.

Wyon re-told the story of the old Presbyterian scholar who was often afflicted with doubts about whether he was worthy to receive communion. One Sunday as he sat in his pew worrying about this, he noticed a young girl sitting nearby who was weeping bitterly, and he saw that she hesitated to take the

---

[14] Ibid., p. 122.
[15] Olive Wyon, *The Altar Fire: Reflections on the Sacrament of the Eucharist* (London: SCM Press, 1954), p. 18, quoting P. T. Forsyth, *The Church and the Sacraments*, pp. 224-25.
[16] Wyon, *Altar Fire*, p. 24.

bread as the elder offered the plate. He leant forward, his own scruples forgotten, 'Take it! Take it!' he whispered, 'it's for sinners.' It is a story that deserves re-telling, for the wonder of the eucharist is precisely that. It can never be about our worthiness. It can only ever be about God's grace and love, about God's reaching out to us. Adoration and thanksgiving have their roots there, in the gratitude of forgiven, renewed people who come time and again to the table.

The second element, memorial, is one which has received honour in the Reformed tradition. The reformation of worship in the sixteenth century was about recreating the Lord's Supper as it is recorded in the New Testament writings, and the institution narrative became the warrant for what the churches did. It was because the Lord commanded, 'Do this in remembrance of me', that the Lord's Supper was celebrated. It was, Zwingli reminded the people of Zurich, a simple memorial. However, as Wyon noted, 'memorial' and 'remembrance' don't fully capture the meaning of the Greek word *anamnesis*. There is a certain emptiness about the English words. They suggest something past and gone. The Greek is rather about a 'calling to mind' or a 're-calling' - that is to say, it is about making present again. *Anamnesis* is about the past becoming present again and affecting us. It is a 'telescoping' of time, bringing together the historical fact of Jesus' death and the reality of Christ's sacrifice – '…not as the pathetic death of a young prophet, hounded down by his enemies, but as the mighty act of redemption, in which evil has been conquered and the way to God thrown open for all humanity, past, present and to come.'[17] The Lord's Supper is grounded in history, yet takes us far beyond history into the very workings of Christ in fulfilling God's purposes for the universe.

God and humanity meet at the table of the Lord in Olive Wyon's theology, and that leads her into reflections on the nature of sacrifice. In a detailed exposition of the Lord's words in the Passion story she draws out the way in which he willingly laid down his life, obedient always to the Father's will, caught up in the awesome dynamics of his Messianic devotion. What, she asks, compelled him to this

> It was love - love only - and love to the uttermost. His purpose was pure love, the profound desire and purpose to heal the broken relationship between God and man - broken by man's sin - by the breaking of His Body and the offering of Himself in sacrifice. His love is so great that it goes to the extreme of identification with sinful man. Never did His love and sacrifice reach greater heights than when He cried out on the Cross in the darkness, 'My God, my God, why hast thou forsaken Me?' Yet the cloud passed, and in His last words at the very end there is a cry of triumphant achievement: 'It is completed!....Father, into Thy Hands I commend My spirit'.[18]

---

[17] Wyon, *Altar Fire*, p. 37.
[18] Ibid., pp. 46-47.

The meaning of the cross and the meaning of the eucharist are bound up together. God's acceptance of Christ's self-offering on the cross is the defeat of all the powers of darkness and death, the victory of Easter and the empty tomb, and (as the author of the epistle to the Hebrews so brilliantly expounds it) Christ our High Priest enters heaven for us. She explores that thought. The cross is a finished work, a perfect sacrifice made once for all, but it is also the beginning of a priesthood which will continue until time ends and God's purposes are fulfilled. That priesthood in the heavenly places is undertaken by a Christ with nail-torn hands. The one who intercedes for us is one who knows inside out what it means to be human. In early Christian writings one finds again and again that the dominant conception of eucharistic worship centres on the figure of Jesus the Great High Priest serving at the heavenly altar. It is that heavenly ministry which is made manifest in the eucharist. That ministry is still fashioned from obedience to the Father, the working out of the Son's unique vocation. As we feed on the bread and wine, we are being strengthened to offer ourselves in our continuing and varied vocations, growing into the shape of the one who is our Master and Lord.

That priesthood of Christ demands a human response. The church is that response. In the New Testament the church as a whole is described as a royal priesthood. It bears the same relationship to human society as the Jewish priesthood bore to the community as a whole - '...you are a chosen race, a kingdom of priests, a holy nation, a people to be a personal possession to sing the praises of God who called you out of darkness into his wonderful light.' (1 Pet. 2:9). An exceptionally well-read theologian, she gently corrected the tendency towards individualism which is so characteristic of Western Protestantism by stressing the way in which the New Testament always speaks of the priestly activity of the *whole* church. It is the whole church which is intended in the good purposes of God to bring God to humanity and humanity to God.

However, it is as she explores the nature of the priestliness of the church that the riches she had gleaned from a life-time of ecumenical dialogue become clear. She writes with excitement of the Communion of Saints as she had discovered it within the Roman and Eastern Orthodox communions. She brings her deep knowledge of early Christian history to her argument that the offertory in early liturgies meant much more than our practice suggests. She draws a picture of a wonderful symbolic moment. As the bread and wine are offered, everyone in the congregation 'from the bishop down to the last confirmed member of the church' is giving themselves anew to God. It was a corporate offering of the whole church as a body. She quotes Augustine in a sermon to the newly confirmed at Easter - 'There *you* are upon the Table; there *you* are in the chalice.' We speak of communicants. The primitive church spoke of offerers. There is, as Wyon points out, a world of difference - that between spectators and active participants. The offertory, the bringing of bread and wine to the table, things that human hands, agriculture and industry have made, was a moment when the whole of life was offered to God. There was no division between Sunday and Monday, no assumptions about what was sacred and what secular. In a prophetic word that is as relevant now as it was fifty years ago when she wrote her book, Olive Wyon pleads for a renewed awareness that '...Christ is Lord of all life, and that the whole of life must be brought under His sway.'[19]

It is the reception of heavenly food, the holy communion, that completes the eucharist, for it is the moment of meeting between Christ and his people, and the meeting of the faithful with each other. This is the point when God takes all that we have offered, and '...in infinite mercy and gentleness, takes what is offered, consecrates and transforms it.'[20] This is, as all who have meditated on or written about communion know, a holy mystery. It is therefore with due diffidence that Wyon offers her own understanding. Using John 6 as her guide she muses that Jesus's words about eating his flesh and drinking his blood were as strange to their original hearers as they are to us. She suggests that eating Christ's flesh means to receive his spirit of self-sacrifice and self-giving to God and humanity and that drinking his blood means receiving his living, resurrection power. 'So in the act of Communion we receive Christ in all his living power. Through this Sacramental Communion He wills to dwell with us for ever. We are therefore to 'feed on Him in our hearts', and to abide in Him continually.'[21] Calvin, who could have been a tremendous help to her here, is ignored (as indeed he is in most of her writing).

She concludes her meditation on the eucharist with the sixth of Underhill's aspects, the mystery of the presence. Here she is on safer, more familiar ground, gathering from the world church experiences of Christ's presence during communion - from Russian Orthodoxy, the Franciscans, Lutheran hymnody, and Soren Kierkegaard (always one of her favourites). Their thoughts are echoed in the journal of an unknown nineteenth century Free Church of Scotland woman, 'At the Sacrament to-day I had the substance of the Feast, my very Christ, who is more precious than words can tell...To-day He has been made known to me in the breaking of bread.' Here speculation and theological definition are eschewed, for all that matters is that Christ *is* present in the eucharist, not exclusively but paradigmatically.

Olive Wyon deserves to be remembered. She was a rare guide to the spiritual realities of the Reformed tradition at the very moment that it was rediscovering itself as part of the one, holy, catholic and apostolic church. Yet she belongs also to the world church, which she served so faithfully. As the New Testament scholar C.F.D. Moule remembered, 'You could not possibly conceive of attaching an ecclesiastical label to her. She was at home wherever

---

[19] Ibid., p. 62.
[20] Ibid., p. 81.
[21] Ibid., p. 84.

Christ was Lord.'[22] As an unofficial chaplain to women students at Cambridge during the war (at Charles Raven's suggestion) she was a member of St Columba's Presbyterian Church of England. In retirement she found her spiritual home in the pews of Great St Mary's, the University Church. But she remained beyond labels. When an Anglican bishop criticised a Free Church communion service, she turned and said quietly '...at Cheshunt [College] in a very simple Lord's Supper, the very Shekinah of the Lord was there.'[23]

She ends her meditation on the eucharist by asking why Christ comes to us

> He comes to make us like Himself. This is a very costing thing and He cannot do much with us unless we give Him a free hand. All He asks from us is an entire surrender, in docility and confidence. If we do not shrink from His saving and transforming action, He will do His creative and redeeming work in us, shaping us according to His will. So our constant prayer at every communion will be: 'Behold, the handmaid of the Lord, be it unto me according to His word.'[24]

---

[22] Oates and Foster, *Chronicle*, p. 25.
[23] Oates and Foster, *Chronicle*, p. 23.
[24] Wyon, *Altar Fire*, p. 91.

CHAPTER 8

C.H. Dodd and W.D. Davies: Two Welsh Congregationalists on the Nature of the Church[1]

John Tudno Williams

Undoubtedly, the two greatest New Testament scholars to emanate from Wales in the twentieth century were Charles Harold Dodd and William David Davies and they were both nurtured within the Congregationalist tradition. Dodd was born and bred in the largest town in North Wales, Wrexham, while Davies came from Glanaman in Carmarthenshire, from an area where, until comparatively recently, what was claimed to be the best anthracite coal in the world was mined. Dodd's family belonged to the English-speaking section of the Congregationalists in Wales, although there is ample evidence to show that he had a working knowledge of the Welsh language.[2] George Caird states in his British Academy memoir that 'Dodd was proud to record that his was the fifth generation to belong to the same chapel'.[3] The chapel was Salem, Pen-y-bryn, which was to be replaced during his boyhood by a new complex of buildings to

---

[1] I offer this modest contribution by way of tribute to one who was for nearly ten years a valued colleague at the United Theological College, Aberystwyth. I do so with thanks for all that I learned from him and for the wider perspectives on academic and church life I experienced through his generosity.

[2] See my article 'Charles Harold Dodd – Welshman', *Expository Times*, 113 (2001/2), pp. 270-72. In the Introduction to *The New English Bible: New Testament* (Oxford/Cambridge: University Presses, 1961), p. x, Dodd had written: 'No one who has not tried it can know how impossible an art translation is.' It appears he had debated a great deal with regard to the advisability of including the word 'impossible' at this point. Davies, in a survey of the course of New Testament studies during his lifetime, comments on this remark by Dodd, who was his mentor in Cambridge: 'We were both bilingual and, therefore, knew that translation is always a betrayal' ('Reflections on Thirty Years of Biblical Study', *Scottish Journal of Theology*, 39 (1986), p. 46).

[3] G.B. Caird, 'C.H. Dodd', *Proceedings of the British Academy*, lx (1974), p. 497.

be known as Salisbury Park Congregational Church.[4] On the other hand, Davies was nurtured within the Union of Welsh Independents and for his theological training for the Congregationalist ministry attended firstly the Memorial College, Brecon, and then Cheshunt College. He began his ministry at Fowlmere and Thriplow Congregationalist churches in Cambridgeshire in 1941, remaining there until his appointment to teach the New Testament at the Yorkshire United Independent College, Bradford, in 1947.[5]

Dodd had no doubt that it was to be within the Congregationalist tradition that he was to exercise his future ministry. In reply to the question posed at his ordination in 1912 at Brook Street Congregationalist Church, Warwick, as to why he chose to serve in a Church of that tradition, he replied: 'I am persuaded that the independent or congregational church-order, at its best, conserves most fully the spirit of the primitive Church and the liberty of the Gospel: and that it gives the fullest opportunity for the exercise of a spiritual ministry, unfettered by superfluous forms whether of Church government, of ritual or of Dogma.'[6] In his assessment of his ecclesiological standpoint at the end of his life, Dillistone, his biographer, concludes: 'There is no sign that he wavered in his high regard for Independency, but gradually, as he gave more serious study to the doctrine of the Church and Sacraments, he came to an increasing recognition of its dependence upon a full-orbed theology.'[7]

In his contribution to the volume of essays issued in commemoration of the Centenary of the Congregational Union of England and Wales in 1931, Dodd evaluated the evidence for the church in the New Testament. He stated that

> we do not know exactly how any church of New Testament times was governed. All we do know is that they were governed in a great variety of ways.... But one thing is clear, that the governing idea in the New Testament is that of the one Church – a unique society constituted by acts of God in history. That is where we must start. We are not thereby bound to the corollary which was drawn by the Jewish-Christian community in its first days, that the Church must have a rigid constitution with a centralized government. Paul liberated the Church from that idea. If we follow him, we shall value the particular local church as a fellowship of the Spirit and a visible embodiment of the one Church. As Independents we have always held to the spiritual competence of the particular church as united to Christ and guided by His Spirit, and here I think we should have Paul with us, though not James. But we could not claim Paul's support, or that of any New Testament teacher, if we wished to leave it at that. He desired and expected that the free local *ecclesia* should not only feel itself one in spirit with all other

---

[4] F.W. Dillistone, *C.H. Dodd: Interpreter of the New Testament* (London: Hodder and Stoughton, 1977), pp. 13-14.
[5] Cf. R. Rooke, *Mere Independents: A History of Fowlmere and Triplow United Reformed Church* (privately printed, 1996), p. 39.
[6] See Dillistone, *C.H. Dodd*, p. 61.
[7] Dillistone, *C.H. Dodd*, pp. 221-22.

Christians, but should take practical steps, so far as in it lay, to give a body to that spirit.[8]

He reminded us that the word *ecclesia* 'does not admit of a plural. "The Church" is seated at Jerusalem, while its members may reside elsewhere. There is no other church.'[9] However, it was claimed that the entry of substantial numbers of Gentiles altered the situation in the early church. 'It is noteworthy', he said, 'that the Acts uses *ecclesia* for the first time strictly as a common noun in speaking of the church at Antioch.'[10] 'The communities [Paul] founded were predominantly Gentile. The term *ecclesia*, as a common noun, both in the singular and in the plural, is freely used of these communities both in Paul's own letters and in the Pauline parts of Acts, as well as in the Johannine Epistles and Apocalypse, which belong geographically to Paul's sphere of influence.'[11] Thus he concluded: 'We may fairly say that the Pauline churches represent autonomous communities guided by the Spirit in place of a local community dependent upon the hierarchy of the Mother-church.'[12] 'Although Paul uses *ecclesia* as a common noun, admitting of a plural, he also uses it as a proper noun, denoting a unique thing in the world',[13] and he referred to the evidence of Ephesians and Colossians and of 1 Corinthians. Thus the question was raised whether 'the universal or the local idea of a church is primary',[14] and he proposed that 'the striking phrase of the Corinthian epistles, "the Church of God which is at Corinth", is seen to form the true transition from the older sense of *ecclesia* as a proper noun to its derived use as a common noun'.[15]

Clearly, therefore, the question posed at the beginning of his essay, 'Would it then be a legitimate inference that the fact and the idea of the Catholic Church are a creation of the second age of Christianity, and that the original New Testament order was a pure Independency?'[16] represents a much too simplistic assessment of the biblical evidence and needs to be nuanced considerably, as was indeed accomplished by this most lucid and able of New Testament scholars. As a result of his research in the field of the New Testament Dodd clearly reached 'an exalted view of the whole Church as the Body of Christ, as a living organism indwelt by the one Spirit' and also of the importance of the Eucharist 'as the central outward expression of the Church's

---

[8] Dodd, 'The Church in the New Testament', in *Essays Congregational and Catholic* (ed. A. Peel; London: Congregational Union of England and Wales, 1931), pp. 15-16.
[9] Ibid., p. 6.
[10] Ibid.
[11] Ibid., p. 7.
[12] Ibid., p. 9.
[13] Ibid., p. 11.
[14] Ibid.
[15] Ibid., pp. 12-13.
[16] Ibid., p. 5.

life'.[17]

In a contribution to the volume on *Christian Worship* produced by members of Mansfield College to celebrate its jubilee he outlined the evidence for 'The Sacrament of the Lord's Supper in the New Testament', and insisted that 'a non-sacramental Christianity tends to become non-supernatural, or else takes refuge in a mysticism which is not distinctively Christian because it has lost the living link with history.'[18] Further, in his contribution to the third of a series of conferences of German and English theologians held between the two world wars – the one held at Chichester, 23-28 March, 1931, he wrote on 'The Eucharist in relation to the Fellowship of the Church'.[19] Here again he stressed the central place of the Eucharist in the life of the Church: 'The Church as the unity of believers is most truly itself in the Sacrament of communion, in which its individual members are nourished with the life of God in Christ which is His common gift to them all. In a particular local congregation the sharing of one Loaf and one Cup establishes the unity of that congregation.'[20] Moreover

> the single congregation, entering into the Church's corporate memory of its Lord, shares the experience of the whole Body as a living community, continuous and identical in time as well as in space. And as that experience is of the eschatological order, discovering the end in every stage of the process, the congregation knows itself to be in the presence of the whole Church triumphant, and so is lifted above all particularity of space and time. Thus the Sacrament is a witness that the Catholic church is no aggregate of parts, but lives as a whole in every congregation of Christian people which breaks the bread and pours out the wine with the sincere intention of showing forth the Lord's death until He come and making a communion of His Body and Blood. The Eucharist, rather than the episcopate, is the true *sacramentum unitatis.*[21]

Two important aspects of Dodd's thought are prominent in this quotation: the first is the eschatological element, which, of course, featured so prominently in his whole work from the time he first raised it in his contribution to an earlier Conference of German and English theologians in 1927.[22] Such Platonic language, as is found here, featured later in his work also,

---

[17] Dillistone, *C.H. Dodd*, p. 222. Dillistone, *C.H. Dodd*, p. 195, also comments: 'No one who reads his writings comprehensively can fail to be impressed by the prominence given to the Eucharist in his theology and his devotion.'
[18] Dodd, 'The Sacrament of the Lord's Supper in the New Testament', in *Christian Worship: Studies in its History and Meaning, By Members of Mansfield College* (ed. N. Micklem; Oxford: University Press, 1936), p. 79.
[19] Dodd, 'The Eucharist in relation to the Fellowship of the Church', *Theology*, xxii, no. 132 (1931), pp. 333-36.
[20] Ibid., p. 336.
[21] Ibid.
[22] See Dodd, 'The This-Wordly Kingdom of God in Our Lord's Teaching', *Theology*, xiv (1927), pp. 258-60.

when, whilst stressing the element of 'realised eschatology' in Jesus' teaching, he intimated that those sayings of his which appear to imply a future Kingdom of God did not refer to a coming in this world, but rather to something beyond space and time.[23] He expanded on this statement in his discussion of the concept 'the Day of the Son of Man', which, he said, stands for a timeless fact: 'So far as history can contain it, it is embodied in the historic crisis which the coming of Jesus brought about. But the spirit of man, though dwelling in history, belongs to the eternal order' (this, we may interpose, appears to be a Platonic rather than a biblical idea)[24] 'and the full meaning of the Day of the Son of Man, or of the Kingdom of God, he can experience only in that eternal order. That which cannot be experienced in history is symbolized by the picture of a coming event.'[25] So the Sacrament of the Lord's Supper is closely associated with eschatology, for it is 'in origin...the sacrament of a transformed eschatology. As such, it places us in the presence of the eternal, supernatural order – the Kingdom of God....[The] mediation of the eternal through the temporal [i.e. the eating of bread and drinking of wine] is the presupposition of the Sacrament.'[26]

The second significant aspect raised here is his clear stand on the need to promote the ideal of Christian unity. In his Introduction to *The Roads Converge* Dodd wrote of the idea of the Reunion of a divided church: 'There is no subject which commands wider interest among Christians of all communions at the present time,'[27] he said. Despite the slow progress, indeed stagnation, of the movement towards the union of separated churches a 'leaven was working',[28] and he proceeded to give examples of significant progress in relationships and attitudes. Notable was the amount of mutual understanding between scholars from Catholic and Protestant backgrounds in the field of New Testament studies.[29] His concern for the unity of the church reflected a central concern of

---

[23] Dodd, *The Parables of the Kingdom* (London: Nisbet, rev. edn, 1953), p. 56.

[24] Cf. R.H. Fuller, *The Mission and Achievement of Jesus* (SBT 1/12; London: SCM Press, 1954), pp. 20, 33; and N. Perrin, *The Kingdom of God in the Teaching of Jesus* (London: SCM Press, 1963), p. 68, n. 3.

[25] Dodd, *Parables*, p. 108; cf. also pp. 209-10; and Dodd, *The Coming of Christ* (Cambridge: University Press, 1951), p. 27. See further Dodd, *Coming*, p. 17; *Parables*, pp. 108-109; *The Apostolic Preaching and its Developments* (London: Hodder and Stoughton, new ed., 1956), p. 36; and *History and the Gospel* (London: Nisbet, 1938), pp. 170-78.

[26] Dodd, 'The Sacrament of the Lord's Supper', p. 79; cf. also Dodd, 'The Eucharist in relation to the Fellowship of the Church', p. 333.

[27] Dodd, Introduction to *The Roads Converge: A Contribution to the Question of Christian Reunion* eEd. P. Gardner-Smith; London: Edward Arnold, 1963), p. 1.

[28] Ibid., p. 2.

[29] Ibid., p. 3.

his studies, which was for the unity of the New Testament writings;[30] indeed, his emphasis on the kerygmatic unity of the New Testament provided a major impetus to the growth of biblical theology.[31] He believed that the analytical criticism of the liberal critics of the early twentieth century paradoxically provided 'the indispensable preliminary to the discovery of [the] wholeness [of the New Testament]',[32] in that as a result of the work of the form critics, who appeared to be working towards the complete disintegration of the Gospels, there were produced three primary elements which introduced the formal patterns of *kerygma*, *didache*, and liturgy (the form of the church's worship).[33] He said of the analysis of liberalism that we had been 'presented with a New Testament of bits and pieces. Each separate constituent was characterized and appreciated in depth, often to its great illumination, but they scarcely seemed to form a whole. The relation they bore to one another was obscure.'[34] Thus, it was in reaction to this older liberal criticism with its emphasis on the search for sources and analysis of the material that he forged a principle of unity for the New Testament writings. In fact, Dodd turned the methods of the form critics 'to more constructive use'.[35] Of liberal criticism he said: 'It has given us back a richer unity, which is the concrete unity of a living and active society, expressing itself in manifold ways: unity in diversity.'[36] And it was precisely this view of the pattern of unity in Christendom 'to which we aspire', he said,[37] and he quoted Hans Küng approvingly: 'Unity is not sameness but the very opposite…While unity is desired outside the Catholic Church as well as inside, uniformity certainly is not.'[38]

Dodd played a significant role in a body called the Friends of Reunion. In 1933 a conference of representatives from different denominations agreed to form 'a society of those who seek the unity of the Church of Christ, and who promise to further that end in any way that may be open to them'.[39] It was he who was called upon to deliver the main conference address on 'The Basis of Reunion'. The grounds on which a conceivable visible unity might be

---

[30] Cf. J.A.T. Robinson, 'Theologians of Our Time: xii. C.H. Dodd', *Expository Times*, lxxv (1963/4), pp. 100-101.

[31] Cf. W.D. Davies' tribute to Dodd in *New Testament Studies*, xx (1973/4), p. iii.

[32] Dodd, *The Roads Converge*, p. 5.

[33] Ibid. For Dodd's theories about *kerygma* and *didache* see his *Apostolic Preaching* and *Gospel and Law: the relation of faith and ethics in early Christianity* (Cambridge: University Press, 1951).

[34] Dodd, *The Roads Converge*, p. 4.

[35] G.B. Caird, 'C.H. Dodd', in M.E. Marty and D.G. Perman (eds), *A Handbook of Christian Theologians* (Cambridge: Lutterworth, 1984), p. 324.

[36] Dodd, *The Roads Converge*, p. 5.

[37] Ibid.

[38] H.Küng, *The Council and Reunion* (trans. C. Hastings; London/New York: Sheed and Ward, 1961), p. 247.

[39] Dillistone, *C.H.Dodd*, p. 196.

established were to be based on three propositions: the faith proclaimed in the Scriptures and safeguarded in the classical creeds; the Sacraments of Baptism and Holy Communion; and the ministry 'potentially capable of becoming acknowledged by the whole Church as possessing not only the inward call of the Spirit but also the outward commission of Christ'.[40] So 'he looked for a Church of the future which would incorporate the good from each tradition while rejecting the inessential or the false'.[41] At subsequent meetings of the Friends of Reunion he increasingly turned his attention to the so-called 'non-theological factors' which obstructed the path towards church unity,[42] and it was these factors which he addressed in an interesting and significant letter he penned soon after the end of the second world war.

The letter was addressed to Oliver S. Tomkins, Secretary of the Commission on Faith and Order of the World Council of Churches at the time, and later to be Bishop of Bristol. In it Dodd expressed his fears about there being 'an element of unconscious or unavowed motive which prevents us from "following the argument whithersoever it leads".'[43] He pointed out that the ground of debate so often shifts in ecumenical discussions.[44] He outlined a suspicion of such unavowed motification with regard both to confessional or denominational loyalty and also to social and political traditions: indeed, he claimed, some of these were so deep-seated in the English *psyche* that they went back to the Civil War with terms such as 'priest' and 'bishop' remaining emotive words.[45] In the final resort, he asked, do 'we care more about saving the face of our denomination than about the *Una Sancta*?'[46] Did intense pride in our own tradition prevent us reaching agreement with others? We harboured such a fear of reaching agreement that we tended to change the subject of discussion.[47] In the final resort we needed 'to ask whether our tenacity in defending certain positions may be due to something other than pure doctrinal logic'.[48] This letter of C.H. Dodd evoked such interest that it resulted in the Faith and Order Commission meeting in Chichester in 1949 'deciding', according to Tomkins, its Secretary, 'that although it was too late to make this subject the material for a separate theological commission it should continue to be borne in mind in the preparations for the Lund Conference [on Faith and

---

[40] Dillistone, *C.H. Dodd*, pp. 196-97.
[41] Ibid., p. 197.
[42] Ibid., pp. 197-98.
[43] Dodd, 'A Letter concerning unavowed motives in Ecumenical Discussions', *The Ecumenical Review*, ii (1949-50), p. 53 (reproduced in C.H. Dodd, G.R. Cragg and Jacques Ellul, *Social and Cultural Factors in Church Divisions* (London: SCM Press, 1952), pp. 7-11.
[44] Dodd, 'A Letter concerning unavowed motives', p. 52.
[45] Ibid., pp. 53-55.
[46] Ibid., p. 53.
[47] Ibid., p. 54.
[48] Ibid., p. 55.

Order, 1952]. Subsequently the American Committee for Faith and Order began some correspondence on the subject, and finally convened a study conference in the summer of 1951. The fruit of their work was brought by three of their number to another conference, primarily of European and British church members, which was held at the Ecumenical Institute at Bossey, Switzerland, in November, 1951. This conference, which consisted not so much of professional theologians (though they were included in its number) as of historians, economists, psychologists, etc., produced the report' [entitled 'Non-Theological Factors that may hinder or accelerate the Church's Unity': Report of a Conference held at the Ecumenical Institute at Bossey in November, 1951].[49]

'The Faith and Order Movement, the Conference on Life and Work, the International Missionary Council which eventually came together in the World Council of Churches were movements in which Dodd was a valued Counsellor, and to which he was a lively contributor', says John Marsh.[50] Along with Karl Barth he was invited to speak to introduce the main theme of 'Man's Disorder and God's Design' in the First Assembly of the World Council of Churches at Amsterdam in 1948.[51] He was also appointed a member of the Faith and Order Commission at Amsterdam,[52] and he had a hand over a period of three or four years in preparing for the Second Assembly at Evanston in 1954 with its theme: 'Christ – The Hope of the World'.[53] He contributed one of four talks on Evanston, broadcast during July, 1954.[54] It is no surprise, therefore, to find the Bishop of Bristol (Oliver Tomkins) writing in *The Times* newspaper after his death and stating: 'May I be allowed to emphasize the contribution which [Dodd] made as one of the "backroom boys of theology" to the change of climate in the relations between churches?'[55]

A year before he died the United Reformed Church was formed. A letter written to his minister at the time and reproduced in Dillistone's biography reveals his joy at this development: 'It is the consummation of an ideal which I cherished for years before it was talked of. I have long felt it to be a nonsense

---

[49] Tomkins in his Preface to *Social and Cultural Factors*, p. 5. The Report is published in *Social and Cultural Factors,* pp. 26-33. It is interesting to note that Oliver Tomkins' father, Leopold Tomkins, had been minister of the Congregationalist churches at Fowlmere and Triplow, where W.D. Davies was also to minister, from 1914 to 1917 after missionary service in China. Subsequently in 1920 he entered the priesthood of the Church of England (cf. Rooke, *Mere Independents*, p. 30).

[50] J. Marsh, 'Charles Harold Dodd: The Man and his Work', in *C.H. Dodd, 1884-1973: The Centenary Lectures* (Mold: Clwyd Library and Museum Service, 1985), p. 32.

[51] J. Bowden, *Karl Barth* (London: SCM Press, 1971), p. 94.

[52] Dillistone, *C.H. Dodd*, p. 200.

[53] G.K.A. Bell et al., *We Intend to Stay Together* (London: SCM Press, 1954), p. 12.

[54] Published in *We Intend to Stay Together*.

[55] *The Times*, 28 September 1973.

that our churches should remain apart.'[56] He had indeed witnessed the 'Presbyterianizing' of his own denomination and conceded that 'the Congregationalism of to-day, centralized and bureaucratic, is as different from the Independent Congregationalism of old days as chalk from cheese and it is quite certainly more like Presbyterianism as I now know it'.[57] Long before, at the conclusion of his contribution to the volume commemorating the Centenary of the Congregational Union in 1931, he had entered a plea for a greater effort to work for the reunion of Christ's divided body.[58]

In response to Daniel Jenkins' claim in *The Gift of Ministry* that Christians urgently need 'a recovery of the conviction that Church order is divinely ordained for the true governing of the Church according to God's will in a fallen world',[59] W.D. Davies questioned 'whether and in what sense, if any, the New Testament presents us with a normative pattern for Church life'.[60] In a brief review of studies of the church in the New Testament he concluded that by about 1880 a consensus had been reached on the basis of the contributions of Lightfoot and Hort and of Hatch that the church was no longer to be considered a divine ordinance but rather a social necessity.[61] Later with J.V. Bartlet's study, *Church- life and Church- order during the first four centuries* [62] emphasis was placed on the primacy of the possession of the Spirit in contrast to Catholic Christianity's stress on order.[63] Thus there developed a new concentration on the nature of the church rather than on the form of its life.[64] Davies noted the influence of the ecumenical movement on New Testament scholarship in this matter[65] and gave credit to two scholars in particular, namely the English Methodist, R. Newton Flew, and the Scottish Presbyterian, George Johnston, for drawing attention to the unity of the New Testament doctrine of the church.[66] In this way, the essential nature of the church as the eschatological people of God in Christ came to be widely recognized; but disagreement arose as to how this people was organised, if, indeed, they were 'organised'.[67]

---

[56] Dillistone, *C.H. Dodd*, p. 199.
[57] Ibid.
[58] Dodd, 'The Church in the New Testament', p. 16.
[59] D. Jenkins, *The Gift of Ministry* (London: Faber and Faber, 1947), p. 174.
[60] W.D. Davies, *A Normative Pattern of Church Life in the New Testament: Fact or Fantasy?* (London: James Clarke, 1950), p. 1.
[61] Ibid, p. 2.
[62] J.V. Bartlet, *Church-life and Church-order during the first four centuries: with special reference to the early Eastern church-orders* (Oxford: Blackwell, 1943).
[63] Davies, *Normative Pattern*, pp. 4-5.
[64] Ibid., pp. 5-6.
[65] Ibid., p. 5.
[66] Ibid., p. 7. Cf. R.N. Flew, *Jesus and His Church* (London: Epworth Press, 1938) and G. Johnston, *The Doctrine of the Church in the New Testament* (Cambridge: University Press, 1943).
[67] Davies, *Normative Pattern*, p. 7.

Davies concluded: 'No... form of Church government or order regarded as sacrosanct by our Puritan forefathers can claim the unique sanction of the New Testament. We must state, quite brutally, that neither Congregationalists nor any other Free Churchmen can claim to be the sole heirs of the New Testament in their Church life.'[68] He added

> This has been forcibly brought home to us by those scholars who have insisted that there is no one form of Church life presented to us in the New Testament, and that, on the contrary, the New Testament presents us with many forms of Church life. The dichotomy in New Testament studies between the unity of our conception of the nature of the Church and our disagreements as to its form or forms is no mere accident, but a necessity, because the Churches of the New Testament are like a coat of many colours, they vary both in foundation and in organization.'[69]

This position reflected the view of the Anglican scholar, B.H. Streeter, *The Primitive Church*, who, in pointing to a primitive diversity in Christian institutions, said that in this diversity 'the Episcopalian, the Presbyterian, and the Independent can each discover the prototype of the system to which he himself adheres'.[70] Of course, Free Churchmen would welcome such a position.[71] Thus, Davies can conclude his brief monograph with the following words: 'The New Testament would not seem to present us with a single fixed pattern of Church order which we are to regard as normative: but it does provide us with certain criteria which can guide us.'[72] He set out the following five criteria by which to judge any form that the church may assume:

(1) The church in the New Testament was not a purely spiritual society and so had a measure of form and order[73].
(2) There was no single ordered pattern of liturgy and worship in the early church. In fact, variety was the order of the day.[74]
(3) 'The variety of Church orders and life in primitive Christianity did not

---

[68] Davies, *Normative Pattern*, p. 10.
[69] Ibid.
[70] B.H. Streeter, *The Primitive Church: Studied with special reference to the Origins of the Christian Ministry* (London: Macmillan, 1930), p. ix; cf. Davies, *Normative Pattern*, p. 11. Dodd, 'The Church in the New Testament', p. 3, gave his support to this view; cf. also further Davies, *Normative Pattern*, pp. 13-14; and T.W. Manson, *The Church's Ministry* (London: Hodder and Stoughton, 1948), pp. 60, 65.
[71] Davies, *Normative Pattern*, pp. 11-12.
[72] Ibid., p. 22. See also P.T. Forsyth, *Congregationalism and Reunion* (London: Independent Press, 1952), p. 63, quoted by A.P.F. Sell, *Testimony and Tradition: Studies in Reformed and Dissenting Thought* (Aldershot: Ashgate, 2005), pp. 295-96.
[73] Davies, *Normative Pattern*, pp. 15-16.
[74] Ibid., pp. 16-17.

destroy the awareness of the essential unity of Christians.'[75] It was a unity 'which transcends all merely organizational differences'. Moreover, 'unity in the faith and universalism in appeal are not broken by diversity in organisation. The Church is a unity in diversity.'[76] Thus, Daniel Jenkins' view of one divinely ordained church order was untenable.[77]

(4) Church order in the New Testament evolved.[78]

(5) The church according to the New Testament is a society called into being by the direct act of God in Christ.[79] Dodd had said: 'One thing is clear that the governing idea in the New Testament is that of the one Church – a unique society constituted by an act of God in history.'[80]

In 1963 Davies contributed to a Roman Catholic – Protestant Colloquium at Harvard in which he offered reflections 'in relation to the rapprochement which, like a thaw after a long winter, seems to be cracking the icy barriers which have long plagued Christendom'.

'My method', he said, 'will be to point out certain areas where, it seems to me, a challenge to dialogue is issued by recent study of the New Testament.'[81] He claimed that it is from a reappraisal of the relation of Christianity to Judaism in the New Testament that he had been led to a new openness towards Catholicism.[82] He reiterated the importance of the rediscovery of elements of order in the primitive church and added two further conclusions he had come to as a result of his study of the New Testament in the ecumenical climate of the middle of the twentieth century: firstly, the need to see Gospel and Law not as antithetical but as conjoined, and, secondly, the recognition of the importance of tradition within the church.[83] Indeed, the direction in which Pauline studies have gone in the latter half of the twentieth century with regard to the so-called 'New Perspective on Paul' owes much to the pioneering studies of W.D. Davies into the nature of the Rabbinic Judaism in which the Apostle was immersed.[84] Thus, 'it is no longer just a matter of justification by faith versus the Pharisaism of Rome, but a Paul for whom justification and loyalty to a

---

[75] Davies, *Normative Pattern*, p. 17.
[76] Ibid., p. 18.
[77] Ibid., p. 19.
[78] Ibid., p. 19.
[79] Ibid., p. 19.
[80] Dodd, 'The Church in the New Testament', p. 15.
[81] Davies, 'Challenge to Dialogue in the New Testament', in *Ecumenical Dialogue at Harvard: The Roman Catholic – Protestant Colloquium* (ed. S.H. Miller and G.E. Wright; Cambridge, Mass.: Harvard University Press, 1964), p. 110.
[82] Davies, 'Challenge to Dialogue', p. 113.
[83] Ibid., pp. 113-17.
[84] W.D. Davies, *Paul and Rabbinic Judaism: Some Rabbinic Elements in Pauline Theology* 4th ed. (Philadelphia: Fortress Press, 1980).

tradition co-existed'.[85] Thus, the age-long grip of Lutheran exegesis of Paul has, if not been entirely broken, certainly been loosened as a result.[86]

Clearly these two Congregationalists displayed an ecumenical approach to New Testament ecclesiology and to contemporary research in this field. The primary motivating factor in their whole study of the New Testament documents was to uncover the essence of the faith of the early church. The concept of the church was central to their understanding of the life of the early Christians as it is portrayed in the New Testament documents. The church was a fellowship of the Holy Spirit, and individual churches were in fellowship with others as they belonged essentially to the same body. Thus, it was recognized that the Catholic church lives in every congregation, with the Eucharist assuming a central position in its life. Dodd observed that the two most characteristic activities of the primitive church were the proclamation of the gospel and the administration of the Sacraments: 'The Church enters history with the apostolic kerygma as the expression of its life outwardly to the world, and the communion of "the breaking of bread" as the expression of the same life inwardly among its members.'[87] This, Dillistone believes, was the constraining conviction which motivated all Dodd's efforts to promote unity among the churches of Britain and to support the work of the ecumenical movement world-wide.[88]

In their work there is a real concern for the contemporary church. Hagner in his assessment of Dodd's contribution remarks: 'Scholarship for Dodd was to be pursued not for its own sake but for the sake of the church.'[89] It is also worth recording that Davies' first published contribution listed in the Bibliography of his publications in the *Festschrift* dedicated to him[90] is an article in the Welsh journal of the Student Christian Movement in which he appeals to the Movement to go back to its roots and rekindle a zeal for the foreign mission of the church.[91]

Finally, it is sad to note the response of contemporary Congregationalists in Wales, more specifically, the Union of Welsh Independents, towards recent proposals in the document *The Way Forward* for the organic union of all the

---

[85] Davies, 'Challenge to Dialogue', p. 150.
[86] For a recent detailed assessment of the whole debate see Stephen Westerholm, *Perspectives Old and New on Paul: The "Lutheran" Paul and His Critics* (Grand Rapids, Michigan: Eerdmans, 2004).
[87] Dodd, *History and the Gospel*, p. 161.
[88] Dillistone, *C.H. Dodd*, p. 196.
[89] D.A. Hagner, 'Dodd, C.H.', in *Historical Handbook of Major Biblical Interpreters*, D.K. McKim, ed. (Downers Grove /Leicester: IVP, 1998), p. 480.
[90] R. Hammerton-Kelly and R. Scroggs eds, *Jews, Greeks and Christians: Religious Cultures in Late Antiquity: Essays in Honor of William David Davies*, Studies in Judaism and Late Antiquity 21 (Leiden: Brill,1976).
[91] Davies, 'Myfyrwyr a'r Genhadaeth', *Yr Efrydydd*, vol.1, no.1 (October, 1935), pp. 42-46. The *Festschrift* gives the date of the article incorrectly as 1941.

Free Church denominations in Wales. They rejected them in 2002 and many of these Independent churches even added that further discussions along these lines were 'a waste of time'! Salutary are the words of W.D. Davies: 'The kind of isolationism prevalent in many Independent Churches...[is] a denial of the Christ we have learned'.[92]

---

[92] Davies, *Normative Pattern*, p. 22.

CHAPTER 9

Jesus Before Parents: Finding the Right Priority When Seeking Unity in the Family

Peter Balla

It is a great honour to me to contribute to the volume in honour of Professor Alan Sell, because it gives me also an opportunity to greet him in the name of all his Hungarian friends. He has visited us many times during the past decades and we thank for all his lectures at our theological faculties in the capital and in the countryside of Hungary. We pray God's blessing upon his life, and we hope that he can continue to offer lectures for us so that we can learn from his wisdom and biblical teaching, as well as from his vision for the unity of Christianity.

The present essay is offered as a modest example of the unity of the church, a unity that is hoped for also by New Testament scholars. In the vision of the present author, biblical scholarship in the future shall bring together representatives of different denominations in a common search for the Scriptures that testify about the Son of God incarnate.[1]

In recent decades there has emerged an increasing interest in the family relationships in antiquity.[2] Monographs and collections of essays have dealt with aspects of the Roman family. The number of publications on the Jewish

---

[1] The present essay was delivered as a guest lecture at Trinity Evangelical Divinity School in Deerfield (Illinois, USA) in September 2004, and at the University of Deusto (Bilbao, Spain) in December 2005. I thank the Protestant and Catholic brethren, respectively, for these two privileging invitations. I thank Jonathan S. Marshall (TEDS) for improving the English text of the manuscript.

[2] This essay summarises and develops the ideas presented in my habilitation thesis: P. Balla, *The Child-Parent Relationship in the New Testament and its Environment*, WUNT 155 (Tübingen: Mohr Siebeck, 2003); American reprint edition (Peabody, MA: Hendrickson, 2005). I thank the Alexander von Humboldt Foundation for helping me to return for research leaves to Heidelberg University in July 2004 and July 2005, where I could continue to work on the topic I had developed when I worked on the thesis with the help of their scholarship in 1999-2000.

family in antiquity has increased as well. Publications of papyri and inscriptions allow insights into the life of Greek and Jewish families. Classical philologists, sociologists and biblical scholars alike have turned their attention to the sociological dimensions of ancient family life.[3] Some aspects have been studied extensively, such as, for example, the legal situation in the Roman family.

In general, the child-parent relationship has been presented primarily from the perspective of the parents. In contrast to this prevailing emphasis in scholarship, in previous work I have focussed on the child-parent relationship especially from the point of view of the child, asking the question: How did they experience and fulfil the duties towards their parents? Or, to put it in another way: How did children honour their parents?

Within the New Testament we may encounter two layers of tensions regarding the expectation that parents should be revered. On the one hand, there is a difference between reverence toward parents among the first followers of Jesus and in the settled congregations. The latter is represented, for example, by the Household Codes in the epistles to the Ephesians and Colossians, where children are addressed together with their fathers. This implies that the obedient children are together with their parents at home and even at the worship services of the household churches. This can be contrasted with passages in the Gospels that narrate that the first disciples of Jesus left their family homes when they followed their master.[4]

The second layer of tension presents itself within the Gospel texts themselves. In several instances one finds Jesus subscribing to the commandment 'Honour your father and mother' (see e.g. Mark 7:9–13 par. in relation to the *Corban*; and Mark 10:17–27 par.: the passage concerning the 'rich young ruler'). But, conversely, one also discovers radical sayings concerning 'leaving' one's parents attributed to Jesus (see e.g.: Mark 10:29 and parallels) and also an extremely radical saying in Luke 14:26 about the necessity of 'hating' one's father and mother.[5]

Already in these few examples we can see that the duties of children to their parents applied to them even when they were grown-ups. This is reflected in

---

[3] For a recent collection of essays, see David L. Balch and Carolyn Osiek eds., *Early Christian Families in Context: An Interdisciplinary Dialogue* (Grand Rapids: Eerdmans, 2003).

[4] For a detailed argumentation concerning the continuity between the early phase of the Jesus movement and the Pauline house churches, see e.g. John H. Elliott, 'The Jesus Movement Was Not Egalitarian But Family-Oriented', *Biblical Interpretation* 11 (2003), 173-210.

[5] See also Santiago Guijarro Oporto, 'Kingdom and Family in Conflict. A Contribution to the Study of the Historical Jesus', in: J.J. Pilch ed., *Social Scientific Models for Interpreting the Bible. Essays by the Context Group in Honor of Bruce J. Malina.* BIS 53 (Leiden: Brill, 2001), pp. 210-38; P. Balla, 'Did All the First Christians Have to Leave Their Parents?', *European Journal of Theology* 7 (1998), 101-11.

the Greek term τέκνον that can refer to the child-parent relationship irrespective of the age of the 'child'. Accordingly, I use the term 'children' to refer to children in their relationship to their parents. Children, then, remain 'children' to their parents as long as their parents are alive; and even after this when they venerate the memory of their deceased parents.

Although most of the New Testament texts that contain references to our present field of study were not written with the purpose of describing family relationships, nevertheless they do reflect child-parent relationships among the early Christians. In my study, New Testament texts are examined in relation to non-biblical family ethics and practices in order to find answers to the questions: To what extent did early Christianity fit into the pattern of its environment?; and, What were the characteristics peculiar to the first few generations of the followers of Jesus?

My primary question is: How did children honour their parents? Or, to put it in a more concrete way, did the first Christians fulfil the expectation to honour their parents? I do not discuss the relationship from the side of the parents, for example, I do not cover the more extensive field of the education of children.

In order to understand the difficult sayings of Jesus concerning the call to leave one's parents, I shall briefly point to some texts in the non-Christian environment of the early Christians. In this environment we find that parents were highly respected also in the pagan world. After the short overview about the environment, I shall refer to some NT texts outside the Gospels to show that early Christianity after Jesus' time continued to revere parents.[6]

I suggest that these two sides – the non-Christian environment, and early Christianity after the time of Jesus – should serve as a background against which we have to read the radical sayings of Jesus about leaving one's family. My point is that the later child-parent relation shows how early Christians interpreted Jesus' teaching. After a discussion of some key Gospel texts I shall arrive at a conclusion. I should say that even I was surprised during my studies when I arrived at these conclusions.

I

First, let us examine some texts from the non-Christian world around the time of the early Christians.[7]

Diogenes Laertius writes (VII. 120, in the section on Zeno): 'The Stoics approve also of honouring parents [γονέας σέβεσθαι] and brothers in the second place next after the gods [ἐν δευτέρᾳ μοίρᾳ μετὰ θεούς]. They further

---

[6] I note that in my book, *The Child-Parent Relationship*..., I have structured the material in a different way: in the second part of the book (dealing with the NT), the Gospel tradition is dealt with first, then traditions in the Pauline corpus, and then the rest of the NT are discussed.

[7] For further examples, see ch. 2 in P. Balla, *The Child-Parent Relationship*, pp. 41-79.

maintain that parental affection for children is natural to the good, but not to the bad'.[8] We note the reference to nature as a reason why parents love their children; this implies the same reason why children should return that love. The very connection expressed by the phrase 'next after the gods' may also imply that the gods are the ground of honouring parents.

We can find further examples in the writings of Hierocles, the Stoic. The titles given by him to each section imply a certain ranking: he first discusses conduct towards the gods then conduct towards one's country. Then he writes: 'After considering the gods and our country, what person deserves to be mentioned more than, or prior to our parents? ...No mistake, therefore, will be made by him who says that they are as it were secondary or terrestrial *divinities*' (οὕς δευτέρους καὶ ἐπίγειους τινὰς θεοὺς εἰπὼν οὐκ ἂν ἁμάρτοι τίς).[9] Although between the gods and parents there is mention of the fatherland, it is nevertheless clear that parents are also related to the gods. The text implies honour as a duty, and the gods also serve as a 'reason' for the duty. Cicero has a similar sequence (a certain prioritization) of the triad, gods – country – parents, in *De officiis* 1.45.160: 'even in the social relations themselves there are gradations of duty [*gradus officiorum*] so well defined that it can easily be seen which duty takes precedence of any other: our first duty is to the immortal gods; our second, to country; our third, to parents; and so on, in a descending scale, to the rest.'[10] He can also refer to the 'fatherland' (*patria*) and parents without mentioning the gods (*Off.* 1.17.58): 'Now, if a contrast and comparison were to be made to find out where most of our moral obligation is due, country would come first, and parents; for their services have laid us under the heaviest obligation; next come children and the whole family, who look to us alone for support and have no other protection....'[11]

We note the argument that parents support and protect their children; this implies that children owe them a return. The speaker is under an obligation to his parents and he is to protect his own children: this implies an on-going process in which children of ever new generations are expected to return provision to their parents. It can be argued that honour is not simply one duty among others, but is an all-encompassing term: other duties are aspects of the duty of honouring one's parents.

Let us see another famous pagan author: Seneca. He writes: 'not to love

---

[8] Diogenes Laertius, *Lives of Eminent Philosophers*, R.D. Hicks trans, Vol 2 LCL (London: William Heinemann/Cambridge, MA: Harvard University Press), p. 225.

[9] David R. Fideler ed., *The Pythagorean Sourcebook and Library: An Anthology of Ancient Writings Which Relate to Pythagoras and Pythagorean Philosophy,* Kenneth S. Guthrie comp and trans (Grand Rapids: Phanes, 1987), p. 277. For the Greek text see Karl Praechter, *Hierokles der Stoiker* (Leipzig: Dieterich'sche Verlags-Buchhandlung, Theodor Weicher, 1901), p. 45.

[10] *Cicero in Twenty-Eight Volumes XXI: De Officiis*, Walter Miller trans, LCL (London: William Heinemann/Cambridge MA: Harvard University Press, 1968), p. 165.

[11] Ibid., p. 61.

one's parents is to be unfilial' (*parentes suos non amare impietas est*; *De beneficiis* 3.1.5).[12] Thus love and *pietas* are inseparable. Seneca also says that children 'owe' their parents the provision of care. In *Ben.* 6.23.5 he writes: 'We owe filial duty to our parents' (*debemus parentibus nostris pietatem*).[13] In this latter context he refers to the gods as well as to nature as our providers; inasmuch as they give life to children through their parents, the gods and nature can be seen as the ground for saying that children owe their parents provision in return. Seneca argues that we are indebted to our parents for our lives even if they did not 'plan' our birth.

Let me just mention one more pagan source. The papyri from Egypt provide many examples of letters written to family members. Two duties of children frequently recur in our sources (occasionally they occur together): 1) to provide for their parents when they get older; and 2) to bury them when they die. We have a beautiful expression of these duties in a letter of a son to his father. The editors of the papyrus provide the background information: the son, Philonides, was living in Alexandria; the father, Cleon, was a chief engineer in the Fayum. (The papyrus is dated about 255 B.C.)[14] Before the son urges his father to come to him and spend at least a season with them, he addresses his father in this way: 'Nothing truly will be dearer to me than to protect you for the rest of your life in a manner worthy of you and of myself, and if the fate of mankind befalls you, to see that you enjoy all due honours [τυχεῖν σε πάντων τῶν καλῶν]; this will be my chief desire, honourably to protect you [προστατῆσαι] both while you live and when you have departed to the gods.' Writing a personal letter, Philonides expresses in a roundabout way – but nevertheless clearly – that he will provide for a burial that would express the honour due to his father.

Having seen some examples from the pagan environment, let me refer to some Jewish authors who affirm the obligation to honour one's parents.[15] Philo of Alexandria is a very interesting testimony because although he exposits the Ten Commandments, he adds some motifs which are not there in the text of the OT. To offer but a few quotations: In a way similar to what we have seen in pagan authors, Philo also 'ranks' parents; they come immediately after God (*On the Special Laws* 2.235): 'Honour therefore, he says, next to God (μετὰ θεόν) thy father and thy mother, who are crowned with a laurel of the second

---

[12] *Seneca in Ten Volumes. Moral Esssays*, Vol 3 (*De Beneficiis*), John W. Basore trans., LCL (London: William Heinemann/Cambridge MA: Harvard University Press, 1975), p. 129.

[13] Ibid., p. 409.

[14] *Select Papyri*, A. S. Hunt and C. C. Edgar trans, LCL Vol. 1: *Non-literary Papyri: Private Affairs* (London: William Heinemann; Cambridge, Mass.: Harvard University Press, 1970), p. 279.

[15] See also P. Balla, *The Child-Parent Relationship*, pp. 80-111.

rank assigned to them by nature, the arbitress of the contest'.[16] It is interesting to observe here that even in a passage where Philo refers to the commandment itself, he expounds it with his own interpretation by referring to 'nature'.

Philo emphasizes the duty of honouring parents according to the Fifth Commandment. I note that although the Ten Commandments are not numbered in the Old Testament, Philo numbers them. I adopt his numbering, which coincides with the numbering in my home church, and in the Reformed churches in general. (The Catholic and the Lutheran churches refer to the commandment to honour father and mother as the Fourth Commandment.) Philo deals with this commandment in *De Decalogo* 106–120, introducing this section with the following summary (106): 'After dealing with the seventh day, He gives the fifth commandment on the honour due to parents'. We note that Philo summarises the reference to 'father and mother' in the Fifth Commandment as 'parents'. He divides the Ten Commandments into two sets of five. Concerning the Fifth Commandment, he affirms (106): 'This commandment He placed on the borderline between the two sets of five; it is the last of the first set in which the most sacred injunctions are given and it adjoins the second set which contains the duties of man to man.' This implies a very high view on parents, since the duty toward them is placed as the conclusion of the list of duties toward God. Inasmuch as the OT does not tell us how the commandments are divided on the two tables of stone, Philo goes beyond the OT when distinguishing the Fifth Commandment from other commandments concerning duties towards fellow human beings, and placing it on the 'border-line between the mortal and the immortal side of existence' (*Decal.* 107). Philo argues by referring to the procreative function of parents (107): They belong not only to the mortal, but also to '...the immortal [side of existence] because the act of generation assimilates them to God, the generator of the All.'[17]

Having considered Philo, let us now look at a few intertestamental Jewish sources. The *Letter of Aristeas* refers to the duty as required by God's commandment. The letter has a long section that relates how, during the seven days of a banquet the Egyptian king put questions to each of the translators of the Septuagint (Aristeas 187–294). In Aristeas 228 we read that the king 'asked the sixth guest to answer. His question was, "To whom must one show favour?" The answer was, "To his parents, always, for God's very great commandment concerns the honor due to parents. Next (and closely connected) he reckons the honor due to friends, calling the friend an equal of one's own self. You do well if you bring all men into friendship with yourself".' Here we observe the significance of friends; but also the priority of parents. We note the reference to

---

[16] *Philo in Ten Volumes (and Two Supplementary Volumes)* LCL Vol 7 (*De Decalago; De Specialibus Legibus I-III*) F. H. Colson, trans (London: William Heinemann/ Cambridge MA: Harvard University Press, 1950), p. 453.

[17] Ibid., p. 61.

God's commandment as the reason for the duty.

The *Sibylline Oracles* have a passage which exhibits a certain 'ranking', which possibly comes from Egypt as well. In the third book, lines 573–574 provide the context for our relevant passage: 'There will again be a sacred race of pious men who attend to the counsels and intention of the Most High.' Then in lines 593–594 we read: 'and they honor only the Immortal who always rules, and then their parents.' We note that in these two examples the appearance of the duty right after the duty of honouring God can be seen as a ground for that duty. We have met this phenomenon also in the non-Jewish environment.

Pseudo-Phocylides provides further evidence for the presence of this duty in Alexandria, expressed in a form that we may call a 'ranking'. Line 8 reads: 'Honor God foremost, and afterward your parents' (πρῶτα θεὸν τιμᾶν, μετέπειτα δὲ σεῖο γονηέας). I note that Pseudo-Phocylides is a significant source in the realm of ethical conduct in the household, on which he has a long passage (lines 175–227).

In one last Jewish source, let us look at a fragment from Qumran: In 4Q416, frag. 2, col. iii, lines 15–19a we read

> Then thou shalt know what is bitter for a man, And what is sweet for a *person*. Honour thy father in thy poverty, *16* And thy mother in thy *low estate*. For as God (*scarcely* 'the Father') is to a man, so is his own father; And as *the Lord* is to a person, so is his mother; For *17* they are 'the *womb* that was pregnant with thee'; And just as He has set them in authority over thee And *fashioned (thee)* according to the Spirit, So serve thou them, And as *18 they* have uncovered thy ear to the mystery that is to come, Honour thou them for the sake of thine own honour And with [*reverence*] venerate their *persons*, *19* For the sake of thy life and of the length of thy days. *vacat*."[18]

I think these examples have sufficiently shown that in the pagan and Jewish environment of early Christianity, parents were highly respected, but God was given a priority over against parents.

II

In our second section I shall give some NT evidence that the early Christians after Jesus' time shared this same view of children's duty to honour their parents.[19] I have already mentioned the Household Codes in my introductory sentences. I shall not quote them here, since it does not need any arguing that they affirm children's duties toward their parents. I rather point to an indirect evidence in our NT texts, namely, that the early Christians used the language of

---

[18] *Qumran Cave 4, XXIV: Sapiential Texts, Part 2 (Discoveries in the Judaean Desert XXXIV)*, Ed.-in-chief: Emanuel Tov (Oxford: Clarendon Press, 1999), p. 113 (italics and brackets added by the editor).

[19] See further P. Balla, *The Child-Parent Relationship*, chs. 5 and 6, pp. 157-228.

the family to refer to their relationships to one another in the congregation. They were like a large family, we might say, the family of God, *familia Dei*.[20]

We will consider just a few examples from Paul and then from the Catholic Epistles. In Romans 16:13, in a long list of persons to be greeted, Paul mentions a certain Rufus, whose mother he also calls his own mother: 'Greet Rufus, eminent in the Lord, also his mother and mine.' At the end of the verse there is a compressed expression in the Greek. The verse can be translated like this: 'Greet Rufus, the chosen (one) in the Lord, and greet his mother (who is) also mine.' Paul never refers to his earthly parents in a concrete way (see the autobiographical sections at Phil 3:3–6; Acts 21:3). But, he uses family imagery in a figurative sense here. Perhaps Paul was grateful for the loving care experienced from Rufus's mother. Thomas Schreiner suggests: 'presumably Rufus's mother either helped Paul in a specific situation or ministered to him regularly at some point in his labors.'[21] Although we do not know the reason why he calls her his mother, it is clear that Paul wants to describe a close relationship by alluding to the strong bond between a mother and her child. This supposes a high view of the role of a mother, and also the natural expectation that a son would love his mother and remain grateful for her care.

Paul also uses family imagery to express a caring role in connection with his congregations and disciples. For example, in 1 Cor 4:14–16 we read: 'I do not write this to make you ashamed, but to admonish you as my beloved children. (15) For though you have countless guides in Christ, you do not have many fathers. For I became your father (ἐγὼ ὑμᾶς ἐγέννησα) in Christ Jesus through the gospel. (16) I urge you, then, be imitators of me.' In other words, Paul expects the Corinthians to learn from him as from their father (note especially v. 16). Schrage rightly points out that the child-parent imagery implies an unchangeable relationship.[22] The term 'beloved children' is applied in the singular to Timothy in the same context in v. 17 (otherwise it does not appear in the Pauline Corpus). These texts, then, can be seen as indirect evidence for Paul's positive view of the role of parents; and, accordingly, for his expectation that 'children' should follow their parents' instructions. We could discuss many similar Pauline texts, e.g. 2 Cor 6:13 ('I speak as to children'), or 2 Cor 12:14-15 ('I will not be a burden, for I seek not what is yours but you; for children ought not to lay up for their parents, but parents for their children ... If I love you the more, am I to be loved the less?'), or Gal 4:19: 'My little children, with whom I am again in travail (οὓς πάλιν ὠδίνω)

---

[20] Cf. also David G. Horrell, 'From *adelphoi* to *oikos theou*: Social Transformation in Pauline Christianity', *Journal of Biblical Literature* 120 (2001), 293-311. I note that Horrell works with the hypothesis that there are only seven genuine Pauline epistles (see p. 294).

[21] Thomas R. Schreiner, *Romans*, BECNT (Grand Rapids: Baker, 1998), p. 793.

[22] Wolfgang Schrage, *Der erste Brief an die Korinther*, EKKNT VII/1 (Zürich: Benziger Verlag; Neukirchen-Vluyn: Neukirchener Verlag, 1991), p. 354.

until Christ be formed in you!'

However, let us examine some similar examples from the Catholic Epistles as well.[23] In 1 Peter 1:14 we read: 'As obedient children (ὡς τέκνα ὑπακοῆς), do not be conformed to the passions of your former ignorance'. The expression 'obedient children' has a similar genitival structure in the Greek to the phrase 'the sons of disobedience' (υἱοις τῆς ἀπειθείας) in Eph 2:2. Thus it may be that it is idiomatic, describing the readers as an 'obedient people'.[24]

In the Epistles of John the recipients are addressed frequently as 'children'. John calls them his own children, and he also refers to them as God's children. In 1 John 2:1 the author presents the purpose of his writing. It is significant that this is the first time in 1 John when the author calls his readers 'children' (with a diminutive form, 'my little children', τεκνία μου): 'My little children, I am writing this to you so that you may not sin; but if any one does sin, we have an advocate with the Father, Jesus Christ the righteous.' By this way of addressing his recipients, John implies that he has a loving relationship to them, and also that he writes with the expectation that they will obey him.

We note that in the same verse John refers also to God as 'father'. Thus the author uses the child-father imagery in a twofold way. First, he himself is the 'father' of his addressees in a spiritual sense. We observe that he does not refer to himself as 'father', but refers to his addressees as his 'children' (so also later in 2:12-14, in a clearly structured passage). Second, Christians are regarded as the children of God. This is implied in the first two chapters and is expressed explicitly in 3:1a.2: 'See what love the Father has given us, that we should be called children of God; and so we are ... (2) Beloved, we are God's children now; it does not yet appear what we shall be, but we know that when he appears we shall be like him, for we shall see him as he is.' These examples show that in early Christianity after the time of Jesus it was taken for granted that Christian families should not be dissolved, rather even the congregations should live like a family, as children of God and brothers and sisters of one another.

If this be the case, how should we understand Jesus' sayings about the disciples' leaving their parents? I suggest that we read those difficult passages in the light of what we have seen so far.

III

So, thirdly, and finally, let us look at some texts from the Gospels concerning the child-parent relationship.[25]

According to the Synoptic Gospels, right from the beginning of his public

---

[23] See also P. Balla, 'Child-Parent Imagery in the Catholic Epistles', *The Southern Baptist Journal of Theology* 6 (2002), 66-77.

[24] See e.g. Ramsey Michaels, *1 Peter*, WBC 49 (Waco, Tex.: Word Books, 1988), p. 56.

[25] See also P. Balla, *The Child-Parent Relationship*, ch. 4, pp. 114-56.

activity, Jesus called certain people to follow him as his disciples. In some cases this call resulted in the disciples leaving their parents. At first sight, this seems to witness to a radically anti-family attitude on Jesus' side. Gerd Theissen has coined the phrase 'Wanderradikalismus', itinerant radicalism, to describe the phenomenon that while people literally followed Jesus, they left behind their home, family, and fortune.[26] In the following, the radicalism of Jesus' ethos will not be questioned; rather, it will be discussed with the question in mind whether this radicalism meant a break with the duty of honouring parents.

Jesus Calls his First Disciples

We find a report of Jesus calling his first disciples in all four canonical gospels; Mark 1:16–20 and Matt 4:18–22 are similar enough to be called parallels, but Luke and John have different stories concerning the call (Luke 5:1–11; John 1:35–51). It is explicitly stated about James and John that they 'left their father' (Mark 1:20b). Matthew says they left the boat and their father, but he does not mention the hired servants. Luke says in a concluding sentence (5:11) that they left 'everything' (πάντα; the term 'everything', a neuter plural, can include persons as well).

First we note that one pair of brothers, James and John, were working in the same trade as their father: they were fishing together. Although it is not stated explicitly, we may presume that the same was true for the other pair of brothers, for Simon (Peter) and Andrew. They are reported to have left the boat, but there is no mention of their father.[27] There is no enmity between children and parents implied in the calling narratives. James and John continued to be called the sons of Zebedee even after they became disciples of Jesus, right until the end of the Gospels, according to the following passages: Mark 10:35 par. Matt 20:20; the Lukan parallel does not refer to concrete disciples; but see also Matt 26:37; Luke 5:10; John 21:2, where the references to the 'sons of Zebedee' are clearly later than the time when they left their father.

In a similar way, Peter cared for the ill mother of his wife (Mk 1:29-31 par.). It is narrated with a certain naturalness that Peter's mother-in-law lived with them in their house. Nothing compels us to presuppose that these disciples would not have provided for their parents later if any need should have arisen. Peter was prepared to return to his fishing business after Jesus' death.

---

[26] See e.g. Gerd Theissen, 'Wanderradikalismus. Literatursoziologische Aspekte der Überlieferung von Worten Jesu im Urchristentum', in: G. Theissen: *Studien zur Soziologie des Urchristentums* 3rd ed. (Tübingen: J. C. B. Mohr /Paul Siebeck, 1989) pp. 79-105, esp. p. 90. I thank Professor Gerd Theissen, my 'Humboldt *Gastgeber* Professor', for his manifold support to me during my research visits to Heidelberg.

[27] Codex Bezae and the Old Latin witnesses have πάντα in Mark 1:18; this may be an assimilation to Luke 5:11.

Irrespective of the question of the authenticity of this scene reported only by the Fourth Gospel (John 21:3), it makes best sense if we presuppose that the author of the Fourth Gospel did not think that there was any enmity between Peter and his family (although it has to be emphasised that we do not hear anything about the parents of Peter in the Gospels). We note that according to 1 Cor 9:5, many years later Peter's wife accompanied him on (at least some of) his journeys. We do not know how early she began to follow her 'wandering' – itinerant – husband; it remains important that (if we can trust the sequence of the Gospels) Peter and his wife fulfilled the duty of providing for old or ill parents even after Peter was called to follow Jesus.

We emphasise again that the scene concerns Jesus calling disciples. In their first context, texts about *Nachfolge*, the following of Jesus, may be regarded as referring to exceptional cases, i.e. they do not apply to all disciples. David Mealand contends that the group of those who 'left behind their home and family...probably exceeded twelve in number', but he adds that 'not all Jesus's hearers followed him in the literal sense.'[28] Jesus had two kinds of disciples: some who had to follow him, and those who returned to their homes right after they became disciples of Jesus. Thus not every saying applied to all of them. And even those who left their family in a literal sense, did not cut off all connections to them, did not initiate enmity toward them.[29]

A New Family?

In the Synoptic Gospels, there is a report of a direct confrontation between Jesus and his mother and brothers (Mark 3:31-35 par. Matt 12:46-50 and Luke 8:19–21). There is no agreement among scholars as regards the historicity of this passage, or to what extent it reflects the situation of the household churches. It can be argued that it presupposes the separation of the Christian community from the synagogue.[30]

However, it can also be argued that it is not likely that the early church created a story with such a negative attitude from Jesus' family.[31] The other two synoptic Gospels introduce this scene in another context. It is significant that a preparatory comment is only to be found in Mark (3:21): 'And when his family heard it, they went out to seize him, for they were saying, "He is beside himself".' The Greek text, οἱ παρ' αὐτοῦ ('those with him'), is not

---

[28] David L. Mealand, *Poverty and Expectation in the Gospels* (London: SPCK, 1981), p. 73.
[29] See also Santiago Guijarro, 'The Family in the Jesus Movement', *Biblical Theology Bulletin* 34 (2004), 114-121.
[30] So e.g. Walter Schmithals, *Das Evangelium nach Markus* ÖTK 2/1 (Gütersloh: Gütersloher Verlagshaus Gerd Mohn; Würzburg: Echter Verlag, 1979), p. 212.
[31] So e.g. Gerd Theissen and Annette Merz, *Der historische Jesus: Ein Lehrbuch* (Göttingen: Vandenhoeck & Ruprecht, 1997), p. 104.

unambiguous: it can refer to the disciples or to the relatives of Jesus. It is more likely that the latter sense is to be applied here, because otherwise the scene reported in 3:31–35 is difficult to understand: why does Jesus refuse his mother and brothers if they had not given any reason for wanting to call him away? For our understanding of vv. 31–35, the inclusion of vv. 20–21 means that Jesus' identification of his true family was not meant to involve the abandoning of his blood relations. It can be seen as an answer to the intended action of his non-understanding parents. Taeseong Roh has rightly pointed to the difference between Jesus' own attitude and that which was expected from the disciples. Whereas Jesus defines his own new family (v. 34: 'And looking around on those who sat about him, he said, "Here are my mother and my brothers!"'), there is no expectation of any breach with one's family on the side of the listeners.[32] We may add that Jesus was provoked by his 'non-believing' family to praise those who were accepting what he taught.[33] Thus this passage does not address the child-parent relationship in the case of the disciples. In Jesus' case, it was not his own initiative; rather it was a response to hostile behaviour on the side of his family. He did not follow them when they wanted to hinder him in his teaching ministry. The content of his teaching is not narrated, but from the concluding word we may infer that it was the priority of the will of God, the heavenly Father, that caused him to be disobedient to his mother and brothers. This decision was not without some pain for Jesus (see Mk 6:1-6a par., where it is reported that Jesus had to face enmity also from his country).[34]

Conflict Suffered as a Consequence of Discipleship

There are several sayings attributed to Jesus that affirm that children will rise against their parents. Some have strong similarities, e.g. Mark 13:12 par. Matt 10:21. This verse is printed without an indication of a variant in NA27 in the Markan text, and there is a little grammatical variation in the Matthean version. The verse reads (RSV): 'And brother will deliver up brother to death, and the father his child, and children will rise against parents and have them put to death'.[35] What is striking in this case is that the verse is part of a longer unit

---

[32] Taeseong Roh, *Die* familia dei *in den synoptischen Evangelien: Eine redaktions- und sozialgeschichtliche Untersuchung zu einem urchristlichen Bildfeld*, NTOA 37, Freiburg (Schweiz): Universitätsverlag (Göttingen: Vandenhoeck & Ruprecht, 2001), p. 112.

[33] For a tradition that Jesus' brethren did not believe in him during his earthly ministry, see also John 7:5.

[34] For a similar view, see John H. Elliott, 'Household/Family in the Gospel of Mark as a Core Symbol of Community', in: David B. Gowler et al. eds., *Fabrics of Discourse. Essays in Honor of Vernon K. Robbins* (Harrisburg/London/New York: Trinity Press International, 2003), pp. 36-63, esp. 47-52.

[35] The variant in Matthew is more likely a grammatical correction: the majority of the witnesses give the verb 'rise' in the third person plural, whereas the Codex Vaticanus

Jesus Before Parents

that has a parallel in Matthew in a different context: Mark 13:9–13 is part of the 'little apocalypse', whereas its parallel, Matt 10:17–22 occurs in Jesus' speech concerning the sending out of the disciples.

To be sure, the expression 'children will rise against parents and have them put to death' indicates enmity within the family to the bitter end. This is an extremely hard saying as regards children's behaviour. We have to observe, however, that the context clearly shows that the enmity arises against the followers of Jesus: It is because of Jesus' name that they will be persecuted. This persecution is carried out with such emotion that even family members turn against one another. This does not imply that Jesus' own followers would turn against their parents; rather, Jesus warns his disciples that they will be persecuted by their parents or even by their children.

Thus when Jesus speaks here of an enmity between children and parents, he refers to the consequences of discipleship, which are not intended by the disciples, but have to be suffered by them unavoidably.

The Urgency of Discipleship

There is a passage with a radical saying of Jesus, arguably a double tradition, i.e. it is witnessed in both Matthew and Luke. The content is similar but the wording is different in the two Gospels. Since the different expressions of the same content will be significant for our exposition, we quote both. Matthew 10:37–38 reads: 'He who loves father or mother more than me is not worthy of me; and he who loves son or daughter more than me is not worthy of me; (38) and he who does not take up his cross and follow me is not worthy of me.'[36] Luke 14:26–27 contains one of the most striking sayings of Jesus, often understood as a witness to his radical anti-family ethos: 'If any one comes to me and does not hate his own father and mother and wife and children and brothers and sisters, yes, and even his own life, he cannot be my disciple. (27) Whoever does not bear his own cross and come after me, cannot be my disciple.' Luke 14:26 and Matt 10:37 are either witnesses of independent traditions or 'Lukan' and 'Matthean' versions of a common tradition. The latter view is held by scholars who assign the saying to Q.[37] I accept that Luke 14:26 and Matt 10:37 are parallels; perhaps they are editorial adaptations of a Semitic original. We can find in them the same idea expressed by different idioms:

---

and some other codices bring the more correct third person singular, because the subject, 'children' (a plural neuter in the Greek) would require this.

[36] The original hand of Codex Vaticanus, Codex Bezae and a few other witnesses omit the second half of v. 37, probably due to homoioteleuton, as both half-verses end with the word *axios*. As v. 38 ends with the same word, the omission in P19 until the end of v. 38 is probably due to haplography as well.

[37] So e.g. Ulrich Luz, *Das Evangelium nach Matthäus*, EKKNT I/2 (Zürich: Benziger Verlag; Neukirchen-Vluyn: Neukirchener Verlag, 1996), p. 134.

'loves more' in Matthew equals 'does not hate' in Luke. The Semitic background of the term 'hate' would suggest that it is about a priority and not about emotions in the modern sense. As Craig Evans has put it: 'This may be an example of the Semitic expression of preference by means of antithesis – "I love A and hate B" meaning "I prefer A to B" (cf. Gen. 29:30ff; Deut. 21:15; Rom. 9:13) – which has been altered, but correctly interpreted, in the Matthaean form (Matt. 10:37).'[38] God places second the one whom he 'hates' as opposed to the one whom he elects (cf. also Mal 1:2–3), as we shall argue below. Howard Marshall points to further parallels (2 Sam 19:7; Prov 13:24; Isa 60:15; 1 John 2:9) and translates the term as 'to love less'. (See also Deut 24:3 and Eph 5:29.) He adds that the Hebrew original also means 'to leave aside, abandon': 'The thought is, therefore, not of psychological hate, but of renunciation.'[39] If a disciple loves Jesus then he should not love his family more than he loves Jesus; he must place his family second after Jesus (in Luke's words: he must 'hate' his family).

It has to be acknowledged that in the majority of the seven occurrences of the term μισέω in Luke the term refers to 'hating.' Nevertheless, it can be argued that the close context is against this meaning in Luke 14:26. Here it is affirmed at the end of the list that one has to hate even one's own life. This cannot mean real hating; it must mean a willingness to sacrifice even one's own life for the sake of Jesus. As Darrell Bock argues: 'The call to "hate" is not literal but rhetorical.... Otherwise, Jesus' command to love one's neighbor as oneself as a summation of what God desires makes no sense (Luke 10:25–7).'[40] Thus, the saying is about priorities: Jesus must be more important to the disciple than the disciple's own life. As Luke has many OT allusions (especially in the case of the infancy narratives),[41] he was probably capable of seeing the meaning of 'putting to the second place in preferences' also in the case of μισέω. God hated Esau, but nevertheless he made him a nation as well (though he did punish the nation when it turned against the chosen people) according to the Old Testament tradition (Mal 1:2–3). This tradition was understood as pointing to priorities in election, as it is witnessed to by Paul who cites this passage from Malachi in Rom 9:13. To sum up, I argue that Luke 14:26 refers to the priority of Jesus' call to one's own family ties. It does not express a general rule, but the urgency of the call to some of Jesus' disciples.

There are further texts concerning which I would argue in a similar way that

---

[38] Craig F. Evans, *Saint Luke*, TPINTC (London: SCM Press; Philadelphia: Trinity Press International, 1990), p. 577.

[39] I. Howard Marshall, *The Gospel of Luke: A Commentary on the Greek Text*, NIGTC (Exeter: Paternoster Press, 1979), p. 592.

[40] Darrell L. Bock, *Luke*, BECNT, 2 vols, Grand Rapids, Mich.: Baker Books, vol. 1: 1999 (second printing of 1994 orig.), vol. 2: 1998 (second printing of 1996 orig.), quotation from vol. 2, p. 1284.

[41] See e.g. Bock, *Luke*, vol. 1, p. 68.

they are not directed against the family, but instead elevate the priority of the Kingdom of God, or of Jesus himself. For example, in Matt 8:21-22 par. Lk 9:59-60, the saying concerning leaving the dead to bury their own dead as an answer to a would-be disciple who wanted to bury his father may sound shocking at first hearing, but it is also clear that it is about priorities: Jesus called the man to follow him and that was a once and for all possibility in this man's life. Perhaps later he would not have met Jesus again, and would not have heard his words a second time: 'but as for you, go and proclaim the kingdom of God' (Lk 9:60). Discipleship has to take precedence; people who would have remembered the example of how God has precedence in the case of the Nazirites, could understand a radical call to become preachers of God's Kingdom.

So at last I arrive at my conclusion. If Jesus required priority not only for God and his Kingdom, but also for himself, this may be seen as further indirect evidence that he held that he was the Son of God. We have seen in the environment of the early Christians that God had a priority even over parents. So does Jesus. In his radical call his disciples must have heard the claim of divine Sonship. That is why the early Christians in their writings outside the Gospels did not require disciples to separate from their families. They remembered well that Jesus affirmed the Fifth Commandment in the *Corban* pericope and also in his conversation with the rich young ruler. Later Christians also remembered that in the Synoptic Gospels immediately after the pericope of the rich young ruler there follows the saying concerning the cost of discipleship. In the name of the disciples Peter said (Mk 10:28-30): 'Lo, we have left everything and followed you.' Jesus said, 'Truly, I say to you, there is no one who has left house or brothers or sisters or mother or father or children or lands, for my sake and for the gospel, who will not receive a hundredfold now in this time, houses and brothers and sisters and mothers and children and lands, with persecutions, and in the age to come eternal life.' This is our new family, the family of God, in which even in the Jesus tradition the validity of the Fifth Commandment is maintained. Jesus comes before parents; but this does not dissolve the *unity* in the family. We have to find *this right priority*, the priority of Jesus, the Son of God, when we seek unity in the Christian family, even in the larger 'family' of all the children of God.

CHAPTER 10

Weber, Troeltsch, and the Maintenance of Hegemony in the Marketplace of German Religion: A Preliminary Analysis

Irving Hexham

By religion I mean Christianity; by Christianity I mean Protestantism; by Protestantism I mean the Church of England as established by law.

Henry Fielding, *Tom Jones*, III. 3.

Introduction

Professor Stuart Mews, of the University of Lancaster, England, discovered a sure-fire way of engaging his seminar in discussions of Max Weber's *Sociology of Religion*. He began by introducing himself as a member of the Methodist Church. Then he would ask if any participants in the seminar belonged to the Lancaster University Inter-Varsity Fellowship (IVF). Usually two or three people, about a third of the seminar, would admit to IVF membership.

Having solicited this profession of faith Mews would then tell them that as evangelical Christians they were sectarians who belonged to sects or even worse cults. This statement produced howls of disagreement. If anyone was a sectarian surely it was Mews the students would argue. After all, they argued, Methodism broke away from the Anglican Church in the eighteenth century. That made it a sect. Further, most IVF members were Anglicans. So how could they be a sect when the Church of England was the State Church with the Queen as its official head?

This heated debate was usually followed by a similar one the following week, when indignant IVF members would bring along their Bibles to convince Mews that their theology was based upon scripture. In the New Testament, they argued, there was a clear distinction between the Church and sects that did not match his definition of either church or sect. Unimpressed by such theological arguments Mews would carefully explain Weber's theory of ideal types and the distinction Weber made between church, sect and cult.

When he explained Weber's ideas Mews, like thousands of other sociologists, stressed the contrast between Weber's 'scientific' approach and the unreflective historical or theological arguments used by his students. The distinctiveness of Weber's definition of 'church,' 'sect,' and 'cult,' it was claimed, was that Weber based his work on a careful analysis of the data and empirical observations not theological or other prejudices. Anyone who reads an introductory anthropology or sociology that discusses this issue will know that Mews' argument is repeated *ad nauseam* in the literature.

Theology and Prejudice[1]

Henry Fielding's comment, which heads this chapter, illustrates the problem of defining cults and sects by making a joke about religious prejudice. He draws attention to the ease with which people define religion in terms of their own beliefs and practices. No doubt, if we substituted the Roman Catholic Church, or the Berlin-Brandenburg Landeskirche, for 'the Church of England,' many Irish Catholics and German Protestants could easily adopt Fielding's view as their own.

The problem with this sort of definition is that by identifying religion with one particular tradition we exclude all others. Yet when people, including many scholars, begin to talk about 'cults' or 'sects' today the definitions they use are often no better than Fielding's. The case of Salman Rushdie, whose book *The Satanic Verses* led to a sentence of death by the Iranian Government, illustrates how dangerous such sectarian definitions can be. Western governments reject the claim that Islamic scholars have the right to pass the death penalty on anyone on purely theological grounds.[2] But, when we come to cults and sects we find that the very people who are appalled by the judgement on Rushdie are often quite prepared to argue that Western governments ought to accept milder, but nonetheless theological, judgements on cults as a basis for legislation. This is particularly so in continental Europe.

The Use of 'Cult' in Old Testament Biblical Criticism

The word 'cult' has a long history of different meanings. During the nineteenth century various theologians used cult to describe ritual practices associated with religious centres. Behind the long development of the concept of the cult

---

[1] This paper develops the argument found in Irving Hexham and Karla Poewe, *New Religions as Global Cultures* (Boulder: Westview, 1997). To make the argument more accessible to English readers wherever possible English translations of German texts were used although the German was consulted.

[2] *The Observer* (19 February 1989).

in Biblical studies stands the towering figure of the German philosopher Hegel (1770-1831). Under his influence the development of critical studies of the Bible were given a great impetus. Hegel's students, including Bruno Baur (1809-1882) and D.F. Strauss (1808-1874), forged the tools which made the analysis of the Bible as a secular text possible.

The significance of Hegel's influence lies in his early theological writings where Hegel displays an undisguised disgust for Judaism.[3] In Hegel's view the Germans made a fundamental mistake when they converted to Christianity.[4] True, he admits that Jesus was an unusual Jew. [5]Nevertheless, he laments the 'servile' and essentially life denying influence of the Jews on German society.[6]

The implicit and often explicit anti-Semitism of Hegel is an important factor in our understanding of the development of the concept of 'cult' as it used by theologians. Behind many nineteenth-century critical theological studies there seems to be an unacknowledged desire to distance Christianity from Judaism which, because of its exclusive nature, is seen as a cult.

Thus the great German Old Testament scholar Julius Wellhausen, who was openly anti-Semitic, sharply distinguished between the cultic nature of Jewish legalism, which was highly exclusive, and the freedom of prophetic religion that developed an open outlook.[7] Apart from philosophical influences from the Hegelian tradition, the chauvinistic politics of the German National Movement and Wellhausen's political conflict with and dislike for his own teacher at Göttingen, Georg Heinriich August Ewald (1803-1875), a converted Jew, may well have contributed to the development of his views on the Old Testament.[8]

Later, starting with the German scholars Hermann Gunkle (1862-1932) and Hugo Gressmann (1877-1927), a concerted attempt was made to identify liturgical texts, such as the Psalms, and place them in the context of cultic rituals.[9] This usage of cult, as a means to understand the development of Israelite religion, is found in many modern studies such as John Bright's now classic *A History of Israel*.[10]

In his influential work Bright argues that in the Bible 'the cult of the

---

[3] Hegel [1793, 1797, and 1800] 1961: pp. 68-69 and 182-205. The references to Hegel before 1800 are to manuscripts. As a result the dates are approximations. All dates given in [ ] are to the date of the original manuscript or first published edition. The date outside the square brackets is to the published edition we used.

[4] Hegel, [1793] 1961: pp. 145-151.

[5] Ibid., p. 69.

[6] Ibid., pp. 68-70 and 177-79

[7] Lou H. Silberman, 'Wellhausen and Judaism', *Semina* 23 (1983), pp. 75-79; cf. Soloman Schechter, *Seminary Addresses* (Cincinnati: Arc Publishing, 1915).

[8] Rudolf Smend, 'Julius Wellhausen and his *Prolegomena to the History of Israel*', Semina 23 (1983), p. 6.

[9] R.K. Harrison, *Introduction to the Old Testament* (Grand Rapids: Eerdmans, 1969), pp. 46-66.

[10] John Bright, *The History of Israel* (London: SCM, 1962).

patriarchs is depicted as exceedingly simple.' It was, he tells the reader 'always the cult of the ancestral deity of the clan'.[11] With this introduction to his usage of cult Bright develops the idea that the 'symbols of that early cult were symbols of ... kingship'.[13] The idea of kingship and the Kingdom of God, which Bright sees as central to the Old Testament, is shown to develop into the full blown theology of the royal cult centred on the Davidic Kingdom.[15]

Bright's usage the word cult is fairly neutral and can be seen as simply describing the development of Hebrew religion. Nevertheless, when read carefully it can be seen that on the one hand he identifies cults and cultic practices in terms of their exclusivity while the development of prophetic religion is seen as a move towards inclusiveness.

The Use of the Term 'Cult' in New Testament Biblical Criticism

A similar development of the use of the term 'cult' is found in the work of New Testament scholars who located the origins of Christianity in a prophetic rebellion against the deadening rituals associated with the Temple cult located in Jerusalem. Once again, cult was used to identify liturgical performances and religious rituals, which enforced a restrictive ethos within an exclusive community.

These theories originated in the late eighteenth century with English Deism. In Germany Deism was often mediated by American writers like Tom Paine (1737-1809). Thus Paine's *Age of Reason*[16] had a profound effect in German universities like Göttingen. Here Tom Paine is important because of the strong objections he raised to Jewish exclusivism, which he contrasted with the openness of Jesus' inclusive ethic.[17]

When Biblical criticism entered theological faculties radical views about the Bible were embraced by a number of leading thinkers influenced by Hegel and his followers. Thus, the reliability and apostolic authorship of the gospels were rejected and what Albert Schwietzer (1875-1965) called *The Quest for the Historical Jesus*[18] began.

One of the key arguments in this quest was the rejection of the primary role previously assigned to Matthew's Gospel in Christianity. From as early as the

---

[11] Bright, *The History of Israel*, p. 92.

[13] Ibid., p. 135.

[15] Ibid., pp. 204-207.

[16] Tom Paine, 'The Age of Reason' in William M. van der Weyde (ed.), *The Life and Works of Thomas Paine* VIII (New Rochelle: Thomas Paine National Historical Association, 1925 [Part One originally published 1794 and Part Two in 1796]).

[17] Paine, 'The Age of Reason', pp. 11-12, 155-74.

[18] Albert Schweitzer, *The Quest for the Historical Jesus* (trans. Montgomery; New York: Macmillan, 1968 [first German edition 1906, first published in English 1910]).

second century Christian writers like Irenaeus (130-200 A.D.), Clement of Alexandria (150-215 A.D.) and later Eusebius (d. 341-342 A.D.) had insisted that the Gospel of Matthew was the first written gospel. They also taught that the author was Matthew, the Jewish tax collector, who is mentioned in the gospel itself (Matt. 10.3). Thus, on the basis of their arguments, both the reliability of the gospel and the Jewish background of Christianity are firmly rooted in Christian thought.

Probably the most important development in New Testament criticism during the nineteenth century was the rejection of this traditional view of Matthew's Gospel. Instead theories of Markan priority and speculation about the possibility of an earlier testament to the sayings of Jesus, which scholars called 'Q' from the German *Quelle,* or source, were developed (Farmer 1964).

At the time that the theory of Markan priority was created, although not necessarily today, everyone agreed that Matthew was the most Jewish of all the Gospels. Therefore, to deny the authenticity of Matthew was to cut Christianity off from its Jewish roots and the cultic, or exclusive, aspects of Judaism.[19] Similarly, Adolf von Harnack (1851-1930) convincingly argued that it was imperative for modern Protestantism to remove the Old Testament from its cannon of sacred scriptures.[20] Although von Harnack was not a Nazi such views lent considerable force to the growing pro-Nazi German Christian Movement.[21]

What went unnoticed in subsequent New Testament studies was the anti-Semitic undertone of these theories. Of course, this was not a crude anti-Semitism. Rather, it depended on sophisticated views about political culture and the requirement of nationhood. Consequently, the Jews, and other exclusive or sectarian groups, were seen as disruptive elements that strained social order.

Nevertheless, despite the obvious undertones of such theories, their political nature is not addressed in standard works on the history of Biblical criticism.[22] Only recently has the political aspect of the debate about Markan priority been recognised by scholars[23] and the anti-Semitism of much Biblical criticism

---

[19] Cf. Rudolf Bultmann, *Theology of the New Testament: Volume One* (trans. Kendrick Grobel; New York: Charles Scribner's Sons, 1951 [first published in German in 1948]), p. 115; also Rudolf Bultmann, *Theology of the New Testament: Volume Two* (trans. Kendrick Grobel; New York: Charles Scribner's Sons, 1955 [first published in German in 1953]), p. 125.

[20] Wilhem Pauck, *Harnak and Troeltsch* (New York: Oxford University Press, 1968), pp. 37-38.

[21] Doris L. Bergan, *Twisted Cross: The German Christian Movement in the Third Reich* (Chapel Hill: University of North Carolina Press, 1966), p. 143; Karla Poewe, *New Religions and the Nazis* (London: Routledge, 2005), pp. 21-29.

[22] Cf. John Rogerson, *Old Testament Criticism in the Nineteenth Century: England and Germany* (London: SPCK, 1984); William Baird, *History of the New Testament. Research: Volume One: From Deism to Tübingen* (Minneapolis: Fortress Press, 1992).

[23] Henning Graf von Reventlow and William Farmer, *Biblical Studies and the Shifting of Paradigms, 1850-1914* (Sheffield: Sheffield Academic Press, 1995), pp. 15-49.

pointed out.[24]

From these observations we see that words like 'cult' came into general and theological usage loaded with the negative connotation of exclusiveness. Thus cult was used to represent 'dead religion' or 'formal rituals' which were contrasted with the 'vigour,' 'health' and 'openness' of prophetic movements. The spontaneity of faith, said to characterise Christianity, was also contrasted with the legalistic works of Judaism.[25]

The Theories of Weber and Troeltsch

Today anthropological and sociological discussions about the classification of various forms of religious organisation are strongly influenced by the work of Max Weber (1864-1929) and Ernst Troeltsch (1865-1923). To distinguish between different categories of organisation these scholars devised a method of social analysis based on the use of ideal types. An ideal type is an approximation that Weber and Troeltsch believed expressed the essence of an organisation in its pure form.[26]

On the basis of this methodology they developed the classic terminology of church, sect and cult. Most social scientists using these terms see them as scientifically neutral in contrast to the ideologically loaded terms used in theology and Biblical studies. But, a careful examination of Weber and Troeltsch's work shows that this understanding is incorrect.

Many introductory texts describe Troeltsch as Weber's student, pupil, or disciple.[27] This is wrong and, as we will see, very misleading. One reason for the neglect of Troeltsch is perhaps the fact that Talcott Parsons (1902-1979), who dominated American sociology for many years, devotes an entire volume of his *The Structure of Social Action*,[28] to Weber, while relegating Troeltsch to four short footnotes.

In fact, Weber moved to the University of Heidelberg in 1896 two years after Troeltsch had occupied the Chair of Theology. Both men were already working on similar topics as were a group of like-minded friends.[29] In 1904

---

[24] von Reventlow and Farmer, *Biblical Studies*, pp. 132-48.

[25] Ernst Troeltsch, *The Christian Faith* (based on lectures given at the University of Heidelberg, 1912-13; trans. Garrett E. Paul; ed. Gertrud von le Fort; 1991), p. 29.

[26] Thomas Burger, *Max Weber's Theory of Concept Formation* (Durham, North Carolina: Duke University Press, 1976), pp. 115-40.

[27] John J. Macionis, Juanne Nancarrow Clarke and Linda M. Gerber, *Sociology* (Scarborough, Ontario: Prentice-Hall, 1994), p. 468; Michael Hill, *A Sociology of Religion* (London: Heinemann Educational Books, 1973), p. 51; Kurt Samuelsson, *Religion and Economic Action* (New York: Harper and Row, 1957), p.20.

[28] Talcott Parsons, *The Structure of Social Action* (New York: The Free Press, 1968 [1937]).

[29] Harry Liebersohn, *Fate and Utopia in German Sociology, 1870-1923* (Cambridge, Massachusetts: MIT Press, 1988), pp. 52-62; Wolfgang J. Mommsen and Jürgen

they spent 'five weeks or so' together on a trip to America and for a number of years their families shared the same house.[30]

Weber's essay *The Protestant Ethic and the Spirit of Capitalism* appeared *after* the American trip. In this work Weber introduced the distinction between 'church' and 'sect.' As a result many writers attribute the use of this terminology to Weber.[31] Other writers attribute this distinction to Troeltsch.[32] Today it is probably impossible to discover which of the two originated the terminology. What is clear is that they owed a lot to each other.[33] The relationship between them and the way it has influenced subsequent scholarship is not unimportant.

If, as most texts wrongly state, that Troeltsch was Weber's student, then anyone reading their works naturally assumes that Weber taught Troeltsch to think sociologically. On the other hand if Weber was in any sense a student of Troeltsch, a theologian, we need to re-think our understanding of the 'scientific' nature of the concepts they developed through their co-operation.

Commenting on this possibility Friedrich Graf argues that Weber's reliance on Troeltsch is established by a careful examination of Weber's footnotes to *The Protestant Ethic*.[34] He then suggests that in fact a careful study of Weber's work and its sources would reveal a far greater reliance on Troeltsch's theological judgements than is usually recognised.

The importance of this observation is that it illuminates the negative connotations of 'sect' and 'cult' found in both Weber's and Troeltsch's work. Rather then being completely disinterested observations, it is highly probable that their conception of sect and cult were influenced by preconceived theological judgements based in the theological system of Troeltsch and the understanding of cult and sect by Biblical scholars. In other words notions about the exclusiveness Judaism and open nature of Christianity that had significance in both theology and German social life may have influenced the formation of ideal types as used by both Weber and Troeltsch.

Weber and Troeltsch's German Christian Ideology

Contrary to popular opinion neither the research of Weber nor Troeltsch was

---

Osterhammel (eds), *Max Weber and his Contemporaries* (London: Unwin Hyman for the German Historical Institute, 1987), pp. 215-33.

[30] Mommsen and Osterhammel (eds), *Max Weber and his Contemporaries*, p. 217.

[31] Meredith B. McGuire, *Religion: The Social Context* (Belmont: Wadsworth, 1981), p. 107; Reinhard Bendix, *Max Weber: An Intellectual Portrait* (London: Methuen, 1962), p. 314.

[32] Milton J. Yinger, *The Scientific Study of Religion* (London: Macmillan, 1970), p. 252; Thomas O'Dea, *The Sociology of Religion* (Englewood Cliffs: Prentice Hall, 1966), p. 68.

[33] Mommsen and Osterhammel (eds), *Max Weber and his Contemporaries*, pp. 223-24.

[34] Mommsen and Osterhammel (eds), *Max Weber and his Contemporaries*, p. 222.

motivated by abstract intellectualism. Behind both men lay a passionate commitment. Together they recognised that Germany and German Christianity faced grave dangers. Thus, Troeltsch argued that on the one hand the old 'system of *absolute establishment*' which created a monopoly situation through the close union of church and state was dead. On the other hand, an American or French style of *disestablishment* was seen by Troeltsch as un-German. This left a 'system of *mixed establishment*' as the only viable option.[35]

In particular Troeltsch hated American-style free churches which he saw as 'based on Baptist and Puritan ideas ... a democracy that is as individualistic as it is egalitarian, and on an enlightened relativism.'[36] Although Troeltsch doubted that it was possible to transplant American ideas to Germany he was very worried about the American system of church and state.

He observed that churches in America were dominated by orthodox groups similar German Pietists. These groups, he argued, were always strong among the laity. Therefore, in America, where the laity had free reign conservative theologians dominated the churches. Such conservatism was, he believed, dangerous because it rejected 'scientific education.' In making this comment he seems to have meant German higher criticism of the Bible.[37]

To counter the Americanisation of German religion Troeltsch believed it was essential that the state prevent the growth of American-style churches dominated by the laity. Therefore he advocated that the Government select a small number of churches that would be granted 'corporate privileges grounded in public law.' These churches were to be selected on the basis of their 'contribution to public life' and the education of their ministers carefully controlled through university-based faculties of theology. Thus, in return for 'a considerable degree of state control' the churches would be provided with 'the material base of support.'[38]

In Troeltsch's view 'The separation of church and state can be no separation of state from Christianity.'[39] Rather, the 'concept of revelation' represented a holistic fusion of life and history in a manner worthy of Kant and Goethe. This reality, he argued, set Germany forever apart from France and America.[40]

When moving from Troeltsch's sociological work to his theological writings, one finds a parallel discussion of church and sect. It also becomes clear that while it may be unfair to describe Troeltsch as a philosophical Hegelian he follows Hegel in his understanding of the relationship between Christianity and Judaism.

---

[35] Ernst Troeltsch, *Religion in History,* trans. James Luther Adams and Walter F. Bense, (Minneapolis: Fortress, 1991), pp. 109-17.
[36] Ibid., p. 111.
[37] Ibid., p. 112.
[38] Ibid., p. 109.
[39] Ibid., p. 115.
[40] Ibid., p. 116.

Thus, in his 1912-1913 *Glaubenslehre* lectures at the University of Heidelberg, published in English as *The Christian Faith*,[41] Christianity's break from Judaism is constantly emphasised.[42] Christianity is, in his view, a universal religion that separated itself from the nationalism of Judaism and other ancient cults.[43]

Following Wellhausen he sees Judaism as 'the most legalistic of all religions.' On the other hand, Christianity is a religion of freedom imbued with the prophetic spirit.[44] It is against this theological background that Troeltsch develops his ideas about church and sect.[45]

A definite political agenda lies behind Troeltsch's views. Therefore it is no surprise that his comments on sects were less than enthusiastic. To be fair he saw the problems with established churches and understood the appeal of sectarian movements. But, behind his apparent scientific spirit is an apologetic thrust shaping his conclusions.

Weber appears to have been more sympathetic than Troeltsch towards sects and the American religious model which seems to have intrigued him. In his view, sects gave 'American democracy its own flexible structure and its individualistic stamp'.[46] Like Troeltsch, however, he believed that German religion and society had developed in its own unique way. This meant that it was both impossible and undesirable for American-type sects to develop in Germany. With Troeltsch, Weber, agreed that by definition, sects were anti-intellectual.[47]

Although Weber recognised the piety and commitment expressed by members of sects, he believed that the only viable option for an educated person was church membership. For him, commitment to a sect was, by implication, intellectually inferior.[48]

Weber and Troeltsch's Definition of Church and Sect

The sociological definitions of church, sect and cult propagated through the work of Weber and Troeltsch clearly show the influence of Troeltsch's ideological concerns and dislike of American religion. They use 'church' to refer to any religious organisation that is universal in its scope and inclusive in membership. Thus, a church is a religious body that counts as members anyone

---

[41] Troeltsch, *The Christian Faith*.
[42] Ibid., pp. 25, 29.
[43] Cf. Troeltsch, *The Christian Faith*, pp. 87, 93, 293.
[44] Ibid., pp. 279, 29.
[45] Ibid., pp. 20-23.
[46] Max Weber, '"Churches" and "Sects" in North America: an Ecclesiastical Socio-Political Sketch', *Sociological Theory* 3.1 (trans. Colin Loader; Spring, 1985 [1906]), p. 10.
[47] Ibid., p. 11.
[48] Ibid., p. 12.

living within a certain geographic area. It is also remarkably similar to the prophetic form of religion identified by Biblical critics.

This definition uses the indiscriminate baptism of infants, or some similar rite, as one basis for identifying a religious group as a church. Consequently, Orthodox Churches, Roman Catholicism, and many older, often called 'mainstream,' forms of Protestantism, including almost all Lutheran and German *Landeskirchen*, and many Episcopalian, Presbyterian and Congregational churches have little difficulty in being recognised as churches.

On the other hand, all evangelical groups which preach conversion, be they Anglican, Lutheran, Presbyterian, Pentecostal, German pietist, or independent Charismatic Churches are by definition, sects. A sect, in Weber and Troeltsch's view, is characterised by the exclusive nature of its membership. Thus sects reflect the characteristics found by Biblical critics in Judaism and other ancient cults.

According to this school of thought any evangelical or pietistic Christian group is *by definition* a sect, sectarian movement, or cult. Thus the early Methodism in England is a classic example of a sectarian movement. Other groups defined as sects include the Puritans, German Pietists, the Plymouth Brethren, Baptists, and so on.

Using this type of definition it now becomes clear why, in contemporary Germany, independent churches like the Church on the Way in Berlin, are *Sekten*, or sects. So too, according to Weber and Troeltsch, are many Episcopalian congregations, for example, All Souls, Langham Place in London, Southern Baptist congregations in America, and all African Indigenous Churches.

Sociologically these churches are sects because their ministers preach conversion. In this sense, Wolfhard Margies who founded the Church on the Way, Billy Graham, George Carey the former Archbishop of Canterbury, and even Archbishop Desmond Tutu are all sectarian leaders because they preach the necessity of conversion and a new birth through Jesus Christ.

Germany and 'the Cults'

The historical development of German churches in the twentieth century is exceptionally complex (Sholder 1988).[49] Nevertheless, it is clear that an understanding of church-state relations similar to the one advocated by Weber and Troeltsch was widely accepted. Following the defeat of Nazi Germany, as a result in part of the heroic opposition of many churchmen, the three Western allies approved the creation of a legal framework remarkably similar to

---

[49] Klaus Scholder, *The Churches and the Third Reich*, Vols 1 and 2, trans. John Bowden (London: SCM, 1988); Erich Geldback, *Freikirchen – Erbe, Gestalt und Wirkung* (Göttingen: Vandenhoeck and Ruprecht, 1989); Otto Piper, *Recent Developments in German Protestantism* (London: SCM, 1934).

Troeltsch's ideal.[50]

Today the principal of 'religious freedom' is recognised and guaranteed in the *German Basic Law*[51] and German authorities are adamant that there is 'no state church in Germany.' Nevertheless, both the Evangelical Church in Germany (EVD) and the Roman Catholic Church (RCC) 'have a special status as independent public corporations.' Further the status of the EVD and RCC 'is often described as a partnership' in official publications.[52]

In other words, *de jura*, Germany lacks a State Church. But, *de facto* there are two State Churches, the EVD and RCC. Other churches and religious bodies exist alongside these privileged groups. Some, such as the so-called 'free churches,' mainly Baptists and Methodists, are also recognised as 'public corporations,' but many other groups are not. Only the EVD and RCC share a special relationship or partnership with the state and are supported by a government-collected church tax.

The unification, or re-unification, of Germany in 1991 saw the introduction of a hefty tax to finance reconstruction in the former German Democratic Republic (DDR) of East Germany. Responding to this additional tax burden many Germans have opted to formally withdraw from church membership thus exempting themselves from paying church tax.[53] It is against this background of a mass exodus from the established churches, the EVD and RCC, that current concerns about cults and sects in Germany must be viewed.

Not long ago German bookstores, such as Elwert's in Marburg, carried only a few books on cults or sects. By 1997 the number of books devoted to 'exposing' the danger of cults filled several shelves and has continued to grow. During the same period numerous popular magazine articles and TV shows also contributed to the growing concern about cults in Germany.[54]

Numerous local and national government agencies have also published exposés of 'dangerous' religious groups.[55] Finally, in 1966 the Federal

---

[50] Arno Kappler and Adraine Grevel, *Facts about Germany*, trans. Kathleen Müller-Rostin (Bonn: Societäts-Verlag, 1995), pp. 382-85.

[51] For an extended discussion of current legal issues see: Norber Kirsch, *Christ and Recht* (Berlin: Zussammenarbeit Christlicher Juristen und Rechtsberater, 1995).

[52] Kappler and Grevel, p. 383.

[53] 'Der Himmel Muss Warten', *Der Spiegel* 10 (1995), pp. 76-104; 'Religion, Glaube ohne Kirche', *Focus* 15 (1996), pp. 52-104.

[54] 'Die Sekten-Falle', *Focus* 17 (1994), pp. 40-48; "Die teuflische Macht der Sekten,: *Stern*, (4 May 1995), pp. 3 and 32-42; 'Guru, yogische Flieger, Scientologen und okkultische Ufo-Fans', *Frankfurter Rundschau* 9 (Samstag 14 Juni 1997).

[55] Monika Schipmann (ed.), *Informationen über neue religiöse und weltanschauliche Bewegungen und sogenannte Psychogruppen (Information Brochure on 'New Religious and Ideological Movements, and so-called Psycho Groups')* (Berlin: Senatsverwaltung für Jugend und Familie, 1994); 'Bericht der Landesregierung Tätigkeit von Seckten in Schleswig-Holstein: Psycholkulte, Sekten, "Jungendreligione", Extremguppen', *Die Ministerpräsidentin des Landes Schleswig-Holstein* (Kiel: Carius Druck, 1997);

Government in Bonn established a Special Commission on So-Called Sects and Psyco-Groups.[56]

In North America, concern about the treatment of religious groups in Germany has focused on Scientology because of that movement's media campaign.[57] This is unfortunate because it diverts attention from other groups and basic questions about the nature of churches, sects and cults. Scientology, in fact, is not the only group under investigation by the German government. Nor is Scientology necessarily the most threatened religious group. Other small religious movements and churches such as the growing Charismatic movement are also designated 'cults' or 'sects' making it very difficult for them to function in a normal manner.[58]

The German government responds to the criticism that some religious groups are persecuted in Germany today by pointing to the guarantees of religious freedom in the *Basic Law*. But critics like the Berlin lawyer Norbert Kirsch argue that since 1989 higher Courts in Germany have consistently reinterpreted the *Basic Law* to restrict the activities of small religious groups which they identify as sects or cults.[59]

Attempting to discuss this issue with many Germans, pastors and academics, can be very frustrating. In many ways it seems that we talk completely different languages. In Germany, the definitions created by Weber and Troeltsch take on social reality. This means that in Germany the debate about religious freedom is framed within a specific set of assumptions. These assumptions involve social norms that isolate popular religious movements that appear exclusive. Consequently, it is easy for official and semi-official bodies to warn the public against them using the language of church, cult, and sect, impunity.

By establishing the primacy of privileged churches through their sociological terminology, Weber and Troeltsch effectively prevented the acceptance of free churches and other religious groups in German society.[60] Free churches are tolerated. Other religious movements have to constantly justify their existence.

The fact that the terms used to label these movements are rooted in

---

'Sogenannte Sekten und Psychogruppen: Die Mun-Bewegung, K', *Bundersministeriums für Familie, Senioren, Frauen und Jungend vom Bundesverwaltungsampt* (1996).

[56] 'Zwischenbericht der Enquete-Kommission, Sogenannte Sekten und Psychogruppen', Enquete-Kommission 170 (Bonn: Deutscher Bundestag Drucksache, 13 August 1997).

[57] E.g. 'What America needs to know about Discrimination in Germany', *Church of Scientology* (Los Angeles: 1977); 'Does Germany have something against these guys?', *Time* (10 February 1997), pp. 28-29.

[58] 'German Charismatic Churches Face Persecution, Threats of Violence', *Charisma* 18 (November 1995); Kirsch, 'Religious Freedom under Threat?'.

[59] Kirsch, *Christ and Recht*.

[60] Cf. Rodney Stark, 'German and German-American Religiousness: Approximating A Crucial Experiment', *Journal for the Scientific Study of Religion* 36:2 (1997), pp. 182-93.

nationalist ideologies and anti-Semitism should not go unnoticed.[61] It is time, as Stark and Bainbridge[62] argue, to reject the ideologically-loaded methods of Weber and Troeltsch and replace them with more scientific concepts. Thus church historians and theologians need to heed current sociological discussions and use value-neutral terms that identify religious movements without invoking hidden theological prejudices in their works.

---

[61] Cf. Gary A. Abraham, *Max Weber and the Jewish Question* (Urbana and Chicago: University of Illinois Press, 1992); Paul Lawrence Rose, *Revolutionary Antisemitism in Germany from Kant to Wagner* (Princeton, New Jersey: Princeton University Press, 1990).

[62] Rodney Stark and William Sims Bainbridge, *The Future of Religion: Secularisation, Revival and Cult Formation* (Berkeley, California: University of California Press, 1985); Rodney Stark and William Sims Bainbridge, *A Theory of Religion* (New York: Peter Lang, 1987).

Ecumenical and Eclectic: Resonances

CHAPTER 11

Two Decades of Ecumenism in Europe: A Promising Past with an Uncertain Future

Keith Clements

It perhaps comes as a slight shock to realise that 'history' is not just something we study, but a reality which we share in and help to make; and that the history which is worth studying is not only that of distant ages past, but the events and developments of our own lifetimes. What future historians will make of the past 20 years of the ecumenical life of Europe, we cannot tell. But it is certainly a story which already merits attention and appreciation – and the future of which requires considerable thought.

My starting point is the Ecumenical Encounter organised jointly in 1984 by the Conference of European Churches (CEC) and the Council of Catholic Episcopal Conferences in Europe (CCEE) at Riva del Garda, near Trento in Italy.

As one who was not present at Riva del Garda, my own pictures of that event have been formed by reading the accounts and documents,[1] but no less by the vivid recollections passed on by some who did participate. They tell how moving it was for many Protestants to come to Trento, a city whose name is inevitably associated with the hardening of dogmatic and ecclesiastical divisions in the aftermath of the 16th century Reformation. They tell of the inspirational worship services of common prayer, including prayers of repentance. They speak of the richly informative theological lectures by Dr R.P.C. Hanson and Professor Werner Löser, and other addresses. They record the sense of real achievement in the production of the text 'Our Credo – Source of Hope' – and much else.

But first, Riva del Garda 1984 must be set in its historical context as the starting point for this brief survey of the European churches in ecumenical

---

[1] *Confessing the Faith Together – A Source of Hope*. Report of the Third European Ecumenical Encounter, 3-8 October 1984, Riva del Garda, Italy (Geneva and St Gallen: CEC and CCEE, 1985).

pilgrimage these past 20 years. It was the third Ecumenical Encounter organised jointly by CEC and CCEE, following those at Chantilly, France, in 1978 and at Logumkloster, Denmark, in 1981. It should be borne in mind that both CEC and CCEE at that time were still relatively young organisations, still feeling their way in promoting ecumenical dialogue. It was, moreover, humanly speaking a very bleak climate in which they dared to speak about unity among the churches and peace in Europe. Not only was Europe still politically - and seemingly for ever - divided between east and west but the Cold War was now entering a newly alarming phase of military confrontation. The threat of nuclear warfare hung over all. As yet *glasnost* and *perestroika* were unknown words.

Chantilly and Logumkloster had focused on the calling of the churches to unity in one hope, that the world might believe. It was a bold and decisive step that was taken, to make the theme of Riva del Garda not the production of a new statement about unity, but a return to a study of the ancient confession of faith common to all Trinitarian Christians: the Niceno-Constantinopolitan Creed. This choice of topic should not be seen in isolation from the wider awakening of interest in the creed around that time. The Faith and Order Commission of the WCC was launching the study process 'Towards the Common Expression of the Apostolic Faith Today' based on a new ecumenical explication of the creed (a process in which, along with Alan Sell, I was privileged to take part for several years).[2] Both the WCC and the Vatican Secretariat for Unity had proposed that this study also be implemented in continental, regional contexts. Riva del Garda can therefore be seen as a venture in Europeanising the wider programme. But it also had a momentum and a specific motivation of its own. Divided churches in a dangerously divided continent; churches which by their divisions had historically contributed to the wider human divisions; churches which seemed powerless in face of the ideological divides and the nuclear arsenals – what had they to say, what *could* they say, with integrity? How could they bring hope into a seemingly hopeless situation? What 'common witness' could they bring?

At first sight, it must have seemed that to return to an ancient creed of 381 was an escape from the brutal and fearful realities of the present day. The architects of Riva del Garda were under no illusions that the project might be laughed at and dismissed. What is remarkable is that they refused to see the creed as merely a historical monument, or even just as a liturgical text enshrined in tradition, but regarded it as a sign and source of hope: it still had a future, and it offered a future. As the 'Message to the Christians of Europe' from Riva del Garda stated: 'This common confession of our faith is certainly not the immediate answer to the questions nor is it the solution to all the

---

[2] For the summary results of this study process see *Confessing the One Faith. An Ecumenical Explication of the Aposotolic Faith as it is Confessed in the Nicene-Constantinopolitan Creed (381)* (Faith and Order Paper 153; Geneva: WCC Publications, 1991).

problems which arise today in a divided Europe. It does however remind us of God's love for all men; and it encourages us to go further together along the road which will lead Europe and the world to peace and reconciliation.'[3] This was a recognition that if the churches *do* have anything of relevance to say to one another in their search for unity and to the world in its longing for peace, it must arise from the faith confessed in this creed. The churches' witness cannot just be a recasting of one form or another of human philosophy or political ideology. It has to have a specific theological grounding in the Trinitarian faith. This was a decisive clearing of the ground and a laying of the foundations for so much which was to come in the two following decades. The churches of Europe were recovering a truly theological confidence for their witness, even if at that time many aspects of that witness remained unclear and uncertain. Above all, it was a witness *in hope* that was being recovered. As the theological text says in its concluding paragraph on the resurrection and new creation: 'We realize that this patient expectation of the new creation does not exonerate us from working with others for the establishment of a more just and human world. Indeed, this liberates us for this task.... The courage to live has its source in the hope of eternal life.'[4]

Riva del Garda reverberated with a two-fold harmony: the faith confessed in the creed as the source of hope, and the calling for that hope to be translated into concrete action in responsibility for Europe: 'Our common confession of the faith challenges us to find new ways of responding together to the questions raised by the modern world and of providing together the service of aid and sharing which Christ commands. Peace, disarmament, human rights, the place of women in church and society, unemployment, poverty, the environment – these are some of the difficult questions to which we as Christians should seek answers together.'[5]

The recognition of this agenda was indeed to prove prophetic, as further developments from the mid-1980s showed. Again, these developments cannot be isolated from the wider ecumenical world scene but in Europe they were to take a dramatic turn. The 6th Assembly of the World Council of Churches in Vancouver, 1983, had recommended that the churches enter into a 'conciliar process of mutual commitment to justice, peace and the integrity of creation'. It was in Europe that this call was to be taken up in a specially important way, and the initiative was to be provided by the churches in the two countries which represented the division of Europe in its starkest form: the German Democratic Republic and the Federal Republic of Germany. It should be remembered that in fact the European churches had already been accompanying very closely the implementation of the Helsinki Final Act and the work of the Conference on Security and Cooperation in Europe (CSCE), which at that time represented the

---

[3] *Confessing the Faith Together*, p. 8.
[4] Ibid., p. 26.
[5] Ibid., p. 8.

only real hope on the political level of countering the Cold War divide. But the German initiative, especially on the GDR side, came with a special challenge to the churches themselves. In part it was because among German Protestants the memory had been alive of what had happened in 1934 at the conference on the Danish island of Fanö of the Universal Christian Council for Life and Work. There, Dietrich Bonhoeffer had spoken on the need for a universal ecumenical council of the churches to be summoned, to declare God's will of peace among the nations and to outlaw war.

At the 9th Assembly of the Conference of European Churches in Stirling, Scotland, in 1986, representatives of the churches in the two German republics presented resolutions calling for a European Assembly as part of the worldwide process for justice, peace and the integrity of creation. The Assembly itself adopted a resolution proposing that CEC and CCEE together should call an ecumenical Peace Assembly for all the churches in states which were signatories to the Helsinki Final Act. Thus was set in train the process that led to the 1st European Ecumenical Assembly, organised by CEC and CCEE, which met in Basel, Switzerland, in May 1989 under the theme 'Peace with Justice'.[6] It was an epoch-making event in several respects. Not since the great east-west schism of 1054 had Christians from all over Europe met in such numbers – Catholics, Orthodox, Protestants and Anglicans – as the 700 official church delegates and hundreds more gathered for that week of prayer, celebration, study and affirmation of faith and responsibility. But it was also of course significant in the more immediate historical context. The tremors of change were already being felt across Europe. In the west there was increasing criticism of the military standoff. In the east, Poland had been transformed by 'Solidarity' while *glasnost* and *perestroika* were indeed now familiar terms. Basel took up many of the items spelled out for the Christian agenda at Riva del Garda: peace, disarmament, human rights, reconciliation. But one concern which received relatively little attention at Riva del Garda now took at least an equal place with all the others: the integrity of creation, to be made concrete in the care of the environment and its preservation for future generations. This new recognition of creation was quite decisive in giving European Christians a sense that they belonged to one continent, which was part of the one interdependent world of nature and humanity. The Chernobyl disaster of 1986 had spread radioactivity far beyond the borders of the Soviet Union. There was a new realization of the significance that land and soil, sea and air, are held by all in common. The Danube rises in western Germany and flows through Romania into the Black Sea. Whose river is it?

Basel celebrated the one faith of all European Christians, and Christians celebrated that unity – the unity they already had and the unity they still hoped

---

[6] See *Peace with Justice* (The official documentation of the European Ecumenical Assembly, Basel, Switzerland, 15-21 May, 1989; Geneva: Conference of European Churches, 1989).

for. They went on pilgrimage across the three borders between Switzerland, France and Germany to symbolize their vision of a new Europe *sans frontières*. A new language was being spoken, heard for example in one of the prayers prepared for Basel that echoed words of Pope John Paul II. 'We thank you that the peoples of the East and the peoples of the West share a common home in Europe. Lord, help us to know that peace between East and West in Europe will help to solve many conflicts outside Europe. Keep us from accepting division and tension.'

If Basel in May 1989 took place at a time of rising excitement and hope, few could have anticipated that by the end of that same year the Berlin Wall would have collapsed, and change would have swept through Hungary, Romania, Czechoslovakia and other countries in the east. But it is important to acknowledge that the churches of Europe, while taken by surprise at the speed of events, were not simply following in their train. Just as the revival in the Russian Orthodox Church did not wait for the events of 1990-91, nor even for the policies of President Gorbachev, but was already under way in preparation for the celebrations in 1998 of the 1000th anniversary of the conversion of Russia, so too Basel anticipated much of what was to come in Europe as a whole. The European churches were finding each other anew, and realising they had a common responsibility for Europe, their common home.

As Wordsworth said of the early days of the French revolution, 'Bliss was it in that dawn to be alive...'. But the full light of day challenged the euphoria. While Basel had declared that there were no problems or tensions in Europe which justified violence as a solution, soon we had the bloody conflicts attending the break-up of the former Yugoslavia, conflicts which tragically did have a religious dimension to them. It seemed that with the breakdown of the political and ideological divide between east and west the ancient historic fault-line between Orthodox east and Latin west was re-emerging. This did not run only through present-day Bosnia-Hercegovina, but more widely from the Baltic to the Mediterranean. It had cultural elements. It was also taking on new economic aspects, as it became clear that many of the countries in the east were entering not a new paradise of prosperity but a chaos of industrial disintegration, unemployment and breakdown of social welfare. And what of the churches? For many of them, the new scenery was bewildering. The totalitarian regimes had imposed a kind of *de facto* ecumenism where Protestant, Catholic and Orthodox found themselves in natural solidarity, and in which belonging to wider ecumenical bodies like CEC or the WCC had served to enable contact with the western world. Those who had endured or resisted communism found that the new situation of freedom posed new questions to them as to their identity, in relation both to society and to other churches. Who were they meant to be, and to whom should they now relate? The churches in the west, for their part, found that their partners in the east often had quite other priorities than theirs, in for example the need to rebuild their life and ministry in their basic essentials.

In the early 1990s there was talk of the emergence of a 'new confessionalism'. It was certainly significant that during 1991-92 three major confessional gatherings took place: the First Synod of European Catholic Bishops in Rome, the 'Protestant Synod' in Budapest, and the Synod of Orthodox Bishops in Constantinople. This in itself was hardly remarkable. It was only to be expected that those with a shared tradition and identity should seek to reflect on their particular role and responsibility in a quite changed situation. What was more alarming was that at the same time new actual suspicions and disputes were arising interconfessionally. Orthodox were angered at what they saw as invasions by proselytizing Protestant missionaries from the west, or new Catholic designs on their territory. Equally, some churches in minority situations felt that the majority historical churches were seeking to restore their old pre-communist priviledged positions in state and society, without regard for religious freedom and democratic rights. All this, however, did not prevent CEC and CCEE from holding another Ecumenical Encounter in Santiago Compostela in 1991 on the theme 'Mission and Evangelism in Europe Today'.

It was becoming clear that the call made at Riva del Garda in 1984, for the churches to seek again reconciliation and unity as the basis for a credible witness in Europe, was taking on a new urgency in these years. In fact, in addition to their regular annual meetings of the CEC-CCEE Joint Committee, CEC and CCEE maintained a joint working group specifically to monitor the follow-up to the Basel Assembly and to see that its vision was not lost. It was at the meeting of the Joint CEC-CCEE Committee in Leanyfalu, Hungary, in 1994 that the decision was taken to start preparing for a 2nd European Ecumenical Assembly. The final decision was taken at the Ecumenical Encounter in Assisi in May 1995, to hold the Assembly in 1997 and to focus on the theme of 'reconciliation'. This was chosen deliberately as a way of continuing the central concerns of Basel but also to open up new dimensions. The experiences since Basel had made the churches aware that reconciliation was what they needed among themselves, and that the gospel of reconciliation was the most precious gift they could offer to the world.

So we come to Graz, July 1997, where 10,000 Christians from all traditions and from all over Europe came to pray, celebrate and study together under the theme 'Reconciliation - Gift of God and Source of New Life'.[7] It was the largest ever pan-European gathering of this kind, where for the first time east Europeans were together on truly equal terms with the west. But it was noteworthy not only for its breadth but for its depth as well. It was one of those rare occasions when not only the public issues of peacemaking, economic justice, environmental care were studied and debated, but where the need for spiritual formation of those who would be peacemakers and reconcilers was

---

[7] See *Reconciliation – Gift of God and Source of New Life,* Documents from the Second European Ecumenical Assembly (Graz: Verlad Styria for CEC and CCEE, 1998).

made clear. As the final message states

> We came to this ecumenical gathering not just to exchange ideas and share experiences, but to go beyond words to specific measures, aware that our divisions and enmities still provoke conflict and are a serious obstacle to making visible the gift of reconciliation. For this we seek God's forgiveness and express our repentance to those we have harmed. We are sadly aware that these divisions exist not only between our churches but also between members of our churches and between women and men. Since these exist in us as individuals and in our churches, reconciliation must start by the Spirit of God in Christ changing our hearts and minds.[8]

'To go beyond words to specific measures...': Among the recommendations of Graz, was

> 1.2 We recommend that the churches develop a common study document containing basic ecumenical duties and rights. From this a series of ecumenical guidelines, rules and criteria could be developed which would help the churches, those in positions of responsibility and all members, to distinguish between proselytism and Christian witness, as well as between fundamentalism and genuine faithfulness, and help to shape the relationships between majority and minority churches in an ecumenical spirit.[9]

Equally significant was the stated rationale for this: 'The ecumenical fellowship is currently in a difficult situation as a result of various factors. This requires conscious counter-strategies. It seems necessary to foster an ecumenical culture of living and working together, and to create a firm basis for it.'

Thus was conceived what was born and became known as the *Charta Oecumenica. Guidelines for the Growing Cooperation among the Churches in Europe*.[10] The *Charta* is an attempt to set out in concrete terms what growing together in dialogue, cooperation, fellowship and shared responsibility towards Europe mean for the European churches today. No less than its content, the way it was produced was an effort to exemplify these values. The process was launched at the annual meeting of the CEC-CCEE Joint Committee in Rome in January 1998. Its drafting was entrusted to a joint group of Protestant, Orthodox and Roman Catholic theologians who laboured through much encounter and debate to produce a first text which was circulated to all the Bishops' Conferences and CEC member churches in the summer of 1999, giving them more than year in which to respond with their comments,

---

[8] *Reconciliation*, p. 32.
[9] Ibid., p. 49.
[10] St Gallen and Geneva : CCEE and CEC, 2001. For a discussion of the *Charta* and its reception see Viorel Ionita and Sara Numico, eds, *Charta Oecumenica. A Text, Process and a Dream of the Churches in Europe* (Geneva: WCC Publications, 2003).

criticisms and suggestions. A large number these were received, in the light of which the text was revised and submitted for final amendment and approval by the CEC-CCEE Joint Committee in January 2001. It was launched upon the world at the Ecumenical Encounter held by CEC and CCEE in Strasbourg just after Easter 2001. This was an encounter between 100 European church leaders and an equal number of young people, who gathered to celebrate and affirm the meaning of Christ for the new millennium under the theme 'Lo, I am with you always, to the end of the age.' Many of those present for the ceremony at which it was signed by the then Presidents of CEC and CCE, Metropolitan Jérémie Caligiorgis and Cardinal Miloslav Vlk respectively, felt not so much that they had come to the end of a process but to a new beginning, a new stage on the ecumenical pilgrimage.

For an ecumenical document the *Charta* is a relatively short text - perhaps that is one reason why it has become so popular. It has been translated into at least 30 languages and been studied and discussed all over Europe, and even officially adopted by some churches. It comprises three main sections: 'We believe in "One Holy Catholic and Apostolic Church";' 'On the Way Towards the Visible Fellowship of the Churches in Europe;' and 'Our Common responsibility in Europe.' It states both the obstacles towards unity and the means of grace by which alone they can be overcome, the renewing power of God's Spirit in our hearts and lives. It lays down the importance of meeting together, struggling on difficult ethical and theological issues together, praying together. It sets out Europe's reality as a diversity of peoples and cultures and religions, in which peace is to be sought through dialogue, and the needs and rights of all to be respected. Thus it implicitly recognises the process of European integration in which the enlarging European Union is playing a key role but at the same time seeks to provoke questions about the values which must sustain a united Europe. But the core of this text, what makes it unique, lies in the *commitments* which it invites the churches and Christians to make their own: from recognising freedom of conscience to praying for one another and for Christian unity; from counteracting any form of oppressive nationalism to adopting a lifestyle free of consumerism; from strengthening the position of women and equal rights of women to dialogue with Jews and Muslims. In some circles, the *Charta* has been criticised for allegedly saying little that is new, and in one sense that is true for it gathers up much of the thought and experience on the ecumenical journey from Riva del Garda onwards. What is new, is the series of commitments which churches are challenged to make in specific directions. It is a mirror against which they can look at themselves and their real actions, or lack of action. Certain churches, once they have started to do this, have admitted that while they think they may know and already do what is in the *Charta*, when measured against the actual praxis called for by the *Charta* they are found wanting. It indicates the direction in which they still have to walk.

From Riva del Garda to the *Charta Oecumenica* was one journey. The starting point of the *Charta Oecumenica* is the same as the theme of Riva del Garda, for the *Charta* opens its first section by declaring: 'With the Gospel of Christ, according to the witness if Holy Scripture and as expressed in the ecumenical Nicene-Constantinopolitan Creed of 381, we believe in the triune God: the Father, Son and Holy Spirit.' Much had happened since Riva del Garda. There in 1984 the churches of Europe were brought together. Since then they have journeyed together. And if in some ways new problems have arisen between the churches, it is precisely because they have been brought so much closer together. You only really *argue* with people next to you, not those far away. At Riva del Garda the churches came together on the basis of a given text, the ecumenical creed. With the *Charta* they have created a text of their own. At Riva del Garda they looked forward in broad terms to a greater unity in a more united Europe. With the *Charta Oecumenica* they are committing themselves to concrete acts of cooperation and common responsibility. So it is a journey from confession to actions which are themselves new forms of confession. It cannot claim to have left dialogue behind. The *Charta* in fact it calls for still deeper dialogue. While at Riva del Garda the churches of Europe expressed their longing to be together, they now know they cannot do without each other, cannot get away from each other, and cannot understand themselves without one another. At Riva del Garda in 1984 it was said: 'Our creed supports our hope in a quite special way. It witnesses to God the Holy Trinity who gives a future and hope to all, and at the same time commits each of us to perform acts of hope.' The *Charta Oecumenica* is but the continuation of this way, being itself an act of hope, and specifying those actions which here and now lead us towards visible unity, towards peace and human dignity for all, towards reconciliation and the care of creation, and all to the glory of the one God, Father, Son and Holy Spirit.

These two decades of European ecumenism indeed constitute a promising past. But the future of the story is uncertain, even as we look forward to the 3rd European Ecumenical Assembly being planned by CEC and CCEE for Sibiu, Romania, in 2007 under the theme 'The Light of Christ Shines Upon All – Hope for Renewal and Unity in Europe.' It is a truism now to say that the ecumenical movement is more beset by questions and doubts than driven by confident expectations. What has to be asked is whether the journeying of the kind undertaken thus far has enough energy to ride these uncertainties and find answers. Or, to put it another way, does the *Charta Oecumenica* with its repeated emphasis on dialogue represent simply a contentment to mark time, or a determination to push ahead? Level-headed wisdom counsels against undue pessimism: 'The ecumenical movement is simply having to cope with its own success' one hears it said, and suchlike. Maybe, but questions are now being raised about the whole nature of the ecumenical movement as such.

Some of these questions arise from the context in which we now find ourselves, and of course not only in Europe. But there are some particular reasons why European ecumenicals are uneasy at the moment within the perspective of the global scene. The WCC, under its then general secretary Konrad Raiser, in 2002 initiated a debate about the 'reconfiguration' of the ecumenical movement. By this was meant a reconsideration of the different structures and organisations now acting as instruments of the ecumenical movement – as well as the WCC itself, the regional ecumenical organisations such as CEC, the world confessional bodies (Lutheran World Federation, World Alliance of Reformed Churches, etc), national councils of churches and so on. The question was asked: at a time of diminishing resources (especially financial of course) can the churches afford continuing support such a range of bodies? Is there not need, at the very least, of more careful division of labour and greater coordination? But a prime mover of this debate was the greater ecumenical role now being claimed by a number of the church-related development agencies (or 'specialised ministries' as they now prefer to be called). These largely northern-based bodies such as Christian Aid (UK) and Bread for the World (Germany) were now no longer content simply to support the existing ecumenical organisations and to channel their funds through them, but were now desirous of creating a new kind of coalition among themselves which would itself carry out advocacy work at the international level. This would, at first sight at least, appear to set up an ecumenical structure alongside the WCC and its cohorts, not only implying a diversion of resources from these 'traditional' ecumenical bodies but taking over some of their agenda as well. At the same time there has been a return to the concern manifested in the earlier study under WCC auspices, 'A Common Understanding and Vision of the WCC' for a widening of the ecumenical movement in the sense of a more visible and organised inclusion of the large and increasing Christian constituency outside the present ecumenical structures. Here is meant particularly of course the Roman Catholic Church and the burgeoning Pentecostal and evangelical movements.[11]

It is not clear just where the 'reconfiguration' debate is presently heading. Little more has been done so far than a thorough mapping exercise of the multiplicity of organisations and their inter linkages.[12] The arrival of Konrad Raiser's successor as WCC general secretary, the Kenyan Samuel Kobia, signals yet another factor being brought into the discussion: what appears to be the wholesale shifting of the centre of gravity of Christianity away from Europe and the rest of the north, to the south. To what extent this is actually happening, and what is its real significance if it is so, may be contestable. But European

---

[11] See *Towards a Common Understanding and Vision of the World Council of Churches* (A Policy Statement, adopted by the Central Committee of the World Council of Churches and commended to member churches and ecumenical partners for study and action; Geneva: WCC, September 1997).

[12] See *Ecumenism in the 21st Century,* Report of the Consultation Convened by the World Council of Churches, Chavannes-de.Bogis, Switzerland, 30 November to 3 December 2004 (Geneva: World Council of Churches, 2005).

ecumenism during the next few years may well have to cope with the sensation that in the eyes of much of the rest of the Christian world it is a mere sideshow re-enacting old historical story-lines while the real dramas are elsewhere.

This is not all. The assumption that even the *whole* of the *Christian* world and 'Christian unity' constitute the highest priority for ecumenism is now being challenged by the claims of inter-faith dialogue. This was becoming so long before the events of 11 September 2001 and the upsurge in popular demands for inter-faith understanding which these provoked. Several years before that, a German newspaper carried a headline 'God has a new address' over an article which argued that within Europe itself the interesting religious questions had moved out of the churches into the arena where Muslims, Jews and Buddhists as well as Christians encountered each other. But it cannot be denied that in a world fraught with conflicts, actual and potential, in which religious identity plays a crucial role inter-faith dialogue is an urgent priority. The work of Hans Küng, arguing for a global ethic supported by all the major world religions, is but one example of this concern: 'There can be no peace among the nations without peace among the religions. There can be no peace among the religions without dialogue between the religions.'[13] Should inter-faith dialogue now replace inter-confessional Christian dialogue and cooperation as the ecumenical priority? Many are now saying 'yes'.

In such a climate, the kind of ecumenism which has been born and bred in Europe, and which can be well illustrated by the account of the last two decades, would seem to have little chance of much further progress - or even, maybe, survival. But it is not just the environment which is unpromising. It is the lack, among the churches themselves, of any real ideas on what concretely unity might actually mean.

For example, one of most striking features of the ecumenical landscape at the moment is the virtual disappearance from it of interest in unity conceived of as *conciliar fellowship*, which was such a feature of WCC Faith and Order work during the 1970s and which flourished from the mid-1980s in the movement and programmes for Justice, Peace and the Integrity of Creation (JPIC). Central in all this was the notion of churches, which were themselves united, becoming bound together in common decision-making processes and accountable to one another in their decision-making. Perhaps the JPIC process attempted too much too soon and, as some allege, succumbed to socio-political rhetoric rather than enquiring what truly prophetic action required. Something deeper, however, was at work. The end of the Cold War in Europe, as stated earlier in this paper, brought not only liberation but a new quest for self-identity on the part of many churches. This put the notion of conciliarity on the margins of concerns. Mutual accountability has to rest on an assurance that one's conciliar partners are as truly 'church' as oneself, albeit understood in a

---

[13] Hans Küng, *Global Responsbility. In Search of a New World Ethic* (London: SCM Press, 1991).

diversity of ways, and that truly common interests are at stake. It is precisely that which is now in question. Ecclesiology and ecumenical commitment have moved apart, and may even be set at odds with each other. The most striking instance of this was the publication of the Vatican document *Dominus Iesus* in 2000 which, while indeed it may have represented essentially a re-statement of classic Roman Catholic self-understanding, took the Protestant and Anglican world by surprise and caused widespread dismay by its tone as much as by its content.[14]

It is not enough, however, to point the finger at Rome with accusations of anti-ecumenical aspirations. The fact is that all the main confessional traditions in Europe display a manifest *defensiveness* at the present time, with a tendency for them to define the nature and goal of unity mainly on their own terms. The Roman Catholic Church is concerned to defend the integrity and authority of its hierarchical structure inherent to which is its understanding of the sacraments. Orthodoxy defends vigorously its canonical territories which it sees as essential to its being church. Among some Protestants one can find an equally rigorous defense of the historic confessions to be preserved in all their particular minutiae. All this makes the prospects for pursuing the goal of visible unity somewhat bleak. One can of course opt for the notion of 'reconciled diversity', which one can realistically, if not somewhat cynically, view as a theological justification of the status quo – but at what cost for the pursuit of truth?

The fact is that at the moment there is no single, over-arching concept of the goal of ecumenism within which all can find their onward paths; no vision transcending all present differences and calling us forward together towards the horizon of unity. In the past the ecumenical movement has had a series of such visions. At the World Missionary Conference in Edinburgh in 1910, generally accepted as the birthplace of the modern ecumenical movement, it was the vision of evangelisng the whole world for Christ, a task in which all could and should work together regardless of particular confession. In the Life and Work movement which grew up in the 1920s it was the goal of serving the social needs of humanity, a service which would itself draw the churches more closely together. Simultaneously the Faith and Order movement began the project of theological dialogue, in which many joined on the premise that the different understandings and practices of the churches were all but partial expressions of the one, deeper and greater truth of Christ yet to be apprehended by them all. The World Council of Churches was founded to draw all these streams together, as were a regional organisations such as CEC, whose Constitution states in its Preamble

The member churches of the Conference seek by the grace of the Triune God to

---

[14] This paper was completed shortly before the election on 19 April 2005 of Cardinal Joseph Ratzinger, generally identified as the author of *Dominus Iesus*, as Pope Benedict XVI.

pursue together the path of growing conciliar understanding on which they have set out. In faithfulness to the Gospel...they seek to continue to grow in the fellowship (koinonia) of faith, hope and love. Faithful to this Gospel, they also seek to make a common contribution to the mission of the Church, to the safeguarding of life and the wellbeing of all humankind.[15]

All this is down on paper, but there is a lack today of any one meta-narrative to enthuse and inspire. This, of course, may be said to be simply one more manifestation of the post-modernist culture we inhabit, a context in which meaning can be found only in the particular, the partial or even fragmentary elements of experience granted to us. Therefore it may be asked, why should the ecumenical movement be any different? Was not the earlier ecumenical movement unconsciously expressing the western, liberal, modernist mindset seeking to impose one grand rationality upon everyone and everything? Why should we not joyously allow confessionalist particularities and enthusiasms to flourish uninhibitedly if that is what people want?

There can be no question that faith is received and lived out in particular, concrete forms, confessional and cultural. There is no abstract, disembodied Christianity. One believes and worships and lives as a Russian Orthodox, or a Polish Catholic, or an English Baptist, and so on. But what the ecumenical movement stands for is the *active relation between* these forms, and the basis on which they recognise that in all their diversity they do belong to one other, in Christ. Put most fundamentally, ecumenism is about people embodied in these particular, diverse forms loving one another through identification with the other and accepting each other as part of the whole which claims them all. The *Charta Oecumenica*, in two of its sets of commitments, states very clearly what must surely be the minimum ecumenical duty here:

- to pray for one another and for Christian unity;
- to learn to know and appreciate the worship and other forms of spiritual life practiced by other churches;
- to move towards the goal of eucharistic fellowship.

- to continue in conscientious, intensive dialogue at different levels between our churches, and to examine the question of how official church bodies can receive and implement the findings gained in dialogue;
- in the event of controversies, particularly when divisions threaten in questions of faith and ethics, to seek dialogue and discuss the issues together in the light of the Gospel.

Such invitations to commitment signal that a decisive point on the journey has been reached. It is now a matter of nerve as to whether it will be pursued

---

[15] *Constitution of the Conference of European Churches* (Geneva: CEC, 2003), p. 3.

further. Notwithstanding all the questions about such ecumenism acknowledged a few paragraphs earlier, it would be an act of monumental irresponsibility by the European churches to abandon the pilgrimage now. Additional tasks indeed have to be accepted but not as diversions from this central path. The question of 'reconfiguring' the ecumenical movement in terms of its organisational structures is still secondary to that of what the churches and other living expressions of Christian community themselves want *from each other*, not just from the ecumenical instruments which they themselves have set up and then all too frequently ignore, or fail to resource properly, or castigate for their alleged shortcomings. The Christian centre of gravity may be moving from the north to the south, but that should serve to concentrate the European ecumenical mind even more sharply on what its particular needs and responsibilities are and not to give up the ghost on its own endeavours in guilt-laden resignation masquerading as modesty. The urgency of inter-faith dialogue and the search for a global ethic are indisputable. But the case for their usurping the priority of intra-Christian ecumenism is not only not proven, it is self-contradictory, for how can any one world faith claim to be a dialogue partner with other faiths if it is not at least on the way to unity with itself? As the late Pope John Paul II tirelessly repeated, there is no alternative to the ecumenical path, and that way must be trodden in dialogue.

The crucial question for the further journey is, just what is involved in the great, endlessly repeated term 'dialogue'? If it is simply a never-ending exchange of views on theological and practical issues that of itself it is unlikely to produce really new results. There will be, at best, an elegant dance in which participants move around, perhaps successively exchanging partners but finally ending up exactly as before albeit with a reverential bow to one another as the music ends. We may perhaps understand a little more of what one another's 'positions' are, but the positions are unlikely to have changed. We shall therefore need to look more seriously into what kind of *logos*, speaking, must now make up truly ecumenical dia*logue*.

At this point, one must note a term that is now coming into vogue in ecumenical discourse, at least in Europe, and mainly from the Roman Catholic side: 'spiritual ecumenism'. This betokens a welcome recognition that prayer and spirituality must be at the heart of ecumenical encounter and endeavour, and not just abstract theological discussion or structural reorganization. At first sight, it might also arouse suspicion that an emphasis on the 'spiritual' is being offered as a diversion from tackling the thorny, divisive issues of ecclesiology, ministry, sacraments and so forth. One cannot but notice, for example, that in gatherings of one of the most attractive and popular movements drawing Catholics and other Christians together in Europe today, the Focolari movement, there is joyous and wholesome celebration that communion in Christ is real despite all doctrinal differences – while at the same time there seems to be a studied avoidance of the question 'If this is so, then why cannot we celebrate the eucharist together?' The implication of such an attitude would seem to be either that we *should* be at the Lord's Table together here and now, or that the question of eucharistic communion does not really matter so much after all – a position which it is hard to credit being held by the many Catholic bishops who identify with Focolari!

There is, fortunately, a more profound and realistic exposition of what 'spiritual ecumenism' means, to be found for example in the presentation of Bishop Kurt Koch (of Basel) to the Plenary of the Pontifical Council for Promoting Christian Unity in November 2003. Koch both clearly recognises the solidity and unavoidability of the issues which separate the churches and at the same time calls for a spirituality which will precisely energise the tackling of them. He states candidly

> ...[T]he ecumenism of truth and love and the ecumenism of life in the sense of a renewed ecumenical spirituality are intextricably linked. Over and above that, an ecumenical spirituality can not be an alternative to theological dialogue within ecumenism, for the simple reason that the ecumenical spirituality has never existed, and the often cited conviction that theology separates while spirituality unites is impossible to verify even historically. For behind the church schisms of the 11th and the 16th centuries there were not only different theologies but also and especially different spiritualities. That is still true even today, above all in the relationship between eastern and western Christendom. On the level of theology we are indeed very close to the Orthodox churches, while on the level of spirituality and the culturally determined way of life we are very far apart. In the relationship with the churches and ecclesial communities which resulted from the Reformation, the situation is exactly the reverse. But how can a renewed ecumenical spirituality help us to make progress in this situation?[16]

Bishop Koch's question can only be answered by delving further into what the actual content will be of the spirituality which impels more creative dialogue. Prayer, yes; 'exchange of gifts', yes. But is there not also a dimension to the New Testament understanding of *logos* which should haunt and disturb us? *Logos* according to the Scriptures is ultimately Jesus Christ, and *ho logos sarx egeneto*: the Word became flesh (John 1:14). Christian dialogue must take the same route. Dialogue where *logos* simply remains *logos*, speaking, is no longer enough in the light of this gospel of incarnation. The Scottish poet Edwin Muir had in his immediate sights the hyper-Calvinist highland church where in doctrinal polemic

> The Word made flesh is here made word again,

---

[16] Kurt Koch, 'Recovering the Soul of the Whole Ecumenical Movement (UR8). Necessity and Perspectives of an Ecumenical Spirituality', Pontifical Council for Promoting Christian Unity Information Service 115 (2004/1-11) (Vatican City, 2004), p. 35.

A word made word in flourish and arrogant crook.[17]

But there are collateral implications wider than Protestant verbosity, and ecumenical discourse too must heed the warning. The churches must take the risk of making experiments in sharing their actual ways of being church. Perhaps we need a new term: not just dialogue, exchange of words, but *diazoë*, exchange of life. I have to confess that I myself can as yet barely glimpse what this might mean in practice But, for example, could not the churches, meeting in conciliar fellowship, jointly commission an 'order' of persons to whom would be assigned the mission of sharing for a period of time in the life of churches other than their own, experiencing from within and to the full the liturgical, pastoral, diakonic and missionary life of those churches, and then bringing their experiences and reflections into the ongoing ecumenical dialogues? The integrity of the different churches and their traditions would be maintained while at the same time a *diazoë* would be enabled that could fructify ecumenical encounter with quite unforeseen possibilities.

That, of course, 'is only an idea' and there may well be (and I hope there are!) better ones. But the ecumenical movement, certainly in Europe, needs new ideas at the moment if the promising past is to have a fulfilling future.

---

[17] Edwin Muir, 'The Incarnate One'. Source: *Penguin Book of Religious Verse*, ed. R.S. Thomas (London: Penguin Books, 1963), p. 55.

CHAPTER 12

The Challenge of the Culture of Dialogue

Alan Falconer

Introduction

It is a great privilege to have been invited to contribute to a volume honouring Alan Sell on his seventieth birthday. Alan played a very important role in international ecumenical dialogue in his capacity as Theology Secretary for the World Alliance of Reformed Churches. In that position he was responsible for overseeing a number of bilateral dialogues with representatives of other Christian World Communions and Churches. He also took the opportunity to co-ordinate a response on the part of Reformed Churches to the Faith and Order report *Baptism Eucharist Ministry*[1] through a suggested series of questions which Reformed and Presbyterian Churches might address in their individual response, thus facilitating a coherent and helpful reception on the part of the churches of the confessional tradition.[2]

It was in his capacity as Theology Secretary that Alan invited me to take part in two of the bilateral dialogues in which the World Alliance was engaged – viz. those with the Disciples of Christ, and with the Roman Catholic Church. This was my first experience of direct involvement in bilateral dialogues. I had been on the staff of the Irish School of Ecumenics, based in Dublin, for some ten years where I was responsible for teaching Faith and Order issues and analysing the results of bilateral and multilateral dialogues, both national and international. Much of this analysis emerged from a complex process of detective work, since, on the whole, access to the papers and drafts of the dialogues was restricted. It was therefore a great privilege to be invited to participate in these dialogues at first hand and gain a sense of the mechanisms

---

[1] *Baptism, Eucharist, and Ministry*, Faith and Order paper 111 (Geneva: WCC, 1982).
[2] Alan Sell, 'Responding to Baptism, Eucharist and Ministry: A Word to the Reformed Churches' in *Studies from the World Alliance of Reformed Churches*, 3 (Geneva: WARC, 1984).

and tensions of the dialogue process.

On appointment to the post of Director of the Faith and Order Commission of the World Council of Churches, much of my work became centred on the organization, publication and reception of international ecumenical theological dialogues, and involvement in a number of bilateral dialogues – including membership of the Joint Working Group between the Roman Catholic Church and the World Council of Churches. The Faith and Order Commission was also responsible for the publication of the final reports of the international bilateral dialogues sponsored by the different Christian World Communions[3] and for bringing together those involved in these dialogues every three or four years. In the Bilateral Forum, as it was called, the agenda, insights and difficulties of the respective dialogues were shared, and attention was paid to the development of processes of reception.[4]

However, at the beginning of the 1990s, involvement in international ecumenical theological dialogues had become an enterprise that was widely questioned. Towards the end of what had been deemed the century of ecumenism, why were the churches no closer to union than they had been the century before? After a quarter of a century of bilateral dialogues involving the Roman Catholic Church why had the results of dialogue been so seemingly negligible? The enterprise of dialogue was a costly process - both financially and in terms of human resources and time. Churches were beginning to question the cost of that involvement. The criticism of dialogues has been further exacerbated by the failure of churches to incorporate the results of the dialogues into their own teaching and understanding.

It seemed appropriate, therefore, in this essay to reflect on the processes and prospects of dialogue in this contribution, since Alan Sell was greatly involved in encouraging dialogue, promoting bilateral dialogues in a theologically rigorous manner, and introducing a number of Reformed theologians to this world.

Ecumenical Dialogues – A Variety of Types

As churches began to develop methods for engaging in dialogue from the beginning of the twentieth century, a number of different methods emerged. These tended to depend on the previous relations of the partners in the

---

[3] *Growth in Agreement. Reports and Agreed Statements of Ecumenical Conversations on a World Level*, Faith and Order Paper 108 (Geneva: WCC, 1984); *Growth in Agreement I. Reports and Agreed Statements of Ecumenical Conversations at World Level 1982-1998*, ed. Jeffrey Gros, FSC, Harding Meyer, William G. Rusch Faith and Order Papers 187 (Geneva: WCC, 2000).

[4] See e.g. 'Report of the Seventh Bilateral Forum' in Alan Falconer (ed.), 'Report of the Seventh Bilateral Forum', *Emerging Visions of Visible Unity in the Canberra Statement and the Bilateral Dialogues*, Faith and Order Paper 179 (Geneva: WCC, 1997).

dialogue. In the first stage of ecumenical dialogue, the churches, particularly through the Faith and Order movement, sought to move from a situation of competition with each other towards acceptance of each other's existence and co-existence by adopting an approach which was at root 'comparative'. Churches compared their stances on doctrinal positions with each other. Thus in the early Faith and Order conferences such an approach was evident. Each tradition presented papers on its confessional understanding of the topic under consideration. A wide range of positions was evident. It was a comprehensive approach. Each Church or confessional tradition was enabled to present its understanding in its own terms and with its own particular accent. On the basis of the presentations, the reports of the conferences – e.g. Lausanne 1927, Edinburgh 1937 and, to a certain extent, Lund 1952 – were then attempts to garner what the churches could say together on the subject. A common statement was presented, and the issues that still divided the Churches were delineated for future work. Such an approach was essential for the churches as they began to emerge from isolation into a situation of communication and communion.

However, ultimately, such an approach is at root not one of dialogue, but of monologue. It can be characterised as 'we will accept you as long as you are the same as us, but we will reject you at the points of difference'. The Scots poet, Edwin Muir phrased this well in *The Solitary Place*

> If there is none else to ask or reply
> But I and not I
> And when I stretch out my hand, my hand comes towards me
> To pull me across to me and back to me,
> If my own mind, questioning, answers me,
> If all that I see
> Woman and man and beast and rock and sky,
> Is a flat image shut behind an eye,
> And only my thoughts can meet me or pass me or follow me,
> O then I am alone
> I, many and many in one
> A lost player upon a hill.[5]

With our own perspectives as the only acceptable positions, it was possible only to affirm the status quo – the 'solitary place'. The comparative method evident in doctrinal and church and society discussions in the first phase of the ecumenical movement moved interchurch relations from conflict, competition and co-existence to comparative acceptance. However it was evident that such a method could not effect a real relationship of communion.

At the Lund Faith and Order Conference, therefore, a different methodology

---

[5] Edwin Muir, *Collected Poems* (London: Faber, 1960), p. 81.

was adopted – although the preparatory papers had basically been written on the basis of the comparative method.[6] Theological discussions began to proceed on the basis of the attempt to reach consensus – not simply to map the status quo. As it discussed the nature of the Church, particularly on the understanding of the Church as the pilgrim people of God, the Conference noted

> We cannot build the one Church by cleverly fitting together our divided inheritances. We can grow together towards fullness and unity in Christ only by being conformed to Him who is the head of the Body and Lord of His people.[7]

The statement then explored the complementarity of the various understandings, identified the one-sidedness of many approaches, and called the Church to reassert its nature as the pilgrim people

> Those who are ever looking backward and have accumulated much previous ecclesiastical baggage will perhaps be shown that pilgrims must travel light and that, if we are to share at last in the great Supper, we must let go much that we treasure. We cannot know all that shall be disclosed to us when together we look to Him who is the Head of the Body. It is easy for us in our several churches to think of what our separated brethren need to learn. Christ's love will make us more ready to learn what He has to teach us through them.[8]

This approach to doctrinal matters was matched also by the attempt to act as churches in a co-operative and consensual manner. The Lund Conference adopted what came to be known as the Lund Principle

> Should not our churches ask themselves whether they are showing sufficient eagerness to enter into conversation with other churches, and whether they should not act together in all matters except those in which deep difference of conviction compel them to act separately?[9]

As a result of this a new methodology in multilateral conversations was adopted. In this the churches sought to do their theology together. No longer was a topic to be examined on the basis of what the different teachings of the churches were, but on an exploration through scripture and the tradition of the churches on the topic under investigation. This method therefore brought scholars from different Christian and confessional traditions together to probe, test and seek to find a language – above all from scripture- which predated that of the dividing controversies and thus would provide a wider framework in which churches might explore the issue.

---

[6] E.g. R. Newton Flew (ed.), *The Nature of the Church* (London: SCM, 1952).
[7] Oliver Tomkins (ed.), *The Third World Conference on Faith and Order, Lund, 1952* (London: SCM, 1953), pp. 20ff.
[8] Ibid., p. 21.
[9] Ibid., p. 16.

After examining the relation between Scripture and Tradition itself,[10] the Faith and Order Commission explored, among other topics, Baptism, Eucharist and Ministry. In examining the issue of the eucharist – to take an example to demonstrate the methodological implications - the work proceeded on the basis of an exploration of the biblical terms 'anamnesis' and 'leitourgia', and was set within a framework of the meal tradition of Jesus in the New Testament, and phrased within a trinitarian framework – thanksgiving to the Father (thus taking up the theme of 'blessing' in the bible), anamnesis or memorial of Christ, and invocation of the Spirit (thus taking up the theme of 'epiclesis'). After an extended period of discussion and communication with the churches at key stages on the way to the development of the text, a statement was agreed at Lima in 1982, and sent to the churches to be received.

On the whole, and despite the very carefully worded questions to the churches, the churches responded by applying a comparative method. How does this statement echo 'our' church teaching? Some churches did understand the process by seeing that the questions invited the churches to move to a new position: How does this statement challenge your understanding of the eucharist and what are the implications for the teaching and the practice of your community as you celebrate the Sacrament and welcome the stranger into your midst?

The multilateral international theological discussions were not the only forum in which interchurch dialogue was being pursued. Throughout the twentieth century, a number of churches were engaged in discussions about the possibility of church union - either as bilateral dialogues, or as multilateral initiatives. Some of these dialogues through persons who were also involved in the international multilateral dialogue were able to draw on the discussions within the World Council of Churches Faith and Order Commission as they undertook their work.[11] Others took a decision after a period of intense theological examination, which concluded that there was sufficient agreement at the core on the different churches' expression of the gospel to unite and on the basis of their new shared life to explore adequate ways of phrasing their doctrinal understanding[12] as a community. Yet others sought to lay a substantial theological agreement as the basis of which the different churches could unite.[13] It was clear that in each of the developments of church union proposals the previous history of the relation between the communities determined the topics to be explored and provided the atmosphere in which the discussions

---

[10] See P.C. Rodger and Lukas Vischer (eds), *The Fourth World Conference on Faith and Order: The Report from Montreal 1963* (London: SCM, 1964), and Ellen Flesseman-van-Leer (ed.), *The Bible: Its Authority and Interpretation in the Ecumenical Movement* (Geneva: WCC, 1980).

[11] E.g. the discussions leading to the formation of the Uniting Church in Australia.

[12] E.g. the Church of South India

[13] E.g. the Church of North India.

proceeded.

Alongside the international ecumenical theological discussions and the discussions in particular contexts of church union initiatives, there also began a series of international – and to a lesser extent, national-bilateral theological dialogues. In the light of the Second Vatican Council such international bilateral dialogues began to proliferate, as the Roman Catholic Church, for example, entered discussions with officially appointed theologians of the different confessional families. The agenda for such discussions was to a great extent determined by the previous relations between the Roman Catholic Church and the dialogue partner, as was the methodology adopted. Thus the dialogue between the Roman Catholic Church and the Anglican communion began with an overview in which it was declared that basically the churches of these traditions confessed the same core faith but that certain issues needed to be resolved before communion or union could be conceived. These issues included the understanding of the eucharist with regard to the sacrifice of Christ and the presence of Christ, the issue of ordination to the ministry, and authority.[14] These topics emerge as critical in determining relations between the communities in The Thirty-nine Articles, but also in every tentative exploration of the difference between the communities undertaken since the Reformation.[15] It was not surprising that these topics therefore have provided the agenda of the Anglican–Roman Catholic International Commission's work (though they have subsequently also discussed approaches to moral questions; the church as communion and Mary and the Saints). The intention of the theologians of these traditions was not simply to repeat the formulae adopted in opposition and isolation, but to develop where possible a new vocabulary which went behind the divisive expressions. Once again, through persons who were members also of the international multilateral dialogues, insights from the Faith and Order discussions were able to be fed into the bilateral discussions, and vice versa. Thus the wider horizon of theological reflection and agreement on the topic provided a language and perspective which managed to break through the impasse of previous denominational positions. Where churches or confessional traditions had not directly divided from each other, but the division had already been established and they had inherited the division and subsequently little direct contact had been evident then the agenda of the bilateral dialogue was of a wider more exploratory nature. In such conversations – for example, between the Roman Catholic and Methodist traditions - the topics have examined issues

---

[14] See 'The Malta Report 1968' in *Called to Full Unity: Documents on Anglican-Roman Catholic Relations 1966-1983* (Washington, D.C.: United States Catholic Conference, 1986).

[15] The study undertaken at the request of Pope Urban VIII by Fr. Leander Jones; the discussions between William Wake and Drs Du Pin and Girardin at the beginning of the eighteenth century; the discussions between Abbe Portal and Lord Halifax in the 1890s, and the Malines Conversations (1922-26).

at the very foundations of the Christian faith.[16]

Clearly in the bilateral dialogues in particular, the agenda and method of dialogue have been determined by the previous relations between the communities and by the aim or goal of the dialogue itself. For some, the hope is that the dialogues may achieve unity, for others communion - where there will be a continuing existence of each partner in the dialogue though better relations will have ensued between the churches.

Throughout this century of ecumenical dialogue, a complex situation has developed, through the adoption of different expectations from the dialogues, different methodologies and agenda and different modes of receiving the results of those engaged in the dialogues. This has led to a crisis in dialogue.

The Crisis in Ecumenical Dialogue – Some Features

There are a number of features in the practice in ecumenical dialogue that have made it difficult to harvest the results and have led to a questioning of the enterprise.

The first concerns the dialogue partners. Within the multilateral dialogue of Faith and Order, the members of the Commission who engage in dialogue are recommended for appointment by the member Churches of the World Council of Churches, by the Roman Catholic Church and by some non-member churches in rotation according to an acknowledged formula. Since not all churches can in fact be directly represented, the Commission is chosen according to a percentage balance taking into account theological expertise – and the balance of the theological disciplines particularly in the light of the agenda; confessional tradition; region of the world; gender and youth.[17] Once appointed, however, the members are not primarily involved in the Commission to represent their tradition, but on the basis of their tradition to contribute to a theological exploration of the issues involved. There is an expectation that a corporate personality of the Commission will evolve around the common exploration of the issues being explored. The Faith and Order Commission cannot take decisions on behalf of the member churches. It can only commend its studies on the basis of the wisdom offered and invite the churches to move towards a new understanding. The churches themselves then need to explore how far the insights can help them to move into new relationships with other churches. Thus on the basis of the insights of *Baptism Eucharist Ministry* a number of churches were enabled to enter new agreements

---

[16] Also the Roman Catholic-Disciples of Christ; Roman Catholic-Pentecostal dialogues – the reports of all these are found in the 2 volumes of Growth in Agreement.

[17] Thus in the period 1998-2006, a number of liturgical scholars were appointed and involved due to the exploration of baptism and ordination.

of communion.[18] The churches, however, tend to act in ecumenical relations in ways rather similar to autonomous nations in the sphere of the United Nations. The first element of the crisis in ecumenical dialogue is that the understanding of Faith and Order as a corporate personality whose task is to provide a wider framework in which the churches can then find a new language to explore the issues between them – issues evident in international bilateral dialogues and church union schemes – has on the whole been difficult to maintain and sustain. Many members of the Commission and their churches assume that this forum is a space in which their particular understanding must provide the limits for the concluding document. The danger for the Commission is that it becomes the space whereby a topic is explored on the basis of a wide variety of bilateral conversations posited on a methodology of seeking to overcome very specific historical differences. Of course in every Faith and Order study, the results of the international bilateral dialogues are examined,[19] but that examination is conducted in the context of a wider horizon.

A second difficulty that contributes to a critical period in ecumenical dialogue and arises from the nature of the Faith and Order Commission itself is that the member churches of the World Council of Churches seem reluctant to allow others to act on their behalf. While it is clear that it not possible for all the member churches to be directly involved in the work of the Commission, it is evident that it is easier to engage in the analysis of the issues when draft papers are sent for comment and reflection if the church concerned has a member who is a member of the Commission. If not, then very often the work of the Commission is regarded as remote.

Within the context of the international bilateral dialogues, there have arisen issues of representation also and also of coherence. As with the World Council of Churches, membership of Christian World Communions does not imply that the Communions can take decisions on behalf of the member churches. Representation on the various working parties and ecumenical dialogues in which the communions participate is subject to the same difficulties as those faced by the Faith and Order Commission – though exacerbated by the fact that since the theological and ecumenical committees of the Christian World Communions are smaller that those of Faith and Order even fewer churches feel themselves to be directly involved.

Because of the character of the dialogue process itself, where the members

---

[18] E.g. Meissen, Porvoo, Reuilly, Waterloo agreements; the Reformed-Lutheran Agreement in the USA – see the speech by Dr Mary Tanner at the 75th Anniversary Celebration of Faith and Order in Lausanne 2002 and her article in Alan Falconer (ed.) *Eighth Forum on Bilateral Dialogues. The Implications of Regional Bilateral Agreements for the International Dialogues of Christian Word Communions, Annecy, France, May 2001*, Faith and Order Paper 190 (Geneva: WCC, 2002), pp. 46-56.

[19] See e.g. Tamara Grdzelidze (ed.), *One, Holy, Catholic and Apostolic: Ecumenical Reflections on the Church Faith and Order*, paper 197 (Geneva: WCC, 2005).

have moved from position A to position B, those churches not directly involved find it difficult to discern the process that has taken place. On the whole the international bilateral dialogues have been reluctant to publish the papers presented in the course of the dialogues themselves or to provide an interpretative commentary on the agreement to facilitate understanding. Because detective work then seems necessary for some churches to receive the results of the dialogue, suspicion of the process occurs.

A further difficulty faced by the partners of the different theological ecumenical bilateral dialogues is that different theologians represent the Communions in different dialogues and issues of coherence have been raised. Are the Christian World Communions saying different things to the different partners with whom they are in dialogue? Are the different agreements consonant with each other and compatible? Until the 1990s, coherence was largely achieved through the membership in different dialogues - multilateral and bilateral - of significant key ecumenical theologians. They were in a position in themselves to draw together from the different fora in which they were involved what was happening in ecumenical discussions on the topic under consideration. However with the proliferation of dialogues and different expectations of ecclesiastical and academic institutions, this is no longer the case. A challenge in ecumenical dialogue will be to find a forum within the Christian World Communions and the World Council of Churches to provide a space for reflection on the results of the various dialogues. While the Bilateral Forum offers such a possibility, the Communions have been resistant to giving it a function of finding coherence and commonality, since that might be seen to detract from the autonomous character of the communities involved in dialogue.

These and other difficulties emerging in the various ecumenical dialogues have been recognized by the participants in the dialogue and have been the subject of a number of informal discussions arranged by the Ecumenical Institute of Strasbourg over the last decade.

Alongside the problems faced within the dialogues themselves, as I mentioned at the beginning of this essay, a critical situation is now facing the whole enterprise of international theological ecumenical dialogue itself. Many churches from the two-thirds world assert that the dialogues are taking up issues that are the responsibility of the European and North American churches rather than themselves. They do not feel that they are directly involved since they inherited the division of the church and were not direct parties to those events of division. They suggest that they have more pressing issues to be addressed. On a number of occasions I had the opportunity to listen to the leaders of some of these churches who told me that the unity agenda was not their priority. When I probed with them further about what the issues were that they were facing, what very often emerged was that their major preoccupation was with competing churches establishing themselves in close proximity to their churches; or different churches being associated with different ethnic groups and developing theologies in opposition; or different understandings of church membership and the implications of this especially with regard to baptism and full participation in the eucharist; or what the nature and mission of the church was in their situation and their relationship with other churches in different parts of the world. In effect a major preoccupation for them was the unity agenda, although they did not always immediately recognize that nor did they necessarily find it easy to insert their way of phrasing their concerns within the framework of the bilateral discussions to date.

Further, there has undoubtedly been disappointment that the results of the patient work of dialogue have not had the crucial impact on the life, worship and teaching of the churches that might have been anticipated. The process of 'reception' among the churches has been slow and the mechanisms at times cumbersome. It has led many to feel that the churches are fundamentally resistant to change. Do the agreed statements figure significantly in the theological education of the churches? Do churches explicitly note that their worship or practice has been or could be enhanced by the adoption of the thought or practice of another community? Are the churches moving into a situation where they are accountable to each other for their life and witness nationally and internationally? Are the churches prepared to reflect theologically on their developing common life in councils of churches in respect of worship, thought and the practice of the church? Are the churches prepared to be involved in ecumenical discussions which go beyond stating their own positions, as in the comparative methodology outlined earlier? Certainly one church - the Russian Orthodox Church - has recently reiterated its claim to be the One Holy Catholic and Apostolic Church to which every other church must return, and thus for it dialogue is simply stating and restating its own historical postures.[20] For them and for others the major question to be examined is that of the nature and mission of the church, the clash of different ecclesiologies and attitudes to dialogue itself.

Increasingly there is also a difference in understanding the nature of the unity sought. Is it simply 'reconciled diversity' where after intense dialogue the churches celebrate communion with each other at local, national and international level, while maintaining their own autonomous structures? Or is the vision of unity that of a conciliar fellowship where churches truly united at local and national level are in a relationship of mutual admonition and affirmation at international level, an implication being that denominational structures will collapse to be replaced by structures which are inclusive and focus on the life and witness of the church in a geographically defined area?

And yet despite these difficulties, no church can afford not to be seen to be engaged in ecumenical dialogue. Throughout the twentieth century there has

---

[20] E.g. see the documents worked out at joint sessions of the Commission of the Moscow Patriarchate on a dialogue with the Russian Orthodox Church Abroad...in *Europaica* 70:29 (June 2005).

emerged what can only be called a 'culture of dialogue'.

A Culture of Dialogue

The Joint Working Group between the Roman Catholic Church and the World Council of Churches was formed in 1965. It began its work by reflecting on the nature of dialogue. In 1967 it published a report entitled *Ecumenical Dialogue* which has served since that time as a useful reference. In the period 1999-2005 the Joint Working Group again took up the subject, in the light of the experience of forty years of dialogue experience and in the context of a crisis facing ecumenical dialogue.[21] The process for this report began with two stimulating and suggestive presentations by Dr Konrad Raiser, then General Secretary of the World Council of Churches and Bishop Walter Kasper, then Secretary of the Pontifical Council for Promoting Christian Unity, at the first meeting of the Group in Beirut, 2000.[22] The report outlines some of the ways in which ecumenical dialogue has helped to change relationships between some churches and understanding between others. It then explores the nature of dialogue and develops a spirituality of dialogue – all in the attempt to promote a culture of dialogue.

Throughout the first half of the twentieth century, the philosophical, cultural, and theological presuppositions for such a culture of dialogue were elaborated. In his recent book, *To heal a Fractured World,* the Chief Rabbi of Great Britain and Northern Ireland, Jonathon Sachs, has offered valuable insights for the roots of such a culture.[23] The Chief Rabbi points to the detail in the sanctuary. The holiest item of its furniture was the ark, containing as it did, the tablets of the Torah. Above the ark were two figures, cherubim. He notes that the Torah says that their faces were turned towards each other, and he goes on to comment

> The sages say they were like children, or in another interpretation, that they were intertwined like lovers. It was between the two cherubs that God spoke to Moses. The message of this symbol was so significant that it was deemed by God himself to be sufficient to outweigh the risk of misunderstanding. *God speaks where two persons turn their face to one another* in love, embrace, generosity and care. God's presence is everywhere. But not everywhere are we ready to receive it. When we open our 'I' to another's 'Thou' – that is where God lives. We discover God's image in ourselves by discerning it in another. God lives in *the between* that joins self to self through an act of covenantal kindness.

---

[21] See *Eighth Report of the Joint Working Group bewween the Roman Catholic Church and the World Council of Churches (1999-2005) Geneva* (Rome: WCC and Pontifical Council for Promoting Christian Unity, 2005), pp. 73-89.
[22] See *Ecumenical Review* 52:3 (2000), pp. 287-292, and 293-299 respectively.
[23] Jonathon Sachs, *To Heal a Fractured World: The Ethics of Responsibility* (London: Continuum, 2005), p. 54.

Conversation and dialogue therefore are not simply modes of stating one's own ideas and postures, but involve the transforming understanding, which emerges from the face-to-face encounter.

To enter dialogue is to take humanity and God seriously. Christian faith asserts that human beings are created in the Image of God. Our understanding is that God is communion of three persons, however we seek to find words for the inexpressible or unutterable. To speak of human beings made in the Image of God is to speak of Imago Dei Trinititatis. As human beings we are created in and for community. We cannot exist without each other. As Walter, Cardinal Kasper noted in the article cited above: 'We not only have encounter, we are encounter. The other is the limit of myself: the other is part of and an enrichment of my own existence. Dialogue thus belongs to the reality of human existence. Identity is dialogical.'[24] The Word of God, the word of and to the churches, emerges from the dialogue, and is not a presupposition of it. Dialogue is a venture of risk and of grace. To enter such a process does involve a certain disposition. In a famous interview with Olivier Clement, Patriarch Athenagoras identified this as the spirit of Christ - humility, dispossession of self and the disinterested welcome of the other.[25] The underlying Christology for such a disposition is that evident in the Philippian Hymn (Philippians 2:5-11) – a kenosis or self-emptying, a life of transfiguration. Such a mode of living, of dialogue, emphasises the being of each Christian as interdependent through seeking to have the same mind of Christ. In this process of transformation, each becomes vulnerable to the other. Each is transformed in the process.

Dialogue is a complex process. As an aspect of human existence and of faithfulness to our calling in Christ we cannot dispense with it. It has the potential to transform and transfigure the churches. But it is important that as the churches engage in processes of dialogue they are prepared to be guided by that which happens between the conversation partners and do not seek to control the process. Such an understanding of dialogue emphasises the pilgrim or journeying nature of faith and church life, and seeks understanding rather than assuming a possession of the truth. Only by returning to the roots of the nature of dialogue will the crisis of dialogue be overcome, and a culture of dialogue emerge.

---

[24] *Ecumenical Review* 52:93 (2000), p. 293.

[25] Olivier Clement Dialogues with Patriarch Athenagoras cited in Rene Girault, *One Lord, One Faith, One Church* (Maynooth: St Paul, 1993), p. 141.

CHAPTER 13

New Perspectives in the Lutheran-Reformed Dialogue[1]

Botond Gaál

In this paper, I intend to address a topic whose subject matter deals principally with the Lutheran-Reformed dialogue about the question and practice of Holy Communion. I must immediately recognize that in this I shall have to grapple with one of the most difficult tasks in theology. That is, the dividing line between different Christian denominations falls precisely at the point which should unite these denominations into one community, the community of the body of Christ. The point itself is the event of the Holy Communion, that at-table community which emphatically expressed and expresses a sense of unity. The deepest fissure which separates Christians from one another in our time is that caused by the interpretation and practice of Holy Communion. For this very reason the question of whether the discussions at Nagygeresd and Leuenberg brought any result is to be considered a most valid question; and if there were any results, it would be good to know what they were and whether we can expect any further developments along these lines. In response to this unsettling question posed already here at the beginning, I shall rejoin with an affirmative, that is, I shall endeavour to outline an encouraging solution to this objectionable situation.

I shall thus begin with the more difficult part of the task at hand. This means returning to the 16th century and attempting to enter into discourse with Luther, Zwingli and Calvin. Before doing that, however, let us trace the historical strands from the Reformation to the present so that we may better grasp the purpose of our analysis. In using more weighted expressions and taking the faith-heritage of our Reformational fathers seriously, together we can avow that our historical memory ought never be deficient. This is why we must ask them

---

[1] First presented at Révfülöp, Hungary on 9 November 2005 at the Lutheran Pastors' National Conference, with the subtitle, 'Nagygeresd, Leuenberg – Have we achieved anything, are we to expect anything?'

also whether they foresaw that their teachings concerning the Holy Communion would result in the unremitting separation of succeeding generations much the way it does today. My estimation is that they did not foresee this turn of events. In their own time they were thoroughly disquieted by the fact that there was no accord among them in the Holy Communion question. In this they had already refused the idea of *transubstantiation* and as a consequence they had distanced themselves from the Roman Catholic Church. Yet all of them must have perceived this disaccord as a mere academic question and surely never suspected that this would so thoroughly permeate itself into the conscience of the community of believers. It is most probable that the great reformers never dreamed that the differences in these teachings would later become the well-defined dividing line among the children of the Reformation and that this disagreement would harden into the presently consolidated divisions. As the subsequent generations came and went the divide only became deeper. Many of the faithful, however, retained an inner longing for a sense of unity, nurtured by the knowledge that all of them had flourished from the same root. Almost unconsciously many of them felt what others, through their faith in Paul's words, adhered to: '... if the root is sacred, so are the branches' (Romans 11:16). The search for each other was underway.

The result of this search as it manifested itself in Germany on the 300th anniversary of the Reformation is well known. In Hungary this same search yielded the Concord of Nagygeresd in 1833[2] for those of the Augustinian and Helvetian Confessions. The theological discourse of this latter occasion was not carried forward, being either not yet applicable or no longer applicable, for nothing more happened here than the mutual recognition of the existence of brotherly bonds. In the 20th century, the search for the lost brother became much more vocal and the result was the launching of countless events featuring inter-denominational dialogue whose intellectual ripples have not entirely subsided even today. The verity of this is perhaps best demonstrated by how the situation evolved in Germany. It is known that members of the Confessing Church – despite their unusually difficult predicament – initiated a type of dialogue on the question of the Holy Communion. After the Second World War this dialogue broadened to such an extent that a whole series of dialogues was soon in progress. 'The Theses of Arnoldshain as pertaining to the Holy Communion' in 1957, the 'Clarification' of these same theses in 1962 and 'The

---

[2] The exact title is *The Concord of Nagygeresd in the year 1833, between those adhering to the Augustinian Confession and those adhering to the Helvetian Confession, both in West-of-the-Danube Church Districts*. It appeared in Protestáns Egyházi és Iskolai Lap (PEIL), in the issues of January 10, 24 and 31, 1864 in three installments. It had similarly appeared in three installments in the PEIL. in 1846.

Concord of Leuenberg' in 1973[3] were all noteworthy outcomes of this intellectual stirring. Theologians from the Lutheran and Reformed Churches of Hungary participated in the formulation of the latter document. In tracing the evolution of this within Hungary itself, it is the decision of the National Committee of Elders of the Lutheran Church which must be mentioned first, which takes a clear stance on how the Lutherans perceive their own situation within the ecumenical movement in Hungary. This declaration issued in 1974 does not refer to Nagygeresd but clearly alludes to its historical significance

> The National Committee of Elders has corroborated that the Lutheran Church of Hungary has lived in true community with the Reformed Church of Hungary in terms of its pulpit and Holy Communion practices which are based on the historical tradition of many former generations and with this same openness has continuously maintained contacts with churches of the Reformed persuasion in other lands. As a consequence, the wording of the Concord of Leuenberg cannot be directly applied to the situation of the churches within Hungary.[4]

Following this, the National Committee of Elders ratified the Concord's formulation of 'the church community which includes the community of the Holy Communion and of the pulpit, the mutual recognition of ordination and the sanctioning of *intercelebratio*'.[5] Nonetheless, in the following paragraph, an element of caution appears, in my estimation, justly

> in the case of a community of churches of Reformed persuasion, the National Committee of Elders deems sufficient a concensus in the interpretation of the Gospel and of the sacraments, according to the wording in points 6-16 of the first section of the Concord of Leuenberg. In the interpretation of the Holy Communion and the concepts of Christology and predestination, the Committee indicates, much as points 17-34 of the second section of the Concord of Leuenberg stipulate, the need for further theological discussion so that the accords outlined in the formal articles may evolve into veritable consensus.[6]

Now Lutheran pastors are not the only ones who must ask: have the formulations as found in our Church's articles of theological teaching evolved to a level of true concordance? This question is all the more relevant when it refers to the Holy Communion. And in this particular case our answer would have to be that the desired level has not been reached. This shortcoming is not due to a lack of desire but to a lack of concerted effort. The intentions of the

---

[3] Cf. Eckhard Lessing, *Abendmahl* (Bensheimer Ökumenische Studienhefte 1; Göttingen: Vandenhoeck, 1993), pp. 19-41, in Michael Welker, *What Happens in Holy Communion?* (Eerdmans: Grand Rapids, 2000), p. 22.
[4] *A Leuenbergi Konkordia elfogadása* (Ratification of the Concord of Leuenberg), Theologiai Szemle, XVII. évf. 1975. 5-6. sz., p. 180.
[5] Ibid.
[6] Ibid.

formulators of the Concord are summarized in four lengthier chapters. It is in the third chapter where the large differences in the perception of the Holy Communion and the topics of Christology and predestination are noted to have had a central role in preventing the Lutheran Church and the Reformed Church from establishing their potential church community. In my judgement mediation in this matter by the Hungarian Ecumenical Council was less than helpful, seeing that this forum is in the thrall of church politicians and thus is basically a quiescent body. The Hungarian National Committee of Elders had requested a 'theological discussion' but this was realized in very feeble fashion if at all there was any in the three aforementioned questions. There is some work to do in examining these questions together so we may try to ascertain how our positions can begin to move closer to one another's and in this way help the Concord of Leuenberg's goal become a reality.

Let us now pose three questions: What was the reason for the inablitity to agree in the question of the Holy Communion? How do we perceive our situation today? Which direction should we pursue in seeking a resolution? It is necessary to pose all three questions in order to eventually be able to make a declaration which will touch upon not only our identity but also on having found one another within the context of a brotherly community. Everything and all that can be forthrightly said concerning these questions at present is a direct result of the international discussion which was sparked by the Concord of Leuenberg. Unfortunately, very little of this discussion ever entered the lifestream of Hungarian theology. It was clearly the desire to reach mutual understanding which led to assuring and promising developments at an international level, or more precisely, within the flows of international, academic theological reflection. We would do well to not leave this unnoticed.

The Legacy of the Past

A major discrepancy in the interpretation of the Holy Communion had already reared its head at the very beginning. To grasp this it is basically sufficient to reflect upon the disagreements among Luther, Zwingli and Calvin in this matter. Calvin, who was a generation younger than the former two, joined the fray of an already existing dispute. Harsh judgements to the extent of accusations were flung at one another –even by their progeny years later– and it is these waves which we still feel today. In trying to move forward in this, let us not be swayed by inadvertent winds which may fill our sails but, to some extent, let us make an effort to be independent thinkers, much as the apostle Paul was.

I myself am a mathematician, physicist and theologian and I endeavour to use my acquired knowledge to gain a better and more profound interpretation of God's Word. I view as instruments all that which I have as a gift received, much as the leaders of the Reformation avowed the same. And our difficulty begins here in that at the time of the Reformation, much like at any time, there existed a certain culture, a certain mode of intellectualization and a certain body of knowledge. The leaders of the Reformation were all very well educated, they possessed a great amount of knowledge and were among the outstanding thinkers of their time. When we look at any of Luther, Zwingli or Calvin, we cannot help but see imbued in them and driving each of them the common motivation to point to and give witness of the sacrifice of the veritable self-giving Jesus Christ. The recognition of this caused them to be humble before both God their fellows. On one hand they recognized the infinite wealth of God's Word, while on the other hand it was obvious to them that their theology inevitably bore the imprints of the human understanding of faith and the shortcomings of human obedience through faith. It was for this reason that they recommended to Christians living in any age to measure all teaching by the standard of the Scriptures. This tenet they later imbedded within the Reformational principle of *Sola Scriptura* which for them signified a *Scriptura valde prima* perception[7], that is, the Scriptures above all else. And we have now come to the point where we can ask them why the end result of their reflections on the teachings of Jesus Christ became the end result that it did.

In ancient Greece the knowledge available at the time grappled with a trying difficulty. Interpreting space, time and the veritable material world in which humanity physically existed proved to be problematic. Plato had elevated space to a position of importance, wanting to designate it as the dimension bridging the natural world to the world of ideas but he finally abandoned this tack and settled for classifying it as something of a 'transitional' nature. It does not move, it is a vessel without motion. Aristotle said that space was something which encompassed bodies, it was of measurable quantity and it exerted an influence on any given body. It is a vessel but it is not without motion. The Stoics perceived space as something which a body brings into existence for its own existential needs. The body expands and thus sets the cosmos in motion, otherwise it would be at rest. On the basis of this the Greeks all arrive to the idea of a god. God for them is either the concept of Good or the foremost motivator who is at rest [ie. without motion] or the force which is present in all things. This was the world into which Christianity stepped and it was amidst these conditions that it had to define the incarnation of Christ. On the basis of the teaching of creation arising from nothingness, it was entirely clear that God Himself could not be envisioned according to the Greek model; that is, God could not be perceived as an entity existing relative in space and in time to the universe. Resorting to classical Greek concepts, the following can be said: nothing subsumes God but much more so it is God who subsumes everything. This subsumption is not of a physical nature but occurs through His strength

---

[7] Cf. Michael Welker, 'Sola Scriptura? The Authority of the Bible in Pluralistic Evironments', *A God So Near. Essays on the Old Testament Theology in Honor of Patrick D. Miller* in B.A. Strawn and N. R. Bowen, eds, (Eisenbrauns: Wiona Lake, IN, 2003), p. 377.

and His power (Col. 3:3). For the theologians of Nicea –and it suffices here to think of Athanasius– the concept of space as the Greeks had postulated it was of little use because God became incarnate in Jesus Christ by stepping into our human space; that is, He became man without having vacated His 'place' as God, which is to say that He remained what He had always been: infinite, omnipotent and eternal, a being who ultimately cannot be enclosed within the framework of finite existence. He is a creative power who is above all space and all time while man in his own station of creature is in thrall to both time and space. From this it becomes clear that the Greek concept of the vessel cannot be applied to the secret of God's incarnation.[8]

Here, then, is where the paths diverge. There was no place accorded to Aristotelian tenets in Nicean theology, yet we see that after a given time they surface and, with the appearance of Thomas Aquinas, the concepts of substance and accidents are integrated into the Holy Communion. Because these two concepts had to be separated from one another, the issue of *realis praesentia* posed an immediate difficulty. As we know, Thomas resolved this by distinguishing and according a special presence to Christ whereby Christ is physically present in both the bread and the wine. But because this state is neither a metric nor quantitative presence, it could only be interpreted as something without extension, exactly like a mathematical point.[9] This perception of things was quite common at the end of the 15th and beginning of the 16th centuries and surely Martin Luther must have been familiar with this.[10] However, he decidedly opposed the teaching of the principle of transubstantiation. Luther was not enamoured with Aristotle's foremost-motivator-at-rest idea either, and in this way he came to a crossroads. The question of how the integral unity of Christ's human nature and Christ's godly nature could be reconciled must have taxed his mind. This must have been when he decided that the guarantee of this unity could be found in the 'Man-Christ' concept, that is, in the baby of Bethlehem. As he moved towards his final conclusion he realized that, despite being opposed to the concept of transubstantiation, he also feared Zwingli's radical symbolism, so he continued to cling to the formulation whereby Christ is physically present in the Holy Communion: 'To this we cling, and we also believe and teach that in the Holy Communion we eat and take unto ourselves Christ's body in a veritable and

---

[8] This question is discussed in detail by Thomas F. Torrance in *Space, Time and Incarnation* (Oxford: Oxford University Press, 1969), pp. 1-21.

[9] In Euclid's famous book entitled *Elements* we read the following about the point: 'The point has no parts.' We do not know whether this was known in Martin Luther's time or if this observation about the point was borrowed from elsewhere. First Latin Translation of Elements was published in 1482 by a German printer Erhardus Ratdolt in Venice, Italy.

[10] Cf. Torrance, *Space, Time and Incarnation*, pp. 22-51. Torrance's ideas pertaining to the space demarcated by this vessel or receptacle were generally accepted in academic circles.

physical way.'[11] We know that the explanation he supplied for this was the omnipresence of Christ.[12]

In arriving at his theological position, he declined to borrow the explanatory concept of the absolute point of rest as purported by the Scholastics, but offered an interpretation from the perspective of God's absolute power and of God's capacity to act. This was in harmony with the interpretation of the ascended Christ, something which Luther understood to be a state of perfect fellowship, where there is neither time nor space and where Christ Himself, while standing before God in physical form, is no longer subject to the constrictions of either time or space.

The Roman Catholic, the Lutheran and the Reformed Churches unilaterally emphasize complete union with Christ in the sacrament of the Holy Communion.[13] In the case of the Roman Catholic Church, Christ's appearance is invoked by consecration, the Lutheran Church avows the concept of omnipresence and the Reformed Church consistently vows from the time of Calvin that complete union with Christ in the Holy Communion is guaranteed by the presence of the Holy Ghost. This latter will require an interpretation from us as it is the teachings of the Holy Communion from the Lutheran and Reformed Church perspectives that is at issue here. If we revert to the Concord of Leuenberg which mentions the problems associated with the Holy Communion, and the questions of Christology and predestination, we must conclude that, beyond their own merits, all three raise Christological questions also. This is especially true of the first two because they are closely related. It can thus be said that the essential questions concerning the differences in Calvinist and Lutheran theology can be condensed into the following three expressions: the so-called *extra-Calvinisticum* tenet, Christ's 'place' in heaven, and the problems of eucharistic parousia. These three are all related to the issue of Holy Communion, the dispute over this issue providing the wider backdrop. Calvin's reflections took a divergent direction. Using Biblical logic, he organized his theological cogitations into a system. Of the Lutheran formulation he was of the opinion that, in the incarnation and in the Holy Communion, it presented a Christ who was limited in space and restricted to place. In using terms used in philosophy, we might describe this as an imagined vessel. Calvin viewed this differently, establishing that God Himself was incarnated in Christ, who was veritable God and veritable man, but, in respect to His own God-ness, he never left His heavenly throne. Here, the term extra-Calvinisticum took its root. This was due to the fear of the representatives of

---

[11] M. Eugene Osterhaven, *Az egyház hite* [*The Faith of the Church*] (Budapest: Kálvin Kiadó, 1995), 162. Quotation: LW, XXXVII, p. 29.
[12] Cf. Botta István, *Méliusz Péter ifjúsága* [*Péter Méliusz's Youth*] (Budapest: Akadémiai Kiadó, 1978), pp. 142-149.
[13] Cf. Alan P.F. Sell, *A Reformed, Evangelical, Catholic Theology* (Grand Rapids: Eerdmans, 1991), pp. 154-60.

the Lutheran standpoint that in this formulation the unity of Christ's human and god-like character was threatened. Yet, according to Calvin, Christ cannot be physically hidden in the bread of the Holy Communion because He is physically in heaven.[14] At this point the supporters of the Lutheran position began to see a Christ 'locked into heaven' and out of this evolved the problems of the famous *localis inclusio*. Calvin and his later followers interpreted the incarnation as the Son of God having entered the dimensions of time and space without having lost God's transcendence over time and space. Similarly did the ascension translate into the Son's transcendency over time and space without Him having lost his participation in time and space in His incarnated form.[15] In the Holy Communion, it is Christ Himself who thus lifts us to Himself by means of the Holy Spirit and this is how he is veritably present amidst His own children. The Holy Communion also means that Christ will return on the final day exactly as the Scriptural liturgical text states. Calvin endeavours in his arguments to be strictly biblical.

Before us then are two different approaches to the same tenet of faith, a tenet which an earlier generation at Chalcedon had already formulated. The reason for pursuing this path and mode in examining the issue is that this is what the discussions at Leuenberg singled out: the question of Jesus' nature (God-like and man-like) and the unity of His person. It can be seen that the Concord is on the right track when it designates as its goal a newer realization of the intention of the fathers of the Reformation. This end can only be attained if we invest more energy in trying to understand each other's theological stances and consequently discovering those common traits whose substantiation was the mutual goal of the Reformation fathers.

The Situation at Present

It is worthwhile to examine the possibility of mutual understanding from two perspectives: first of all, in the light of congregational life and, secondly, in the light of theological ties or purpose. In casting a glance at congregational life, many positive and worthy things can be said of the links between Lutheran and Reformed Church congregations. These ties may have been stronger in the past, notably at the youth organizations level, and Holy Communion was celebrated jointly on different occasions. It is somewhat rare to hear of such things nowadays. In the sixties and seventies my father often assisted the small Lutheran Church community in Mátészalka by leading Bible studies for them, filling in for their pastor who could not always be present. In Debrecen the two denominations together celebrate World Women's Prayer Day in the context of which Holy Communion was jointly celebrated a few times but it seems that no new noteworthy rapprochement in the spirit of the Leuenberg Concord has

---

[14] Cf. Calvin, *Institutio*, IV, p. 17.

[15] Cf. Torrance, *Space, Time and Incarnation*, pp. 31-32.

occurred. In fact, the members of our congregations know very little about this. And we each lead our lives, side by side, in a quiet and peaceful fashion. To summarize the situation briefly: It is unsatisfactory. If we examine the rapprochement at a theological level and ask whether we have achieved anything, then we could respond with both a 'yes' and a 'no'. On this level our ties are friendly, in fact, brotherly. Stepping into the University of Lutheran Theology in Budapest, I have never felt as if I were entering an institution belonging to a denomination other than my own. Nonetheless, I myself am aware that there is a definite lack of dialogue within our circle, dialogue which could facilitate a rapprochement between the two denominations.

If we analyze the situation today as it is, further questions are likely to be raised by both the Lutheran and Reformed sides. There is a kind of mutual wariness in regards to the idea of community in Holy Communion, which is surely due to some negative reflex or subconscious reason. 'They are different', think many people, so we cannot participate in 'their' celebration of the Lord's Supper. In my assessment, the principal reason for declining to participate is that our church members are not entirely clear about the essence of Holy Communion. What, for instance, do the different declarations of the institutional Scriptures actually mean: the Lord Jesus gave thanks, this is my body, broken for you, this is my blood, spilled for you, this cup is the new testament, in remembrance of me, proclaim the Lord's death until He comes? If there is the possibility of ushering change into the life of the congregation, then, before anything else, it is these tenets of the Lord's Supper that must be taught and entrenched jointly in members of both denominations. I emphasise this because as long we approach the whole by its separate parts, and then wish to couple or paste together the Lutheran and Reformed denominations in some way, the best we can hope for is the formation of a civil association. Perhaps instead we could make our point of departure the thought that the fathers of the Reformation had all originally wanted one thing: that the human soul of the believer establish direct channels to the Lord and thus not require other mediators beyond Jesus Christ, through whom we have been declared before God to be just. In this light we ought not to allow our differences to dominate the foreground and thus view these differences as dividing walls between us. Theological differences of opinion cannot be allowed to stand as a watershed in the relations between our two denominations.

Nonetheless, in viewing the relations of the two denominations at a distance in a detached and concrete manner, the conclusion that I draw is that the picture, in terms of practical congregational life, is decidedly complex. The source of this complexity is most likely and most pointedly a result of the interpretation of the Holy Communion. Of this the average believer perceives nothing more than that difficulties do exist but these he hardly understands, much less grasps. Thus the division represents a situation which needs to be simplified. The solution in any matter cannot be established dogmatically and over the heads of our members, informing them that they have no choice but acceptance. Taking this tack is nothing less than the cloistering of our denominations' believers within the walls of intellectual immaturity.

Outlook for the Future

In which direction is the solution to be found? With this question our attention is directed towards the future. The last third of the 20th century witnessed much by way of dialogue and ecumenical bonding. Even the theologians were finally given their say. All of this was most productive because many facts, perceptions and other matters surfaced which may help resolve, or at least give a positive push, towards the future. It is here that I would like to denote three essential things that might help us to answer the questions posed early in this article: have we achieved anything; are we to expect anything?

1. The ecumenical dialogue during the last third of the 20th century in the question of the Holy Communion has steered the attention of the larger church communities towards an encouraging direction. The first observation was that on the path leading to rapprochement there are inordinately many obstacles rooted in stances which are unbending. Yet even this yielded a positive result in that a great number of questions had to be scrutinized in their own right in theological depth and this motivated the theologians to delve deeper into the theology of their denomination while, at the same time, gaining familiarity with the stance of the other denomination. A direct consequence of this, on one hand was the shedding of light on many questions which are, in final analysis, commonly avowed articles of faith in the matter of the Holy Communion but which had not been aptly recognized in each other's theological doctrines. On the other hand, the new light helped define much more plastically the differences between the denominations. Once the final result was tallied, the conclusion drawn was that the points in common are far more dominant than the differences.[16] This spurred the formulation of a new perception which, when positively weighted with the dominance of common traits, would review everything and re-evaluate the relationship between the two denominations. The relative value of the differences was not to be diminished but simply accorded lower priority than those points which assure a common base. In my perception this is both just and encouraging.

2. All of the above was instrumental in ushering in a new perception, atmosphere, and spirit to ecumenical meetings, relationships and dialogue. Yet, it still does not seem to go far enough with respect to achieving results in the future. Progress has unmistakably resulted in 'ecumenical peace'[17] but it is not yet sufficient for the establishment of a church community of consequence. We are very much aware of this because this type of 'ecumenical peace' has already existed between us since the decisions of Nagygeresd, that is, one

---

[16] Cf. Welker, *What Happens in Holy Communion?* pp. 22-25.

[17] Ibid., p. 23.

hundred forty years before it was formulated in the Concord of Leuenberg. However, from the dialogue itself, there resulted a more encouraging development, which though inherent in hidden form, became perceptible only later. This development is the decided determination to legitimize the biblical perspective in the process of the dialogue. It appears that there is a tendency now gaining momentum which, beyond wading through the speculative and theoretical interpretations, is now seeking to return to the original source, to the Scriptures and is asking: what is it that is veritably transpiring within the Holy Communion? In adhering to this process, light was shed on much of the extraneous baggage carried by the way that Holy Communion was practiced and theoretically interpreted, this baggage having been accumulated through peripheral, non-relevant, inessential and even distorting elements of interpretation. The different traditions of different groups, the passing on of inexact teaching and the assimilation of the local community's characteristics all attributed a meaning to the Holy Communion which it had never had. Such a situation is not tenable and therefore it is fitting if, operating on the principle of consensus, we seek direction within the Scriptures. It is worthwhile to note that it was not only the churches issuing from the Reformation which defined these criteria but also the pre-Reformation and counter-Reformation churches.[18] We can thus note that the exclusive 'ordering principle' in this unusually complicated question can be none other than the teachings of the Scriptures. In our particular case this is somewhat encouraging because, in the final analysis, both Luther and Calvin would have liked to have found an underpinning theological explanation, but, both being men of their particular age, it was precisely their cultural and intellectual differences which caused them to lock their intellectual and spiritual antlers. It has been four hundred fifty years now that no satisfactory solution has been found.

3. The third encouraging item I am denoting is the question of scholarly justification. It is rather disconcerting, perhaps even vexing, that, despite the open and free thinking of the fathers of the Reformation, a somewhat rigid set of doctrines was formulated. The introduction to the Second Helvetian Confession of Faith says that 'in expressing our thanks we are prepared to obey and align ourselves in the Lord to those who teach us from God's Word that which is better.' This question must be directed firstly to church leaders, because they have become the responsible, practical, intellectual and spiritual sentries of congregations. The question at hand has an aspect which, because of its very nature, we cannot delegate to the members of the congregations. Its responsibility rests primarily on the shoulders of leaders: there exist certain theological questions which demand to be examined and analysed theologically. My decided opinion is that the churches which today stand on the foundations of either Luther's or Calvin's teachings have strayed from the veritable spirit of Martin Luther and John Calvin, which has led to our present

---

[18] Ibid., p. 21.

divisions and unyielding positions. Our Reformational fathers moved forwards while we always wanted to go back to them for answers. To greatly simplify the matter: it is not to them that we need to go back except that we also move forward, like them. We see that in both denominations there exists a seemingly static, unmoving theological order or tradition to which belongs perhaps the most obvious example: the interpretation of the Holy Communion. Both denominations' order in this question appears to be unmoveable, its intellectualization having stiffened into dogmas on which is built our separation. Were I to formulate my opinion more harshly, I would say that both orders of doctrines have stiffened into ideologies, and this is the foremost obstacle to the rapprochement of the two denominations. But then let us think this through also.

Every intellectual order has basic tenets on which it rests. With respect to their function, these basic premises serve the same purpose as axioms in science. Using the example of mathematics, it can be shown –especially as demonstrated by one of the greatest Hungarian mathematicians, János Bolyai– that closed systems can be opened up to allow truly worthy developments to ensue. Generally speaking, if a field of knowledge possesses a system of axioms, involving this system is most helpful in completing or even enlarging that particular field. Euclidean geometry, which is taught in secondary schools, is a case in point. It is known that acquired knowledge built on certain systems of axioms can result in a closed field, that is, the system allows its user to acquire only a certain amount of knowledge. Stepping beyond this, to a higher level of knowledge, can only be achieved if the closed field is opened. Effecting the opening is only possible if the tenet which prescribes the closedness is identified. The genius of János Bolyai lay in his ability of being able to find the point of Euclidean geometry which limited it to a closed field and to a state which did not allow its user to step out of this system. He deduced that it was the axiom of parallels which needed to be changed. He effected this without eliminating the axiom yet at the same time allowing him to take a step higher in knowledge. It was after this that he wrote to his father, exactly on 3 November 1823, that, 'from nothing I have created a different new world!' We can also apply this as an analogy. Our veritable ecumenical –may I say most worthy– task would be to seek out jointly those points of our denominations' theological order which destine them to be closed systems of thought. Then, with a new perspective based on the Scriptures, we should begin to replace or modify the axioms identified as the ones preventing us from stepping higher', so that the theological order of both denominations is able to be released to the infinite freedom which we have won in Jesus Christ.

For further concrete progress to be realized it would appear to me that the keepers of Lutheran theology will have to make more significant steps in the field of the eucharist, while the Reformed side will have to provide additional clarification in their doctrine concerning predestination. Should I wish to assess the present situation from a perspective of modern academic knowledge, I would say, that the possibility for this exists, and this is what the fathers of the Reformation themselves desired from the beginning.

CHAPTER 14

Universalism or Tribalism? Christian Social Ethics in an Era of Globalisation[1]

Anna M. Robbins

'Globalization' may be narrowly defined in economic terms as the increasing integration of economies across national borders through trade in goods and services, the migration of labour and the investment of capital. More widely, it also involves the spread of cultural influences and ease of communication across borders.

The principal cause of globalization has been the dramatic reduction in both durations and costs of international transport and communication – be it the container ship or the Internet. Since the interwar period, the average real charge for ocean freight tonnage has fallen by 70 per cent, average revenue per air passenger mile by 85 per cent and the cost of a 3-minute transatlantic telephone call by 99 per cent. These technological enhancements have been accompanied by a reduction in regulatory barriers to trade, financial flows and investment.[2]

In our contemporary world, the very processes of globalisation, driven as they are by economic power, depend on universal principles, and develop universalising tendencies. Sameness permeates our world, soaking into once diverse cultures under brand names and advertising. Sociologists and others highlight the recognition of a common youth culture that is seen to be developing globally, in addition to the common economic culture that emerges

---

[1] This paper builds on research presented at the Tyndale Fellowship Ethics and Social Theology Group and at the Fellowship of Evangelical European Theologians in Germany in 2004; it was presented at the Ethics Commission of the Baptist World Alliance in Mexico, 2006. I am grateful to participants in all of those venues for their feedback and encouragement.
[2] Paul S. Mills, *Cambridge Papers* 14/1 March 2005.

from the application of principles of capitalism.³ Telecommunications and information technology introduce us to concepts and images that are the same the world over, offering icons as the symbols around which we organize our common identity. As Max Stackhouse comments

> The process we call globalisation seems to be creating the conditions for a new super-ethos, a worldwide set of operating values and norms that will influence most, if not all, peoples, cultures, and societies. It is quite possible that most of the contexts in which humans now live, and their roots in particular sets of values and norms, will be modified by a new comprehending context that owes its allegiance to no particular society, local ethos, or political order, even if it is advanced by 'western' influences.⁴

The development of this universal 'super ethos' has not been welcomed by everyone. Indeed, many interpretations of globalisation 'see in it the triumph of a "global capitalism" that manifests the interests of the already rich, leads to the exploitation of the less rich, pollutes the environment, commodifies every resource and relationship, creates worldwide inequality, and generates a cultural homogeneity that devastates regional diversity.'⁵ Moreover, as Kofi Annan pointed out 'many see globalisation less as a term describing objective reality about the creation of a new social order or civilizational possibility than as "an ideology of predatory capitalism" which they experience as a kind of siege.'⁶

Stackhouse has identified a backlash against the universalising tendencies of globalization, which he suggests takes three forms: 'growing nationalism sometimes threatening multiethnic states; call for strong leaders seldom democratic who seek to mobilise these national interests against internationalism; an attempt to use globalisation as a scapegoat for all the political and social ills that in fact have domestic roots.'⁷ Others, however, welcome the developments, suggesting that we need to learn to live well with this new reality, arguing that eventually, it will benefit all those who participate in it.⁸ It should not surprise us that there is no consensus on this process.

So, on the one hand, the world is growing more and more connected, more

---

³ See for example, Marcelo Vargas, 'Can the Global Replace the Local?: Globalisation and Contextualisation' in *One World or Many? The Impact of Globalisation on Mission*, ed. Richard Tiplady (Pasadena: William Carey Library, 2003), pp. 203-209.
⁴ Max Stackhouse, ed., *God and Globalisation Vol 1: Religion and the Powers of the Common Life* (Harrisburg: Trinity Press, 2000), p. 19.
⁵ Ibid.
⁶ Cited in ibid., pp. 4-5.
⁷ Ibid.
⁸ See for example, Peter Heslam ed., *Globalization and the Good* (London: SPCK, 2004); and Philippe Legrain *Open World: The Truth About Globalisation* (London: Abacus, 2002), amongst others.

Universalism or Tribalism?

and more homogeneous. On the other hand, the world seems to be fragmenting through the recognition of difference, plurality and the significance of context and culture. Even in the realm of Christian ethics, it is no longer true that what must be done is evident and obvious to all, even if how it ought to be done has always been somewhat more complex.[9] Moreover, we wonder now if we even are speaking the same language across diverse contexts, let alone employing the same concepts or engaging the same rationality. We are more and more the same, and yet more and more wanting to stress our difference and the truth of plurality as the only truth. So how do these opposing tendencies relate together? Do they relate at all? And what is the relevance for the way we approach ethics as Christians in the contemporary world?

The matter of defining the problem of adjustment between the global or universal and the tribal or plural, is complex. There is a primary tension between the global-universal and the tribal-plural tendency that has profound implications for ethics. At least some ethical aspects of this primary tension may be identified and explored through the following three categories (see Table below): Moral Ontology – ways of being; Moral Epistemology – ways of knowing; Moral Praxis– ways of doing.

Within each category, we may more clearly describe how the tendency towards global or universal culture contrasts with a simultaneous pull in the opposite direction towards tribal or plural culture. This may help us to reflect further on how the church might relate to these tensions, and hopefully, we may gain some insight for how we might approach the ethical task in a globalised world.

GLOBALISED FRAGMENTS	GLOBAL-UNIVERSAL	TRIBAL-PLURAL
ONTOLOGY (WAYS OF BEING)	THE CONSUMER SELF THE PASSIVE SELF	THE MORAL SELF THE ACTIVE COMMUNITY
EPISTEMOLOGY (WAYS OF KNOWING)	FOUNDATIONALISM UNIVERSAL VALUES	DIFFERENCE LOCAL VALUES
PRAXIS (WAYS OF DOING)	ECONOMIC POWER NEW IMPERIALISM	POLITICAL POWER NEW INDEPENDENCE

---

[9] See Douglas John Hall, 'The State of the Ark: Lessons from Seoul,' *Between the Flood and the Rainbow: Interpreting the Conciliar Process of Mutual Commitment (Covenant) to Justice, Peace, and the Integrity of Creation*, compiled by D. Preman Niles (Geneva: WCC, 1992), p. 37. Hall highlights the need for churches to be able to relate across contexts in order to meet uniquely global challenges.

Ontology

Let's begin with the ontological tension, reflecting on how 'ways of being' play themselves out in response to the two tendencies. We will do this by considering how the self of the globalised-universal world differs from the self of the contrasting tribal-plural realm. It is my contention that the self of the global-universal world is formed by a frontier context, while the self of the tribal-plural realm is formed by a local, bordered context, thus producing a tension within the self that compromises moral responsibility.

In a globalising world, human persons are identified by their consumer patterns and practices. This identification is both external and internal. It is reflected externally through the categorisation of peoples and populations by economic and political researchers, who maintain databases of spending, consumption and voting patterns, or income and educational levels. For example, major supermarket chains keep track of our spending through loyalty cards, and attempt to direct marketing at us on the basis of a determined set of characteristics. People are identified according to their consumer habits. Moreover, political parties demarcate populations according to defined characteristics derived from sociological and commercial data. They are able to chart, with unsettling accuracy, how an individual will vote in an election on the basis of these external identifications. Such information drives the marketing and advertising which then goes on to continue to shape the self in the direction of these gathered indicators. In many ways, these external characteristics define the consumer self. The stability of the global economy depends on the creation of the consumer self through media and advertising; the self who will purchase and consume in an ongoing cycle of unsatisfied desire. So even while the majority of the world's population does not actively participate in consumer structures due to poverty and powerlessness, to bring them within the parameters of a consumer identity is part of the agenda of economic and political globalisation.

These external factors then, go on to shape the internal self. Through branding and imaging, the consumer uses the signs of the global culture to express who they think they are. As individuals purchase and rearrange the signs of the global economy in attempts at self-expression, the process of identity creation is ongoing.[10] But in such a context, the choice is actually limited by the products that companies choose to offer, and prescribed by the forces of advertising, which subtly erodes the moral sense of the self as one who truly has freedom to choose.

In a consumer culture it is important to maintain the illusion that moral authority rests with the individual self. The individual is seen to possess authority because the individual is the one who chooses from amongst the signs and images of a global market culture. Yet, it is clear that choice is limited and

---

[10] See D. Slater, cit. Gordon Wenham in *Christ and Consumerism,* Craig Bartholemew and Thorsten Moritz eds. (Carlisle: Paternoster, 2000), p. 121.

prescribed, at least to some degree.[11] The consumer self, then, is discouraged from active, creative responsibility as a moral agent. Instead, the moral self is conditioned by marketing to become morally passive, interested in moral action only insofar as it may be expressed through consumer habits (as in commitment to purchase fair trade products for example) or insofar as it is an acceptable media-generated trend that expresses something positive about the moral self (as in the Live 8 concerts, for example). Individual loyalty to global signs and symbols shifts moral authority away from local communities and even away from national institutions. Their moral influence is consequently eroded, but the consumer self as a passive self is not able to fill the moral gap.

The consumer self becomes the morally passive self through the constant manipulation of image. The image of the self is easily disconnected from the real self, and the image is constantly created and recreated through the symbols of global culture.[12] We become enchanted with our own image, and unaware of the world around us. The consumer culture depends on us becoming mesmerised with out own image, in order for it to propagate itself. From the resulting anomie, there is an emerging sense of normlessness that results in community and individual fragmentation. The global context needs to be addressed by a global moral sense, which fragmented communities and selves are unable to provide. We become fragmented moral selves submerged in a homogenising collective, without the moral resources to grasp, let alone confront, the accompanying global issues. Active communities coordinate and negotiate the needs of individual members in light of the whole, but in a global culture, such responsibility is easily surrendered to the media and marketers to coordinate. The consumer self is fashioned then, in opposition to foundationalism and universal values, even though consumer culture operates out of such assumptions. There is the possibility of some active participation at the local level, but it is more often expressed in fragmented form, than sustained, interested involvement.

In many ways, the moral self is deferred, or is expressed in assertions of difference and contextualisation. In the west, such expressions may be liquid in nature, akin to Bauman's 'peg communities', which form and dissolve at tribal levels.[13] Elsewhere, they may be found in assertions of difference in the face of globalisation, through attempts to preserve some valued aspects of rapidly-fading cultures, or in assertions of nationalism or various fundamentalisms. They may even be asserted as badges of difference, like images left slowly fading from a screen after the power has been shut off. The most committed are

---

[11] Ibid., p.130.

[12] For an analysis of the self-replicating nature of the image as the 'hyperreal' see Jean Baudrillard, *The Consumer Society* (London: Sage, 1998). Baurdrillard is here dependent, at least in part, on Marshall McLuhan's work on the media in *Understanding Media: The Dimensions of Man* (Falmouth: Abacus, 1973).

[13] See Zygmunt Bauman's *In Search of Politics* (Oxford: Polity Press, 1999), pp. 47-48.

left discouraged and dismayed at the lack of moral progress they are able to generate. There is a recognition that the moral self rooted in the active community is the basic 'way of being' that corresponds with a sense of moral responsibility.[14] There is an acknowledgement that many such communities exist in parallel, and share borders with one another. Some are convinced that the way to counter the passive moral self of the global culture is to reinforce local activity. And yet we cannot fail to miss the fact that wherever television goes, the global economy follows. How are such local communities able to prevent and confront the passive moral self from developing an allegiance to the symbols of the consumer society? Moreover, how does the active community equip potentially fragmented moral selves to address the ethical issues of a global world? There is clearly an ontological tension that is not easily overcome.

Epistemology

If we find a tension emerging in our 'way of being' as moral selves in the contemporary world, we may discover it is exacerbated when we move on to consider matters of epistemology, or our 'way of knowing'.[15] Here, we see the same tension work itself out in terms of our access to, and understanding of, that which we know. Our epistemology goes on to inform the way that we respond to the world in which we find ourselves. In some respects, epistemology then, could also be thought of as a tension between basic assumptions about the nature of our worldviews.[16]

On the tribal-plural level, there may be an emphasis on local values within a culture or community. The local community is the context in which access to knowledge and understanding is formed. The culture that exists in a particular place and time conditions the way that the world is understood. One assumption is that only that which is local and contextual can be known, since it is impossible for any single person or community to perceive the whole. Moral values then, are also local and contextual, if not culturally relative. Since epistemology at the local-tribal level is considered to be culturally conditioned and endemic to a particular time, place and environment, communities who

---

[14] See Marcia Y. Riggs 'Living into Tensions: Christian Ethics as Mediating Process' in *Many Voices One God,* Walter Brueggemann and George W. Stroup eds. (Louisville: Westminster/John Knox Press, 1998), pp. 181-192.

[15] This is not unrelated to ways of being. Certainly, how we understand ontology will influence our understanding of epistemology, and vice-versa.

[16] A discussion on worldviews is relevant here, but space prohibits it. See James Sire, *Naming the Elephant: The Concept of Worldview* (Downers Grove: IVP, 2004), and David Naugle's *Worldview: The History of A Concept* (Cambridge: Eerdmans, 2000). Of course their thought is preceded by that of Kant and Dilthey amongst others.

engage with each other may well encounter the other as 'different'.[17] Encounters may enable them to compare and contrast their values, to understand how and why they differ, while at the same time reinforcing their allegiance to be 'different' from others around them. Reinforcing difference may become a means of forging a common local identity in the face of the moral passivity discussed earlier. This may be understood positively as a means of developing healthy local values in the face of globalised values. It may be understood negatively as reinforcing sectarianisms that may lead to conflict, or as becoming so ruggedly contextual that moral relativism, fragmentation and disorientation results. For some, the relativism that is implied, particularly in a world where those who are 'different' are encountered at every turn, may simply lead to moral paralysis or even nihilism. If our values are simply the projected hopes and fears of our communities, what meaning is there for the ethical life in the contemporary world?

A tribal-plural understanding of moral values is reinforced by much of contemporary scholarship. One of the more pervasive influences has been that of Alasdair MacIntyre, whose understanding of cultures and ethics is very much one that reinforces the local-plural dimension.[18] Such a perspective is further reinforced by several postmodern ethicists who not only emphasise the local fragmentation of ethics, but also suggest the impossibility of transcending the culturally conditioned self with regards to epistemology and ethics. The notion is that since all we can know is what we have experienced, we are unable to generalise from our local context to a wider context in any way that does not do violence to another self or community. Any attempt at dialogue becomes simply a disguised effort to impose our views on others. The best we can do is to divest ourselves of self-interest, and encounter the ethical 'other'. In the 'other' one finds one's true self.

It seems, however, that such a localised, experience-based approach differs significantly in its epistemology from that of the universalised experience of globalisation. The processes of globalisation depend on an epistemology often dismissed by scholars as 'modern' and passé, as they hail the end of the enlightenment project in grand, sweeping generalisations. While epistemology fragments even within local communities, convincing them of the 'myth' of progress, globalisation progresses on assumptions and conditions of

---

[17] The ethical importance of the term *difference* is a popular topic within postmodern philosophy, including the work of Paul Ricoeur and Jaques Derrida.

[18] See Alasdair MacIntyre, *After Virtue* (London: Duckworth, 1985); cf. MacIntyre, *Whose Justice, Which Rationality?* (Notre Dame: University of Notre Dame Press, 1988). In the latter work, MacIntyre allows for dialogue across contexts, though its potential is not really made clear. In a recent article in *Studies in Christian Ethics*, Michael Taylor highlights the contrast between MacIntyre and Ronald Preston, with relevance for the present discussion. See Michael Taylor, 'Faith in the Global Economic System,' *The Future of Christian Social Ethics: Essays on the World of Ronald H. Preston 1913-2001, Studies in Christian Ethics*, 17/2, 2004, pp. 197-215.

universality.

Foundationalism is the term given to an epistemology that begins with first principles of knowledge gained through reason. Once these first principles are accessed, they can be laid down like the cornerstone of an edifice, and built upon with other assumptions of reason that depend upon them. The scepticism of causality that was raised by Hume, and carried on in diverse forms by other philosophers found particular manifestation in the nihilistic thought of Nietzsche, who seems to have been resurrected in contemporary times as a postmodern guru. His programme of radical doubt wanted to push DesCartes to the point even of self-doubt, such that no aspect of reasoned thought could have any confidence that it is necessarily rooted to reality. Thus, the cornerstone of reason was itself called into question, which led to the entire edifice crumbling. Some contemporary understandings of foundationalism are consequently suspicious of ethical systems that rely on universalisms of any kind.[19] Where foundationalist approaches to reason exist, it is suggested that a belief in progress, and the general ability of humanity to harness all the powers of nature to serve itself, at the expense of the other is folly, if not self-deception. The lack of moral progress in history is posited as evidence that foundationalism is an illusion. Some suggest that it leads only to imperialism and violence. In response, many have emphasised instead the local-plural dynamic of contextualism that we discussed previously as a means of countering violent claims of universalist moral truth.

Much of this discussion provides a philosophical explanation of what we see happening at the grassroots and what we experience ourselves in our lives today. However, a globalising world actually depends for its survival and growth on a foundationalist approach, with universal assumptions and applications. The assumptions of global capitalism for example, grow out of a reasoned approach to human nature, growth, competition, desire and accumulation. As such, it depends on stability, reliability and predictability. It not only assumes a certain universality of reason and human behaviour, it reinforces universal principles and universal values, whether they be values of consumerism, development, or even greed. Through the icons of advertising, for example, a global culture emerges that may appear diverse and fragmenting, but that actually promotes similarity over difference, sameness over diversity. The homogenising influence allows its foundationalist values to replicate themselves, and a local pluralist ethic of difference is not able to counter its more destructive aspects. For if ethics are local and contextual only, what voice is there to critique prophetically, and constructively, the instruments of global

---

[19] Even some secular ethicists who have no biblical reason for doing so, attempt to establish some sort of universalism for ethics. See, for example, John Rawls, *A Theory of Justice* (London: Oxford University Press, 1972) and attempts by Hans Küng and others to establish a universal ethic on global human rights. See for example, Hans Küng *Yes to a Global Ethic* (London: SCM, 1996).

capital that often leave the weak and hungry despairing in their wake? How can a voice that emphasises the 'difference' of knowledge be heard in the corridors of the power of those who believe in the 'sameness' of knowledge, in a way that actually connects with the concerns of those who occupy such corridors? Moreover, how does one community that finds itself in a position of power relative to another community overcome contextuality in order to stand together against exploitation and injustice? The tension is a real one in the contemporary world.

Praxis

Again, we see the tension between the global-universal and the tribal-plural emphasised in the way global ethics may work out in an era of globalisation. On the tribal-plural level, there is a sense of emerging independence amongst some that may lead to a complete disenfranchisement amongst others. In any case, a sense of being in control of one's own affairs may be a positive achievement in a world where many communities feel forgotten and left out of the global picture. There may be, amongst such communities, a belief that public, or social ethics must be discussed at, and addressed to, the local or national political authorities. Political involvement, protest, and social action are all designed to encourage governments to change policies, and generally to 'make the world a better place.' In a community that emphasises its difference, this may happen on a relatively local level, though it sometimes may extend to national governments. Often times, Christians lobby governments on the basis of their local knowledge, but demonstrate a distinct lack of sophistication or savvy in terms of how politics work. Or, they are so ruggedly contextual, that their appeals have little more than minimal relevance to a wider population. The Berlin Group that emerged from an assembly of disgruntled ethicists in the WCC lamented the contextuality they encountered amongst Christians and Christian bodies that displayed a distinct naivity about global politics and economics. Their observations have become rather acute when applied to the contemporary world. Theology, whilst helpful cannot replace good knowledge about the universal power of economics, nor is a contextual praxis able to address the universalising issues of a new imperialism from a perspective that is wider than itself.

An example of how this tension works itself out in praxis may be seen in an incident from just a few years ago. An international company was called to account by a news organisation that discovered it was, in essence, trading child slaves in West Africa order to harvest cocoa. In an interview on the evening news, the anchor questioned both a managing director of the company, and a representative from UNICEF who was amongst those documenting the atrocity. When the UNICEF rep was asked why he hadn't raised the issue before, he suggested that in fact, he had been doing so for quite some time. He insisted that he had been lobbying the British government for years on the matter. The company director interrupted, suggesting that he wished the UNICEF representative had approached him instead, insisting he had no knowledge of the situation until it was recently 'discovered.' 'Did you ever confront him with what you'd discovered?', the news anchor demanded. The answer was one word, 'No'. Leaving aside the issue of whether the director was aware of the situation or not, watching this newscast left me rather downcast. Why do organisations, including the church, direct all of their activities towards political groups and governments, while increasingly, the real power is held in the hands of a few, massive, multinational companies, whose global tentacles stretch far beyond the authority of any single political body or government? Surely there is a place for local and national political action. But how well is the church equipped to meet the challenge of discussing ethical issues with multinational corporations with a degree of wisdom, savvy and expertise? Do we even recognise the need to expand our ethical interest beyond the level of governments to address the almost universal power of economics?

If we hope for our social ethics to have any effective outcomes, we will need to address the nature of the global-universal/local-plural tension in terms of praxis. So where do we go from here? I suggest that we may approach ethics in the contemporary, globalising world from one of three perspectives: frontiers, borders, or networks.[20] Let's consider each of these in turn.

Frontiers

Come with me, if you will, to the frontier. We saddle up our horses, and ride out, blazing a trail across the plains. Everything is a new world to be discovered...and to be conquered. It is a great adventure. Our encounters with others are rare, and often result in confrontation, either because of misunderstanding, or because one wishes to conquer the other and impose a certain cultural and moral 'sameness' upon the other. There is no pretending that we have anything significant in common with the ones we meet. Our differences are obvious and mutually acknowledged, even with a certain respect, if not fear or hatred. The values we take with us we hold dear, and we wish to see them taken up by others. Our values are the truth. They are what give us our identity, and our difference. We are willing to suffer and to die – or even to kill - for that difference, and we believe in a future that will see our values realised everywhere and by all.

On the positive side, the frontier conjures up the exciting images of uncharted territory; the notions of challenge and adventure. The frontier is most closely associated with images of the American wild west, where brave

---

[20] I introduced this typology in *Sharing the Feast* in relation to doing theology in the contemporary world. However, I think it involves a more developed conceptualisation than was presented in that more popular level work. See Anna Robbins, *Sharing the Feast* (Authentic: Milton Keynes, 2005).

individuals and families rode out into the wild blue yonder, looking to blaze a trail to a new life. They had a belief that they were moving into free land in order to stake their claim. There, they could remove any who impinged upon their freedom to live and establish life according to their own ideals. To conquer, rather than encounter, was the norm. The real goal was self-determination; a desire to forge out an authentic existence true to the individual or community vision. But the myth of the frontier, though well entrenched in western culture, both through the wild west metaphor, and the European notion of empire, demands critique.

Theologian Roberto Goizueta offers a helpful initial critique of the frontier myth in western culture. First, he cites the romantic notion of the frontier epitomised in the words of Tennyson's *Ulysses*

And this gray spirit yearning in desire
To follow knowledge like a shining star
Beyond the utmost bound of human thought.
...Come my friends,
'Tis not too late to seek a newer world.
Push off, and sitting well in order smite
The sounding furrows; for my purpose holds
To sail beyond the sunset, and the baths
Of all the Western stars until I die
To strive, to seek, to find, and not to yield.

Giozueta refers to the romantic frontier myth as our foundational myth of modernity – our creation myth.[21] Although the great frontier no longer exists in reality, its image remains. He suggests we should awake to the reality of its demise, and turn our attention instead to the existence of borders, which bring people into direct encounter on an equal footing. Certainly the idea of conquering and defeating an enemy for reasons of self-determination is not a popular one in our contemporary world.

But should we dispense so readily with the image of the frontier as a metaphor for our socio-ethical engagement just because it is unpopular? Has it ceased to exist in reality? Niall Ferguson has recently elaborated a thesis that posits the role America plays in the contemporary globalising world.[22] He defines the globalisation process as America's new empire-building process. Though he suggests there are positive aspects to America's role in the international order, he admits there are also problems, mostly owing to lack of

---

[21] Roberto Giozueta, 'There You Will See Him: Christianity Beyond the Frontier Myth,' in *The Church as Counterculture*, Michael Budde and Robert Brimlow eds. (Albany: SUNY, 2000), p. 174.
[22] Niall Ferguson, *Colossus: The Price of America's Empire* (New York and London: Penguin, 2004).

commitment to the outposts of empire, and confidence to see the empire clearly established. It seems he is calling for a renewal of a frontier mentality in order to make globalisation work for those who seem at present to endure it rather than enjoy it. Moreover, recent world events suggest that we are not far removed from a world of conflicting value systems that seem resolved only by severe clashes of ideology.[23] At very least, there are still many people in the contemporary world who have strong ideological commitments, and who engage the world as though it were a frontier to be conquered by the moral values of an 'empire'. Not least, we have already demonstrated how the global-universal suggests a frontier mentality in terms of its desire to take its foundational, universal values around the world.

And yet, Giozueta seems to have a valid point in beckoning us to consider a different paradigm of public ethical engagement, particularly when we consider Fergusson's description of the weaknesses of the new imperialism. Although the world seems ever full of conflict and confrontation, and it seems reasonable to stake out our territory – even to conquer new territories – there is no doubt that we have more neighbours to contend with than ever before, and our contact with those from outside of the moral tradition where we are most comfortable has increased in a world of plurality and mobility. Rather than simply facing a global-universal frontier, perhaps we do also live in a world of regular border crossings that influence the way we engage God's world.

Borders

We stand at the border and peer across to the other side. Travelling under the identity of the passport in our hand, we move into unknown territory, excited by what we may discover. We encounter all sorts of people from different backgrounds, and they encounter us, as they travel across our border too. We share many things, and yet we are different. There is so much mobility it is hard sometimes to remember where we are, or who we are. But we travel light, and so we can always check our passport, and go back home for a while. Even there, things have changed.

Perhaps the metaphor of borders is preferable to that of frontiers, as it acknowledges the value of the tribal-plural context. It acknowledges an unavoidable confrontation between cultures and values. It recognises that Christian morality encounters other moralities in a context where they all exist, in a manner of speaking, as cultures, with their own commitments and self-defining languages. It recognises the reality of pluralistic existence, and yet in maintaining its own identity, a Christian morality is able to make its own claims about reality, and engage the ethical task.

Doing social ethics at the borderlines implies several things. For example, it

---

[23] See, for example, Samuel Huntington, *The Clash of Civilizations and the Remaking of World Order* (London: Simon & Schuster, 1997).

implies an initial confidence in the task, with a clear sense of identity, and potential for idea exchanges. It indicates an openness to learn from others, and not only to teach or impose a single worldview. There is a degree of mutual trust; if one does not impose morality by force, they may expect respect of their value system in return. Inevitably there is an ongoing, integral dialogue.

Doing theology at the borderlines also provides several insights through numerous mutual exchanges of cultural practice, ideas and beliefs. It provides a measure of objectivity that may highlight moral differences between individuals and groups. Yet, at the same time, it may artificially harmonise observed similarities. We seek points of contact and mutuality with others, but without commitment to them, and rejecting responsibility for them. When anything is demanded of us, it is possible to withdraw behind the borderline of encounter to more familiar territory. Our contacts may clarify allegiances through reinforced tribal identity, whilst encouraging us to find at least artificial commonalities. If it is at all true that we know and are known through our relationships, then it must also be true that our public theology is best defined and through an examination of its relations with other views. A border context makes this a real possibility.

For example, Kathryn Tanner alludes to the potential of positive identity-giving functions in her discussion of Christian identity in virtue of a cultural boundary.[24] She believes the critical caricature of postliberals regarding the self-contained and self-originating character of Christian identity, is at least in part an accurate reflection of reality. While postliberals might want to acknowledge the composite nature of the Christian way, they will not acknowledge the composite nature of their identity. She writes, 'By taking two strategies, postliberals are able to suggest that, while a Christian way may not be self-contained and self-originating, Christian identity still is; though Christian practices are mixed-up for example, with wider cultural spheres, the Christian identity of those practices – what makes them Christian – has nothing to do with such mixing.'[25]

In contrast, she wishes to argue that the boundaries are indeed essential in understanding Christian – and consequently theological and ethical – identity. Boundaries, or borders, imply differences. 'The nature…of any boundary distinguishing Christian from non-Christian ways of life cannot be determined by looking at Christianity alone…Boundaries are determined, in sum, by how a Christian way of life is situated within a whole field of alternatives. The boundaries distinguishing a Christian way of life from others will shifts with shifts in the practices of the other ways of life making up the field.'[26]

---

[24] Kathryn Tanner, *Theories of Culture: A New Agenda for Theology* (Minneapolis: Augsburg Fortress, 1997).

[25] Ibid., p. 105.

[26] Ibid., p. 111. While we may wish to go beyond Tanner and say that the essential *content* of Christian theology is at least in some respects self-defining, (or God-defined

Following Michel De Certeau, Tanner suggests that the appropriation of cultural material is not a passive activity, rather there is a 'creativity of consumption.' 'Material borrowed from elsewhere is twisted and turned, used in different ways, when set in a different context.'[27] For contemporary public theology, this activity represents a clear and present danger: there is often no recognition that the material passed off as theology has but a bare semblance to it. Perhaps there is a need to recognise the dangers of consumptive behaviour for public theology at the borders.

The tendency towards identity consumption in the border context suggests several problems presented by this metaphor. First, in the metaphor of public encounter as border crossings, we can behave merely as tourists, and so never really engage the differences of others. We may fail to gain any external critique from our encounters, and similarly perceive no responsibility for the other in our travels.[28] Secondly, travelling without responsibility means that we may be little more than consumers generating a false image for our identity: we may have a reputation for ethical concern, or even a spoken one, but we risk a separation of image from reality if we are not willing to enter authentic transformative relationships rather than capitulate to a consumerist attitude to others.[29] Thirdly, frequent, almost constant border crossings can undermine our confidence in our moral values, and can confuse our identity. Unlike the frontier, the border metaphor may have the effect of watering down identity as it harmonises differences, highlighting the cultural relativity of moral values. Rather than divide and conquer, we unite and cohere. Or, according to Bauman, we can become fearful, uncertain, and insecure.[30] If, as Jean Baudrillard suggests, we consume others (or at least their images) and we allow others to consume ours, do Christians in a border context risk losing our distinct identity, and our ethical voice altogether? If, in the uncertainty of relativism we retreat from making any public proclamation, do we end up like the student of Prague, committing ethical suicide, and with it whatever public voice we might have in

---

insofar as it relates to the revelation of the gospel), the *activity* of theology, especially public theology, is one of relationship with other insights and disciplines. Indeed, Archbishop Rowan Williams rightly suggests this recognition is essential to integrity in moral discourse, and that the activity of discourse itself presupposes such relationships. See Rowan Williams, *On Christian Theology* (Oxford, Blackwell, 2000), p. 4-5.

[27] Tanner, *Theories of Culture*, p. 112.

[28] Zygmunt Bauman has identified the stroller, vagabond, tourist and player as alternative identities to that of the pilgrim in postmodern life. See Bauman's *Life in Fragments: Essays in Postmodern Morality* (Oxford, Blackwell, 1995).

[29] This calls to mind Jean Baudrillard's four orders of simulation that results in the separation of image from reality: the image first reflects reality; then masks reality; then masks the absence of a profound reality; then has no relation to reality whatsoever (hyperreality). See Jean Baudrillard, *Simulacra and Simulation* (Ann Arbor: University of Michigan, 1994).

[30] Zygmunt Bauman, *In Search of Politics*, pp. 9-57.

society?[31]

This is not simply a vague possibility, but a real one, similar to that which some members of the evangelical church have experienced before.[32] In his exposition of Abraham Kuyper's American public theology, John Bolt indicates the situation that resulted from the great reversal of the 1960s and 70s in America. We have something to learn from their experience, just as we have must to learn from the experience of the ecumenical activists in the WCC from the same period, who faltered in their social engagement for the opposite reason. Where one group began to lose confidence in public theology, the other became ruggedly ideological. Both ended up failing the enterprise, as eventually they swapped roles; the WCC losing its confidence, and evangelicalism turning to ideology. Bolt reminds us that

> ...moving through the later decades of the twentieth century, American evangelicals have increasingly been marginalized from public life by a dominant liberal-secular mind-set. This has not occurred without some complicity on its own part, as evangelical Christianity in its conflicts with modernism retreated into fundamentalism Along the way, the public identity and character of America, historically seen by many as "Christian America," was fundamentally altered. The process of change, hidden for many years as the nation continued to live under the influence of Christian America's moral capital, became obvious in the counter-cultural upheavals of the 1960s. In the 1970s and 1980s, shocked to discover that "their" America had been taken from them, conservative American evangelicals reacted by forming political action groups – moral majorities and Christian coalitions. Politically engaged evangelical Christians, particularly in the so-called "Christian Right," have become a significant force in American political life in the last decades of the twentieth century. The boldness of evangelical activism was not always supported by clearly thought out, principled political strategy. In addition to covering too many issues to do any of them full justice, evangelical activists often failed to set political and strategic priorities in their campaigns. It soon became clear that not only were they out of practice for the political battles and culture wars they entered, they were also – by some of their leaders' own admission – theologically and philosophically ill-equipped for the task.[33]

This conclusion coheres with my own research on social ethics in the WCC

---

[31] See Jean Baudrillard, *The Consumer Society: Myths and Structures* (London: Sage, 1998).

[32] I would suggest this possibility is particularly real in the life of popular British evangelicalism at the moment, much of which brings to mind the social gospel emerging from 19th Century Liberal Protestantism. Cf. Gary Dorrien, *The Making of American Liberal Theology: Imagining Progressive Religion 1805-1900* (Louisville: WJKP, 2001).

[33] John Bolt, *A Free Church, A Holy Nation: Abraham Kuyper's American Public Theology* (Cambridge and Grand Rapids: Eerdmans, 2001), p. xiv.

– and offers us caveats for the present time.[34] The retreat into fundamentalism (at one time evangelicalism, but now in all forms, including liberalism) may have the effect of abandoning the institutions of society to secularization.[35] Once that retreat has taken place, Christians of all sorts, including evangelicals, will need to discover new methods for engagement, since the moral capital once latent in the culture, cannot be expected to linger. Moreover, Christians will need to continue to find ways of addressing the terrorism that has recently been directed against the Western world, but which some of our brothers and sisters have endured for generations. Driven by contextual ideology, the public enterprise is bound to fail, a fact admitted on the evangelical side by writers Cal Thomas and Ed Dobson, and on the broadly ecumenical side by a whole host of writers and ethical participants.[36] Despite its relevance, simply trading a metaphor of frontiers for one of borders, therefore, does not seem offer much promise for successful public ethical engagement that takes global power seriously.

Networks

Our lives are made up of countless connections, some random, some intentional. Within the parameters of space and time, we have limitless mobility, and a seemingly liquid identity. Depending on the company we keep, we can be very different things to different people. We have close contacts around the world, and may live far away from families and traditions. In the comfort of a sparsely furnished room at home, we do our shopping, conduct our business, and engage relationships with a global community. This is truly a different context from the frontier or even the border. I am an online activist. I can engage the world at the touch of a button. But I haven't actually seen

---

[34] Anna Robbins, *Methods in the Madness: Methodological Diversity in Twentieth-Century Christian Social Ethics* (Carlisle: Paternoster, 2004).

[35] Secularisation is defined by Peter Berger as 'the process by which sectors of society and culture and removed from the domination of religious institutions and symbols.' Berger, *The Sacred Canopy: Elements of a Sociological theory of Religion* (Garden City NY: Doubleday Anchor, 1967), p. 106.

[36] In particular, a group of ecumenical participants formed the *ad hoc* 'Berlin group,' which convened on several occasions to explore the future of social ethics in the WCC. They acknowledged that ideology and dogmatism are insufficient equipping for the task of public theology, and highlighted instead the crucial role of dialogue in reversing the ideological and contextual trend. In particular, they highlighted several issues of dialogue that I have adapted as elements of practical unity within a model of moral integrity. The first report of the Berlin Group was issued as *A Statement to the World Council of Church on the Future of Ecumenical Social Thought: Report of an informal discussion of church leaders, theologians, social ethicists, and laity*. Berlin, May 29-June 3, 1992. The majority of their documents and official responses are unpublished. Cf. Roger Shinn, 'Friendly Dialogue,' *One World* (April 1994), p. 13.

anybody today. This is the network society.

As individuals and communities, we occupy myriad communities and engage in countless, seemingly random encounters and deeper relationships. There is a sense of connectedness, but not with linearity. We find ourselves engaged in the contemporary network – not completely unrelated to an early description by Harvey Cox as the secular city with its networks of traffic, and both casual and meaningful connections.[37] More recently, the rise of the network society has been described in depth by Manuel Castells.[38] Information technology, and globalisation have led people into new forms of communicating and relating in the contemporary world. Regardless of whether one accepts all of Castells' observations and conclusions, there can be little doubt that 'as a historical trend, dominant functions and processes in the information age are increasingly organised around networks'.[39] With an increasing dominance over the social structure of globalized society, networks are dominated by flows rather than power,[40] and presence in the network, and the interaction of networks defines control. In Castells' observation, network society becomes characterised by social morphology rather than social action.[41]

But what is a network? According to Castells, it is a set of interconnected nodes, with infinite possibilities for communication. In his words, they are 'open structures, able to expand without limits, integrating new nodes as long as they are able to communicate within the network, namely as long as they share the same communication codes (for example, values or performance goals). A network-based social structure is a highly dynamic, open system, susceptible to innovating without threatening its balance.'[42] He suggests that the appropriateness of networks to global culture will go on to shape the structure of society itself.

What might a network context suggest for social ethics? It will define relationships as intentional, based around common interests and goals. Power for change will be in the hands of those who participate in the network, and control the entry of new nodes into the network. There exists the possibility to compare differences universally, rather than simply with those sharing a border, as the potential for relationship within the network is limited only by who has the capacity to participate, and identification of shared goals. Relationships may be temporary, and utilitarian, suggesting that once goals are achieved, they

---

[37] Harvey Cox, *The Secular City: Secularization and Urbanization in Theological Perspective* (London: SCM, 1965).
[38] Manuel Castells *The Rise of the Network Society* (Oxford: Blackwell, 1996).
[39] Ibid., p. 469
[40] Castells describes this as the dominance of the 'power of flows over the flows of power.' Ibid., p. 469.
[41] Ibid.
[42] Ibid., pp. 470-71.

may dissolve with the network.⁴³

We can see positive and negative potential in a network context. The potential for universality, and for providing power to the potentially marginalised voice is significant. Shared goals may forge relationships on a global level, increasing flows and the opportunity to make a social impact beyond one's immediate neighbourhood. On the other hand, it may simply provide a new and complete form of marginalisation to those who, for whatever reason, lack the ability to participate in a network society. The opportunity to compare differences may reinforce identity, but it may also leave it fluid, as networks appear and dissolve according to shifting goals and values. The lack of permanence in relationship means that rather than cultures consuming one another, there is potential for individuals to consume one another through relationships that are forged and dissolved according to whim or interest.⁴⁴ We may or may not like what we may become as Christians in a network society. But we must reckon with its challenge nonetheless, not least because of its potential to weaken moral discernment and community commitment.

In fact, I believe that the church is uniquely poised to approach ethics through a network method; to make the most of its opportunities, and to ameliorate its excesses. I further suggest that engaging a network method in a globalising world is the only means we have of overcoming the divide that emerges from the global-universal/tribal plural tension.

The Networked Church

In his work on apologetic method in the contemporary world, Alan Sell suggests a model of the church that connects the local and global, the plural and the universal.⁴⁵ Balancing reason, faith and experience, his work suggests that the church functions as a community of local experience, but that filters the development of faith through an understanding of reason that is not necessarily foundationalist, but that offers evidence for its belief beyond fideistic claims. Such evidence does not establish the church, however. All reason, faith and experience must be filtered through revelation, a universal reality that stands outside of, and critiques, all experience, even as it enters into our experience of the church, and breathes into God's life into ours. As such, the global-local

---

⁴³ This is exemplified in Bauman's description of the 'peg-style community' as a liquid form of political action in a postmodern age. See Zygmunt Bauman, *In Search of Politics*, pp. 9-49, especially pp. 47-48.

⁴⁴ The existence of 'liquid' church models in theory, and emerging church networks in practice, are examples of varied responses to these cultural trends, and provide evidence for their influence on Christian life and thought.

⁴⁵ Alan P.F. Sell, *Confessing and Commending the Faith* (Cardiff: University of Wales Press, 2002). Although he does not specifically make this point, such conclusions may be extrapolated from his work.

tension or divide is overcome: in the church, the moral self and the active self is the self of community; in particular the community that confesses that Jesus Christ is Lord. In praxis, the church is formed by the action of confession, that further overcomes the divide between universal principles and the particularities of lived experience: Christians are those who confess what it means to follow Jesus Christ is Lord in various contexts and circumstances, and yet we also recognise in our contacts with one another that we have been found by the good news of Jesus Christ beyond our local circumstances. The body that confesses Christ is local and global, plural and universal. As we confess, we express in every language that which is beyond expression, as a statement of worship. The words 'Jesus Christ is Lord' stand beyond linguistic analysis as a first order statement, an utterance of praise. But this is not to say that the utterance is meaningless. To the contrary, the act of confession points to the fact of the confession – the ontological reality that Jesus Christ really is Lord, within and beyond all of our attempts to understand and explain who he is and what he has done. He is not Lord because we say that he is; he is Lord because He Is. He incarnates into all of our contexts in the person of the Holy Spirit, and yet his work is of universal relevance, for the whole of the cosmos.

The church then, perhaps uniquely in the contemporary world, is poised to be an already-established network that unites the global and the local, the universal and the plural. As a body that recognises its calling to be morally active in the local community, it also finds itself in international expression. It is a hub of networks that potentially makes connections between the rich and the poor, the powerful and the weak, the hungry and the satisfied. And it is through the intentional development and use of networks that it may find a way of addressing the needs of local Christians while addressing prophetically those who could do a lot more to ameliorate those needs. It is difficult to say exactly what such intentions should look like. Indeed, some broader Christian identities are already being formed as global urban communities, evangelical and Pentecostal expressions in particular unite a global Christian community of urban poor; a reality that is slowly being recognised by Christians in the West, though its ethical implications remain largely unexplored by both rich and poor.[46]

The church depends on such a network for its own survival: being a network is part of the essence of the church. Particularly for baptistic Christians, with no central authority apart from Christ, and with little or no denominational hierarchy, the network is a particularly important way of viewing the church. But embracing this reality in a globalised world, and directing it with ethical intention will mean fostering our international denominational links at a time when locally, denominationalism is falling on seemingly hard times; it will mean Christians from all denominations forging network links with other like-minded Christians, such as we are already witnessing between evangelicals and

---

[46] Andrew Davey, *Urban Christianity and Global Order* (London: SPCK, 2001), p. 30.

Pentecostals who are emerging as a new global culture; it will mean encouraging the comfortable to get out of their comfort zones and to assume greater responsibility for brothers and sisters around the world by changing personal and local community behaviour within a global consumer culture; it will mean finding ways as international networks to connect Christians and economists and politicians rather than retreat into our respective epistemological hubs (and such expertise certainly is available in the Christian world, if theologians avail themselves of it); it will mean finding more ways of connecting like-minded Christians across contexts to share ideas and stories while pushing beyond the narrative to ask the question, 'What does this story mean for me; demand of my community?'; it will mean finding way of connecting diverse Christians across contexts to not only encourage but to challenge one another (the former is often much easier than the latter); it will mean reaffirming our confidence that a body that affirms its powerlessness in a world of power can actually make a difference, not for its own glory but for the glory of Christ.

For baptistic Christians, among others, all of this may entail particular challenges and opportunities. For example, what does the principle separation of church and state mean for those of us who live in democracies where, I would suggest that, we have not only the legal right but also the moral obligation to be politically involved on behalf of our brothers and sisters who do not enjoy the same freedom of worship and assembly? If we do not use our rights and defend our liberties are we bound to lose them? How can we be publicly active communities whilst respecting the liberty of individual members of the community to dissent? How do we account for the diversity in our ethical perspectives when we all claim to be 'people of the book'?

Perhaps some of us have occasionally hid behind our ecclesiological principles in order to avoid some of the tough questions rather than allow them to direct and influence our ethical endeavours. If we are a priesthood of believers, do we not have the obligation to prevail upon the authorities on behalf of one another in a globalised world as part of our priestly function and to present a biblical worldview in a prophetic, and perhaps even constructive manner? Equally, if we are to be willing to confront the principalities and powers, we must be willing to divest ourselves of power too, establishment and otherwise. This is costly for those of us who think we have much to lose. How precious is the freedom of self-determination, expressed through the economics of a consumer society, to those of us who don't have to think too hard about whether we can afford to attend international conferences and meetings year on year? What does it mean for me, when I'm buying my new iPod, that I've just met a pastor from a country where many of his friends have been martyred in the previous few years? Our networks, if they are to mean anything, have to be of the mutually life-changing kind. They must involve more than platitudinous statements: they must have real implications for action at the grassroots.

Let us do all things possible to ensure that our emerging connections become hubs of networks that not only inform and radically challenge our ethics, but that lead to effective ethical action in local contexts, and global ones. For despite its fallen condition, this is the world that Christ yet surveys and cries, 'Mine!'[47]

---

[47] Recalling Abraham Kuyper's famous phrase, 'There is not a square inch in the whole domain of our human experience over which Christ, who is Sovereign over ALL, does not cry, "Mine!"' as cited in Bolt, *A Free Church,* p. xiii.

CHAPTER 15

A Case for the Cross? Passionate Apologetics[1]

Gabriel Fackre

While reading Alan Sell's penetrating work, *Confessing and Commending the Faith*, this appreciative reviewer wondered what such a double move might look like today.[2] Is there some current notable effort to be both a witness to the 'cross-resurrection event'[3] central to confessing the faith, and one that commends it to the wider public in the latter's own idiom? A venture of this sort that actually might gain a significant hearing for the gospel?

Whatever one might think of the traditionalist Roman garb in which Jesus is fitted out, surely the film, *The Passion of the Christ*, is such an attempt, and one that has managed to get the ear and eye of multitudes across the world. Indeed it begins, unabashedly, where Alan Sell holds apologetic should begin, 'the only satisfactory starting point: the confession of what God in Christ has done....'[4] And if one measure of effective apologetic is the attention to such matters of Christian faith won in a public venue, including passionate attacks on it, then surely this film qualifies.

Are there some apologetic subtleties there in *The Passion of the Christ* seeking to connect with public touchstones, whether they be in our own cultural context or universal human sensibilities? A re-run here of the kind of violence in Mel Gibson's *Braveheart* that echoes the headlines in our newspapers and thus resonates with the audiences who know about these things firsthand? A bridge to the small hope in every heart in the too-brief glimpse of the risen Lord at the close of the film, itself a reprise of the 30 second redemption of the Episcopal priest when he puts his collar back on in another Gibson film, *Signs*?

---

[1] Portions of this chapter were first presented at an October 2004 conference on the Trinity in First Church of Christ, Wethersfield, Connecticut.
[2] The review appears in *The New Mercersburg Review*, XXXV (August 2004), pp. 56-59.
[3] Alan P.F. Sell, *Confessing and Commending the Faith: Historic Witness and Apologetic Method* (Cardiff: University of Wales Press, 2002), p. 150.
[4] Sell, *Confessing and Commending*, p. 6.

A tear from the heavens that says our own tears are understood? A doctrine of common grace in the Reformed tradition warrants communication of this sort. No knock-down argument for the gospel based on such, of course - only the Holy Spirit through the Word proclaimed does that convincing - but a wake-up call, nevertheless, that may open some ears for the hearing of the gospel.

Hearing the gospel entails an interpretive Word. That's why the Reformers required audibilites as well as visibilies in sacramental practice; at the Table, the Word preached as well as the bread and wine served. Applying that to *The Passion*'s very Catholic visibilies, I will argue that the film can be an occasion for confessing and commending the faith if treated as a Reformation-like 'teaching moment', the interpretive Word conjoined to the visible Word. What then are the pedagogical possibilities for both confessing and commending offered by this film on the screens and in DVD slots around the world?

The Passion of One both Human and Divine

It has long been held that Jesus Christ in his *human nature* underwent the humiliation that happened on the road to Calvary and on the cross. But did not the *divine nature*—Jesus as God—in some profound sense also participate in the back that was bloodied, the hands that were pierced, the cry of dereliction, and the death that Jesus died?

Mel Gibson's film focuses on the suffering of the humanity of Christ. What else can a visualization of the passion do than show the human visibilities? And the portrayal of that follows the producer's own spirituality: the 'five sorrowful mysteries' of the rosary—'the agony of the Lord in the garden, his scourging, his crowning with thorns, the carrying of the cross to Calvary, the crucifixion'[5] (Mt. 26:36-46; Mt. 27:26; Mt. 27:29; Mt. 27:31-32; Mt. 27:33-50), with their backdrop in the stations of the cross. Also formative of the film are the visions of the Venerables Mary of Agreda (1620-1665) and Anne Catherine Emmerich (1774-1782), the latter manifesting the stigmata.[6] But there is more here than meets the eye. I want to explore a small hint in the film that pushes the passion to its deepest point--into the very heart of God. We'll bracket the debates about the producer's intentions to promote his tridentine Catholicism, charges against him of anti-Semitism and the like, even the ardent defences of the film, and consider it instead as an occasion to dwell on the meaning of the cross, and in back of that the teaching about the being and doing of the triune God at the centre of confessing the Christian faith.

We begin with the earlier question: was God in some way a participant in the suffering of Jesus? No, said a large part of the church for a long time. 'Patripassianism', a belief in the suffering of the Father held by the Sabellians,

---

[5] See Donald Attwatter, ed., *A Catholic Dictionary* (New York: Macmillan, 1961), p. 470.

[6] On the latter, *The Dolorous Passion of Our Lord*, Internet accessible.

and the 'theopaschitism' (the pain of God) of another group, the Monophysites, were considered over the line.[7] Indeed, a new attack on them and defence of the 'impassibility' of God—the idea that God has no emotions and therefore *cannot* be said to suffer—is mounted today again by some prominent theologians.[8] Yet, in the 20th century, especially since World War I with its introduction of technological means for mass killing that eventuated in 70 million casualties, then the Nazi juggernaut, the Stalinist atrocities, World War II and the Holocaust, the cry of 'the crucified God!' has been heard in the church.[9] How could the heart of God *not* be broken by these horrendous events? So pondered G.A. Studdert—Kennedy, World War I chaplain, in a poem written in the trenches

> How can it be that God can reign in glory,
> Calmly content with what His Love has done,
> Reading unmoved the piteous shameful story,
> All the vile deeds men do beneath the sun?
> Are there no tears in the heart of the Eternal?
> Is there no pain to pierce the soul of God?
> Then must He be a fiend of Hell infernal,
> Beating the earth to pieces with His rod...[10]

And theologian Georgia Harkness in the midst of World War II

> I listen to the agony of God—
> But know full well
> That not until I share their bitter cry—
> Earth's pain and hell—
> Can God within my spirit dwell...[11]

---

[7] The third century Sabellius held that the one Person of God went through three successive manifestations and therefore the Father suffered in the subsequent form of the Son. The Monophysites absorbed the human nature into the divine nature.

[8] So Thomas Weinandy, *Does God Suffer? A Christian Theology of God and Suffering*, (South Bend: University of Notre Dame Press, 2000). See also his article in *First Things*, 117 (November 2001), pp. 35-41.

[9] So John Kenneth Mozley, *The Impassibility of God* (London: Cambridge University Press, 1926) as an earlier survey and argument with Kazoh Kitamori, *Theology of the Pain of God* (London: SCM Press, 1966), and Jürgen Moltmann, *The Crucified God: The Cross of Christ as the Foundation and Criticism of Christian Theology*, R.A. Wilson and John Bowden, trans. (London: SCM Press, 1974) being formative works.

[10] G.A. Studdert-Kennedy, 'The Suffering God' in *The Unutterable Beauty* (London: Hodder and Stoughton, 1927), p. 4.

[11] Georgia Harkness, 'The Agony of God' in *World Call* (October 1942), p. 48.

The Tear of God

And what of the film? For those with the eyes to see, there is in it a kindred poignant moment. It comes during the scene on Golgotha when a tear falls on the mount from Above. Had Gibson read Studdert-Kennedy's poem about 'tears in the heart of the eternal'? To meditate on that drop is to be drawn to the depths of 1 Cor. 5:19: 'God was *in* Christ, reconciling....' Put that passage together with the cross, and the desolation of Christ was, and is, in some sense, the desolation of God. Indeed, if, as the church has always taught, Christ is one Person in two natures that actually inhere in one another, how can what is said about the human nature not be said about the divine nature?[12] So the early church seemed to think when it declared that Mary, the mother of Jesus, was also to be called *theotokos*, 'God-bearing', and thus the 'mother of God'.[13]

To carry this teaching of the divine-human unity of the Person of Christ to all stages on the journey to Calvary: do we have to do with *God* in agony in the garden, *God* knocked down, dragged along, lashed ever and again, *God* crowned with thorns, *God* carrying his own cross, *God*'s blood, *God* crucified? How dare we talk this way! If Jesus Christ is truly God as well as truly human, how can we *not* talk this way? It boggles the mind, and wrenches the heart.

And who had a hand in all this torture and death? In a television interview with Diane Sawyer about the film, we learned from Mel Gibson that it was, literally, in cameo, *his own hand* that drove the spike into Jesus. By doing it the producer said that he sought to show that it was all of us, not the Jewish people as such, who are responsible for the suffering and death of Jesus Christ. One wonders why Gibson did not also show his own face to make that point even more vividly.

Universal human sin, our culpability before God, that *is* the problem. And it takes us right into the drama that lies behind the passion of Christ: the dealings of the triune God with a world capable of such an act. Some have called it 'the trinitarian history of God'.

The Trinitarian Drama

The 'trinitarian history'? I shall try to show how that phrase describes events on both macro and micro scale. In the first case, we have to do with the sweep of a 'cosmic drama' from creation to consummation. This is the language of Gustaf Aulen who argues in his important book, *Christus Victor*, that such is the New Testament teaching, the patristic understanding of the story of salvation, and

---

[12] The view of the 'mutual interpenetration of the natures' found in the early Fathers, Luther and Calvin, though expressed differently with varied interpretations. For a discussion of this see Wolfhart Pannenberg, *Jesus: God and Man*, Lewis L. Wilkins and Duane A. Priebe, trans. (Philadelphia: The Westminster Press, 1968), pp. 296-323.

[13] The description finding its way into the Chalcedonian Formula of 451 as in 'begotten from the Virgin Mary, *Theotokos*...'

A Case for the Cross?

the belief of Martin Luther as well. In the second case, the trinitarian history has to do with the inter-relations of the Father, the Son and the Spirit in the event of the passion of Christ itself. To get to this latter drama, we begin first with the Grand Narrative of God's deeds, the cosmic Story.

The three paragraphs of the ancient creeds—Apostles and Nicene—display in terse fashion the macro-trinitarian history of God: God the Father as Creator, God the Son as Reconciler, God the Holy Spirit as Sanctifier, the divine 'economy' as it has been called, the outworking of the divine purposes.[14] This is the 'economic Trinity', the threefold *doing* of God, that grows out of the threefold *being* of God, the 'immanent Trinity'. Of course, as the Three Persons of God's own inner life are One, so the three defining Deeds of God in the economy are not done by separate Persons without the participation of the Others. Like the togetherness within the inner being of the tripersonal God, 'the *works* of the Trinity are one'.[15]

Let's take a closer look at these three great 'missions' of God, transposing their description into the language of theater, as suggested by the imagery of cosmic drama. The missions become three Acts in the drama. But acts include scenes. Especially so when we look to the script of the drama, the Bible. In his durable study for a lay readership, *The Unfolding Drama of the Bible*, Bernhard Anderson has done just that.[16] Here they are arranged a little differently, but his lead will be followed.[17]

Interestingly, it is possible to portray this cosmic drama of Scripture and the creeds using the symbol of the hand that we've noticed figures significantly in the Gibson film. In this case, however, we have *two* hands. One is ours, that of the filmic universal humanity. The other is the hand of God. We can shape the latter in trinitarian fashion with three fingers and a circle made by thumb and little finger, as in the liturgical gesture of pastors who pronounce such in Christian worship.

The threesome in the circle of inter-relationship signify the three Persons who have such an intimate Life Together, a trinitarian 'coinherence' that the Trinity is at the same time a Unity. So St. John speaks of God as 'Love'. (1 John 4:8) Thus God is not only 'loving', but Love itself—a community so together that the Three *are* One, not a They but a Thou.

According to the Script, the Bible, this triune God does not choose to dwell alone but wills to bring to be another to share in this Life Together. So comes

---

[14] On both the importance and the limitations of historic creeds, see Sell, *Confessing and Commending the Faith,* pp. 27-29.

[15] The 'law of the Trinity'.

[16] Bernhard Anderson, *The Unfolding Drama of the Bible* (Philadelphia: Fortress Press, 1988). However, our scenes will be different though Anderson has noted the similarities of my treatment of 'the story' to his own. Ibid, p. 17.

[17] I believe that that this Grand Narrative is integral to Sell's characterization of the faith in its 'long form', as in Sell, *Confessing and Commending the Faith*, pp. 303, 359.

the first scene of the biblical drama: The hand of God the Creator reaches out in creation to join with our hand, as is portrayed in Michelangelo's painting on the ceiling of the Sistine Chapel. Thus the drama in Act I, Scene 1 is about creation, the love of a Maker that brings to be a partner, one even created in the divine image. We were made for a loving handclasp with God, who invites us to a comparable bonding with the rest of creation.

Do we clasp that divine hand? Not according to Act I, Scene 2. Instead we make a fist and shake it in the face of God. Already at the beginning of time, we have a portent of the Gibson hand-to-come. Here is our 'No' to God's invitation, our desire instead to 'play God' in response to the serpent's beguiling word. (Genesis 3:5) We name such 'original sin', as it marks the whole of cosmic history from its beginnings forward, the balled fist rather than the clasped hands.

But note, this scene in the drama is about a failed gesture, a stumble and 'fall' of the fist-maker. 'Young man- Young man- Your arm's too short to box with God,' said the poet James Weldon Johnson.[18] The fall is the consequence of sin, entailing 'death', that is, our estrangement from God. And such eventuates in our alienation from one another, as current as the headlines of today's paper. We must include, in the fall the fracture of nature too, as evidence the disease and devastation that is our constant companion. And also, the distortions in supernature as well as nature and human nature--the mysterious demonic powers and principalities that run riot in our world.[19]

Act I, Scene 2, the fist, the stumble, the fall. But our drama goes forward to a Scene 3. In it, the hand of God is not withdrawn but arcs over the fallen world. In the words of the spiritual, 'God gave Noah the rainbow sign.' The rainbow of Genesis 9 is the symbol of the Creator's promise not to give up on creation. The arm that tries to box with God and our consequent stumble and fall are not the last act/Act. Scene 3 is the account of God's resolute love for the world, the divine patience with us despite our rebellion, a 'long-suffering' love as described by the Psalmist (Psalm 86:1 5KJV). And that includes the giving of many and varied graces to us in our fallen state, signalled by the multi-coloured rainbow of Genesis 9. We have to do here not with the rise of the sun with the fullness of light and truth that is yet to come, but rather with glimpses of the good, the true, the beautiful and the holy available to the human race in many and varied rainbow colours. This 'common grace', as it is called in some Christian traditions, is the covenant with Noah that allows the drama to unfold further, a 'grace of preservation'. Indeed, it is the warrant for the kind of modest apologetics here presumed in which those who confess the faith connect

---

[18] 'The Prodigal Son', in *God's Trombones* (New York: Penguin Books, 1927).
[19] Gabriel Fackre, *The Christian Story*, I (Grand Rapids: Eerdmans, 3rd rev. ed, 1996), pp. 85-87.

with universal sensibilities of both realism and hope.[20] A symbol above us, the loving arm of God over us, but also under us in the very manual imagery we are using as is expressed in yet another spiritual: 'He's got the whole world in hands!' And where does the rainbow touch down? Where else the rainbow's end than a point chosen by God - among a 'chosen people'. So the word comes to Abraham: 'I will establish my covenant between me and you…'(Gen. 17:7).

Scene 4 of Act I takes up two-thirds of the Christian Bible, another covenant, this time of special grace. It's all about a people gathered by a divine hand into a travelling company and led by a guiding hand out of the land of Ur, shielded by that hand during an Egyptian slavery, pointed out of it and through parted waters into a long journey with Moses and on to another stage in the history of promise - a land of milk and honey, but also trial and tribulation. That hand of God blessed this people, raised up among them prophets, priests and kings, pushed, pulled, prodded, protected them, sojourned with them in exile and return, promised them and us the coming of a time when brothers and sisters shall embrace, when 'the weaned child shall put its hand on the adder's den' (Isaiah 11:8), when the hand clasp between God and the world happens and *shalom* finally come to be. Here again is the 'long-suffering' love of God seen in the covenant with Israel as well as the covenant with Noah, so described by Jeremiah (Jer. 15:15 KJV).

There is no cosmic drama without this scene. Does the Gibson film do justice to the special love of God for the Jewish people? Critics say no, defenders say yes. What better occasion, then, for exploring the relation of Christ to the Jewish people? To draw on the immense new literature on 'supersessionism' and 'anti-supersessionism', to attend to Paul's own struggle with the question in chapter 9-11 of his letter to the Romans. What a chance for those inside and outside the church to deepen their understanding of the 'unfolding drama of the Bible'![21]

As the prophets of Israel foresaw, the hand of God will finally clasp our hand. But first, something else has to happen, again with its clues in God's history with Israel as in the prophetic words concerning one who is 'A man of suffering and acquainted with infirmity…wounded for our transgressions, crushed for our iniquities ….and by his bruises we are healed' (Isaiah 53:3, 5).

---

[20] On the same, see the writer's chapter, 'Realism and Vision' and *passim* in *The Promise of Reinhold Niebuhr* (Lanham, MD: University Press of America, rev. ed, 1994).

[21] For an account of the recent struggle of the Churches to think through the relation of Christian faith to the Jewish people, see the World Council of Churches' *Theology of the Churches and the Jewish People: Statements by the World Council of Churches and its Member Churches* (Geneva: WCC Publications, 1988). For the writer's view see, 'The Place of Israel in Christian Faith' in *Ecumenical Faith in Evangelical Perspective* (Grand Rapids: Eerdmans, 1993) pp. 147-153, a chapter that grew out of a two-year study in the United Church of Christ in which both Jewish and Arab Christian thinkers participated with Christian theologians.

This is the text that the film uses to introduce the passion.

In our own manual account, the hand of God must press down at the rainbow's end and *intersect* this fallen world. Only God in the flesh can turn the tale around. So we now come to the centre-point of the trinitarian drama, Act II. Scene 1: God the reconciler, present among us in the divine-human Person of Jesus Christ.

ACT II in the Theatre of Passion

In returning to the film as our entry point for Act II, we meet again at the stage door the critics. How can such 'sadomasochistic' 'pornography' be a route to the heart of the matter? The violence of *Braveheart*, *The Patriot* and *Lethal Weapon 1-4* be a path to the gentle Jesus? Fathered in anti-Semitism and mothered by a pre-Vatican 2 tridentine Latin Mass church? No attention to the Galilean Jesus who mirrored love and light not doom and gloom? Scripted in gore by a fantasizing anti-Semitic stigmatist, rather than following the modest pens of Mathew, Mark, Luke and John of Holy Scripture? At the end of his newspaper column, James Carroll encapsulates the harsh critical evaluations: 'It is a lie. It is sick....'[22]

If this were a movie review we might linger a bit here, examine and weigh the charges. But instead, we are attempting to approach the film as a 'teaching moment', a counsel also, incidentally, of Kenneth Woodward, former religion editor of *Newsweek* to a *New York Times* readership, an audience for apologetic if there ever was one.[23] But teaching about what? Not the whole of the life, death and resurrection of Christ, but that key half-day, the climactic phase of the intersection of eternity and time, the point which those crossed lines themselves suggest. As P.T. Forsyth puts it: 'The key to the Incarnation is not in its cradle but in the cross...in his death he did *the* act of the universe'.[24] Here the finale of the 'at-one-ment' of God and the world happened, the reconciliation of the alienated parties in the grand drama. This is, in our account Scene 2 of Act II, the finishing of the Work of Christ, the 'Atonement'- is done by the incarnate Person of Christ. Of course, the Atonement was more than these 12 hours. As in John Calvin's threefold office of the Work of Christ - Christ as prophet, priest and king[25]- Christ's career entailed a prophetic ministry in Galilee and a royal ministry on Easter morning, as well as the priestly act of passion and death, each, of course coinherent in the

---

[22] James Carroll, 'An Obscene Portrayal of Christ's Passion' in *The Boston Globe*, 24 February 2004. See his repeat critique in *The Boston Globe*, 12 October 2004.

[23] Kenneth Woodward, 'Do You Recognize This Jesus?', Op-Ed Column, *New York Times*, 25 February 2004.

[24] P.T. Forsyth, *The Divine Self-Emptying* (London: James Clarke, 1901), p. 116.

[25] So described in Gabriel Fackre, 'Atonement' in *Encyclopedia of Reformed Faith*, Donald McKim, ed. (Louisville: Westminster/John Knox, 1992), pp. 13-16.

other. But the film we are using as a teaching resource points us to the drama going on the in the crosshairs of Scene 2.

And well it should, especially so these days. So Woodward's observation of our avoidance of the bloody path to Golgotha, citing the indictment of H. Richard Niebuhr

> In sermons…the emphasis all too often is on the smoothly therapeutic: what Jesus can do for me [and he might have added for the moralists among us, what we should do for Jesus]….More than 60 years ago, H. Richard Niebuhr, summarized the creed of an easy-going American Christianity that in our time has triumphantly come to pass: 'A God without wrath brought men without sin into a kingdom without judgment through a Christ without a cross.' Despite its muscular excess, Mr. Gibson's symbol-laden film is a welcome repudiation of all that.[26]

A case can be made that talk about the wrath of God has disappeared from much Protestant preaching and teaching. But God is *tough* Love as well as *tender* Love. Away with 'sloppy agape'! Begone the indulgent Deity of pop Christianity! Judgment *will* fall and the wrath of God *does* descend. Again, P.T. Forsyth had it right: 'Love is not holy without judgment. It is the love of the holy God that is the consuming fire.'[27]

But on whom does the judgment fall? There are piety and theology that seek to tell it like it is, honestly reporting the bad news of judgment. They do so by declaring that God punishes Jesus in our place. That agonizing bloody figure on the road and on the tree stood in for us, receiving the wrath of God that we deserve for our sin.

This sounds right. But something seems to be missing. The Scripture does not say God was above Christ rebuking, but 'God was *in* Christ reconciling…' The only One who could shoulder the cross that dealt with the judgment of God was the One who was himself 'true God' (Nicene Creed). The Atonement presupposes the Incarnation. There is no Scene 2 in Act II, unless there is a Scene 1. It is the incarnate Person - divine as well as human - who does the Work. It was very God of very God, Jesus Christ, the Son whose blood was shed for our sin. Yes, there was a Father above the Son, but God the Father was not *frowning*, but *crying*.

On this matter of in and above, we get some help from Aulen again: 'God does not stand, as it were, outside the drama that is being played out, but Himself takes part in it…. He overcomes evil, not by an almighty *fiat* but by putting in something of His own by Divine Self-oblation…'.[28] The Actor in the patristic tale he is describing is Deity, God as the second Person of the Trinity: 'The Word of God, who is God Himself, has entered in under the conditions of

---

[26] Fackre, 'Atonement'.
[27] P.T. Forsyth, *The Work of Christ* (London: Independent Press, 1958), p. 85.
[28] Gustaf Aulen, *The Faith of the Christian Church,* Eric Wahlstrom, trans. (Philadelphia: Fortress Press, 1960), pp. 53, 48.

sin and death, to take up the conflict with the powers of evil and carry through to the decisive victory.'[29] Aulen describes this divine participation in the passion, first-hand, as 'continuity' between the Persons of the Father and the Son, rather than the 'discontinuity' that he finds in that other theory of the Atonement which portrays God as providing a human sacrifice, Jesus, to take the punishment for our sins. Rather it is 'God Himself' who suffers under the lash and on the cross.

It is striking how Aulen's characterizations anticipate some of the themes and images of Gibson's film: the portrayal of a cosmic drama with a contest going on constantly between Christ and seductive and wily Evil One, the path of suffering, pain, self-denial, vulnerability, all to the fore—something that so irritates our modern sensibilities, a 'divine Self-oblation' at the bloody centre of the drama....

The 'continuity' Aulen speaks of can be interpreted in this way. The Son is the heart of the Father. The passion of Christ the Son, therefore, is the story of *God's broken heart*. We have to do here with the ultimate brokenness, death itself, not the death *of* God but death *in* God. Death is the horror of separation from God, the Son crying out to the Father, the text to which Jürgen Moltmann so often points

> My God, my God, why have you forsaken me? (Mt. 27:46)
> God - torn apart[30]

While the current attempt to remain faithful to the biblical account of the divine passibility—the divine suffering-- has often more to do with relating the gospel to *human suffering*, we are focusing here on its importance in dealing with *human sin*. How else can our radical estrangement be overcome except by a radical action in kind? Such happened when the judgment we deserve was executed by and on the only One so capable. In this scene of the passion, the Judge stepped down before the Judgment seat and received the verdict, 'The Judge Judged in Our Place' as Karl Barth expressed it.[31] This is surely the burden of the Prodigal Son story, the father's broken heart taking into itself the pain of judgment due the erring son, enabling him to rush to greet him with a passionate unconditional love (in this case, *we* are the son, even as the broken heart is the Teller of this tale).[32] In like matter, on the cross, the divine mercy receives into itself in suffering love the divine wrath (Luther).

---

[29] Aulen, *The Faith of the Christian Church*, p. 32.
[30] So Jürgen Moltmann, *The Crucified God*, especially pp. 160-290.
[31] Karl Barth, *Church Dogmatics* IV/2, Geoffrey Bromiley, trans. (Edinburgh: T&T Clark, 1956), pp. 211-283.
[32] See this writer's 'Foreword', in Richard L. Floyd, *When I Survey the Wondrous Cross: Reflections on the Atonement* (San Jose, CA: Pickwick Publications, 2000), pp. vii-xi.

Yes, *wrath* in God, as with H. Richard Niebuhr's indictment of liberal theology. Yet, a love more integral to who God is than wrath, for the latter is the adjective evoked by our sin and *Agape* is the eternal noun. God as 'holy Love' in P.T. Forsyth's familiar phrase. Love in pain, as the judgment we are due is taken into the central being of God. Can that tear from heaven at the scene of Calvary be the empathy of the Father with the Son, a co-suffering in which the Father 'dies a little death'?

While Aulen is concerned to stress in *Christus Victor* the relations of the Father and the Son as the work of the one God, elsewhere he notes the crucial presence of the Holy Spirit, protesting that as the Father and Son have been sundered in too much conventional theology, 'in the same way the work of the Spirit was separated from the Father and the Son.'[33] As in ancient formula, while the three missions or dispensations are identifiable, 'the external works of the Trinity are indivisible' (*opera dei ad extra indivisa sunt*).

The micro-trinitarian history of God that took place in Scene 2 of Act II of the cosmic drama was the passion of God in the Son's suffering and death, the compassion of the Father in solidarity with the Son and the Holy Spirit's power of powerlessness, co-present in this external Work of Atonement. We might add, with the film in mind, that the agony in the face of Mary, the Mother of God, mirrors that of the One she mothers.

An Ancient Analogy

But what of the protest of all this: 'The mighty God is incapable of suffering'? As noted, the teaching of the divine passibility on which we have been meditating reflects a turn in theology echoing some of the formidable Christian thinkers of our own time—Barth, Bonhoeffer, Pannenberg, Moltmann, Robert Jenson.[34] But it continues to be contested, most recently by Thomas Weinandy in the important work earlier cited.[35] As is often pointed out in response to both the older and current rejection of divine suffering, Greek philosophical notions have had undue influence, ones that view purity and deity as beyond participation in the moil and toil of this life. But there are legitimate concerns.

---

[33] Aulen, *The Faith of the Christian Church*, p. 228.

[34] Barth and Moltmann so noted previously. See also Dietrich Bonhoeffer, *Letters and Papers from Prison*, Eberhard Bethge, ed. (New York: Macmillan, 1972), pp. 348-49, 360-62, 370. While questioning Aulen's *Christus Victor* 'motif', Robert Jenson asserts that the story of the crucifixion is 'the story of God's act to bring us back to himself at his own cost...', an event in 'his life and ours'. *Systematic Theology*, I, (New York: Oxford University Press, 1997), p. 189. Evangelical theology increasingly speaks of the atonement in terms of divine participation. So Donald Bloesch, reflecting Barth's careful statement thereof as in Bloesch's *Jesus Christ: Savior and Lord* (Downers Grove: Intervarsity Press, 1997), pp. 170-74.

[35] See also David Bentley Hart, *The Beauty of the Infinite: The Aesthetics of Christian Truth* (Grand Rapids: Eerdmans, 2003), as in his critique of Robert Jenson, pp. 160-166.

Let's look at them.

For one, does the stress on the divine suffering take seriously the *humanity* of Christ as part and parcel of the atoning Work? Good question. Reconciliation cannot be conceived as a transaction over the head and out of the reach of the real agony and real death of the historical Jesus. Here again the early Fathers gave us a good lead on why the humanity of Jesus is so crucial to the Atonement, and how to think rightly about it.

What is it that brings out the truth about the reality of the fall so that it can be dealt with? The ancients made use of a fishhook-bait analogy. The Devilfish was lured out of its hiding place by the tender morsel of the vulnerable Jesus. Much scorn has been poured on this patristic metaphor. However, such disdain misses the profundity of the figure. Innocence, purity and vulnerability invite anger, hatred and hostility. For Evil to be exposed for what it is, set down in front of sinful humanity the perfection for which we were made. Away with this embarrassment! Strike it down! Lash out at it! Drive in those nails.

Surely the scenes in *The Passion of the Christ* of the agony on the road and on the cross portray how vulnerability evokes the cruelty of which we are capable. So Paul's astute observation that when you love your enemies 'you will heap burning coals on their heads' (Rom.12:20). Jesus is the exemplar of that cheek-turning *agape* that enrages its receiver and brings the lash to bear, ever and again, on the already bloodied back. And shows us up for what we really are, and moves us to ponder the words of another spiritual, 'Were you there, when they crucified my Lord?'

'My Lord?' Again, the provocative fishhook-bait imagery of the early Fathers proves illuminating. For one, it means that the knowledge that the effects of our sin reach into the very heart of God overwhelms us. Is that what prompts the tears of worshippers in the theatre pews when they view this film? How else do we know ourselves to be the sinners that we really are unless we see our hand in the very crucifixion of God? And hear from the Victim's lips, 'Father, forgive…'? No power in this world can so drive us to our knees. Only this Power of the divine Powerlessness, the Christ who reigns from the cross.

The fishhook-bait analogy has yet another meaning. The Devilfish did get caught. The power of God in the powerlessness of Jesus accomplished its purpose. So Aulen, interpreting Irenaeus, says: 'The redemptive work is accomplished by the Logos *through* the Manhood of His instrument, for it could be accomplished by no power than by God Himself.'[36] Can we put it this way? God stoops to conquer. God comes into our midst in human form in Galilee and on the road to Calvary in order there to *expose* us for who we are. We see first-hand One who is as we should be and strike out at this embarrassing Presence. Yet it is, paradoxically, only through our lacerating and crucifying ways that God can *disclose* as well as expose, disclose the suffering Love that makes reconciliation possible. The proper emphasis on the suffering

---

[36] Aulen, *The Faith of the Christian Church*, p. 33.

of Jesus when it excludes the suffering of God constitutes the discontinuity Aulen rightly criticizes. Without making the mistake of this discontinuity, we can yet affirm the concern to preserve the role of the humanity of Christ in the Work of salvation, while knowing that it was the God who was 'in Christ' who evokes our repentance and brings forgiveness to the sinner.

There is a second legitimate question posed to the cry of the 'crucified God!' Does the *power* of God get diminished by insistence on the divine powerlessness? Is the omnipotence of Deity given its due by such a show of divine weakness?

Enter the Holy Spirit

An answer to these questions begins with St. Paul's comment, 'God's weakness is stronger than human strength' (1 Cor. 1:25). How come? There must be more to the cosmic drama. So on to Act III, 'the new dispensation, for the gift of the Spirit for the continuation of the Work of God in [our] souls…'for the unity and communion of God and man.'[37] The final Act in the overarching trinitarian drama, with the Holy Spirit now centre-stage, includes scenes of the Pentecostal birth of the church, the giving of the gift of saving grace through the preaching of the Word of the cross and the participation in Christ's body and blood in holy communion, and following Dietrich Bonhoeffer's call to costly discipleship, participating in the sufferings of God out there in the world of human pain, alongside the victims of war, injustice, disease, disaster, hate and hurt.

But what keeps us going in the struggle against sin, evil and death is the *final* eschatological scene that closes the book on all suffering, human *and* divine, and brings in that last scene of the drama the handclasp of God and the world. The contention that the all-mightiness of God is obscured by a belief in the suffering of God overlooks the trinitarian drama with this denouement. But we are never allowed to overlook it at Christian burial. For there we hear the words from St. Paul in their future tense: 'nothing *will be* able to separate us from the love of God in Jesus Christ….'! At the close of the third great Act of the cosmic drama, the Holy Spirit demonstrates the power of powerlessness by bringing an end to the sorrowful mysteries:

> He will wipe ever tear from their eyes
> Death will be no more
> Mourning and crying and pain will be no more
> For the first things have passed away (Rev. 21:4).

At this ringing down of the curtain, 'God himself will be with them' (Rev. 21:3), bringing to be, and sharing in, that joyful new day. There is *no* eternal

---

[37] Aulen, p. 32 with quotation from Irenaeus.

tear in the eye of God. The End wipes such from every eye, human *and* divine.

The defenders of the divine impassibility are right in what they affirm - the tearless power of God at the beginning and end of the cosmic drama, and wrong in what they deny - the God who weeps in and for Jesus at the centre of the Story.

Conclusion

The movie-goer departing the theatre ponders the things seen. What a moment for teaching about the faith filmicly confessed and commended. Will there be an interpretive Word spoken about the sights on that screen? Here, by a common grace, is offered an occasion to meditate on the cross and the path to it, to probe behind the pictures and understand that the lash on the back and the nail in the hand of Christ have to do with the passion of God the Son, the compassion of God the Father—the divine tears--all made endurable and finally triumphant by the power of God the Holy Spirit. Let the apologist seize the day.

Bibliography of Alan P. F. Sell

As far as is known, and excepting items in school magazines and pastoral letters in local church newsletters, this is a complete list of the writings of Alan P. F. Sell. It includes books, chapters in books, academic and popular articles, reviews and letters to the press. The Bibliography was begun on 22 January 1991. It should not be supposed that the author continues to be at ease with everything he has written.

Abbreviations:
CSCT: *Commemorations. Studies in Christian Thought and History*, 1993.
DTLC: *Dissenting Thought and the Life of the Churches*, 1990.
EEE: *Enlightenment, Ecumenism, Evangel. Theological Themes and Thinkers 1550-2000*, 2005.
TAT: *Testimony and Tradition. Studies in Reformed and Dissenting Thought*, 2005.
WARC: World Alliance of Reformed Churches (Presbyterian and Congregational)

1960
'Without tarrying for Calvin. The heart of Reformed worship,' *The Christian World*, 11 February 1960.

1961
Obituary: 'Edwin Bywater Rawcliffe,' *The Congregational Year Book*, 1961, 447-8.
'Commission I : From the camp of the bewildered,' *The Christian World*, 9 November 1961, 8.

1963
'There may be country folk with straw in their hair - but not here,' *The Congregational Monthly*, November 1963, 13-14.
'Christian ethics and moral philosophy: some reflections on the contemporary situation,' *Scottish Journal of Theology*, XVI, December 1963, 337-51.
'*Conscience* in recent discussion,' *Theology*, LXVI, December 1963, 498-504.

1964
'Theological education by degrees,' *The Expository Times*, LXXV no. 7, April 1964, 196-200.
'John Baillie and Christian epistemology,' *The London Quarterly and Holborn Review*, July 1964, 224-31.
Letter: 'Theological education by degrees,' *The Expository Times*, LXXVI no. 2, November 1964, 70.

1969
Letter: 'Ample opportunity,' *The Congregational Monthly*, July 1969, 14.

1972
Congregationalism at Worplesdon 1822-1972, Birmingham, 1972. Pp. 27. The earlier portion reprinted as 'Nonconformity at Worplesdon,' *The Surrey Archaeological*

Collections, LXIX, 1973, 99-112.

'George Burder and the Lichfield Dissenters,' *South Staffordshire Archaeological and Historical Society Transactions*, XIII, 1971-72, 52-60. Reprinted in DTLC, ch. 10.

'Christians, humanists and common ground,' *Journal of Moral Education*, I no. 3, June 1972, 177-85.

1973

'The background of the current RE/ME debate in Britain: an historical sketch,' *Religious Education*, LXVIII no. 1, January-February 1973, 42-56.

'An approach to college counselling,' *Learning for Living*, XII no. 4, March 1973, 11-15. Reprinted in *Counselling in Colleges of Education: A Symposium*, ed. David Warwick, Lancaster: University of Lancaster School of Education, [1973], 37-41, as 'Three case studies in college counselling: (2) West Midlands College.'

'*Agape*, atonement and Christian ethics,' *The Downside Review*, XCI no. 303, April 1973, 83-100.

'Friends and Philosophy,' *The Friends' Quarterly*, XVIII nos. 2 and 3, April and July 1973, 72-82 and 111-122.

'A liberated churchman,' *The Philosophical Journal*, X no. 2, July 1973, 85-96.

'The social and literary contributions of three Unitarian ministers to nineteenth-century Walsall,' *Transactions of the Unitarian Historical Society*, XV no. 3, October 1973, 77-97. Reprinted in DTLC, ch. 16.

1974

Alfred Dye, Minister of the Gospel, London: Fauconberg Press, 1974. Pp. 60.

'Some sermons of Gilbert White,' *The Philosophical Journal*, XI no. 1, January 1974, 10-18.

'*The Christian's Great Interest* - and the preacher's,' *Evangelical Quarterly*, XLVI no. 2, April-June 1974, 72-80.

'The life and work of Robert Mackintosh (1858-1933),' *Journal of the United Reformed Church History Society*, I no. 3, May 1974, 79-90.

'The peril of reductionism in Christian thought,' *Scottish Journal of Theology*, XXVIII, 1974, 48-64.

Review: G. Langford and D. J. O'Connor, *New Essays in the Philosophy of Education*; *Philosophical Studies*, XII, 1974, 301-304.

1975

'Christian and secular philosophy in Britain at the beginning of the twentieth century: a study of approaches and relationships,' *The Downside Review*, XCIII no. 311, April 1975, 122-143.

'*Philosophical Studies* and philosophical frontiers,' *Philosophical Studies*, XXIII, 1975, 7-21.

Review: R. S. Peters, ed., *The Philosophy of Education*; *Philosophical Studies*, XXIII, 1975, 255-60.

1976

Review: J. King-Farlow and W. N. Christensen, *Faith and the Life of Reason*; *Philosophical Studies*, XXIV, 1976, 280-83.

1977

Robert Mackintosh: Theologian of Integrity, Bern: Peter Lang, 1977. Pp. 107.
'Robert Mackintosh, a neglected theologian,' *The Modern Churchman*, XX no. 3, Spring 1977, 95-108.
'Platonists (ancient and modern) and the Gospel,' *Irish Theological Quarterly*, XLIV no. 3, 1977, 153-74.
'Immanentism and the theological enterprise,' *Faith and Thought*, CIV no. 2, Autumn 1977, 119-145.
'Augustine *versus* Pelagius: a cautionary tale of perennial importance,' *Calvin Theological Journal*, XII no. 2, November 1977, 117-143.
'Evolution: theory and theme,' *Faith and Thought*, CIV no. 3, Winter 1977-78, 202-220.
Review: W. D. Hudson, *Wittgenstein and Religious Belief*; *Philosophical Studies*, 1977, 390-92.
Review: W. H. Austin, *The Relevance of Natural Science to Theology*; *Philosophical Studies*, XXV, 1977, 378-9.
Review: N. Timms and D. Watson, eds., *Talking About Welfare: Readings in Philosophy and Social Policy*; *Philosophical Studies*, XXV, 1977, 358-60.

1978

'Augustinian and Pelagian variations from Cassian to Luther,' *Theologia Evangelica*, XI nos. 2 and 3, July-September 1978, 79-100.
'Conservatives, liberals and the Gospel,' *Faith and Thought*, CV nos. 1 and 2, Autumn 1978, 62-118.

1979

'The centenary of Flint's *Theism*,' *Philosophical Studies*, XXVI, 1979, 167-190.
'Priestley's polemic against Reid,' *The Price-Priestley Newsletter*, III, 1979, 19-31. Reprinted in DTLC, ch. 15.
'The heart of the Christian Gospel,' *The Indian Journal of Theology*, XXVIII no. 1, January-March 1979, 15-32. Revised and reprinted in *Memphis Theological Seminary Journal*, XXXIV no. 2/XXXV no. 1, Fall/Spring 1997, 27-43.
'Transcendence, immanence and the Gospel,' *Journal of Theology for Southern Africa*, no. 26, March 1979, 56-66.
'Ritschl appraised, then and now,' *Reformed Theological Review*, XXXVIII no. 2, May-August 1979, 33-41.
'Arminians, deists and reason,' *Faith and Freedom*, XXXIII pt. 1, Autumn 1979, 19-31.
Review: J. L. Segundo, *The Liberation of Theology*; *Philosophical Studies*, XXVI, 1979, 302-305.
Review: D. O. Thomas, *The Honest Mind: The Life and Work of Richard Price*; *Philosophical Studies*, XXVI, 1979, 305-310.
Review: J. Kent, *Holding the Fort: Studies in Victorian Revivalism*; *Reform*, June 1979, 27.

1980

God Our Father, Edinburgh: The Saint Andrew Press, 1980. Pp. 144. Second edn., Shippensburg, PA: Ragged Edge Press, 2000.
'Henry Rogers and *The Eclipse of Faith*,' *Journal of the United Reformed Church History Society*, II no. 5, May 1980, 128-143. Reprinted in DTLC, ch. 17.

'The rise and reception of modern biblical criticism,' *Evangelical Quarterly*, LII no. 3, July-September 1980, 132-148.
'John Howe's eclectic theism,' *Journal of the United Reformed Church History Society*, II no. 6, October 1980-, 187-93. Reprinted in DTLC, ch. 3.
Review: A. Dulles, *Models of the Church*; *Philosophical Studies*, XXVII, 1980, 348-351.
Review: F. Sontag, *What Can God Do?*; *Reformed Review*, XXXIII no. 3, 1980, 188.

1981
'Parables, propositions and information,' *Journal of Theology for Southern Africa*, no. 37, December 1981, 38-49.
Review: A. I. C. Heron, *A Century of Protestant Theology*; *Reform*, January 1981, 26.
Review: W. D. Hudson, *A Century of Moral Philosophy*; *Reform*, Janaury 1981, 26.
Review: K. W. Clements, *Faith*; *Reform*, September 1981, 25.
Review: A. W. Robinson, *The Personal Life of the Christian*; *Reform*, September 1981, 25.

1982
The Great Debate: Calvinism, Arminianism and Salvation, Worthing: H. E. Walter, 1982. Pp. 141. Reprinted Grand Rapids: Baker Book House, 1983; Eugene, OR: Wipf & Stock, 1998. Korean edn., Seoul: Word of Life Press, 1989.
'A kind of ministry,' *Reform*, February 1982, 11.
'Autonomy, immanence and the loss of authority,' *Churchman*, XCVI no. 2, 1982, 123-141.
'Jerusalem *versus* Athens?' *Irish Theological Quarterly*, XLIX no. 2, 1982, 75-90.
Review: J. L. Segundo, *A Theology for a New Humanity* (5 vols.); *Philosophical Studies*, XXVIII, 1982, 270-73.
Review: H. McKeating, *Why Bother with Adam and Eve?*; *Reform*, July-August, 1982, 27.
Review: L. Houlden, *What Did the First Christians Believe?*; *Reform*, July-August 1982, 27.
Review: J. Beer, *Who is Jesus?*; *Reform*, July-August 1982, 27.
Review: R. Harries, *Should a Christian Support Guerillas?*; *Reform*, July-August 1982, 27.
Review: R. Nelson-Jones, *An Introduction to Counselling Psychology*; *West Midlands Journal of Teacher Education*, I no. 2, September 1982, 63-4.
Letter: 'Debt to Methodism,' *Methodist Recorder*, 4 February 1982.
Letter: 'Ancient and mangled,' (on hymn writing), *Reform*, March 1982, 30.
Letter: 'Meetings change minds,' *Reform*, June 1982, 29-30.
Letter: 'A southerner goes trailing,' *Cumberland Times and Star*, 2 October 1982, 18.

1983
Guidelines on Church Discipline, London: The United Reformed Church, 1983. Pp. 15.
The Preparation and Delivery of Sermons, London: The United Reformed Church, 1983. Pp. 10.
Preface to *Partnership in Mission: Learning and Doing. Extracts from Synod Meeting of 12th March 1983 Relating to the Presentation of the World Church and Mission*

Committee, West Midlands Province of the United Reformed Church, 1983, 1.
'Priestley's polemic against Reid: an additional note,' *Enlightenment and Dissent*, II, 1983, 121. Incorporated into DTLC, ch. 15, n. 4.
Report on the annual meeting of leaders of the Christian World Communions, Sofia, Bulgaria, in the Bulgarian Orthodox newspaper, 19 November 1983.
'The Evangelical Congregational Union of Bulgaria: a profile,' *Reformed Press Service*, no. 219, November 1983, 8-9; and in *Reformed Perspectives* in French, German and Spanish, November 1983. Reprinted in *Broadway United Reformed Church Newsletter*, no. 244, December 1983, 7-9.
'Theology and the philosophical climate: case studies from the second century AD,' *Vox Evangelica*, XIII, 1983, 41-66, and XIV, 1984, 53-64.
'The Walsall riots, the Rooker family, and eighteenth-century Dissent,' *South Staffordshire Archaeological and Historical Society Transactions*, XXV, 1983-84, 50-71. Reprinted in DTLC, ch. 11.
Review: J. Comblin, *The Meaning of Mission*; *Philosophical Studies*, XXIX, 1983, 378-81.
Review: A. Cussianovich, *Religious Life and the Poor*; *Philosophical Studies*, XXIX, 1983, 381-3.
Review: J. Coulson, *Religion and Imagination*; *Philosophical Studies*, XXIX, 1983, 300-303.

1984

Responding to Baptism, Eucharist and Ministry: A Word to the Reformed Churches, (*Studies from the World Alliance of Reformed Churches*, no. 3), Geneva: WARC, 1984. Pp. 16. Reprinted in *Reformed World*, XXXVIII no. 3, September 1984, 187-200; and in French and German in *Bulletin of the Department of Theology*, February 1985.
'Rationality,' in *A Dictionary of Religious Education*, London: SCM Press, 1984, 282.
'Locke and Descartes through Victorian eyes,' *Philosophical Studies*, XXX, 1984, 220-29. Reprinted in DTLC, ch. 18.
'Samuel Clarke on the existence of God,' *Enlightenment and Dissent*, III, 1984, 65-75. Reprinted in DTLC, ch. 4.
'BEM : A step toward unity,' *The Church Herald*, 3 February 1984, 6, 7-9.
'Retirement denied: The life and ministry of Noah Jones (1725-1785),' *Transactions of the Unitarian Historical Society*, XVIII no. 2, April 1984, 91-105. Reprinted in DTLC, ch. 12.
'Christian learning in Ireland,' *Reformed Press Service*, no. 255, May 1984, 12-13; and in French, German and Spanish in *Reformed Perspectives*, June 1984.
'Rwanda: the and of eternal spring,' *Reformed Press Service*, no. 226, June 1984, 10-11; and in French, German and Spanish in *Reformed Perspectives*, June 1984.
'What is the World Alliance of Reformed Churches?' *Boletim de Estudios e Informaçoes* (Portugal), II nos. 4 and 5, July-August 1984, 9-11; *Presbyterian Life* (South Africa), September 1984, 3; *The Presbyterian Outlook* (U.S.A.), 10 September 1984, 5; *The Congregationalist* (New Zealand), September 1984, 2-4; *Reformierte Kirchenzeitung*, 15 September 1984, 229-230; *Stedfast* (Scotland), October 1984, 11-12; Tavita (Indonesia), December 1984, 29; *Jednota* (Poland), December 1984, 11, 20; *Broadway United Reformed Church Newsletter*, no. 258, March, 1985, 12-13; *Weekbulletin* (Netherlands), 25 July 1985, 4-5, and 1 August

1985, 5-6; *Kerk Informatie* (Netherlands), January 1986, 17 and February 1986, 17.

'Ecclesiology in perspective: Conversations with Anglicans and Baptists,' *Reformed World*, XXXVIII, September 1984, 168-176; and in French, German and Spanish in *Reformed Perspectives*, September 1984.

'The resolution on racism and South Africa: 2 years on,' (interviewed by Jill Schaeffer), *Reformed Press Service*, no. 228, September 1984, 10-12.

'Cradley Chapel: from Independency to the Establishment,' *Journal of the United Reformed Church History Society*, III, 1984, 120-131. Reprinted in DTLC, ch. 13.

'An Epiphany charge to wise men,' *Reformed World*, CCCVIII no. 4, December 1984, 216-19. Reprinted in French, German and Spanish in *Reformed Perspectives*, December 1984.

'Fostering theological sharing,' *Reformed Perspectives*, December 1984, in French, German and Spanish. Reprinted in *Reformed Press Service*, January 1985.

Review: D. Locke, *A Fantasy of Reason: The Life and Thought of William Godwin*; *Philosophical Studies*, XXX, 1984, 325-7.

Review: D. A. Lane, *The Experience of God: An Invitation to Do Theology*; *Philosophical Studies*, XXX, 1984, 363-5.

Review: S. Talmor, *Glanvill: The Uses and Abuses of Scepticism*; *Philosophical Studies*, XXX, 1984, 323-4.

Review: H. Rikhof, *The Concept of Church*; *Philosophical Studies*, XXX, 1984, 362-3.

Review: A. Conway, *The Principles of the Most Ancient and Modern Philosophy*; *Philosophical Studies*, XXX, 1984, 327-8.

Review: B. Hebblethwaite and S. Sutherland, eds., *The Philosophical Frontiers of Christian Theology*; *Philosophical Studies*, XXX, 1984, 357-362.

Review: J. M. Miller, *What are they Saying about Papal Primacy?*; *Reformed Review*, XXXVIII, 1984, 91.

Review: J. A. Nestigen, *The Faith we Hold*; *Reformed Review* XXXVIII, 1984, 76.

Letter: 'Amen to that,' *Reform*, July-August 1984.

Letter: 'Greetings and News from Switzerland,' *Broadway United Reformed Church Newsletter*, no. 254, December 1984, 3-4.

1985

'Reformierte Kirchen,' (with K. Halaski), in *Ökumene Lexikon*, Frankfurt: Verlag Otto Lembeck, 1985, 1033-40.

'The Reformed family: a profile,' in *Reformed and Disciples of Christ in Dialogue*, ed. Alan P. F. Sell, (*Studies from the World Alliance of Reformed Churches*, no. 6), Geneva: WARC, 1985, 43-52. Reprinted in *Mennonites and Reformed in Dialogue*, eds. H. G. Vom Berg, H. Kossen, L. Miller and L. Vischer, (*Studies from the World Alliance of Reformed Churches*, no. 7), 1986, 23-32.

Notes to R. L. Harrison, 'The Disciples of Christ and the Reformed tradition,' in *Reformed and Disciples of Christ in Dialogue,* (see previous item), 34.

'Roger Williams, 1603-1683,' in *Des Hommes Une Idée: la Réforme*, Geneva: Fondation des Clefs de Saint-Pierre, 1985, 39-41.

'Henry Grove: A Dissenter at the parting of the ways,' *Enlightenment and Dissent*, IV, 1985, 53-63. Reprinted in DTLC, ch. 6.

'Dubious Establishment? A neglected ecclesiological testimony,' *Mid-Stream*, XXIV no. 1, January 1985, 1-28. Reprinted in DTLC, ch. 22.

'An Englishman, an Irishman and a Scotsman...' *Scottish Journal of Theology*, XXXVIII no. 1, 1985, 41-83. Reprinted (and re-titled) in DTLC, ch. 19.
'Fostering theological sharing, II,' *Reformed Press Service*, no. 233, February 1985, 8. Reprinted in French, German and Spanish in *Reformed Perspectives*, February 1985.
'A catechism, a children's address and a college,' *Reformed Perspectives*, February 1985, in French, German and Spanish; excerpted in *Boletim de Estudios e Informaçoes*, II no. 6, May 1985, 2.
'Alfred Dye: A postscript,' *Grace Magazine*, February 1985, 17.
'Sharing theologically through the Alliance,' *Stedfast*, February 1985, 13=14; *Broadway United Reformed Church Newsletter*, April 1985, 12-14; *Kerk Informatie*, March 1986, 18.
'John Wyclif (d. 1384): Anniversary reflections,' *Reformed World*, XXXVIII no. 5, March 1985, 290-300; and in *Reformed Perspectives* in French and German (March) and Spanish (June). Reprinted in *Krestanká Revue* (Prague), LII no. 5, 1985, 104-111; *Theologiai Szemle* (Budapest), XXVII no. 3, 1985, 158-162; *Református Szemle* (Cluj, Romania), LXXVII nos. 5-6, 1984, 396-404; excerpted in *Communio Viatorum* (Prague), XXVIII nos. 1-2, 1985, 94-5.
'Reformed resources,' *Broadway United Reformed Church Newsletter*, no. 260, May 1985, 14-15; *The Congregationalist* (New Zealand), no. 61, June 1985, 1-4; *Presbyterian Record* (Canada), June 1985, 33-4; *Presbyterian Life* (South Africa), August 1985, 8; excerpted in *Ecumenical Press Service*, 7-13 April 1985, item 38; *Presbyterian Outlook*, 10 February 1986, 7, 12.
'John Chater: From Independent minister to Sandemanian author,' *Baptist Quarterly*, XXI no. 3, July 1985, 100-117. Reprinted in DTLC, ch. 14.
'Memorials,' *The Presbyter* (N.E. India), V no. 18, July-September 1985, 5-6; *Reform*, September 1985, 3; *Broadway United Reformed Church Newsletter*, no. 263, September 1985, 4-6; excerpted in *Ecumenical Press Service*, 21-31 July 1985, item 54; *Presbyterian Outlook*, December 1-8 1985, 14-15.
'Robert Travers and the Lichfield-Longdon Church book,' *Journal of the United Reformed Church History Society*, III no. 7, October 1985, 268-278. Reprinted in DTLC, ch. 9.
'Hungarian theologians and pastors meet,' *Reformed Press Service*, no. 240, October 1985, 4; and in French, German and Spanish in *Reformed Perspectives*.
'The Reformed Alliance and the World Council of Churches,' *Boletim de Estudios e Informaçoes*, II no. 8, December 1984, 3-4; *Broadway United Reformed Church Newsletter*, no. 267, January 1986, 9-11.
Review: E. Hong, *Forgiveness*; *Reformed Review*, XXXIX, 1985, 64-5.

1986

Theology in Turmoil. The Roots, Course and Significance of the Conservative-Liberal Debate in Modern Theology, Grand Rapids: Baker Book House, 1986. Pp. 199. Reprinted, Eugene, OR: Wipf & Stock, 1998.
Church Planting: A Study of Westmorland Nonconformity, Worthing: H. E. Walter, 1986. Pp. 172. Reprinted, Eugene, OR: Wipf & Stock, 1998.
Saints: Visible, Orderly and Catholic. The Congregational Idea of the Church, Geneva: WARC and Allison Park, PA: Pickwick Publications, 1986. Pp. 173.
Ed. *Reformed Theology and the Jewish People*, (Studies from the World Alliance of Reformed Churches, no. 9), Geneva: WARC,1986.

'Reformed, Presbyterian and Congregational Churches,' in *1986 Britannia Book of the Year*, Chicago: Encyclopaedia Britannica, 1986, 365

'Some reflections on Reformed-Methodist relations,' *Epworth Review*, XII no.1, January 1986, 30-40. Reprinted in DTLC, ch. 21.

Ed. And contrib. ECSACT (Ecumenical Centre Staff Association bulletin), 24, February 1986.

'Editorial,' *Reformed World*, XXXIX no. 1, March 1986, 453-4.

'Some contemporaries,' *Journal of the United Reformed Church History Society*, III no. 8, May 1986, 362-5.

'The Lord's Supper in the Reformed family,' *Reformed World*, XXXIX no. 2, June 1986, 518-527.

'Some Reformed responses to *Baptism, Eucharist and Ministry*,' *Reformed World*, XXXIX no.3, September 1986, 549-565; excerpted in *Ecumenical Press Service*, 6-10 October 1986, item 68. Reprinted in *Reformierte Kirchenzeitung*, 15 May 1987, 140-46.

'Reformed responses to BEM,' *Presbyterian Record*, October 1986, 27-8; *Presbyterian Outlook*, 1 September 1986, 9-10.

'Theology by slogans,' *One World*, no. 119, October 1986, 18.

'The witness of Reformed theology and theologians today,' *The Near East School of Theology Theological Review*, VII no. 2, November 1986, 91-105.

'The quest for peace,' *Broadway United Reformed Church Newsletter*, no. 277, December 1986, 16-18; *Presbyterian Outlook*, January 5-12, 1987, 6-7; excerpted in *Ecumenical Press Service*, 1-20 January 1987, item 20; *Stedfast*, March 1987, 13-14.

Review: B. D. Spinks, *Freedom or Order: The Eucharistic Liturgy in English Congregationalism 1645-1980*; *Journal of Ecclesiastical History*, XXXVII no. 1, January 1986, 176-7.

Review: G. Yule, ed., *Luther: Theologian for Catholics and Protestants*; *Reformed World*, XXXIX no. 2, June 1986, 546-7.

Book Notes in *Reformed World*, XXXIX no. 2, June 1986, 548; the last two reprinted in *Reformed Press Service*, no. 250, September 1986, 8-9:

J. I. Cook, ed., *The Church Speaks. Papers of the Commission on Theology, Reformed Church in America, 1959-1984*.

D. K. McKim, *What Christians Believe about the Bible*.

A. P. F. Sell, *Church Planting*.

D. O. Thomas and W. Bernard Peach, eds., *The Correspondence of Richard Price, Volume I, July 1748-March 1778*.

T. F. Torrance, *Theological Dialogue between Orthodox and Reformed Churches*.

Book Notes in *Reformed World*, XXXIX no. 3, September 1986, 595-6. Reprinted in *Reformed Press Service*, no. 250, September 1986, 8-9:

H. Hart *et al*., eds., *Rationality in the Calvinian Tradition*.

L. Newbigin, *Foolishness to the Greeks*.

A. P. F. Sell, *Theology in Turmoil*.

A. Vos, *Aquinas, Calvin and Contemporary Protestant Thought*.

D. Visser, *Zacharias Ursinus*.

Mennonites and Reformed in Dialogue.

J. Schaeffer and A. Reber, eds., *Contre la Torture*, (*Studies from the World Alliance of Reformed Churches*, no. 8).

Reformed Theology and the Jewish People.
A. P. F. Sell, *Saints: Visible, Orderly and Catholic.*
Review: B. Ramsey, *Beginning to Read the Fathers*; *The Furrow*, XXXVII no. 10, October 1986, 673-4.
Review: J. Walsh and P. G. Walsh, *Divine Providence and Human Suffering*; *The Furrow*, XXXVII no. 10, October 1986, 674.
Review: J. W. Yolton, *Thinking Matter: Materialism in Eighteenth-Century Britain*; *Philosophical Studies*, XXXI, 1986-67, 438-9.
Review: J. C. A. Gaskin, *The Quest for Eternity: An Outline of the Philosophy of Religion*; *Philosophical Studies*, XXXI, 1986-87, 400-401.
Review: J. Platt, *Reformed Thought and Scholasticism*; *Philosophical Studies*, XXXI, 1986-87, 429-432.
Review: J. D. Hoeveler, Jr., *James McCosh and the Scottish Intellectual Tradition*; *Philosophical Studies*, XXXI, 1987-87, 435-7.
Review: D. O. Thomas and W. B. Peach, eds., *The Correspondence of Richard Price, Volume I July 1748-March 1778*; *Philosophical Studies*, XXXI, 1986-87, 432-5.

1987

Defending and Declaring the Faith. Some Scottish Examples 1860-1920, Exeter: Paternoster Press and Colorado Springs: Helmers & Howard, 1987. Pp. 280.
The Message of the Erskines for Today. An Address delivered on February 10 1987 to Commemorate Erskine Theological Seminary's 150th Anniversary, Due West, SC: Erskine Theological Seminary, 1987. Reprinted in *Evangelical Quarterly*, LX no. 4, October 1988, 299-316. Reprinted in *CSCTH*, ch. 7.
'Reformed, Presbyterian and Congregational Churches,' *1987 Britannica Book of the Year*, Chicago: Encyclopaedia Britannica, 1987, 333-4.
'John Locke's Highland critic,' *Scottish Church History Society Records*, XXX pt. 1, 1987, 65-76. Reprinted in DTLC, ch. 8.
'Doctrine, grace, Gospel, unity,' *Life and Work*, May 1987, 23.
'On ministerial education,' excerpted in *Ecumenical Press Service*, 26-30 April 1987, item 133; *Stedfast*, June 1987, 13-14.
'Some contemporaries,' *Journal of the United Reformed Church History Society*, III no. 10, May 1987, 445-6.
'Anabaptist-Congregational relations and current Mennonite-Reformed dialogue,' *The Mennonite Quarterly Review*, LXI no. 3, July 1987, 321-334. Reprinted in DTLC, ch. 20.
'On practising what we preach,' excerpted in *Ecumenical Press Service*, 1-8 August 1987; *Presbyterian Record*, September 1987, 8-9; *Stedfast*, October 1987, 13-14; *Broadway United Reformed Church Newsletter*, no. 286, October 1987, 9-11.
Introduction to two international bilateral dialogue reports: 'No doctrinal obstacles: Reformed dialogue with Disciples and Methodists,' *Reformed World*, XXXIX no. 8, December 1987, 821-22.
'A concluding theological postscript,' excerpted in *Ecumenical Press Service*, December 1987, item 55; *Stedfast*, January 1988, 13-14; *Presbyterian Record*, July-August 1988, 30-31.
Review: D. F. Wells, ed., *Reformed Theology in America*; *Reformed World*, XXXIX no. 6, June 1987, 738-9.

Review: D. Bloesch, *Freedom for Obedience*; *The Reformed Journal*, XXXVII no. 11, November 1987, 26-7. Also in *Irish Theological Journal*, LVII no. 4, 1991, 331-2.
Book Notes in *Reformed World*, XXXIX no. 6, 174:
  P. Henry, ed., *Schools of Thought in the Christian Tradition*.
  U. Gäbler, *Huldrych Zwingli, His Life and Work*.
  P. Stephens, *The Theology of Huldrych Zwingli*.
  E. J. Furcha, ed., *Papers from the 1984 International Zwingli Symposium*.
  D. Visser, *Controversy and Conciliation*.
  J. van Hoeven, ed., *Word and World: Reformed Theology in America*.
  C. G. Dennison, ed., *The Orthodox Presbyterian Church 1936-1986*.
  C. G. Dennison and R. G. Gamble, *Pressing Toward the Mark*.
  R. K. Churchill, *Lest We Forget*.
Book Notes in *Reformed World*, XXXIX no. 7, September 1987, 786-7:
  M. C. Bell, *Calvin and Scottish Theology*.
  G. M. Tuttle, *So Rich a Soil: John McLeod Campbell on Christian Atonement*.
  R. A. Riesen, *Criticism and Faith in Late Victorian Scotland*.
  S. L. Jaki, *Lord Gifford and His Lectures*.
  D. K. McKim, ed., *How Karl Barth Changed My Mind*.
  R. G. Crawford, *The Saga of God Incarnate*.
  T. Stylianipoulos and S. M. Heim, eds., *Spirit of Truth*.
  A. C. Cochrane, *The Mystery of Peace*.
  M. L. Stackhouse, *Creeds, Society and Human Rights*.
Review: P. K. Jewett, *Election and Predestination*; *Reformed Review*, XLI no. 1, Autumn 1987, 55.
Book Notes in *Reformed World*, XXIX no. 8, December 1987, 841:
  D. G. Bloesch, *Freedom for Obedience*.
  E. J. Furcha, ed., *John Calvin, 1509-64: In Honour of John Calvin*.
  A. F. Holmes, *The Idea of a Christian College*.
  H. K. Markell, *History of the Presbyterian College, Montreal*.
  A. P. F. Sell, *Defending and Declaring the Faith*.

1988

The Philosophy of Religion 1875-1980, London: Croom Helm and new York: Routledge, 1988. Pp. 252. Reprinted, Bristol: Thoemmes Press, 1996
'Presbyterianer,' in *Wörterbuch des Christentums*, Zurich: Benzinger, 1988, 995-7.
Preface (signed by others) to *Towards Closer Fellowship: Report of the Dialogue between Reformed and Disciples of Christ*, (Studies from the World Alliance of Reformed Churches, no. 11), Geneva: WARC, 1988.
Preface (signed by others) to *Reformed and Methodists in Dialogue: Report of the Reformed/Methodist Conversations, 1985 and 1987*, (Studies from the World Alliance of Reformed Churches, no. 12). Geneva: WARC, 1988.
'Reformed, Presbyterian and Congregational Churches,' *1988 Britannica Book of the Year*, Chicago: Encyclopaedia Britannica, 1988, 299.
'God, grace and the Bible in Scottish Reformed theology: A review article,' *Irish Theological Quarterly*, LIV no. 1, 1988, 66-71.
'The Pembrokeshire Congregational Magazine,' *Journal of the United Reformed Church History Society*, IV no. 2, May 1988, 98-103. Reprinted in CSCTH, ch. 9.

'Some contemporaries,' *Journal of the United Reformed Church History Society*, IV no. 2, May 1988, 168 + inside back cover.

'250th anniversary of John Wesley's conversion,' *Canada Lutheran*, September 1988, 24-5; *The Atlantic Baptist*, January 1989, 10-11.

'Confessing the Faith in English Congregationalism,' *Journal of the United Reformed Church History Society*, IV no. 3, October 1988, 170-213. Reprinted in DTLC, ch. 1.

'Homosexuality: the underlying questions,' *Calgary Herald*, 8 October 1988, D9.

'Revival,' *Calgary Herald*, 19 November 1988, H9.

Review: *The Chronicle of the Hutterian Brethren, Vol. I*; *Ecumenical Review*, XL no. 1, January 1988, 112-13.

Review: J. M. Turner, *Conflict and Reconciliation. Studies in Methodism and Ecumenism in England 1740-1982*; *Mid-Stream*, XXVII no. 1, January 1988, 82-5.

Review: R. A. Muller, *Post-Reformation Reformed Dogmatics*; *Reformed Review*, XLII no. 2, Winter 1988, 174-5.

Review: L. Ryken, *Worldly Saints. The Puritans as They Really Were*; *Reformed Review*, XLII no. 2, Winter 1988, 177-8. Repeated ibid., LII no. 3, Spring 1989, 264-5.

Review: *The Brethren Encyclopedia*, 3 vols; *Journal of the United Reformed Church History Society*, IV no. 2, May 1988, 161-5.

Review: D. M. MacKinnon, *Themes in Theology. The Three-fold Cord*; *King's Theological Review*, XI no. 2, Autumn 1988, 71-2.

Review: D. Stanesby, *Science, Reason and Religion*; *Religious Studies and Theology*, VII no. 3, 1988, 49-51.

Review: R. S. Paul, *The Assembly of the Lord*; *Irish Theological Quarterly*, LIV no. 4, 1988, 324-5.

1989

Ed. with others, *Towards a Common Testimony*, Geneva: John Knox International Centre, 1989. Contrib. Ch 11: 'Confessing the faith in English Congregationalism' - an abbreviated version of the 1988 article and DTLC, ch. 1.

'Resurrection and heaven,' *Calgary Herald*, 25 March 1989, F3; *The Atlantic Baptist*, July 1989, 14; *Pioneer Christian Monthly* (Canada), April 1990, 8-9; *Presbyterian Record*, April 1990, 26-7.

'Is history bunk?' *Historic Sites and Archives Journal* (Alberta and Northwest Conference [United Church of Canada] Historical Society), II no. 2, May 1989, 13; *The Atlantic Baptist*, August 1989, 14; *Presbyterian Record*, November 1989, 8-9; revised version in *The Associate Reformed Presbyterian* (U. S. A.), March 1990, 9-10.

'Some contemporaries,' *Journal of the United Reformed Church History Society*, IV no. 4, June 1989, 283 + inside back cover.

'By the Spirit, through the Word, within the fellowship,' *Touchstone*, VII no. 3, September 1989, 32-41.

'Reformed-Mennonite conference,' *Calgary Herald*, 14 October 1989.

'300 years of toleration,' *Reform*, December 1989, 11; *Historic Sites and Archives Journal*, III no. 1, May 1990, 6.

Review: R. E. Brantley, *Locke, Wesley and the Method of English Romanticism*; *Enlightenment and Dissent*, VIII, 1989, 140-144.

Review: G. Shriver, *Philip Schaff, Christian Scholar and Ecumenical Prophet*;

Ecumenical Review, XLI no. 1, January 1989, 141-2.
Review: T. George, *Theology of the Reformers*; *Mid-Stream*, XXVIII no. 1, January 1989, 142-4.
Review: G. Harland, *Christian Faith and Society*; *Touchstone*, VII no. 1, January 1989, 51-53.
Review: T. F. Best, ed., *Instruments of Unity*; *Mid-Stream*, XXVIII no. 2, April 1989, 218.
Review: V. Shepherd, *Making Sense of Christian Faith*; *Studies in Religion*, XVIII no. 2, 1989, 249-50.
Review: K. J. Hardman, *Charles Grandison Finney*; *The Baptist Quarterly*, XXXIII no. 2, April 1989, 99-100.
Review: W. A. Norgren and W. G. Rush, eds., *Implications of the Gospel*; *Mid-Stream*, XXVIII no. 3, July 1989, 326-8.
Review: C. E. Gunton and D. W. Hardy, eds., *On Being the Church*; *Ecumenical Review*, XLI no. 4, October 1989, 626-9.
Review, J. H. Roberts, *Darwinism and the Divine in America*; *Reformed Review*, XLIII no. 1, Autumn 1989, 77-8.
Review: A. C. Kors and P. J. Korshin, eds., *Anticipations of the Enlightenment in England, France and Germany*; *Faith and Freedom*, XLII pt. 3, Autumn 1989, 150-51.
Review: B. Smith, ed., *Truth, Liberty and Religion. Essays Celebrating Two Hundred Years of Manchester College*; *Journal of the United Reformed Church History Society*, IV no. 5, October 1989, 339-40.
Review: R. C. Whittemore, *The Transformation of New England Theology*; *Evangelical Quarterly*, LXI no. 4, 1989, 366-8.
Review: G. G. Scorgie, *A Call for Continuity: The Theological Contribution of James Orr*; *Canadian Theological Society Newsletter*, IX no.1, October 1989, 12-13.
Review: *Brothers Unite*, trans. and ed. the Hutterian Brethren; *Mid-Stream*, XXVIII no. 4, October 1989, 441-2.
Review: J. Durant, ed., *Darwinism and Divinity*; *Irish Theological Quarterly*, LV no. 3, 1989, 251.
Review: K. L. Parker, *The English Sabbath*; *Calvin Theological Journal*, XXIV no. 2, November 1989, 354-7.
Review: B. J. Fraser, *The Social Uplifters: Presbyterian Progressives and the Social Gospel in Canada 1875-1915*; *Studies in Religion*, XVIII no. 4, 1989, 495-6.

1990

Aspects of Christian Integrity, Calgary: University of Calgary Press 1990, and Louisville: Westminster/John Knox press, 1991. Pp. 160.
Dissenting Thought and the Life of the Churches. Studies in an English Tradition, Lewiston, NY: Edwin Mellen Press, 1990. Pp. xii + 713.
'Through suffering to liberty: 1689 in the English and Vaudois experience,' in Albert De Lange, ed., *Dall' Europa Alle Valli Valdesi*, Turin: Claudiana, 1990, 215-236. Reprinted in CSCTH, ch. 5.
'In the wake of the Enlightenment: The adjustments of James Martineau and A. Campbell Fraser,' *Enlightenment and Dissent*, IX, 1990, 63-92. Reprinted in CSCTH, ch. 10.
With Ross T. Bender, 'Reformed-Mennonite Dialogue: Phase two,' *Journal of*

Mennonite Studies, VIII, 1990, 9-10.
'English Dissent: Dissoluble or dissolute?' *The Baptist Quarterly*, XXXIII no. 5, January 1990, 243-6.
'Presbyterianism in eighteenth-century England: the doctrinal dimension,' *Journal of the United Reformed Church History Society*, IV no. 6, May 1990, 352-386. Reprinted in DTLC, ch. 5.
'Some contemporaries,' *Journal of the United Reformed Church History Society*, IV no. 6, May 1990, 404-6.
'J. H. A. Bomberger (1817-1890) *versus* J. W. Nevin: A centenary reappraisal,' *The New Mercersburg Review*, VIII, Autumn 1990, 3-24. Reprinted in CSCTH, ch. 11.
Review: G. N. Schlesinger, *New Perspectives on Old-Time Religion*; Critical Review of Books in Religion, III, 1990, 398-400.
Review: W. Spellman, *John Locke and the Problem of Depravity*; Enlightenment and Dissent, IX, 1990, 134-7.
Review: M. Mow, *Torches Rekindled. The Bruderhof's Struggle for Renewal*; Journal of Mennonite Studies, VIII, 1990, 223-4.
Review: A. D. MacRae, *Making Sense of Life*; Touchstone, VIII no. 1, January 1990, 55.
Review: G. Fackre, *The Christian Story. A Pastoral Systematics, Vol. II*; Scottish Journal of Theology, XLIII no. 1, 1990, 117-19.
Review: A. Kee and T. Long, eds., *Being and Truth. Essays in Honour of John Macquarrie*; Irish Theological Quarterly, LVI no. 1, 1990, 68.
Review: R. Higginson, *Dilemmas. A Christian Approach to Moral Decision Making*; Reformed Review, XLIII no. 3, Spring 1990, 221-2.
Review: D. J. Hall, *Thinking the Faith. Christian Theology in a North American Context*; Reformed Review, XLIII no. 3, Spring 1990, 233.
Review: J. M. Lochman, *The Faith We Confess. An Ecumenical Dogmatics*; Irish Theological Quarterly, LVI no. 2, 1990, 150-51.
Review: G. Wainwright, ed., *Keeping the Faith. Essays to Mark the Centenary of Lux Mundi*; Journal of the United Reformed Church History Society, IV no. 6, May 1990, 379-7.
Review: E. Kaye, *C. J. Cadoux, Theologian, Scholar and Pacifist*; Faith and Freedom, XLIII pt. 3, Autumn 1990, 150-51.
Review: H. D. Rack, *Reasonable Enthusiast. John Wesley and the Rise of Methodism*; The Baptist Quarterly, XXXIII no. 8, October 1990, 396-7.
Review: G. Tourn, *et al.*, *You Are My Witnesses. The Waldensians Across 800 Years*; Journal of the United Reformed Church History Society, IV no. 7, October 1990, 455-6.
Review: R. W. Vaudry, *The Free Church in Victorian Canada 1844-61*; Canadian Theological Society Newsletter, X no. 1, November 1990, 8-9.
Review: J. F. White, *Protestant Worship. Traditions in Transition*; National Bulletin on Liturgy, XXIII no. 123, December 1990, 253-5.
Review: A. Vos, *Aquinas, Calvin and Contemporary Protestant Thought*; Philosophical Studies, XXXII, 1988-90, 377-9.
Review: R. H. Nash, *Christianity and the Hellenistic World*; Philosophical Studies, XXXII, 1988-90, 341-2.
Review: J. Patrick, *The Magdalen Metaphysicals*; Philosophical Studies, XXXII, 1988-90, 350-52.
Review: R. J. Delahunty, *Spinoza*; Philosophical Studies, XXXII, 1988-90, 299-301.

Review: J. W. Trigg, *Origen*; *Philosophical Studies*, XXXII, 1988-90, 370-71.
Letter: 'Is Report being studies?' (re. Anglican-Reformed international dialogue), *Anglican Journal* (Canada), October 1990, 7.
Letter: 'Ecumenical commandment broken,' *Presbyterian Record*, October 1990, 7.

1991

A Reformed, Evangelical, Catholic Theology. The Contribution of the World Alliance of Reformed Churches 1875-1982, Grand Rapids: Eerdmans, 1991. Pp. 304. Reprinted, Eugene, OR: Wipf & Stock, 1998.

Rhetoric and Reality. Theological Reflections upon Congregationalism and its Heirs, (The Congregational Lecture, 1991), London: The Congregational Memorial Hall Trust (1998) Ltd., 1991. Pp. 29. Reprinted in CSCTH, ch. 14.

Ed. with R. T. Bender, *Baptism, Peace and the State in the Reformed and Mennonite Traditions*, Waterloo, Ontario: Wilfrid Laurier University Press, 1991, Pp. 247.

Articles: 'Anglican-Reformed dialogue' and 'Congregationalism', in *Dictionary of the Ecumenical Movement*, Geneva: World Council of Churches Publications and Grand Rapids: Eerdmans, 1991. Articles updated in 2nd edn., 2002.

'The Samoan White Sunday,' *Journal of Pacific History*, XXVI no. 1, 94-7.

'A little friendly light. The candour of Bourn, Taylor and Towgood,' pt. 1, *Journal of the United Reformed Church History Society*, IV no. 9, December 1991, 517-540; pt. 2, ibid., IV no. 10, May 1992, 580-613. Reprinted in DTLC, ch. 7.

Review: D. W. Bebbington, *Evangelicalism in Modern Britain*; *Enlightenment and Dissent*, X, 1991, 115-18.

Review: C. Gunton, *The Actuality of Atonement*; *Irish Theological Quarterly*, LVII no. 1, 1991, 82-4.

Review: J. Driver, *Understanding the Atonement for the Mission of the Church*; *Irish Theological Quarterly*, LVII no. 1, 1991, 82-4.

Review: A. Carden, *Puritan Christianity in America*; *Reformed Review*, XLIV no. 3, Spring 1991, 263.

Review, F. W. Sacks, *The Philadelphia Baptist Tradition and Church Authority 1707-1814*; *Calvin Theological Journal*, XXVI no. 1, April 1991, 227-31.

Review: C. W. DeWeese, *Baptist Church Covenants*; *The Baptist Quarterly*, XXXIV no. 3, July 1991, 142-3.

Review: D. Allen, *Philosophy for Understanding Theology*; *Faith and Freedom*, XLIV pt. 3, Autumn 1991, 140-41.

Review: R. G. Tuttle, Jr., *Mysticism in the Wesleyan Tradition*; *Proceedings of the Wesley Historical Society*, XLVIII pt. 3, October 1991, 103.

Review: A. C. Clifford, *Atonement and Justification*; *Proceedings of the Huguenot Society*, XXV no. 3, 1991, 293-4. Reprinted in *Calvin Theological Journal*, XXVII no. 1, April 1992, 116-17.

Review: M. J. Coalter, J. M. Mulder and L. B. Weeks, eds., *The Presbyterian Predicament. Six Perspectives*; *Reformed Review*, XLV no. 1, Autumn 1991, 70.

Review: J. L. Stotts and J. D. Douglass, eds., *To Confess the Faith Today*; *Reformed Review*, XLV no. 1, Autumn 1991, 72-3.

Review: H. Zwaanstra, *Catholicity and Secession*; Eerdmans Academic Catalogue, 1992, 3.

Review: J. Leslie, *Universes*; *Studies in Religion*, XX no. 2, 1991, 240-41.

Letter: 'Small globe,' *Reform*, July-August 1991, 24.

1992

'The Reformed family today: Some theological reflections,' in D. K. McKim, ed., *Major Themes in the Reformed Tradition*, Grand Rapids: Eerdmans, 1992, 433-41.

'Robert Barclay (1648-1690), the Fathers, and the inward universal saving light: A tercentenary appraisal,' *Journal of the Friends' Historical Society*, LVI no. 3, 210-226. Reprinted in CSCTH, ch. 6.

Articles: 'J. H. A. Bomberger', 'R. Browne', 'J. Caird', 'Congregationalism - British', 'R. W. Dale', 'Dissenting academies', 'A. M. Fairbairn', 'R. Flint', 'Nonconformity', 'J. Oman', 'Savoy Declaration', 'A. M. Toplady', 'World Alliance of Reformed Churches', in D. K.McKim, ed., *Encyclopedia of the Reformed Faith*, Louisville: Westminster/John Knox, 1992.

'Philosophy in the eighteenth-century Dissenting academies of England and Wales,' *History of Universities*, XI, 1992, 75-122.

With R. T. Bender, 'Baptism, peace and the state in the Reformed and Mennonite traditions,' *Mid-Stream*, XXXI no. 1, January 1992, 41-2. This is the press release also prefixed to the item in the *Journal of Mennonite Studies*, 1990, q.v.

With Karen Sell, 'From Calgary to the land of song and preaching,' *Update* (Varsity Acres Presbyterian Church, Calgary), May 1992, 5.

'Some contemporaries,' *Journal of the United Reformed Church History Society*, IV no. 10, May 1992, 640-42.

Review: D. K. McKim, *Ramism in William Perkins' Theology*; *Evangelical Quarterly*, LXIV no. 1, 1992, 81-2.

Review: J. M. Lochman, *Christ and Prometheus?*; *Mid-Stream*, XXXI no. 1, January 1992, 69-71.

Review: T. George and D. S,. Dockery, eds., *Baptist Theologians*; *Calvin Theological Journal*, XXVII no. 1, April 1992, 121-25.

Review: T. Reid, *Practical Ethics*, ed. K. Haakonssen; *British Journal for Eighteenth-Century Studies*, XV no. 1, Spring 1992, 89-90.

Review: M. Beaty and B. J. Farley (trans.), *Calvin's Ecclesiastical Advice*; *Reformed Review*, XLV no. 3, Spring 1992, 234.

Review: Mark A. Noll, ed., *Confessions and Catechisms of the Reformation*; *Reformed Review*, XLV no. 3, Spring 1992, 235-6.

Review: T. Penelhum, *Butler*; *Philosophical Studies*, XXXIII, 1991-92, 398-401.

Review: M. Peterson, *et al.*, *Reason and Religious Belief*; *Philosophical Studies*, XXXIII, 1991-92, 401-02.

Review: V. White, *Atonement and Imagination*; *Irish Theological Quarterly*, LVIII no. 2, 1992, 158-9.

Review: D. Marsha;;, *Secularizing the Faith in Canada: The Protestant Clergy and the Crisis of Belief 1850-1930*; *The Literary Review of Canada*, I no. 9, September 1992, 11-12.

Review: J. Newman, *On Religious Freedom*; *The Modern Churchman*; XXXIV no. 2, 1992, 49-50.

Review: T. Hart and D. Thimell, eds., *Christ in Our Place*; *Reformed Review*, XLVI no. 1, Autumn 1992, 56-7.

Review: M. Westphal, *Kierkegaard's Critique of Reason and Society*; *Faith and Freedom*, XLV pt. 3, Autumn 1992, 130-31.
Review: R. W. Franklin and J. M. Shaw, *The Case for Christian Humanism*; *Calvin Theological Journal*, XXVII no. 2, November 1992, 431-33.
Review: A. Jeffner, *Theology and Integration*; *Faith and Philosophy*, IX no. 3, July 1992, 400-02.
Review: K. Clements, *Lovers of Discord*; *Irish Theological Quarterly*, LVIII no. 4, 1992, 322-3.
Letter: 'Centrally Reformed,' *Reform*, March 1992, 25.
Letter: 'Methodism and the URC,' *Reformed Quarterly*, III no. 1, May 1992, 6.
Abstract: 'Philosophy in the eighteenth-century Dissenting academies of England,' *British Society for the History of Philosophy Newsletter*, VII, Winter 1991-92, 34-6.

1993

Commemorations. Studies in Christian Thought and History. Calgary: University of Calgary Press and Cardiff: University of Wales Press, 1993. Pp. 394. Reprinted Eugene, OR: Wipf & Stock, 1998.
Conservation and Exploration in Christian Theology, (Inaugural Lecture from the Chair of Christian Doctrine and Philosophy of Religion), Caernarfon: Gwasg Pantycelyn, 1993. Pp. 23. Abbreviated in *Memphis Theological Seminary Journal*, XXXIV no. 2-XXXV no. 1, 1997, 27-43; and in Hungarian and English in *Sárospatak Fuzetek*, 1997 no. 1, 85-96. Reprinted in TAT, ch. 1.
'The witness and legacy of Congregationalism,' *Historic Sites and Archives Journal*, VI no. 1, May 1993, 16, 19.
'Edrych yn ôl dros y flwyddyn yng Nghymru,' *Y Goleuad*, 29 October 1993, 5.
Articles: 'D. W. Forrest', 'A. Campbell Fraser', 'J. Fraser', 'J. Iverach', 'J. Kennedy', 'H. R. Mackintosh', 'R. Mackintosh', 'World Alliance of Reformed Churches', in the *Dictionary of Scottish Church History and Theology*, Edinburgh: T. & T. Clark, 1993.
'Some contemporaries,' *Journal of the United Reformed Church History Society*, V no. 3, October 1993, 176-8.
Review: R. M. Gale, *On the Nature and Existence of God*; *International Journal of Philosophical Studies*, I no. 1, March 1993, 143-6.
Review: F. M. Schroeder, *From Form to Transformation. A Study in the Philosophy of Plotinus*; *International Journal of Philosophical Studies*, I no. 1, March 1993, 168-9.
Review: R. Porter, *The Enlightenment*; *British Journal for the History of Philosophy*, I no. 2, September 1993, 160-61.
Review: P. Harrison, *'Religion' and the Religions in the English Enlightenment*; *British Journal for Eighteenth-Century Studies*, XVI no. 1, Spring 1993, 145-6.
Review: D. Dunn et al., *A History of the Evangelical and Reformed Church*; *Journal of the United Reformed Church History Society*, V no. 2, July 1993, 117-19.
Review: M. Mullett, *Sources for the History of English Nonconformity 1660-1830*; *Proceedings of the Huguenot Society*, XXV no. 5, 1993, 518.
Review: D. L. Jeffrey, ed., *A Dictionary of Biblical Interpretation*; *Reformed Review*, XLVII no. 1, Autumn 1993, 56-7.
Review: N. Wisnefske, *Our Natural Knowledge of God*; *The Modern Churchman*, XXXIV no. 5, 1993, 143-4.
Review: A. Ruston et al., *The Inquirer. A History and Other Reflections*; *Faith and*

Freedom, XLVI pt. 2, Autumn 1993, 129.
Review: A. Hill, ed., *Celebrating Life. A Book of Special Services*; *Faith and Freedom*, XLVI pt. 2, Autumn 1993, 132.
Review: J. R. Beeke, *Assurance of Faith. Calvinism, English Puritanism, and the Second Dutch Reformation*; *European Journal of Theology*, II no. 1, 1993, 81-2.
Review: W. H. Conser, Jr., *Church and Confession. Conservative Theologians in Germany, England and America 1815-1866*; *Calvin Theological Journal*, XXVIII no. 2, November 1993, 449-51.

1994

'Fear God and pay him homage,' in J. Pungur, ed., *An Eastern European Liberation Theology*, Calgary: Angelus Publishers, 1994, 320-28.
'Reflections on a year in Wales,' *The Treasury*, XIX no. 1, January 1994, 3.
'Theology in Canada: Random reflections from afar,' *Canadian Theological Society Newsletter*, XIII no. 2, April 1994, 1-4.
'For the work of the ministry: a sesquicentenary,' *Reformed Quarterly*, NS I no. 4, 1994, 17.
'Some contemporaries,' *Journal of the United Reformed History Society*, V no. 4, May 1994, 232-5.
'The role of bilateral dialogues in the one ecumenical movement,' *Ecumenical Review*, XLVI no. 4, October 1994, 453-60.
'Theological adventures in the antipodes,' *The Treasury*, December 1994, 6.
'Anturiaethau diwinyddol yn yr antipodes,' *Y Goleuad*, 2 December 1994, 5.
Review: T. A. Campbell, *The Religion of the Heart*; *The Baptist Quarterly*, XXXV no. 5, January 1994, 256-7.
Review: P. Naylor, *Picking up a Pin for the Lord. English Particular Baptists from 1688 to the Early Nineteenth Century*; *The Baptist Quarterly*, XXXV no. 5, January 1994, 257-8.
Review: P. Riedemann, *Love is Like Fire. The Confession of an Anabaptist Prisoner*; *The Baptist Quarterly*, XXXV no. 6, April 1994, 293.
Review: E. Arnold, *The Individual and World Need*; *The Baptist Quarterly*, XXXV no. 6, April 1994, 293.
Review: J. P. Wogaman, *Christian Ethics. A* [sic] *Historical Introduction*; *Modern Believing*, XXXV no. 2, April 1994, 64-6.
Review: C. Cunliffe, ed., *Joseph Butler's Moral and Religious Thought*; *Ethics*, CIV no. 3, April 1994, 668.
Review: H. Kirk-Smith, *William Brewster, The Father of New England*; *Evangelical Quarterly*, LXVI no. 4, 358-9.
Review: M. Plant and A. Tovey, eds., *Telling Another Generation*; *Reformed Quarterly*, NS II no. 2, Autumn 1994, 14.
Review: I. J. Hesselink, *Calvin's Concept of the Law*; *European Journal of Theology*, III no. 2, 1994, 175-6.
Review: W. D. McNaughton, *The Scottish Congregational Minister 1794-1993*; *Journal of the United Reformed Church History Society*, V no. 5, November 1994, 303-4.
Letter: 'The call and the Church Meeting,' *Reform*, June 1994, 26.
Letter: 'More than a democracy, or a business,' *Reform*, October 1994, 24.

1995

Philosophical Idealism and Christian Belief, Cardiff: University of Wales Press and New York: St. Martin's Press. Pp. 338.

General Editor's Preface to S. Wright, *Friends in York. The Dynamics of Quaker Revival 1780-1860*, Keele: Keele University Press, 1995.

'P. T. Forsyth as unsystematic systematician,' in T. Hart, ed., *Justice the True and Only Mercy. Essays on the Life and Theology of Peter Taylor Forsyth*, Edinburgh: T. & T. Clark, 1995, 110-145. Reprinted in TAT, ch. 7.

'Epilogue' to C. E. Gunton, P. Réamonn and A. P. F. Sell, eds., *The Church in the Reformed Tradition*, (*European Studies from the World Alliance of Reformed Churches*, no. 1), Geneva: WARC, 54-6.

'Y ffydd ddiwygiedig a'I Hetifeddiaeth yn Hwngari a Rwmania,' *Cristion*, no. 68, January-February 1995, 6-7.

'George Tavard on Lewis S. Mudge: a Congregational comment,' *Mid-Stream*, XXXIV no. 1, January 1995, 75-6.

'Conflicting loyalties: Some Anglo-Canadian reflections,' *Uniting Church Studies*, I no. 1, March 1995, 20-21.

'The Presbyterian Church of Wales and the peace question,' *The Treasury*, May 1995, 6.

'Eglwys Bresyteraidd Cymru a mater heddwch,' *Y Goleuad*, 16 June 1995, 5.

'A renewed plea for "impractical" divinity,' *Studies in Christian Ethics*, VIII no. 2, 1995, 68-91. Reprinted in TAT, ch. 9.

Review: D. O. Tmoas, ed., *The Correspondence of Richard Price, II*; *International Journal of Philosophical Studies*, III no. 1, March 1995, 213-15.

Review: W. B. Peach, ed., *The Correspondence of Richard Price, III*; *International Journal of Philosophical Studies*, III no. 1, March 1995, 213-15.

Review: D. Boucher and A. Vincent, *A Radical Hegelian. The Political and Social Philosopgy of Henry Jones*; *British Journal for the History of Philosophy*, III no. 1, February 1995, 201-04.

Review: R. H. Preston, *Confusions in Christian Social Ethics*; *Modern Believing*, XXXVI no. 3, July 1995, 63-7.

Review: H. A. Meynell, *Is Christianity True?*; *Faith and Freedom*, XLVIII pt. 2, Autumn-Winter 1995, 172-3.

Review: A. E. McGrath, ed., *The Blackwell Encyclopedia of Modern Christian Thought*; *European Journal of Theology*, IV no. 2, 1995, 182-3.

1996

General Editor's Preface, M. Mullett, *John Bunyan in Context*, Keele: Keele University Press, 1996.

Ed. and Preface, *Protestant Nonconformists and the West Midlands of England*, Keele: Keele University Press, 1996.

Articles: 'A. J. Balfour', 'K. Barth', 'E. Brunner', 'R. Bultmann', 'R. Eucken'. 'J. Macquarrie', 'E. Mascall', 'B. Mitchell', 'J. W. Oman', 'T. Penelhum', 'K. Rahner', 'H. Scholz', 'R. N. Smart', 'E. Troeltsch' in *Biographical Dictionary of Twentieth-Century Philosophers*, London: Routledge, 1996.

'The Westminster Assembly and Confession of Faith,' *Evangelisches Kirkenlexikon*, Göttingen: Vandenhoeck & Ruprecht, 1996, IV, cols. 1275-8.

'Decision-making in our churches, including matters of faith,' *One in Christ*, XXXII no. 1, 1996, 70-84.

'Some contemporaries,' *Journal of the United Reformed Church History Society*, V no. 8, May 1996, 505-7.
'Should the Presbyterian Church of Wales become a peace church?' *Reconciliation Quarterly*, Autumn 1996, 25-7.
Review: D. J. Atkinson and D. H. Field, *New Dictionary of Christian Ethics and Pastoral Theology*; *Modern Believing*, XXXVII no. 1, January 1996, 61-2.
Review: A. Brown-Lawson, *John Wesley and the Anglican Evangelicals of the Eighteenth Century*; *The Baptist Quarterly*, XXXVI no. 6, April 1996, 310-11.
Review: J. H. Y. Briggs, *The English Baptists of the Nineteenth Century*; *Evangelical Quarterly*, LXVIII no. 2, April 1996, 180-82.
Review: J. Walsh, C. Haydon and S. Taylor, eds., *The Church of England c.1689-c.1833. From Toleration to Tractarianism*; *British Journal for the History of Philosophy* IV no. 1, March 1996, 197-8.
Review: J. C. Weinsheimer, *Eighteenth-Century Hermeneutics*; *British Journal for Eighteenth-Century Studies*, XIX no. 1, Spring 1996, 93.
Review: J. Locke, *Political Writings*, ed. D. Wooton; *British Journal for Eighteenth-Century Studies*, XIX no. 1, Spring 1996, 93-4.
Review: J.W. Yolton, *A Locke Dictionary*; *British Journal for Eighteenth-Century Studies*, XIX no. 1, Spring 1996, 93-4.
Review: V. Chappell, ed., *The Cambridge Companion to Locke*; *Faith and Freedom*, XLIX pt. 1, Spring-Summer 1996, 84-6.
Review: E. Welch, *Spiritual Pilgrim. A Reassessment of the Life of the Countess of Huntingdon*; *The Welsh History Review*, XVIII no. 1, 164-5.
Review: K. Penzel, *Philip Schaff. Historian and Ambassador of the Universal Church*; *Scottish Journal of Theology*, XLIX no. 2, 1996, 257-8
Review: E. Evans, *Fire in the Thatch*; *Cylchgrawn Hanes*, XX, 1996, 77-81.
Review: J. J. Macintosh and H. A. Meynell, eds., *Faith, Scepticism and personal Identity*; *International Journal of Philosophical Studies*, IV no. 2, September 1996, 363-5.
Review: D. K. McKim, *The Bible in Theology and Preaching*; *Irish Biblical Studies*, XVIII, October 1996, 217-18.
Review: J. Marshall, *John Locke. Resistance, Religion and Responsibility*; *Enlightenment and Dissent*, XV, 1996, 112-16.
Review: P. Nockles, *The Oxford Movement in Context*; *Enlightenment and Dissent*, XV, 1996, 128-30.

1997

John Locke and the Eighteenth-Century Divines, Cardiff: University of Wales Press, 1996. Pp. 444.
Mill and Religion, Bristol: Thoemmes Press, 1997. Pp. 268
'Some contemporaries,' *Journal of the United Reformed Church History Society*, VI no. 1, October 1997, 66-7.
'What has P. T. Forsyth to do with Mercersburg?' *The New Mercersburg Review*, XXII, Autumn 1997, 8-45. Reprinted in TAT, ch. 8.
Review: J. A. Bassett, *Theology for Pew and Pulpit*; *Epworth Review*, XXIV no. 1, January 1997, 126-7.

Review: W. Corduan, *Reasonable Faith*; *Calvin Theological Journal*, XXXII no. 1, April 1997, 177-8.
Review: K. Haakonssen, ed., *The Enlightenment and Religion. Rational Dissent in Eighteenth-Century Britain*; *International Journal of Philosophical Studies*, V no. 1, 1997, 142-3.
Review: J. Von Rohr, *The Shaping of American Congregationalism 1620-1957*; *The Congregational History Circle Magazine*, III no. 5, Spring 1997, 50-52.
Review: R. Rican, *The History of the Unity of Brethren*; *Journal of the United Reformed Church History Society*, V no. 10, June 1997, 642-3.
Review: D. L. Gelpi, *The Turn to Experience in Contemporary Theology*; *The Heythrop Journal*, XXXVIII no. 3, July 1997, 327-8.
Review: D. M. Lewis, ed., *The Blackwell Dictionary of Evangelical biography*; *The Baptist Quarterly*, XXXVII no. 3, July 1997, 150-52.
Review: E. Kaye, *Mansfield College Oxford*; *Journal of Ecclesiastical History*, XLVIII no. 3, July 1997, 596-7.
Review: S. Hamstra, Jr. and A. J. Griffioen, eds., *Reformed Confessionalism in Nineteenth-Century America*; *Journal of the United Reformed Church History Society*, VI no. 1, October 1997, 61-63.
Review: W. F. S. Pickering, *What the British Found when they Discovered the French Vaudois in the Nineteenth Century*; *Proceedings of the Huguenot Society*, XXVI no. 5, 683-4.
Review: A. Pettegree, *et al.*, eds., *Calvinism in Europe 1540-1620*; *Calvin Theological Journal*, XXXII no. 2, 517-19.
Review: *Oxford Dictionary of the Christian Church*, 3rd edn.; *Faith and Freedom*, L pt. 2, Autumn-Winter 1997, 156-7.

1998

'Foreword' to *Life and Joy*, Calgary: Varsity Acres Presbyterian Church, iii-iv.
'Some contemporaries,' *Journal of the United Reformed Church History Society*, VI no. 2, May 1998, 151-2.
Letter: 'Isaac Watts and the Trinity,' *The Treasury*, XXIII no. 12, December 1998, 6.
Review: T. F. Torrance, *Scottish Theology from John Knox to John McLeod Campbell*; *Heythrop Journal*, XXXIX no. 1, January 1998, 84-5.
Review: D. West, *An Introduction to Continental Philosophy*; *Modern Believing*, XXXIX no. 1, January 1998, 53-4.
Review: A. E. McGrath, *Christian Theology. An Introduction*; *Irish Theological Quarterly*, LXIII no. 2, 1998, 204-5.
Review: D. A. Pailin, *Probing the Foundations*; *Calvin Theological Journal*, XXXIII no. 1, April 1998, 215-16.
Review: D. Ford, ed., *The Modern Theologians*; *Modern Believing*, XXXIX no. 2, April 1998, 38-40.
Review: D. F. Wright and G. D. Badcock, eds., *Disruption to Diversity*; *Journal of the United Reformed Church History Society*, VI no. 2, May 1998, 147-8.
Review: D. Boucher, *et al.*, eds., *Philosophy, History and Civilization*; *International Journal of Philosophical Studies*, VI no. 2, June 1998, 302-4.
Review: R. T. Bender, *Education for Peoplehood*; *Epworth Review*, XXV no. 3, July 1998, 109-10.

Review: D. Luscombe, *Medieval Thought*; *Faith and Freedom*, LI pt. 1, Spring-Summer 1998, 77-8.
Review: T. R. Tilley, *et al.*, *Postmodern Theologies*; *The Heythrop Journal*, XXXIX no. 4, October 1998, 470-71.
Review: D. W. Musser and J. L. Price, eds., *A New Handbook of Christian Theology*; *Irish Theological Quarterly*, LIII no. 4, 1998, 403-4.
Review: J. W. Yolton, *et al.*, eds., *The Blackwell Companion to the Enlightenment*; *Irish Theological Quarterly*, LIII no. 4, 415-16.
Review: R. D. Lund, ed., *The Margins of orthodoxy*; *British Journal for the History of Philosophy*, VI no. 3, October 1998, 498-9.
Review: B. Carr and I Mahlingam, eds., *Companion Encyclopedia to Asian Philosophy*; *Modern Believing*, XXXIX no. 4, October 1998, 58-9.
Review: P. Kurtz and T. J. Madigan, eds., *Challenges to the Enlightenment*; *Faith and Freedom*, LI pt. 2, Autumn and Winter 1998, 174-5.
Review: V. Nuovo, ed., *John Locke and Christianity*; *The Locke Newsletter*, XXIX, 1998, 181-3.

1999

Series Editor's Preface to *Theological and Miscellaneous Works of Joseph Priestley*, Bristol: Thoemmes Press, 1999.
Series Editor's Preface to *Selected Works of Isaac Watts*, Bristol: Thoemmes Press, 1999.
'The International Congregational Fellowship,' in J-J. Bauswein and L. Vischer, eds., *The Reformed Family Worldwide*, Grand Rapids: Eerdmans, 1999, 705.
Articles: 'Henry Grove', 'John Taylor', in the *Dictionary of Eighteenth-Century British Philosophers*, Bristol: Thoemmes Press, 1999.
Articles: 'J. Orr,' 'P. T. Forsyth', 'M. Dods', 'A. S. Peake', 'C. H. Spurgeon' in the *Dictionary of Biblical Interpretation*, Nashville: Abingdon, 1999.
'Doctrine, polity, liberty: What do Baptists stand for?' in *Pilgrim Pathways: Essays in Baptist History in Honour of Barrington R. White*, Macon, GA: Mercer University Press, 1999, 1-46. Reprinted in TAT, ch. 4.
'P. T. Forsyth: theologian for a new millennium,' (abbreviated from ch. 9 of the 2000 book of the same name), *Réformatus Szemle*, XCII, November-December 1999, 470-476.
Editorial and biographical contributions to R. Benedetto, *et al.*, *Historical Dictionary of Reformed Churches*, Lanham, MD: The Scarecrow Press, 1999.
Review: G. M. Ella, *John Gill and the Cause of God and Truth*; *Evangelical Quarterly*, LXXI no. 1, 1999, 81-2.
Review: P. L. Quinn and C. Taliaferro, eds., *A Companion to Philosophy of Religion*; *Calvin Theological Journal*, XXXIV no. 1, April 1999, 251-255.
Review: D. Cornick, *Under God's Good Hand*; *Congregational History Circle Magazine*, IV no. 1, Spring 1999, 71-74.
Review: G. Wainwright, *Methodists in Dialog*; *Ecumenical Review*, LI no. 2, April 1999, 224-227.
Review: J. W. Yolton, ed., *Philosophy, Religion and Science in the 17th and 18th Centuries*; *International Journal of Philosophical Studies*, VII no. 2, June 1999, 279-280.

Review: J. R. Coggins, *John Smyth's Congregation*; *The Baptist Quarterly*, XXXVIII no. 3, 1999, 155-156.
Review: J. P. Wogaman and D. M. Strong, eds., *Readings in Christian Ethics*; *Modern Believing*, XL no. 3, 1999, 77-78.
Review: G. A. J. Rogers, *Locke's Enlightenment*; *The European Legacy*, IV no. 4, 1999, 102-105.
Review: R. E. Wentz, *John Williamson Nevin, American Theologian*; *Journal of the United Reformed Church History Society*, VI no. 4, July 1999, 303-305.
Review: G. Kelly, *Recognition. Advancing Ecumenical Thinking*; *Ecumenical Review*, LI no. 3, July 1999, 315-317.
Review: G.R. Evans, *Method in Ecumenical Theology*; *Scottish Journal of Theology*, LII no. 3, 1999, 401-402.
Review: M. G. Haykin, ed., *The Life and Thought of John Gill*; *The Baptist Quarterly*, XXXVIII no. 4, October 1999, 203-204.
Review: G. A. Mast, *The Eucharistic Service of the Catholic Apostolic Church*; *Journal of the United Reformed Church History Society*, VI no. 5, November 1999, 377-379.
Review: H. M. Elkins and E. C. Zaragoza, eds., *Pulpit, Table, and Song. Essays in Celebration of Howard G. Hageman*; *Journal of the United Reformed Church History Society*, VI no. 5, November 1999, 379.
Review: T. C. Pfizenmaier, *The Trinitarian Theology of Dr. Samuel Clarke*; *Enlightenment and Dissent*, XVIII, 1999, 270-275.
Review: W. M. Spellman, *John Locke*; *Enlightenment and Dissent*, XVIII, 1999, 270-275.

2000

Christ Our Saviour, Shippensburg, PA: Ragged Edge Press, 2000. Pp. 119.
The Spirit Our Life, Shippensburg, PA: Ragged Edge Press, 2000. Pp. 107.
General Editor's Preface and Introduction to *Henry Grove: Ethical and Theological Writings*, Bristol: Thoemmes Press, 2000. Introduction reprinted in TAT, ch. 5.
Ed. and contrib., *P. T. Forsyth: Theologian for a New Millennium*, London: United Reformed Church, 2000. 267 pp.
Articles: 'R. Barclay', 'J. Goodwin', 'J. Howe', 'P. Nye', 'T. Rowe', 'M. Warren', in the *Dictionary of Seventeenth-Century British Philosophers*, Bristol: Thoemmes Press, 2000.
'Reformed identity: a non-issue of catholic significance,' *Reformed Review*, LVI no. 1, Autumn 2000, 17-27.
Articles: 'A. B. Bruce', 'S. Cave', 'R. S. Franks' in *The Dictionary of Historical Theology*, Carlisle: Paternoster Press, 2000.
'Approaches to moral philosophy among the eighteenth-century Dissenters of England and Wales,' *Jahrbuch für Recht und Ethik*, VIII, 2000, 263-313.
'Andrew Fuller and the Socinians,' *festschrift* paper for D. O. Thomas, ED, XIX, 2000, 91-115. Reprinted in TAT, ch. 6.
Series Editor's Preface to *The Boyle Lectures*, Bristol: Thoemmes Press, 2000.
Series Editor's Preface to *The Philosophy of Edward Stillingfleet*, Bristol: Thoemmes Press, 2000.
Series Editor's Preface to *The Life and Works of William Law*, Bristol: Thoemmes Press, 2000.

Review: C. R. Coats, *Subverting the System. D'Aubigné and Calvinism*; *Reformed Review*, LIII no. 2, 1999-2000, 161.
Review: M. Beaty, C. Fisher and M. Nelson, *Christian Theism and Moral Philosophy*; *Studies in Christian Ethics*, XIII no. 1, 2000, 108-112.
Review: C. E. Gunton, *Theology Through the Theologians*; *Scottish Journal of Theology*, LII no. 2, 2000, 262-264.
Review: John W. Yolton, *et al.*, eds., *Dictionary of Eighteenth-Century British Philosophers*; *International Journal of Philosophical Studies*, XVIII no. 2, 266-269.
Review: J. A. Vickers, ed., *A Dictionary of Methodism in Britain and Ireland*; *Proceedings of the Wesley Historical Society*, LII pt. 6, October 2000, 77-79.
Review: I. Rivers, *Reason, Grace and Sentiment*, II; *Epworth Review*, XXVII no. 4, October 2000, 77-79.

2001

'Some Reformed approaches to the peace question,' in J. Gros and J. D. Rempel, eds., *The Fragmentation of the Church and its Unity in Peacemaking*, Grand Rapids: Eerdmans, 119-136.
'Church and chapel in the eighteenth and nineteenth centuries,' in *The Impact of Christianity on Life in the Dales*, Sedbergh: Sedbergh and District History Society, 7-8.
'Savoy Declaration of Faith and Order,' in D. K. McKim, ed., *The Westminster Handbook to Reformed Theology*, Louisville: Westminster/John Knox, 2001, 204-5 (reprinted from *Encyclopedia of the Reformed Faith*).
'Foreword' to K. Dix, *Strict and Particular*, Didcot: Baptist Historical Society, 2001, ix-xi.
Letter on leaving Aberystwyth, *The Treasury*, October 2001, 4.
Review: R. Gill, ed., *The Cambridge Companion to Christian Ethics*; *Modern Believing*, XLII no. 3, October 2001, 68-70
Review: *The Dictionary of Seventeenth-Century British Philosophers*; *International Journal of Philosophical Studies*, IX no. 4, 553-555.
Review: J. Higgins-Biddle, ed., *John Locke. The Reasonableness of the Christian Religion as delivered in the Scriptures*; *Journal of Ecclesiastical History*, LII no. 4, 2001, 757-757.

2002

Confessing and Commending the Faith. Historic Witness and Apologetic Method, Cardiff: University of Wales Press, 2002. 550 pp.
The Dissenting Witness, Yesterday and Today, London: The Protestant Dissenting Deputies of the Three Denominations, 2002, 23 pp. Reprinted in TAT, ch. 11.
Reminiscence, Reflection, Reassurance, Caernarfon: Gwasg Pantycelyn, 2002. 45 pp. Reprinted in TAT, ch. 13.
Ed. with W. J. Mander, *Dictionary of Nineteenth-Century British Philosophers*, Bristol: Thoemmes Press, 2002. Articles: 'W. L. Alexander', 'Richard Alliott', 'Henry Allon', 'Elkanah Armitage', 'Robert Aspland', 'Henry Batchelor', 'James Bennett', 'E. R. Conder', 'W. L. Courtney', 'A. M. Fairbairn', 'Robert Flint', 'Benjamin Godwin', 'J. H. Godwin', 'J. T. Gray', 'J. M. Hodgson', 'James Iverach', 'James Lindsay', 'Samuel McAll', 'Robert Mackintosh', 'Edward Miall', 'William Parry', 'George Payne', 'George Redford', 'Henry Rogers', 'Joseph Sortain', 'Samuel

Spalding', 'John Stoughton', 'J. R. Thomson', 'Robert Vaughan', 'Gilbert Wardlaw', and 'Ralph Wardlaw'.

'Telling the story: then and now,' in *Story Lines. Chapters on Thought, Word, and Deed for Gabriel Fackre*, Grand Rapids: Eerdmans, 2002, 146-156. Reprinted in TAT, ch. 3.

Letter: 'Marriage and Church Meeting', Richmond Hill, Bournemouth, Newsletter, June 2002.

Letter: 'Reconciling the memories,' *Reform*, July 2002, 10.

Report: 'The Daughters of Dissent project: Dr. Elaine Kaye's report,' *Friends of the Congregational Library Newsletter*, I, no.2, Autumn 2002, 11-12.

Review: E. T. Long, *Twentieth-Century Western Philosophy of Religion 1900-2000*; *Philosophical Books*, LXIII no. 1, January 2002, 74-76.

Review: P. Streiff, *Reluctant Saint? A Theological Biography of Fletcher of Madeley*; *Modern Believing*, XLIII no. 2, April 2002, 54-56.

Review: J. Roxborogh, *Thomas Chalmers: Enthusiast for Mission*, *Evangelical Quarterly*, LXXIV no. 3, July 2002, 287-288.

2003

Ed. With A. R. Cross, *Protestant Nonconformity in the Twentieth Century*, Carlisle: Paternoster, 2003. 398pp. Includes A. P. F. Sell, 'The theological contribution of Protestant Nonconformists in the twentieth century: some soundings,' pp. 33-62.

'The worship of English Congregationalism,' in Lukas Vischer, ed., *Christian Worship in Reformed Churches Past and Present*, Grand Rapids: Eerdmans, 2003, 83-106. Reprinted in TAT, ch. 2.

'*The Gospel its own Witness*: deism, Thomas Paine and Andrew Fuller, in Glenn Wooden *et al.*, eds., *'You Will Be My Witnesses'*, a *festschrift* for Allison A. Trites, Macon, GA: Mercer University Press, 2003, 188-229. Reprinted in EEE, ch. 4.

'From Union to Church: autobiographical recollections on [sic] Congregational ecclesiology in the 1960s,' in D. Bebbington and T. Larsen, eds., *Modern Christianity and Cultural Aspirations*, a *festschrift* for Clyde Binfield, London: Sheffield Academic Press, 2003, 309-344. Reprinted in TAT, ch. 12.

'The ministry, ministers and theological education: 9.5 theses,' *Friends of Northern College Newsletter*, no. 2, Winter 2003, 3.

'Reformed reflections on spirituality,' *Reformed Review*, LVI no. 2, Winter 2002/2003, 139-161. Reprinted in EEE, ch. 8.

'The public worship of God: memories and challenges,' *Sárospataki Füzetek*, 2003 no. 1, 4-14.

'From fields to concrete, from vision to reality: ecumenical pioneering in Milton Keynes,' *The Chapels Society Newsletter*, 28, May 2003, 125-127, and *Ecumenical Trends*, XXXII no. 6, June 2003, 15-16.

'Establishment as a theological issue: the Dissenting witness,' *Theology*, CVI, July/August 2003, 237-249.

'The Alliance in dialogue, 1970-2002 : retrospect and reflections,' *Reformed World*, LIII no. 4, December 2003, 210-228. Reprinted in EEE, ch. 10.

Letter: 'Wrong criteria,' *Reform*, February 2003, 13.

Letter: 'No to teaching ghetto,' *The Times Higher Education Supplement*, 11 July 2003, 17.

Letter: 'Don't rubbish post-92s' efforts,' *The Times Higher Education Supplement*, 15 August 2003, 15.

Review: S. Collini, *et al.*, eds, *History, Religion and Culture. British Intellectual History 1750-1950*; *British Journal for the History of Philosophy*, XI no. 1, February 2003, 161-164.

Review: M. A. Stewart, ed., *English Philosophy in the Age of Locke*; *Transactions of the Unitarian Historical Society*, XXIII, no. 1, April 2003, 480-482.

Review: A. Thiselton, *A Concise Encyclopedia of the Philosophy of Religion*; *Theology Today*, LX no. 1, April 2003, 145.

Review: V. Nuovo, ed., *John Locke. Writings on Religion*; *British Journal for the History of Philosophy*, XI no. 2, May 2003, 345-347/

Review: J. E. Harris, *Analytic Philosophy of Religion*; *Philosophical Books*, LXIV no. 3, July 2003, 285-289.

Review: L. C. Raeder, *John Stuart Mill and the Religion of Humanity*; *International Journal of Philosophical Studies*, XI no. 3, 2003, 356-358.

Review: J. W. Stewart and J. H. Moorhead, eds., *Charles Hodge Revisited*; *Modern Believing*, XLIV, July 2003, 74-76.

Review: J. Webster, *Word and Church. Essays in Christian Dogmatics*; *International Journal of Systematic Theology*, V no. 3, November 2003, 332-7.

Review: G. T. Eddy, *Dr Taylor of Norwich. Wesley's Arch-heretic*; *Journal of Ecclesiastical History*, LIV no. 4, October 2003, 780-781.

Review: R. Waller, *John Wesley. A Personal Portrait*; *Journal of Ecclesiastical History*, LIV no. 4, October 2003, 780-781.

Review: G. M. Newlands, *John and Donald Baillie: Transatlantic Theology*; *Irish Theological Quarterly*, LXVIII no. 4, 2003, 400-402.

2004

Philosophy, Dissent and Nonconformity 1689-1920, Cambridge: James Clarke, 2004. 296 pp.

Mill on God: The Pervasiveness and Elusiveness of Mill's Religious Thought, Aldershot: Ashgate, 2004. 202 pp.

'I bind unto myself,' *Reform*, May 2004, pp. 20-21.

'From worms to sunbeams: the dilution of Calvinism in English Congregationalism 1830-1930,' *Journal of the United Reformed Historical Society*, VII no. 4, May 2004, pp. 253-274. Reprinted in EEE, ch. 5.

'Some theological aspects of the English Enlightenment calmly consider'd,' *Eighteenth-Century Thought*, II, 2004, pp. 255-298. Reprinted in EEE, ch. 3.

'Reformed theology in Britain in the twentieth century: a bibliographical survey,' in G. Harinck and D.van Keulen, eds., *Viscissitudes of Reformed Theology in the Twentieth Century* (*Studies in Reformed Theology*, IX, 2004), pp. 130-146. Reprinted in EEE, ch. 9

Articles revised for *OxfordDNB*: 'A. M. Fairbairn', 'N. Lardner', 'J. Fraser', 'S. Bourn', 'J. Reynolds', 'S. Bourn III'.

Original articles for *OxfordDNB*: 'W. H. Bennett', 'R. Flint', 'J. Kennedy', 'W. J. F. Huxtable', 'H. F. L. Cocks', 'W. G. Robinson', 'J. S. Whale', 'J. Taylor', 'R. Mackintosh'.

'Protestant Nonconformist Texts,' *Friends of the Congregational Library Newsletter*, I no. 6, Autumn 2004, p. 49.

Foreword to Anna M. Robbins, *Methods in the Madness. Diversity in Twentieth-Century Christian Social Ethics*, Carlisle: Paternoster, 2004, xiii-xiv.

Letter: 'Catch the vision,' *Reform*, April 2004, 14.

Letter: 'No surrender,' *Reform*, July/August 2004, 12.

Review: G. Robson, *Dark Satanic Mills? Religion and Irreligion in Birmingham and the Black Country*; *Proceedings of the Wesley Historical Society*, LIV pt. 4, February 2004, 135-137.

Review: W. Sweet, *Religious Belief: The Contemporary Debate*; *International Journal of Philosophical Studies*, XII no. 2, 2004, 228-229.

Review: W. M. Alston, Jr., and M. Welker, eds., *Reformed Theology. Identity and Ecumenicity*; *Theology*, CVII, September/October 2004, 376-377.

Review: G. R. Breed, *Particular Baptists in Victorian England*; *The Baptist Quarterly*, XL no. 8, October 2004, 500-501.

Review: L. Smith, ed., *Unitarian to the Core*; *Faith and Freedom*, LVII pt. 2, Autumn and Winter 2004, 175-179.

Review: M. Goldie, ed., *John Locke. Selected Correspondence*; *The Scriblerian*, XXX no. 1, Autumn 2004, 95-6.

2005

Testimony and Tradition: Studies in Reformed and Dissenting Thought, Aldershot: Ashgate, 2005. 367 pp.

Enlightenment, Ecumenism, Evangel: Theological Themes and Thinkers 1550-2000, Carlisle: Paternoster, 2005. 421 pp.

'Striving for an educated ministry then - and now? A Review article,' *The Baptist Quarterly*, XLI, January 2005, 53-57.

'The ministerial vocation,' *This and That*, May 2005, 3.

Articles: 'W. G. De Burgh', 'W. R. Matthews', 'H. P. Owen', 'F. J. Powicke', 'N. H. G. Robinson' and 'J. Heywood Thomas' for *Dictionary of Twentieth-Century British Philosophers*, Bristol: Thoemmes Press, 2005.

'The Holy Spirit and ecumenism: some catholic ruminations of a Reformed theologian' in D. Donnelly *et al.*, *The Holy Spirit, The Church and Christian Unity*, Leuven: Peeters, 2005, pp. 75-92. Reprinted in EEE, ch. 11.

'Educating the Church today,' *This and That*, August 2005, 8, 13.

Letter: 'Disestablishmentarianism,' *Reform*, July/August 2005, 12.

Review: W. D. McNaughton, *Early Congregational Independency in the Highlands and Islands of North-East Scotland*; *Journal of the United Reformed Church History Society*, *Journal of the United Reformed Church History Society*, VII no. 6, May 2005, 398-401.

Review: M. Fitzpatrick, *et al*, *The Enlightenment World*; *Enlightenment and Dissent*, XXI, 2002,
198-209.

Review: R. T. Jones, *Congregationalism in Wales*; *Friends of the Congregational Library Newsletter*, II no. 2, Autumn 2005, 16-18.

Review: A. Hood, *Baillie, Oman and Macmurray: Experience and Religious Belief*; *The Heythrop Journal*, XLVI no. 4, October 2005, 554-555.

Review: T. M. Gouldstone, *The Rise and Decline of Anglican Idealism in the Nineteenth Century*; *British Journal for the History of Philosophy*, XIII no. 4, 2005, 811-815.

Review: D. Z. Phillips, *The Problem of Evil and the Problem of God*; *Anvil*, XXII no. 3, 2005, 237-238.
Review: D. F. Ford, *et al*, *Fields of Faith*; *Anvil*, XXII no. 4, 2005, 320, 323-324.

2006

Nonconformist Theology in the Twentieth Century, Milton Keynes: Paternoster, 2006.
'The continuing Epiphany,' *This and That*, January 2006, 3.
'What do we expect of our ministers?' *This and That*, June 2006, 3.
Review: W. D. McNaughton, *Early Congregational Independency in Lowland Scotland*, Vol. I; *Journal of the United Reformed Church History Society*, VII no. 8, June 2006, 512-513.
Review: W. D. McNaughton, *Early Congregational Independency in Shetland*; *Journal of the United Reformed Church History Society*, VII no. 8, June 2006, 513.
Letter: 'Full diet' [of worship], *Reform*, February 2006, 12.

Person Index

Aitken, W.H. 98.
Aristotle 237.
Arnold, M. 53-54, 56.
Arnold, T. 53.
Athanasius 238.
Aquinas, T. 238.
Augustine 144, 156.
Aulen, G. 272, 277-281.
Balguy, J. 31-33.
Barth, K. 68, 131, 166, 278.
Baudrillard, J. 260-61.
Bauman, Z. 251, 260.
Baxter, R. 63, 101, 151.
Blackburne, F. 50, 57.
Blackstone, W. 49.
Bock, D. 186.
Bonhoeffer, D. 208, 281.
Bright, J. 191-92.
Buchanan, C. 70-71.
Burke, E. 46, 49.
Butler, J. 37-38.
Calvin, J. 7-23, 101, 233, 236-37, 240, 243, 276.
Caird, G. 159.
Canovan, M. 45.
Carritt, E.F. 26.
Castells, M. 263.
Chapman, J. 153.
Chauvin, E. 29.
Chillingworth, W. 40, 56.
Clarke, S. 38-40.
Cockburn, C. 27-30.
Coleridge, S.T. 55.
Conybeare, J. 31-33, 40.
Cranmer, T. 21.
Davies, W.D. 159-160, 167-69, 171.
DesCartes, R. 254.
Dillistone, F.W. 160, 170.
Disraeli, B. 116.
Dix, G. 154.
Dodd, C. H. 159-167, 170.
Enfield, W. 57.

Evans, C. 186.
Ferguson, N. 257.
Forsyth, P.T. 154, 276-77, 279.
Foust, T.F. 144.
Froude, J.A. 60.
Gibson, M. 269-278.
Gladstone, W. 90, 110, 117.
Gore, C. 96.
Graf, F. 195.
Griffiths, M. 43.
Grove, H. 35-38, 40, 61.
Grove, W. 86.
Harkness, G. 271.
Hegel, G. 191.
Horne, T.H. 61.
Holmes, R. 55.
Horne, G. 44, 50-52, 54-55, 58.
Horsley, S. 44.
Howard, W.F. 65-66.
Hume, D. 254.
Hunsberger, G.R. 129.
Irenaeus 146, 193, 280.
Jenkins, D.T. 68-69, 167, 169.
John Paul II 209, 218.
Keynes, J.M. 130.
Kierkegaard, S. 157.
Knott, E. 56.
Küng, H. 164.
Lessing, G.F. 45.
Lindsey, T. 50.
Luther, M. 233, 236-238, 243, 273, 278.
MacIntyre, A. 253.
Marsh, J. 166.
Maude, F. 140.
Maurice, F.D. 92, 95, 111-12, 120.
McLachlan, J. 57.
McNeill, J.T. 20-21.
Mews, S. 189-90.
Miall, E. 52.
Moberg, D. 79-80.
Mohler, A. 73-74.
Moltmann, J. 278.

Mott, J.R. 69.
Moule, C.F.D. 157-58.
Muir, E. 219-220, 223.
Newbigin, L. 77-78, 129-148.
Newton, I. 38.
Niebuhr, H.R. 277, 279.
Nietzsche, F. 254.
Packer, J. 76-78.
Paine, T. 192.
Pitt, W. 54.
Plato 237.
Polanyi, M. 131, 133, 142, 144.
Potter, P. 69-70.
Price, L. 141.
Price, R. 25-40, 57-59.
Priestley, J. 44-61.
Prior, A.N. 26.
Reid, T. 26.
Roberts, W.P.R. 112-120, 122, 126-128.
Sachs, J. 231.
Sanderson, R. 34-35, 40.
Schlenther, B. 43.
Schreiner, T. 180.
Schwietzer, A. 192.
Sell, A.P.F. 1-2, 7-9, 22, 25-26, 36, 43-44, 61-63, 129-30, 173, 206, 221-22, 264, 269.
Sharp, J. 30-31.
Sharp, T. 27-30.
Smail, T. 75.
Stackhouse, M. 248.
Stephen, L. 96.
Stott, J. 77.
Streeter, B.H. 168.
Tanner, K. 259-60.
Taylor, M. 141.
Temple, W. 66.
Theissen, G. 182.
Thomas, D.O. 59.
Tindal, M. 31-32.
Tomkins, O. 165-66.
Tracy, D. 144.
Troeltsch, E. 194-201.
Tyndale, W. 102.
Underhill, E. 154, 157.
Vischer, L. 21.
Wainwright, G. 129.
Walls, A. 147.

Warburton, W. 48.
Watts, I. 101.
Weber, M. 189-190, 194-201.
Wellhausen, J. 191, 197.
Willans, W.H. 120-127.
Williams, G.G. 73.
Williams, R. 8.
Wyon, O. 149-158.
Zwingli, U. 155, 233, 236-238.

Subject Index

Apologetics 269-82.
Baptism, Eucharist and the Ministry 71-72, 225, 227-28.
Bible 92-93, 108-109, 131, 151-152.
Change 85-128.
Charismatic renewal 73-78.
Charta Oecumenica 211-13, 217.
Christology 269-82.
Church-state relations 47-62, 196-97, 200.
Clerisy 55-56.
Conference of European Churches 72-73, 205-14, 216-17.
Continuity 85-128.
Conscience 30, 34-39.
Conversion 97-100.
Council of Catholic Episcopal Conference in Europe 205-14.
Cult 189-201.
Culture 131-34, 145-148, 250-52, 254-55.
Dialogue 218-20, 221-32, 233-245.
Disciples 182-187.
Dissent 31, 40, 48-62, 96, 99-103, 122.
Division, 15-17, 67-68.
Diversity 13-15, 215-16, 230.
Duty 28-30, 32, 36-39
Ecclesiology, New Testament 160-171.
Ecclesiology, Reformed 8-23.
Ecumenical Movement 68-73.
Establishment 47-56, 86-128, 196.
Election 9-10.
Epistemology 140-145.
Ecumenism, Europe 205-220, 233-245.
Evangelical Movement 78-82.
Evangelism 130-33.
Family 173-187.
Fundamentalism 79-82.
Globalisation 247-267.
Inter-faith dialogue 215-18.
Latitudinarianism 56-59.
Liberty 47-54, 101-103, 107.

Lord's supper (Holy Communion) 17-19, 105-106, 154-58, 162-63, 218-19, 234-245.
Missiology 138-140.
Mission, church 134-136.
Moral philosophy 26-27, 39.
Passion of the Christ 269-82.
Pentecostal Movement 73-78.
Prayer 150-154.
Prayer book 90-111.
Priesthood 105, 156.
Progress 45-47.
Reason 31-40, 56, 131-32.
Relativism 27, 37-41.
Revelation 31-40, 56.
Sect 189-201.
Social ethics 247-67.
Suffering 279-282.
Truth 31, 33, 39-41, 45-47, 56-59, 61, 96.
Unitarians 50-56, 96.
Unity, church 8-9, 50-54, 59-62, 63-82, 136-37, 163-171.
Unity, in Christ 10-11, 65-68.
Unity, of faith 11-13.
Unity, as gift 15-19.
Virtue, 25-41.
Vocation 137-138, 152-153.
World Council of Churches 69-73, 81-82, 150, 166, 206, 207-208, 214-215, 216, 222, 225, 227-28, 229.

Studies in Christian History and Thought
(All titles uniform with this volume)
Dates in bold are of projected publication

David Bebbington
Holiness in Nineteenth-Century England
David Bebbington stresses the relationship of movements of spirituality to changes in their cultural setting, especially the legacies of the Enlightenment and Romanticism. He shows that these broad shifts in ideological mood had a profound effect on the ways in which piety was conceptualized and practised. Holiness was intimately bound up with the spirit of the age.
2000 / 0-85364-981-2 / viii + 98pp

J. William Black
Reformation Pastors
Richard Baxter and the Ideal of the Reformed Pastor
This work examines Richard Baxter's *Gildas Salvianus, The Reformed Pastor* (1656) and explores each aspect of his pastoral strategy in light of his own concern for 'reformation' and in the broader context of Edwardian, Elizabethan and early Stuart pastoral ideals and practice.
2003 / 1-84227-190-3 / xxii + 308pp

James Bruce
Prophecy, Miracles, Angels, *and* Heavenly Light?
The Eschatology, Pneumatology and Missiology of Adomnán's Life of Columba
This book surveys approaches to the marvellous in hagiography, providing the first critique of Plummer's hypothesis of Irish saga origin. It then analyses the uniquely systematized phenomena in the *Life of Columba* from Adomnán's seventh-century theological perspective, identifying the coming of the eschatological Kingdom as the key to understanding.
2004 / 1-84227-227-6 / xviii + 286pp

Colin J. Bulley
The Priesthood of Some Believers
Developments from the General to the Special Priesthood in the Christian Literature of the First Three Centuries
The first in-depth treatment of early Christian texts on the priesthood of all believers shows that the developing priesthood of the ordained related closely to the division between laity and clergy and had deleterious effects on the practice of the general priesthood.
2000 / 1-84227-034-6 / xii + 336pp

July 2005

Anthony R. Cross (ed.)
Ecumenism and History
Studies in Honour of John H.Y. Briggs
This collection of essays examines the inter-relationships between the two fields in which Professor Briggs has contributed so much: history—particularly Baptist and Nonconformist—and the ecumenical movement. With contributions from colleagues and former research students from Britain, Europe and North America, *Ecumenism and History* provides wide-ranging studies in important aspects of Christian history, theology and ecumenical studies.

2002 / 1-84227-135-0 / xx + 362pp

Maggi Dawn
Confessions of an Inquiring Spirit
Form as Constitutive of Meaning in S.T. Coleridge's Theological Writing
This study of Coleridge's *Confessions* focuses on its confessional, epistolary and fragmentary form, suggesting that attention to these features significantly affects its interpretation. Bringing a close study of these three literary forms, the author suggests ways in which they nuance the text with particular understandings of the Trinity, and of a kenotic christology. Some parallels are drawn between Romantic and postmodern dilemmas concerning the authority of the biblical text.

2006 / 1-84227-255-1 / approx. 224 pp

Ruth Gouldbourne
The Flesh and the Feminine
Gender and Theology in the Writings of Caspar Schwenckfeld
Caspar Schwenckfeld and his movement exemplify one of the radical communities of the sixteenth century. Challenging theological and liturgical norms, they also found themselves challenging social and particularly gender assumptions. In this book, the issues of the relationship between radical theology and the understanding of gender are considered.

2005 / 1-84227-048-6 / approx. 304pp

Crawford Gribben
Puritan Millennialism
Literature and Theology, 1550–1682
Puritan Millennialism surveys the growth, impact and eventual decline of puritan millennialism throughout England, Scotland and Ireland, arguing that it was much more diverse than has frequently been suggested. This Paternoster edition is revised and extended from the original 2000 text.

2007 / 1-84227-372-8 / approx. 320pp

Galen K. Johnson
Prisoner of Conscience
John Bunyan on Self, Community and Christian Faith
This is an interdisciplinary study of John Bunyan's understanding of conscience across his autobiographical, theological and fictional writings, investigating whether conscience always deserves fidelity, and how Bunyan's view of conscience affects his relationship both to modern Western individualism and historic Christianity.
2003 / 1-84227-223-3 / xvi + 236pp

R.T. Kendall
Calvin and English Calvinism to 1649
The author's thesis is that those who formed the Westminster Confession of Faith, which is regarded as Calvinism, in fact departed from John Calvin on two points: (1) the extent of the atonement and (2) the ground of assurance of salvation.
1997 / 0-85364-827-1 / xii + 264pp

Timothy Larsen
Friends of Religious Equality
Nonconformist Politics in Mid-Victorian England
During the middle decades of the nineteenth century the English Nonconformist community developed a coherent political philosophy of its own, of which a central tenet was the principle of religious equality (in contrast to the stereotype of Evangelical Dissenters). The Dissenting community fought for the civil rights of Roman Catholics, non-Christians and even atheists on an issue of principle which had its flowering in the enthusiastic and undivided support which Nonconformity gave to the campaign for Jewish emancipation. This reissued study examines the political efforts and ideas of English Nonconformists during the period, covering the whole range of national issues raised, from state education to the Crimean War. It offers a case study of a theologically conservative group defending religious pluralism in the civic sphere, showing that the concept of religious equality was a grand vision at the centre of the political philosophy of the Dissenters.
2007 / 1-84227-402-3 / x + 300pp

Byung-Ho Moon
Christ the Mediator of the Law
Calvin's Christological Understanding of the Law as the Rule of Living and Life-Giving

This book explores the coherence between Christology and soteriology in Calvin's theology of the law, examining its intellectual origins and his position on the concept and extent of Christ's mediation of the law. A comparative study between Calvin and contemporary Reformers—Luther, Bucer, Melancthon and Bullinger—and his opponent Michael Servetus is made for the purpose of pointing out the unique feature of Calvin's Christological understanding of the law.

2005 / 1-84227-318-3 / approx. 370pp

John Eifion Morgan-Wynne
Holy Spirit and Religious Experience in Christian Writings, c.AD 90–200

This study examines how far Christians in the third to fifth generations (c.AD 90–200) attributed their sense of encounter with the divine presence, their sense of illumination in the truth or guidance in decision-making, and their sense of ethical empowerment to the activity of the Holy Spirit in their lives.

2005 / 1-84227-319-1 / approx. 350pp

James I. Packer
The Redemption and Restoration of Man in the Thought of Richard Baxter

James I. Packer provides a full and sympathetic exposition of Richard Baxter's doctrine of humanity, created and fallen; its redemption by Christ Jesus; and its restoration in the image of God through the obedience of faith by the power of the Holy Spirit.

2002 / 1-84227-147-4 / 432pp

Andrew Partington,
Church and State
The Contribution of the Church of England Bishops to the House of Lords during the Thatcher Years

In *Church and State*, Andrew Partington argues that the contribution of the Church of England bishops to the House of Lords during the Thatcher years was overwhelmingly critical of the government; failed to have a significant influence in the public realm; was inefficient, being undertaken by a minority of those eligible to sit on the Bench of Bishops; and was insufficiently moral and spiritual in its content to be distinctive. On the basis of this, and the likely reduction of the number of places available for Church of England bishops in a fully reformed Second Chamber, the author argues for an evolution in the Church of England's approach to the service of its bishops in the House of Lords. He proposes the Church of England works to overcome the genuine obstacles which hinder busy diocesan bishops from contributing to the debates of the House of Lords and to its life more informally.

2005 / 1-84227-334-5 / approx. 324pp

Michael Pasquarello III
God's Ploughman
Hugh Latimer: A 'Preaching Life' (1490–1555)

This construction of a 'preaching life' situates Hugh Latimer within the larger religious, political and intellectual world of late medieval England. Neither biography, intellectual history, nor analysis of discrete sermon texts, this book is a work of homiletic history which draws from the details of Latimer's milieu to construct an interpretive framework for the preaching performances that formed the core of his identity as a religious reformer. Its goal is to illumine the practical wisdom embodied in the content, form and style of Latimer's preaching, and to recapture a sense of its overarching purpose, movement, and transforming force during the reform of sixteenth-century England.

2006 / 1-84227-336-1 / approx. 250pp

Alan P.F. Sell
Enlightenment, Ecumenism, Evangel
Theological Themes and Thinkers 1550–2000

This book consists of papers in which such interlocking topics as the Enlightenment, the problem of authority, the development of doctrine, spirituality, ecumenism, theological method and the heart of the gospel are discussed. Issues of significance to the church at large are explored with special reference to writers from the Reformed and Dissenting traditions.

2005 / 1-84227-330-2 / xviii + 422pp

Alan P.F. Sell
Hinterland Theology
Some Reformed and Dissenting Adjustments

Many books have been written on theology's 'giants' and significant trends, but what of those lesser-known writers who adjusted to them? In this book some hinterland theologians of the British Reformed and Dissenting traditions, who followed in the wake of toleration, the Evangelical Revival, the rise of modern biblical criticism and Karl Barth, are allowed to have their say. They include Thomas Ridgley, Ralph Wardlaw, T.V. Tymms and N.H.G. Robinson.

2006 / 1-84227-331-0 / approx. 350pp

Alan P.F. Sell and Anthony R. Cross (eds)
Protestant Nonconformity in the Twentieth Century

In this collection of essays scholars representative of a number of Nonconformist traditions reflect thematically on Nonconformists' life and witness during the twentieth century. Among the subjects reviewed are biblical studies, theology, worship, evangelism and spirituality, and ecumenism. Over and above its immediate interest, this collection provides a marker to future scholars and others wishing to know how some of their forebears assessed Nonconformity's contribution to a variety of fields during the century leading up to Christianity's third millennium.

2003 / 1-84227-221-7 / x + 398pp

Mark Smith
Religion in Industrial Society
Oldham and Saddleworth 1740–1865

This book analyses the way British churches sought to meet the challenge of industrialization and urbanization during the period 1740–1865. Working from a case-study of Oldham and Saddleworth, Mark Smith challenges the received view that the Anglican Church in the eighteenth century was characterized by complacency and inertia, and reveals Anglicanism's vigorous and creative response to the new conditions. He reassesses the significance of the centrally directed church reforms of the mid-nineteenth century, and emphasizes the importance of local energy and enthusiasm. Charting the growth of denominational pluralism in Oldham and Saddleworth, Dr Smith compares the strengths and weaknesses of the various Anglican and Nonconformist approaches to promoting church growth. He also demonstrates the extent to which all the churches participated in a common culture shaped by the influence of evangelicalism, and shows that active co-operation between the churches rather than denominational conflict dominated. This revised and updated edition of Dr Smith's challenging and original study makes an important contribution both to the social history of religion and to urban studies.

2006 / 1-84227-335-3 / approx. 300pp

Martin Sutherland
Peace, Toleration and Decay
The Ecclesiology of Later Stuart Dissent
This fresh analysis brings to light the complexity and fragility of the later Stuart Nonconformist consensus. Recent findings on wider seventeenth-century thought are incorporated into a new picture of the dynamics of Dissent and the roots of evangelicalism.
2003 / 1-84227-152-0 / xxii + 216pp

G. Michael Thomas
The Extent of the Atonement
A Dilemma for Reformed Theology from Calvin to the Consensus
A study of the way Reformed theology addressed the question, 'Did Christ die for all, or for the elect only?', commencing with John Calvin, and including debates with Lutheranism, the Synod of Dort and the teaching of Moïse Amyraut.
1997 / 0-85364-828-X / x + 278pp

David M. Thompson
Baptism, Church and Society in Britain from the Evangelical Revival to *Baptism, Eucharist and Ministry*
The theology and practice of baptism have not received the attention they deserve. How important is faith? What does baptismal regeneration mean? Is baptism a bond of unity between Christians? This book discusses the theology of baptism and popular belief and practice in England and Wales from the Evangelical Revival to the publication of the World Council of Churches' consensus statement on *Baptism, Eucharist and Ministry* (1982).
2005 / 1-84227-393-0 / approx. 224pp

Mark D. Thompson
A Sure Ground on Which to Stand
The Relation of Authority and Interpretive Method of Luther's Approach to Scripture
The best interpreter of Luther is Luther himself. Unfortunately many modern studies have superimposed contemporary agendas upon this sixteenth-century Reformer's writings. This fresh study examines Luther's own words to find an explanation for his robust confidence in the Scriptures, a confidence that generated the famous 'stand' at Worms in 1521.
2004 / 1-84227-145-8 / xvi + 322pp

Carl R. Trueman and R.S. Clark (eds)
Protestant Scholasticism
Essays in Reassessment

Traditionally Protestant theology, between Luther's early reforming career and the dawn of the Enlightenment, has been seen in terms of decline and fall into the wastelands of rationalism and scholastic speculation. In this volume a number of scholars question such an interpretation. The editors argue that the development of post-Reformation Protestantism can only be understood when a proper historical model of doctrinal change is adopted. This historical concern underlies the subsequent studies of theologians such as Calvin, Beza, Olevian, Baxter, and the two Turrentini. The result is a significantly different reading of the development of Protestant Orthodoxy, one which both challenges the older scholarly interpretations and clichés about the relationship of Protestantism to, among other things, scholasticism and rationalism, and which demonstrates the fruitfulness of the new, historical approach.

1999 / 0-85364-853-0 / xx + 344pp

Shawn D. Wright
Our Sovereign Refuge
The Pastoral Theology of Theodore Beza

Our Sovereign Refuge is a study of the pastoral theology of the Protestant reformer who inherited the mantle of leadership in the Reformed church from John Calvin. Countering a common view of Beza as supremely a 'scholastic' theologian who deviated from Calvin's biblical focus, Wright uncovers a new portrait. He was not a cold and rigid academic theologian obsessed with probing the eternal decrees of God. Rather, by placing him in his pastoral context and by noting his concerns in his pastoral and biblical treatises, Wright shows that Beza was fundamentally a committed Christian who was troubled by the vicissitudes of life in the second half of the sixteenth century. He believed that the biblical truth of the supreme sovereignty of God alone could support Christians on their earthly pilgrimage to heaven. This pastoral and personal portrait forms the heart of Wright's argument.

2004 / 1-84227-252-7 / xviii + 308pp

Paternoster
9 Holdom Avenue,
Bletchley,
Milton Keynes MK1 1QR,
United Kingdom
Web: www.authenticmedia.co.uk/paternoster